"This is a marvellous book by leading authorities who put across
psychology in a thoroughly sensible and accessible way. Teache
it: there's lots in it for you too."

Sir Anthony Seldon, Vice-Chancellor, The University of Buckingham, ...

"This book is a true gift to aspiring educators and school leaders who desire to bring positive
transformation to schools. It addresses the breadth of issues related to positive education
and provides rich theoretical foundations and practical applications. As a positive educator,
I am truly impressed and intrigued by the reflection questions and discussion points at the
end of each book chapter, which allows educators to crystallise their learnings and reflect
meaningfully on their teaching and learning practice."

Matthew Koh, Founder of The Positive Arena, Singapore

"This compendium of positive school philosophies provides a wealth of evidence and inspiration for educators to consider in their teaching approaches, and in terms of whole-school
self-evaluation. It offers practical insights into how wellbeing can be weaved into schools'
work. It is also a powerful call to action for system leaders to consider how this thinking
might be embedded in future policy and resourcing of schools, particularly CPD for teachers
and school leaders. I encourage educators to read it."

Páiric Clerkin, CEO of the Irish Primary Principals' Network, Ireland

"I am delighted to have this opportunity to endorse such a worthwhile compendium of expert
perspectives on the application of positive psychology to schools. The need for this book is
especially important at a time when so many of our children and young people are reporting
threats to their mental health and positivity related to their experiences in the current pandemic, as well as the reported negative impacts of climate change on their futures. Emotional
health and well-being are central to optimal development – intellectual, physical and social.
In terms of education, we cannot learn optimally if we feel threatened, and this edited
collection offers a wide variety of potential solutions for schools (and families) in our
quest to promote a greater sense of positive agency and inclusion in future generations."

Professor Graham F Welch, UCL Institute of Education, UK

APPLIED POSITIVE SCHOOL PSYCHOLOGY

Applied Positive School Psychology is an essential guide to help teachers regain their own and assist the school community in rebuilding their health post-pandemic. While research in positive psychology is thriving, teachers and educational practitioners find it challenging to apply it in their daily practice. This practical book fills the gap between theory and practice and provides practitioners with an evidence-based toolkit on using the positive psychology in their school communities.

With contributions from experts in their field, this important resource explores student wellbeing, teacher wellbeing, inclusion, developing positive relationships, creativity, and therapeutic art.

Written with the practitioner in mind, *Applied Positive School Psychology* is a must read for the teaching community and those interested in positive education. It will also be of interest to academics specialising in wellbeing or education, educational psychologists, and education policy makers.

Andrea Giraldez-Hayes is an accredited coaching psychologist, supervisor, and consultant specialising in positive and coaching psychology. She is the Director of the MSc in Applied Positive Psychology and Coaching Psychology and the Wellbeing and Psychological Services Centre at the University of East London's School of Psychology.

Jolanta Burke is a Chartered Psychologist (British Psychological Society) specialising in positive psychology and an Associate Professor in the Centre for Positive Psychology and Health in RCSI University of Medicine and Health Sciences. She has authored eight books. For more information, go to www.jolantaburke.com.

APPLIED POSITIVE SCHOOL PSYCHOLOGY

Edited by Andrea Giraldez-Hayes and
Jolanta Burke

Routledge
Taylor & Francis Group

LONDON AND NEW YORK

Cover image: Pilar Amusategui-Giraldez

First published 2023
by Routledge
4 Park Square, Milton Park, Abingdon, Oxon OX14 4RN

and by Routledge
605 Third Avenue, New York, NY 10158

Routledge is an imprint of the Taylor & Francis Group, an informa business

British Library Cataloguing-in-Publication Data
A catalogue record for this book is available from the British Library

Library of Congress Cataloging-in-Publication Data
Names: Giráldez, Andrea, editor. | Burke, Jolanta, editor.
Title: Applied positive school psychology / edited by Andrea Giraldez-Hayes
and Jolanta Burke.
Description: Abingdon, Oxon; New York, NY: Routledge, 2022. | Includes
bibliographical references and index. |
Identifiers: LCCN 2022001716 | ISBN 9781032132051 (hardback) |
ISBN 9781032132068 (paperback) | ISBN 9781003228158 (ebook)
Subjects: LCSH: School psychology. | School children—Psychology. |
Positive psychology.
Classification: LCC LB1027.55 .A67 2022 | DDC 370.15—dc23/eng/20220427
LC record available at https://lccn.loc.gov/2022001716

ISBN: 978-1-032-13205-1 (hbk)
ISBN: 978-1-032-13206-8 (pbk)
ISBN: 978-1-003-22815-8 (ebk)

DOI: 10.4324/9781003228158

Typeset in Interstate
by codeMantra

MIX
Paper | Supporting
responsible forestry
FSC
www.fsc.org   FSC™ C013985

Printed in the United Kingdom
by Henry Ling Limited

To the teachers worldwide, who change the world
one child at a time.

CONTENTS

List of tables   xii
List of figures   xiii
About the editors   xiv
About the contributing authors   xv

PART 1
Positive psychology in schools   1

1   **Positive schools: An introduction**   3
    Jolanta Burke and Andrea Giraldez-Hayes

2   **Applying positive psychology in primary schools**   9
    Sue Roffey

PART 2
Connecting with others   21

3   **Positive relationships**   23
    Jolanta Burke

4   **Self-confidence and self-efficacy development in schools**   29
    Suzy Green, Daniela Falecki, and Clive Leach

5   **Courage in positive education**   44
    Cynthia L.S. Pury

6   **Working with strengths in education: Why educators should strength
    spot in their students, and how students feel about this work**   52
    Denise Quinlan and Lucy Hone

7   **Coaching conversations to enhance well-being**   63
    Andrea Giraldez-Hayes

PART 3

Connecting with self   71

8   **Has life no meaning? Cultivating youth life meaning in schools**   73
     Gökmen Arslan and Murat Yıldırım

9   **Embedding compassion in schools: The what's, the why's, and the how's**   81
     Frances A. Maratos, Julie Hurst, Caroline Harvey, and Paul Gilbert

10   **Meditation-based tools for balance, focus, and health**   101
     Padraic J. Dunne

11   **Strengths-based interventions for students and staff**   115
     Christian van Nieuwerburgh and Ashley Green

PART 4

Creativity in schools: Arts, playing, and language   123

12   **Arts and well-being**   125
     Andrea Giraldez-Hayes

13   **Music, technology, and well-being**   134
     Evangelos Himonides

14   **Playing and thriving in school**   142
     Trudy Meehan

15   **Well-being lexicon in schools**   150
     Tim Lomas

PART 5

Inclusion   157

16   **School belonging as an essential component of positive
     psychology in schools**   159
     Kelly-Ann Allen, Christopher Boyle, Denise Wong, Rebecca G. Johnson, and Fiona May

17   **Positive psychology and school bullying**   173
     Jolanta Burke

18   **Positive psychology, strengths-based and
     inclusive practices, and disability**   180
     Michael L. Wehmeyer

19   **Positive solution**   192
     Conor Mc Guckin, Mary Quirke, and Patricia McCarthy

PART 6
The road less travelled for well-being strategies   201

20 **The why and how of whole-school well-being**   203
    Lucy Hone and Denise Quinlan

21 **Pedagogy for well-being: A new model for**
    organic development of well-being in schools   212
    Majella Dempsey and Jolanta Burke

22 **Well-being of school teachers**   220
    Elaine Wilson and Jude Brady

23 **Expertise: The problem with experience**   232
    David Bott

PART 7   239

  Conclusion   241
  Andrea Giraldez-Hayes and Jolanta Burke

  Index   245

TABLES

1   The Three Categories of Meditation Practice as Defined by
    Singer and Engert (2019)   104
2   Literature Review: School Belonging Practices Evidence-Base
    (Teacher-Level Factors)   163
3   Rapid Literature Review: School Belonging Practices Evidence-Base
    (School-Level Factors)   164
4   Teacher Well-being Contributory Factors   222
5   Reflective Questions for New and Experienced Teachers   225

FIGURES

1 Clough et al. (2002) Developed the 4c Model of Mental Toughness
   (Image Used With Permission From AQR International Ltd)   33
2 TES Well-being Framework   37
3 TES Well-being Strategy   38
4 Components of Meaning in Life (Wong, 1997)   74
5 The Basics of ABT Practice   106
6 Navigating Well-being Change Wheel   206
7 Pedagogical Well-being Framework   214
8 Job Demands – Resources Model for Teacher Well-being   229

ABOUT THE EDITORS

Dr Andrea Giraldez-Hayes is an accredited coaching psychologist, supervisor and consultant specialising in the use of arts and creative approaches to positive psychology and coaching psychology. She is Director of the MSc in applied positive psychology and coaching psychology and the Wellbeing and Psychological Services Centre at the University of East London's School of Psychology.

Curious and passionate about learning and personal and professional development, Andrea is a person of many talents built throughout 30 years of experience. She has served in different roles within the arts, education, and coaching psychology sectors, having worked for universities, education departments, and international organisations in Europe, the United Kingdom, and Latin America. She has authored 20 books and contributed to many peer-reviewed papers and articles in positive psychology, coaching psychology, and arts education.

Andrea is an associate editor for *Coaching: An International Journal of Theory and Practice*, *International Coaching Psychology Review*, and the *International Journal of Coaching Psychology* and co-editor of *Philosophy of Coaching*. She is also a member of the British Psychological Society's Coaching Psychology Division committee. For more information, please go to https://www.linkedin.com/in/andreagiraldez/

Dr Jolanta Burke is a Chartered Psychologist with the British Psychology (British Psychological Society) specializing in positive psychology and an Associate Professor in the Centre for Positive Psychology and Health in RCSI University of Medicine and Health Sciences. She has authored eight books and has contributed with over 200 academic, professional and popular publications in the area of positive psychology for such publications as the *Guardian*, *New Zealand Herald*, and *Irish Independent*, and was invited to speak at events worldwide. Her books include "The ultimate guide to implementing wellbeing programmes for school" published by Routledge and "Positive psychology and school leadership" published by Nova Science Publishers. She is an editor-in-chief of the *Journal of Happiness and Health* and she writes a regular blog "The Good Life Ritual: A Healthy Mind, One Step at a Time" for Psychology Today. Dr Burke has won a range of educational rewards, such as the prestigious "Trinity Teaching Excellence Award", many years in a row. For her work in Ireland, she has been acknowledged by the *Irish Times* as one of 30 people who make it a better place. For more information, please go to www.jolantaburke.com

ABOUT THE CONTRIBUTING AUTHORS

Dr Kelly-Ann Allen, PhD, FAPS, FCEDP, is an Educational and Developmental Psychologist, a Senior Lecturer in the Faculty of Education, Monash University, and an Honorary Senior Fellow at the Centre for Wellbeing Science, University of Melbourne. She is also the co-director and founder of the Global Belonging Collaborative and Editor-in-Chief for the Educational and Developmental Psychologist and Co-Editor in Chief of the *Journal of Belonging and Human Connection*.

Dr Gökmen Arslan is an Associate Professor at Burdur Mehmet Akif Ersoy University in Burdur, Turkey, and an honorary senior fellow at The Centre for Wellbeing Science, University of Melbourne, Australia. He is a researcher in the field of counselling psychology, with a core interest in children and adolescent mental health and wellbeing. His research explores how best to provide meaningful programs and resources that promote positive youth development and wellbeing.

David Bott is a sought-after speaker, author, and education consultant who works with government organisations and some of the world's leading schools to help guide wellbeing vision and strategy. David's bestselling book, *10 Things Schools Get Wrong: And How We Can Get Them Right* was published in 2020. David's current work is informed by his five years as Associate Director at the Institute of Positive Education and his 15 years of practical teaching experience in Australia and the United Kingdom where he held senior pastoral and academic leadership positions.

Professor Christopher Boyle, PhD, FBPsS, is Professor of Inclusive Education and Psychology at the University of Adelaide. He is a Fellow of the British Psychological Society and a Senior Fellow of the Higher Education Academy. He *was previously Editor in Chief* of The Educational and Developmental Psychologist (2012–2017) and is currently the co-inaugural founding editor of *Belonging and Human Connection* (with Kelly-Ann Allen) of the journal *Belonging and Human Connection* published by Brill. He is an internationally recognised and respected academic and author on the subjects of inclusive education and psychology. He is a registered psychologist in the United Kingdom and Australia.

Dr Jude Brady was PhD student at the Faculty of Education, University of Cambridge, supervised by Elaine Wilson. Jude taught English in two inner London secondary schools and obtained a Master's degree from Goldsmiths, University of London. She is now a researcher at Cambridge Press and Assessment.

Dr Majella Dempsey is an associate professor at Maynooth University where she specialises in curriculum, teaching, learning, and assessment. She has led many small- and large-scale European research projects on the role of pedagogy in curriculum enactment. She is the author of "Undertaking Capstone Projects in Education: A Practical Guide for Students" published by Routledge.

Dr Padraic J. Dunne is an immunologist (research scientist), practicing psychotherapist and meditation teacher, currently based at the RCSI University of Medicine and Health Sciences, Centre for Positive Psychology and Health. He is interested particularly in meditation-based interventions that combine biofeedback tools, wearable devices, and digital support coaching platforms for promoting health and wellbeing.

Daniela Falecki, founder of *Teacher Wellbeing*, the "keep-it-real" teacher. Specializing in Positive Psychology & Coaching Psychology with more than 20 years' experience as a teacher. Master's in Education (Leadership), Bachelor of Education (HPE), Certificated Rudolf Steiner Education, licensed Mental Toughness, Executive Coach and member of the International Coach Federation and International Positive Psychology Association.

Professor Paul Gilbert, FBPsS, PhD, OBE, is Professor of Clinical Psychology and Director of the Centre for Compassion Research and Training at the University of Derby. In 2006, he established the Compassionate Mind Foundation, an international charity promoting wellbeing through researching and applying compassion. He was awarded an OBE in 2011 and has written and edited many books on compassion.

Ashley Green is originally from Scotland. Ashley now teaches full time in a school in Dubai, United Arab Emirates. Upon completing her master's degree in applied positive psychology and coaching psychology, Ashley is immersed in her passion for improving mental health and wellbeing provision in education. Her website is www.mindfulmissgreen.com.

Dr Suzy Green is a Clinical and Coaching Psychologist (MAPS) and Founder of The Positivity Institute. Suzy is a pioneer and leader in the complementary fields of Positive Psychology and Coaching Psychology. Suzy currently holds Honorary Academic positions as Honorary Visiting Professor in the School of Psychology, University of East London and Honorary Fellow at the Centre for Wellbeing Science at the University of Melbourne.

Dr Caroline Harvey, PhD, fHEA, CPsychol, is a Senior Lecturer in Psychology, researching compassion in the curriculum within Higher Education. Her work is focussed on supporting students and staff to develop more compassionate communication skills and assessing the impact these skills can have in embedding compassion within education.

Professor Evangelos Himonides held the University of London's first ever lectureship in music technology education. He is now Professor of Technology, Education, and Music and teaches Music Education, Music Technology, and Information Technology, at a post-graduate level, at the UCL Institute of Education and also leads the post-graduate course "Music Technology in Education". Publications currently number over one hundred. When time is available, Evangelos works as an electric guitarist, vocalist, and guitar luthier enthusiast!

Dr Lucy Hone is a co-author of the "The Educators' Guide to Whole-school Wellbeing: A Practical Guide to Getting Started, Best-practice Process and Effective Implementation". She received IPPA's Education Impact Award in 2021. Originally from London, she trained at the University of Pennsylvania and is co-founder with Dr Denise Quinlan of the New Zealand Institute of Wellbeing and Resilience, which works globally to build wellbeing in schools. Lucy works internationally as a speaker and educational consultant https://nziwr.co.nz/. Lucy's best-selling book, *Resilient Grieving*, along with her Top 20 TED Talk of 2021, 3 Secrets of Resilient People (over 5 million views), have seen Lucy's resilience work in demand from a global audience.

Julie Hurst, MSc, founded the Work Life Balance Centre, an organisation promoting the use of positive psychology and compassion in schools throughout the United Kingdom. She is currently studying for a PhD at the University of Derby developing a teacher-led compassion curriculum.

Rebecca G. Johnson is a Master of Educational and Developmental Psychology candidate in the Faculty of Education at Monash University. She has a particular research interest in how young people feel that they belong, both in Australia and cross-culturally.

Clive Leach has worked widely within the education sector internationally on the design and delivery of wellbeing and positive education programs. In addition to his work as a coach, facilitator, and author, Clive is a visiting lecturer on the MAPPCP program at the University of East London. He is a graduate of the Master of Organisational Coaching program at the University of Sydney.

Dr Tim Lomas completed his PhD in 2012, focusing on the impact of meditation on men's mental health. Since then, he has published over 80 papers and 11 books relating to wellbeing, involving topics including linguistics, systems theory, neuroscience, mindfulness, Buddhism, gender, art, and cross-cultural enquiry (see www.drtimlomas.com).

Dr Frances A. Maratos, PhD, fHEA, CPsychol, is an Associate Professor and Reader in Emotion Science, whose expertise centres on understanding psychological, neurological, cognitive, and physiological correlates of emotional wellbeing. Her research has contributed to understanding anxiety and its relationship with eating disorders, understanding processes of threat and self-criticism, and the use of compassion for emotion regulation across various populations. She has published over 40 peer-reviewed works in these specific areas and has further been involved in the award of over £1.3 million in grant applications, including that related to progressing 'Compassion in Schools'.

Dr Fiona May, PhD, is an Educational and Developmental Psychologist and Researcher at Monash University and Senior Research Specialist at the Parenting Research Centre. Fiona has over 20 years' experience supporting the mental health and wellbeing of children, families, and educators working in a range of research, policy, project management, and clinical practice roles in Australia and internationally.

Dr Patricia McCarthy, PhD, is a Visiting Research Fellow in the School of Education at Trinity College Dublin, Ireland. Patricia is a recognised expert in the areas of disability and learner experiences of participation in education and society. As a registered blind person,

Patricia is an active advocate for people with disabilities, advising various governmental and civic society organisations. Patricia's doctoral research focused on the educational experiences and transition opportunities of vision impaired/blind young people. Patricia is a member of the National Council for Special Education (NCSE) Consultative Forum on special education matters.

Dr Conor Mc Guckin, PhD, is an Associate Professor of Educational Psychology in the School of Education at Trinity College Dublin, Ireland. Conor convenes the Inclusion in Education and Society Research Group. Conor's research interests include: psychology applied to educational policy and practices, bully/victim problems among children and adults, and inclusive education. Conor is an Associate Fellow of both the British Psychological Society (BPS) and the Psychological Society of Ireland (PSI). Conor is a Chartered Psychologist with both the BPS and PSI and a Chartered Scientist with the UK Science Council.

Dr Trudy Meehan, PhD, DClinPsych, CPsychol, PsSI, is a lecturer in the Department of Positive Psychology and Health at the Royal College of Surgeons. She is a Chartered Clinical Psychologist specialising in Child and Adolescent Mental Health. Her research focuses on play, creativity, and health.

Christian van Nieuwerburgh is Professor of Coaching and Positive Psychology at the Royal College of Surgeons in Ireland, Global Director of Growth Coaching International and Honorary Principal Fellow of the Centre of Wellbeing Science at the University of Melbourne (Australia).

Professor Cynthia L.S. Pury is Professor of Psychology at Clemson University. She has been studying the psychology of courage since 2003 and is the author of numerous articles and chapters on courage, the editor of *The Psychology of Courage: Modern Research on an Ancient Virtue* (with Shane Lopez, APA Books 2010), and an associate editor at the *Journal of Positive Psychology*.

Dr Denise Quinlan is a co-author of the "The Educators' Guide to Whole-school Wellbeing: A Practical Guide to Getting Started, Best-practice Process and Effective Implementation". She received IPPA's Education Impact Award in 2021. Originally from Dublin, she trained at the University of Pennsylvania and is co-founder with Dr Lucy Hone of the New Zealand Institute of Wellbeing and Resilience, which works globally to build wellbeing in schools. Denise works internationally as a speaker and educational consultant https://nziwr.co.nz/. Her award-winning podcast, Bringing Wellbeing to Life, explores wellbeing topics with leading researchers and practitioners from around the world.

Mary Quirke is a PhD candidate in the School of Education at Trinity College Dublin, Ireland. Mary is a qualified career guidance counsellor, having worked with AHEAD (a non-governmental organization advocating for the inclusion of people with disabilities in further and higher education and in the workplace) as Assistant Director for over 15 years. Mary has actively engaged with UDL for many years. Mary is a recognised expert in the areas of inclusive education and employment – built upon over many years through active engagement with learners, teachers, and employers in Ireland and internationally. Mary's primary research interests include UDL, career guidance/professional practice development, and inclusive practices.

Dr Sue Roffey has been a teacher, educational psychologist, academic, and parent. She has written numerous books, chapters, and journal articles on various aspects of school and student wellbeing, including behavior, relationships, and social/emotional learning. Sue works internationally as a speaker and educational consultant www.growinggreatschools-worldwide.com

Professor Michael L. Wehmeyer, PhD, is the Ross and Mariana Beach Distinguished Professor of Special Education; Chair, Department of Special Education; and Director and Senior Scientist, Beach Center on Disability at the University of Kansas. His research focuses on self-determination, positive psychology and disability, and educating students with extensive support needs.

Dr Elaine Wilson is an Associate Professor at the Faculty of Education, University of Cambridge, where she is the Director of the Innovation and Reform team. Elaine has worked on education reform programmes in Kazakhstan, India, and Romania. She has contributed to Initial Teacher Education programmes and supervises doctoral and master's students in the Faculty of Education. Elaine was funded by the Gatsby Charitable Foundation to support new science teachers to remain in schools and has published research about teacher wellbeing.

Denise Wong is a Master of Educational and Developmental Psychology candidate in the Faculty of Education at Monash University. She has an interest in applying research to improve adolescent education and wellbeing outcomes.

Dr Murat Yıldırım is an associate professor and serving as the Head of Department Psychology, Ağrı İbrahim Çeçen University, Turkey. Dr Yıldırım received master and PhD degrees and postdoctoral training from University of Leicester, United Kingdom. His research focuses on individual differences, positive psychology, and wellbeing.

Part 1

Positive psychology in schools

Almost 15 years after the first experiences applying positive psychology in schools (Seligman et al., 2009), we have a consistent body of research and practice to show the benefits of these approaches and their impact on school communities worldwide. Children and young people spend a substantial part of their time in schools, and parents and teachers try to equip them with the knowledge, skills, and capabilities to succeed in life. But what does "success in life" exactly mean? Although professional accomplishments can be a priority for many, they leave out other essential life areas, including relationships, self-worth, personal growth, engagement, autonomy, or purpose in life. Thus, during the last decade, there has been increasing recognition of the need of placing academic development and well-being as equally important endeavours in schools.

The first part of this book includes two chapters, Positive schools: an introduction and applying positive psychology in primary schools. Chapter 1 explores the application of positive psychology in schools, the rapid development of positive education, and the benefits of using these approaches. Chapter 2 focuses on how positive psychology can help schools promote healthy child development, including growing independence, having a strengths-based self-concept, a positive connection with others, or confidence in learning.

As you read this part, you may consider these questions:

- What are the benefits of applying positive psychology theories and interventions in schools?
- Why should schools consider positive education?
- How is teaching linked with emotional health and well-being?

Reference

Seligman, M. E., Ernst, R. M., Gillham, J., Reivich, K., & Linkins, M. (2009). Positive education: Positive psychology and classroom interventions. *Oxford Review of Education, 35*(3), 293-311.

DOI: 10.4324/9781003228158-1

1 Positive schools

An introduction

Jolanta Burke and Andrea Giraldez-Hayes

> This chapter explores the application of positive psychology in schools, the rapid development of positive education, and the benefits of using these approaches.

In today's world, global education faces many critical challenges. However, it has also millions of passionate teachers contributing to their students' cognitive and emotional growth. Using a traditional perspective, we could focus on the challenges and offer ideas to fix them. Nevertheless, we choose to use a positive psychology approach and focus on the strengths of education worldwide, on what is already working and what could help schools flourish and thrive. By doing that, we do not intend to overlook the problems but adopt an appreciative inquiry stance to education and school change and choose to use positive psychology to prevent and overcome some of the main challenges.

Positive psychology has been defined as the "study of what is right about people –their positive attributes, psychological assets, and strengths. It aims to understand and foster the factors that allow individuals, communities, and societies to thrive" (Kobau et al., 2011). Thus, positive psychology focuses on well-being, strengths, positive emotions, flow, meaning, wisdom, creativity, happiness, relationships, kindness or hope of individuals, communities, and institutions. In other words, it focuses on what makes them flourish rather than languish.

The origin of positive psychology as we know it today can be traced back to 1998, when Professor Martin Seligman, appointed as the president of the American Psychological Society, delivered a historical presidential address and invited researchers and practitioners "to work on building wellbeing, not just on the traditional task of reducing ill-being" (Seligman, 2019). It did not take long for educators to become interested in the application of positive psychology within education settings. In 2009, Seligman and his colleagues referred to positive education as a field with its own entity, defined as "education for both traditional skills and for happiness" (Seligman et al., 2009, p. 293) and suggested that there were already "substantial evidence from well-controlled studies that skills that increase resilience, positive emotion, engagement and meaning can be taught to schoolchildren". Since then, the potential of positive psychology in education, and more specifically in schools, has been considered and given rise to an increasing number of programmes, resources, research,

DOI: 10.4324/9781003228158-2

and approaches to supporting well-being. Many publications, including the *Handbook of Psychology in Schools* (Furlong et al., 2009), *Evidence-Based Approaches in Positive Education: Implementing a Strategic Framework of Well-being in Schools* (White & Murray, 2015), *The Ultimate Guide to Implementing Well-being Programmes for Schools* (Burke, 2021), or *The Palgrave Handbook of Positive Education* (Kern & Wehmeyer, 2015) as well as numerous research papers, demonstrate the interest in the field.

The application of positive psychology in education has focused on a wide variety of topics, including resilience (Kibe & Boniwell, 2015), gratitude (Froh et al., 2014), positive communication and character strengths (Fox Eades, 2008; Liesveld & Miller, 2005; White et al., 2019), creativity (Kaufman & Beghetto, 2009), emotional regulation (Morrish et al., 2018), dialogic teaching, and teaching students to make wise judgements (Reznitskaya & Stenberg, 2004) or hope (Lopez et al., 2004). These and other topics are essential in schools to promote students' and teachers' well-being and prevent mental health issues, partly related to the difficulties experienced in VUCA – that is, volatile, uncertain, complex, and ambiguous – world. If according to the main statistics (APPG, 2020; Golberstein et al., 2020; WHO, 2020), mental health in schools was already a problem, other factors, such as globalisation, climate change, economic uncertainty, inequality and, more recently, the COVID pandemic, have had a massive impact on the school communities. Today's schools look very different than they did a few years ago, and the future is difficult to anticipate. However, something seems to be clear: adapting to unpredictable and fast-paced change requires developing emotional, cognitive, and behavioural skills to cope and thrive amid uncertainty.

COVID-19 affected billions of students and educators worldwide (UN, 2020). In the biggest social experiment in distance education (Gouëdard et al., 2020), some teachers and school leaders have struggled, while others thrived by learning new skills, rapidly adapting to changed circumstances and realising they are more capable to deliver online content and educate young people remotely than they had anticipated (Burke & Dempsey, 2020, 2021; Dempsey & Burke, 2021). Positive psychologists reminded everyone that crisis was also time for "buffering, bolstering, and building mental health" (Waters et al., 2021). Within education, it was time to recognise that COVID-19 has also resulted in growth, bringing people closer together, upskilling, and in some cases, higher levels of well-being (Arslan & Burke, 2021). As much disruption as the pandemic brought into our lives, it made many school communities stronger.

The positive psychology field is growing extensively year on year. While it emerged as a call to researchers to explore the positive assets and experiences that result in positive outcomes, its function is aimed to systematically diminish as we integrate it into daily school life. The same way as positive reinforcement was innovative and has become a common practice in many schools today, so will the application of positive psychology in school. In the meantime, however, we hope that the book will offer readers the direction they can choose to take as teachers and school leaders to make a series of small positive changes in their practice that result in positive outcomes.

The idea of this book came from the extensive discussions with teachers and school leaders, many of whom have read books and articles about positive psychology and saw the immense potential it offered for schools but did not quite know how to introduce it in practice. One of the authors (Jolanta) attempted to provide more clarity about the application of positive education, in her book "The Ultimate Guide to Implementing Wellbeing Programmes for School" published recently by Routledge, however, the current volume takes practitioners further towards a more comprehensive integration of positive psychology research in school's daily practice. We did this by ensuring that half of each chapter focused on the theoretical foundations of positive psychology concepts, and the other half provided practical ways in which positive psychology could be used by teachers to enhance students' well-being and help their school community reach their subjective level of optimal human functioning. The contributors have therefore provided research-based practice, in the form of "try this" activities for educators and students, case studies that offer a peek into how other teachers have applied discussed concepts in schools, as well as a range of discussion points to enable readers to reflect on and discuss the presented research with colleagues. We also supplemented each chapter with additional resources, so that readers can expand their knowledge further if they are interested in a specific topic. Overall, the book provides over 50 tools for educators to help them apply positive psychology in schools more effectively.

While our primary objective when editing this book was to help educators apply positive psychology in schools, our secondary objective was to begin a multidisciplinary debate among researchers concerning ways in which they can create positive schools. Often, positive psychology and education researchers work in silos expanding the wealth of knowledge within their discipline and not drawing enough from other disciplines. Although education is unique in that it incorporates multiple fields in its studies, e.g. psychology, sociology, philosophy, and others; nonetheless, the misunderstanding about positive psychology applied in education persists, whereby some educators continue to see it as 'happyology'. This is why we purposefully invited collaborators with varied expertise. Our contributors include academics who specialise in education, inclusion, social psychology, positive psychology, and many others. Furthermore, some of our contributors have invited practitioners to co-create their chapters to ensure they apply to the readers. We, therefore, offer you a volume that views the Applied Positive School Psychology not through a single, but multiple lenses, which provides a more comprehensive perspective.

To ease your understanding, the volume you are about to read is divided into six parts. These parts offer a comprehensive, but not exhaustive, perspective on the application of positive psychology in primary and secondary schools.

In Part 1 of the book, besides this introduction, we offer a chapter about the application of positive psychology in primary schools. In Part 2 of the book, we consider how young people and teachers connect. Connecting with others is the most fundamental source of well-being for teachers and students (Allen et al., 2017; Pyhalto et al., 2010; Soini et al., 2010). In Chapter 3, we introduce the concept of positive relationships. In Chapter 4, we will discuss the role that self-confidence and self-efficacy play in enhancing well-being. Both concepts enable the connection between people (Clem et al., 2021). Chapter 5 introduces the concept of courage and its application in schools. Courage is required for taking risks and as such can help individuals build connections. Chapter 6 considers how educators can use character strengths to connect with students. Finally, Chapter 7 discusses the application of coaching conversations in school, which, apart from helping individuals connect, can also boost the school community's well-being.

Part 3 delves into a different kind of connection, which is the connection with selves. For us to connect with others, we need to have a good relationship with ourselves. As such, Chapter 8 discusses the meaning of life. We often see meaningfulness as a concept exclusive to adults. Yet, cultivating youth life meaning is one of the crucial ways in which they can connect with themselves, their value system, and their lives. In Chapter 9, we consider connection from the point of view of compassion. What does compassion in school look like and how it can be used daily in a classroom. Chapter 10 delves into the meditation-based tools to connect with the self on a deeper level. Finally, Chapter 11 discusses strength-based intervention as a connection with self.

In Part 4, we discuss the topic of creativity in schools. Chapter 12 considers arts in school and its impact on well-being. Chapter 13 makes the case of music and technology as resources to promote well-being. Chapter 14 focuses on the reasons why play is important for children and adults alike and introduces ways in which play can be introduced into the schools' daily life. Finally, in Chapter 15, we turn the creativity in schools on its head by considering how the innovative well-being lexicon can be applied in school's daily practice.

Part 5 focuses on inclusion. We start with Chapter 16, which delves into the concept of school belonging that is essential for supporting young people in feeling that they matter. Chapter 17 discusses emerging research relating to how positive psychology can help reduce bullying and victimisation in schools. Chapter 18 focuses on a specific type of inclusion, which relates to using positive psychology to enhance inclusive education. Finally, in Chapter 19, we present a positive solution for comprehensive strength-based integration of students with disabilities in schools.

In the final Part 6 of this book, we will discuss topics that usually do not appear in well-being books for school. This is why we called it: *The road less travelled for well-being strategies.* In this part of the book, we start by arguing in Chapter 20 about the importance of whole-school well-being and the process educators may take to enable full integration of well-being strategies. Chapter 21 focuses on the organic growth of well-being that relates to altering some of the pedagogies that enable both students and teachers to experience higher emotional and cognitive functioning. In Chapter 22, we discuss the importance of schools looking after their teachers' well-being. Teachers are often disregarded in well-being strategies. Yet, research is indicating that they are part of the school ecosystem that affects each other (Harding et al., 2019). When teachers are unhappy, so are their students and vice versa. Therefore, putting teachers at the forefront of any well-being changes in school is of utmost importance. Finally, Chapter 23 is an ode to the teacher's expertise in making evidence-based educational decisions. While this book focuses on the contribution of positive educational research to teachers' practice, in this chapter, we acknowledge the importance of teachers' expertise in making evidence-based choices.

This book was created with a practitioner in mind. When selecting contributors, topics, and designing the structure of this book, we continually asked ourselves how our choices will help us in your classroom. We hope that this book will assist you not only in implementing lasting changes in the school but that it will also help you to get the best out of yourself and your students and do what teachers do best, which is changing people's lives one student at the time. Enjoy reading it.

References

Allen, K., Vella-Brodrick, D., & Waters, L. (2017). School belonging and the role of social and emotional competencies in fostering an adolescent's sense of connectedness to their school. In E. Frydenberg, A. J. Martin, & R. J. Collie (Eds.), *Social and emotional learning in Australia and the Asia-Pacific: Perspectives, programs and approaches.* (pp. 83–99). Springer Science + Business Media. https://doi-org.elib.tcd.ie/10.1007/978-981-10-3394-0_5

Arslan, G. and Burke, J. (2021) 'Positive education to promote flourishing in students returning to school after COVID-19 closure', Journal of School and Educational Psychology, 1(1), 1–5.

Burke, J. & Dempsey, M. (2020). Covid-19 Practice in Primary Schools in Ireland Report. Maynooth: Maynooth University.

Burke, J. & Dempsey (2021). Wellbeing in Post-Covid Schools: Primary school leaders' Reimagining of the Future. Maynooth: Maynooth University.

Burke, J. (2021). *The ultimate guide to implementing wellbeing programmes for schools.* Routledge.

Clem, A.-L., Rudasill, K. M., Hirvonen, R., Aunola, K., & Kiuru, N. (2021). The Roles of Teacher-Student Relationship Quality and Self-Concept of Ability in Adolescents' Achievement Emotions: Temperament as a Moderator. European Journal of Psychology of Education, 36(2), 263–286.

Dempsey, M. & Burke, J. (2021). Lessons Learned: The experience of teachers in Ireland during the 2020 pandemic. Maynooth: Maynooth University.

Fox Eades, J. (2008). *Celebrating strengths: Building strengths-based schools.* CAPP Press.

Froh, J. J., Bono, G., Fan, J., Emmons, R. A., Henderson, K., Harris, C., & Wood, A. M. (2014). Nice thinking! An educational intervention that teaches children to think gratefully. *School Psychology Review, 43*(2), 132–152.

Furlong, M. J., Gilman, R., & Huebner, E. S. (Eds.). (2009). *Handbook of positive psychology in schools.* Routledge.

Golberstein, E., Wen, H., & Miller, B. F. (2020). Coronavirus disease 2019 (COVID-19) and mental health for children and adolescents. *JAMA Pediatrics, 174*(9), 819–820.

Gouëdard, P., B. Pont and R. Viennet (2020), "Education responses to COVID-19: Implementing a way forward", *OECD Education Working Papers*, No. 224, OECD Publishing, Paris, https://doi.org/10.1787/8e95f977-en.

Harding, S., Morris, R., Gunnell, D., Ford, T., Hollingworth, W., Tilling, K., Evans, R., Bell, S., Grey, J., Brockman, R., Campbell, R., Araya, R., Murphy, S., & Kidger, J. (2019). Is teachers' mental health and wellbeing associated with students' mental health and wellbeing?. *Journal of affective disorders, 242*, 180–187. https://doi.org/10.1016/j.jad.2018.08.080

Kaufman, J. C., & Beghetto, R. A. (2009). Creativity in the schools: A rapidly developing area of positive psychology. In M. J. Furlong, R. Gilman, & E. S. Huebner (Eds.), *Handbook of positive psychology in schools* (pp. 193–206). Routledge.

Kern, M., & Wehmeyer, M. (Eds.). (2021). *The Palgrave handbook of positive education.* Palgrave.

Kibe, C., & Boniwell, I. (2015). Teaching well-being and resilience in primary and secondary school. In S. Joseph (Ed.), *Positive psychology in practice: Promoting human flourishing in work, health, education and everyday life* (2nd ed., pp. 297–312). Hoboken, NJ: Wiley.

Kobau, R., Seligman, M. E., Peterson, C., Diener, E., Zack, M. M., Chapman, D., & Thompson, W. (2011). Mental health promotion in public health: Perspectives and strategies from positive psychology. *American Journal of Public Health, 101*(8), e1–e9.

Liesveld, R., & Miller, J. A. (2005). *Teach with your strengths: How great teachers inspire their students.* Gallup Press.

Lopez, S. J. et al. (2004). Strategies for accentuating hope. In P. A. Linley & S. Joseph (Eds.), *Positive psychology in practice* (pp. 388–404). Wiley.

Morrish, L., Rickard, N., Chin, T. C., & Vella-Brodrick, D. A. (2018). Emotion regulation in adolescent well-being and positive education. *Journal of Happiness Studies, 19*(5), 1543–1564.

Pyhalto, K., Soini, T., & Pietarinen, J. (2010). Pupils' Pedagogical Well-Being in Comprehensive School–Significant Positive and Negative School Experiences of Finnish Ninth Graders. *European Journal of Psychology of Education, 25*(2), 207–221.

Reznitskaya, A. & Stenberg, R.J. (2004). Teaching Students to Make Wise Judgments: The "Teaching for Wisdom" Program. In P.A. Linsey & S. Joseph (Eds) Positive psychology in practice (pp.181–196). Hoboken, N.J.: Wiley.

Seligman, M. E. (2019). Positive psychology. A personal history. *Annual Review of Clinical Psychology, 15,* 1–23. https://doi.org/10.1146/annurev-clinpsy-050718-095653.

Seligman, M. E., Ernst, R. M., Gillham, J., Reivich, K., & Linkins, M. (2009). Positive education: Positive psychology and classroom interventions. *Oxford Review of Education, 35*(3), 293–311.

Soini, T., Pyhalto, K., & Pietarinen, J. (2010). Pedagogical Well-Being: Reflecting Learning and Well-Being in *Teachers' Work. Teachers and Teaching: Theory and Practice, 16*(6), 735–751.

The All-Party Parliamentary Group. (2020). *The Covid generation: A mental health pandemic in the making.* https://fhcappg.org.uk/wp-content/uploads/2021/04/THE-COVID-GENERATION-REPORT-April2021.pdf

UN. (2020). Education during COVID-19 and beyond. Accessed from https://www.un.org/development/desa/dspd/wpcontent/uploads/sites/22/2020/08/sg_policy_brief_covid-19_and_education_august_2020.pdf

Waters, L., Algoe, S. B., Dutton, J., Emmons, R., Fredrickson, B. L., Heaphy, E., Moskowitz, J. T., Neff, K., Niemiec, R., Pury, C., & Steger, M. (2021). Positive psychology in a pandemic: buffering, bolstering, and building mental health. *Journal of Positive Psychology*, 1–21. https://doi-org.elib.tcd.ie/10.1080/17439760.2021.1871945

White, M., & Murray, S. (Eds.). (2015). *Evidence-based approaches in positive education: Implementing a strategic framework for well-being in schools*. Springer.

White, M. et al. (2019). Positive communication and education: Applying character strengths in schools. In J. A. Muniz Velazquez & C. Pulido (Eds.), *The Routledge handbook of positive communication* (pp. 390–398). Routledge.

World Health Organisation. (2020). *Adolescent mental health*. WHO. https://www.who.int/news-room/fact-sheets/detail/adolescent-mental-health.

2 Applying positive psychology in primary schools

Sue Roffey

This chapter focuses on how schools need to mirror and promote healthy child development, including growing independence, supporting children to have a strengths-based self-concept, positive connection with others, having fun together, and confidence in learning.

Introduction

Children's early experiences of the learning environment are critical for their motivation, sense of self, relationships with others, and feelings of belonging, all of which contribute to both wellbeing and achievement.

This chapter focuses on how the wealth of positive psychology research in education might be applied, both within the classroom and in the wider school community, how teachers can welcome everyone, and practical ways in which they can enhance agency, safety, positivity, inclusion, respect, and equity. We highlight the critical issues of positive relationships and social capital throughout the school, including working with families, effective social and emotional learning, teacher wellbeing, and skilled leadership.

This chapter also takes the reader through the impact of adverse experiences in young children's lives, and how educators might respond to the challenges of meeting their needs. This includes the first indication of special educational needs, as well as issues of loss, trauma, and deprivation. These are often indicated by behaviour that is challenging, so we explore how schools might respond in ways that support the wellbeing of both pupils and staff.

All education, but especially in children's formative years, needs to be aligned with what we know about healthy child development in all domains. We make these links to ensure that wellbeing is embedded throughout a student's learning experience.

Theoretical background

Positive Education might be described as experiences that promote both learning and wellbeing, enabling students to flourish both in the classroom and in their lives. It is usually aligned with whole-child/whole-school wellbeing, with proactive interventions applied universally

DOI: 10.4324/9781003228158-3

and embedded within the life of the school. Positive education is not just about programs, however useful they may be. Every interaction is an opportunity to enhance relationships, resilience, and responsibility at every level of the school system (Roffey, 2017a). This requires awareness from educators, especially school leaders, knowledge of positive approaches and what these mean in practice, and skills to manage a wide range of situations, including diverse challenges.

Early school experiences

Children's first experiences of school can happen as early as four years old. What they make of it will depend on many things: the messages they have received at home about learning, their level of development and skill acquisition, their social and emotional wellbeing, and the approaches of early years teachers (Roffey & O'Reirdan, 2001). Young children who have had interactive conversations with adults and other children are likely to have a wider vocabulary, be able to express themselves better and ask questions. Language development underpins cognitive development and those children who have had positive preschool experiences will be at an advantage compared to those who have spent a lot of time in front of a screen at home and/or not mixed with other children. An effective way to both promote positive parent-child relationships and establish a necessary threshold for learning would be to encourage parents to talk to and with their children, right from birth. This would include describing what they are doing, pointing out what they see in the park or the shops, counting buttons or stairs, labelling everything, including colours, toys, animals, and feelings, sharing children's TV, and singing songs together. Such a campaign, hosted by local schools, would cost little, have far-reaching impact, and position parents respectfully as their child's first and most important teachers. It does not matter what language is spoken at home, it is giving children the tools with which to think.

Children learn in the early years by watching, listening, and copying, and also through structured and unstructured play, where they can experiment on their own, try things out with others, communicate ideas, problem-solve, experience and learn to manage a wide range of feelings, and let their imagination roam. Play is essential, not only for both receptive and expressive language, but for social and emotional development and creativity. There is now increasing evidence that unstructured play opportunities also support mental health and resilience (Gray, 2011; N.I. Gov./ Playmatters, n.d.; Howard & McInnes; 2013).

Many early education settings prioritise readiness for school by focusing primarily on the requisite behaviours, attitudes, and basic skills within the cognitive domain that will enable children to quickly adapt to an academic curriculum. Positive education suggests that establishing social and emotional wellbeing, and being guided by children's natural development, maintains children's curiosity and love of learning, which is a powerful foundation for achievement (Shoshani & Stone, 2017; Baker et al., 2017).

In the natural drive towards independence, young children are usually more than keen to do things for themselves. Giving children encouragement and agency where possible is therefore not only one of the pillars of positive psychology (Seligman, 2011), but also a prerequisite for motivation (Ryan & Deci, 2017). Early years teachers, alongside educators of pupils with additional needs, are skilled at scaffolding tasks so children can achieve at least some of the steps involved independently and experience success in doing so.

Safeguarding issues are of concern to teachers across the world, and there are often specific guidelines about touching children. But we also know that physical touch is comforting for many young children and at times they seek this out (Owen & Gillentine, 2011). It makes sense to follow the child's initiative and to be brief and public about any physical contact. This protects everyone. One teacher in Palestine has posted a video (see TeleSUR English, 2019, in the resources section at the end of the chapter) showing a poster on her classroom door with symbols of a handshake, a high five, a fist-bump, and a hug. The children point to the greeting they want each morning – an excellent example of agency in practice.

Communication with families

Positive education looks beyond events in the classroom to engagement with families. This is important throughout a child's education but never more than in the experiences parents have as their child enters school for the first time. The conversations that families have at home can either be supportive or critical of the school, and positive messages heard by children give them greater enthusiasm for being in school. If a mother says, "I met your teacher today and she seems really nice", then not only will parents feel reassured but so too will children. Some parents are anxious about this transition, and unsurprisingly convey this to their children who may then find it difficult to settle. Others are already accustomed to leaving their child and this will not be such a dramatic change. Some parents may not have had good experiences themselves in school and be intimidated by authority, others will have been successful and have confidence in asking questions or even making demands. There may be parents from different cultures, speaking a variety of languages and maybe uncertain about what will happen in school. When communication is clear, positive, inclusive, and respectful, parents feel valued and reassured about their child's safety and learning. This establishes the groundwork for future conversation and collaboration (Roffey, 2002). Communication is two way and parents also need to know they can ask questions and inform staff if there is anything that may be affecting that child's wellbeing, knowing they will not be judged. Teachers can also encourage parents to support their child's learning in ways that do not put stress on anyone – making it a fun time where mistakes are accepted as a step towards learning (Dweck, 2016).

A sense of belonging

Feeling that you belong is now recognised as essential to mental health and wellbeing and there has been a raft of research about what this means in practice in the learning environment (Allen et al., 2018). In brief, it means being welcomed and acknowledged as a valued member of the school community. This can be as simply as smiling warmly at students, using their names, and finding out a little about them so teachers can have brief conversations beyond academics, such as pets, siblings, or favourite toys. It also means structuring opportunities, so all students are able to participate and contribute. This might mean taking action to ensure that everyone is included not only in classroom activities but also in break times.

This illustrates the principle of equity. Treating everyone exactly the same does not account for individual needs or context. Children also need to see themselves progressing with their learning so that school has meaning and purpose for them.

A sense of belonging can also extend to parents, when communication is in their home language, they are invited into school as experts on their own children, and positive messages home about their children's strengths promote their confidence, not only in the school but also in their role as parents. 'Positive postcards home' is an example of a simple strategy that informs a couple of families a day of something positive about their child such as an act of friendship, a noticeable effort, or being especially helpful.

Many schools promote the wearing of a uniform to enhance a sense of pride in belonging to that particular institution. This may be the case if there is sufficient flexibility in what can be worn, respects the cultural traditions of the communities the school serves, and teachers do not discipline students for uniform infringements. This can quickly damage relationships and undermine rather than promote a sense of belonging.

Issues for students in the primary years

There are a number of issues that may arise with primary aged children as they go through school. Here we cover some that teachers will invariably come across, and explore how a positive approach might help students, their teachers, and their families.

Special educational needs: Sometimes there is growing awareness that a child is not progressing as might be expected, or that behaviours being monitored in the early years become more pronounced and challenging. This can be devastating for families, who often go through a grieving process, sometimes expressing denial and anger when presented with difficult information. Discovering that a child is on the autistic spectrum when there are no visible physical problems can be especially hard. Talking things through requires high levels of sensitivity and relationship skills. Some parents need time to accept that their child has a difficulty, some may demand high levels of support that are not available, and others just want to know why – a question that often has no clear answer. The wide range of emotions involved include sadness, anger, guilt, blame, frustration, and confusion. Teachers themselves want to do their best for their students, but may not have the time or resources to meet all needs, and they too may live with both guilt and frustration. Where there is a high level of social capital in a school, teachers will feel supported by colleagues and less likely to be overwhelmed. Parents' concerns and emotions must first be acknowledged and taken seriously: this raises the chances of working together for the benefit of the child. In time, strengths and solution-focused conversations are more helpful for everyone. This means accepting the child as they are and identifying all the strengths and positives that make them unique, rather than focusing solely on what is wrong. Similarly, clarifying what a student can do in various areas and exploring next steps in learning is a more optimistic approach. Working in partnership with families means taking into account their concerns and contexts, ensuring everyone is consulted on decisions about goals and strategies and feeling safe they can share challenges (Roffey & Parry, 2014).

Making progress: When a school is very competitive and focuses primarily on praise for pupils and their teachers who gain high marks, then it isn't only children with special needs who might struggle to maintain a positive sense of self. In order to feel they belong in a school, it has to be meaningful for children; a place where they can see themselves making progress with their learning. Where schools focus more emphatically on 'personal bests', where children compete against themselves (Ginns & Martin, 2018), they are always a winner. Students can be asked to say what was an improvement on previous pieces of work and what they have learnt for the next attempt. Cooperative learning is an instructional technique where students work together on a common project. Evidence suggests that this raises achievement levels and is helpful in maintaining interest, motivation, and positive peer relationships (Woods & Chen, 2010; Quinlan et al., 2012).

Identifying and utilising strengths: Children have different skills and abilities, but if only academic achievements are noticed, then the pillars of learning to be, learning to live together, and learning to transform oneself and society, are marginalised (OECD, 2020). When children are acknowledged for character strengths such as patience, kindness, determination, humour, and creativity, they are more likely to both feel accepted for themselves and tuned into who they are becoming. They can then explore how their strengths might support their learning, help them deal with challenges, motivate and engage them, and contribute to their overall well-being (Seligman et al., 2009). The language of strengths replaces the language of deficits and gives children something to live up to. Tell a pupil she is lazy and that becomes the self-concept she may live out. Tell her you have noticed she is trying harder and is becoming more determined, and that is how she sees both herself and her potential. A strengths approach across a class is not only beneficial for individuals but can also transform relationships and improve class cohesion (Quinlan et al., 2015). Young people's self-concept becomes more fixed as they get older. Strengths-based approaches are therefore especially valuable in the primary school.

Friendship and social emotional learning

Some teachers may believe that the social dynamics of a class are not their concern – but that risks some pupils being marginalised. Simple activities, such as mixing children up to talk to those they don't usually speak to, can change the class climate and promote cohesion. In structured conversations, or using stimulus materials, pupils may be asked to find things they have in common or to identify strengths for each other (Roffey, 2020).

Throughout the primary school friendships change and evolve, but by the time pupils are in Year 2 there is invariably a clear gender divide. Girls tend to mix in small, quite closed communication-based groups, whereas boys are in much looser activity-based groups. Without a structured intervention, those who do not fit or who are somehow different may be the target of bullying. Traditionally, schools have anti-bullying policies to react to these behaviours. Positive education focuses instead on one of the pathways to student wellbeing – social and emotional learning (SEL) (Noble et al., 2008). There is now a wealth of evidence (e.g. Durlak et al., 2011; Schonfeld et al., 2015; UNESCO/MGIEP, 2020) to indicate that not only does SEL improve skills, behaviour, attitudes, and connection to school but also learning outcomes. Effective SEL that goes beyond skills to enable pupils to take responsibility together for developing a safe and positive classroom climate requires a specific pedagogy (Roffey, 2017b; Dobia et al., 2019; Roffey, 2020). ASPIRE sets out the following:

Agency: Students are given activities that promote discussion and reflection so rather than being told what to think, they come to their own understanding about important issues. They are also given group responsibility for class wellbeing.

Safety: This is maintained by pupils working in pairs or groups and using the third person rather than the first. They discuss issues, never incidents. There is no individual competition and no student is ever singled out. Pupils may 'pass' if they choose to remain silent.

Positivity: This combines a strengths- and solution-focused approach alongside promoting positive emotions. All activities are presented as games and Circle Solutions include fun activities where pupils laugh together (Hromek & Roffey, 2009). Identifying strengths for each other is also a powerful tool for inclusion.

Inclusion: Students play a variety of games to mix them up so they work with all their peers not just their own social group. This includes 'pair shares' and 'paired interviews'. There are clear guidelines on responding to those who break the guidelines to ensure maximum inclusion.

Respect: This is demonstrated by everyone listening to whoever is speaking and never putting anyone down. Teachers model respect in all interactions, including those with students not abiding by the guidelines. Respect for culture also matters.

Equity: Some students need support to participate. This requires some flexibility. Equity is also demonstrated by the teacher participating in all activities and modelling what is required from students.

Adverse childhood experiences (A.C.E.s)

These can range from chronic issues such as ongoing neglect, abuse, poverty, family violence, parental mental illness, or addictions, to issues whose immediacy is temporary such as loss or physical illness. Some of these experiences are traumatic and will impact on children's levels of concentration and therefore on memory and learning; they are likely to foster negative emotions which can lead to outbursts of distress or aggression, non-compliance, and social difficulties (Brunzell et al., 2016; Quinlan & Roffey, 2021). We cannot address all these issues individually, so will cover some of the most common before we briefly explore what is effective in response.

Loss and family breakdown: One in four children are likely to have experienced their parents separating by the time they are 16. Children who have been living with high levels of family conflict may benefit from the relationship ending and having a calmer home life, but for many there is confusion, anxiety, and for younger children self-blame. Because of their egocentric stage of development, it is hard for children under seven years not to believe that the disappearance of a parent is not somehow their fault, perhaps because they were not 'good' enough (See Dowling and Elliot (2012) for a comprehensive guide to potential responses at different ages). Some children then have to come to terms with having a step-family. Parents may not explain what is happening, and the dramatic changes in family life can lead to outbursts of distressed behaviour seen in school, but not at home. This is another reason why positive, open relationships with parents are critical, so they feel more willing to let teachers know what is going on in students' lives that may impact on their behaviour and learning.

Poverty and deprivation: Increasing numbers of children are living with poverty and this has been exacerbated following the pandemic. The link between poverty and mental health has been illustrated in many studies (e.g. Kuruvilla & Jacob, 2007; Yoshikawa et al., 2012). Cortisol levels are raised, and many of the other A.C.E.s that children already live with are made worse. Families in dire need are less likely to have the resources that support their children's learning, including technology, books, or space to study.

Trauma: Trauma refers to experiences that are outside the norm, unpredictable, overwhelming, and result in feelings of terror and helplessness. Thoughts, feelings, and images can intrude into everyday life and affect the ability to function 'normally'. Trauma causes psychological injury with wounds that are hard to heal. The experiences include abuse, particularly sexual abuse, witnessing or being involved in incidents of violence, serious accidents, or natural disasters. Powerful and confusing feelings can be triggered by sights, sounds, voices, places, or smells. Often it is hard for a teacher to understand the trigger for unexplained behaviour. The most important thing is to try and bring the child back into the present rather than being overwhelmed by memory and/or imagination. More strategies for supporting students and their teachers can be found in the following: Roffey (2018) and Brunzell and Norrish (2021).

Relationships and behaviour

A behaviourist approach to maintaining discipline gives rewards for desired behaviours and sanctions for unwanted behaviours. For children from consistent and supportive families, this may be effective – though simply being disappointed with them is often enough. For those experiencing A.C.E.s, this approach does not only not work over the longer term, but it can also make things much worse. A zero-tolerance authoritarian approach damages relationships and does not make for a happier or more effective school (Skiba et al., 2006).

The factors that promote resilience and adaptation include having someone who believes in you, opportunities to participate and feel you belong, and high expectations – not giving up on someone (Werner & Smith, 2001). Many of the ideas already covered in this chapter will promote more pro-social behaviour when applied consistently over time, but teachers also need to have specific skills to respond with respect, care, and clarity when challenged.

An emotionally literate response is one that does not threaten a child who may already be in a fight, flight, or freeze mode. Teachers do not invade personal space, they validate emotions so there is less need for them to be expressed more loudly, and offer choices and agency rather than trying to 'control' the child. Educators need training and support to use relational strategies, including restorative approaches. Where schools focus on social capital and the quality of relationships throughout the learning environment, teachers feel supported and do not demand their rights for retribution in the face of challenging behaviour, and students know they will be treated with respect and empathy. Everyone wins.

Although there are a range of behaviours, from difficulty settling to general disruption to emotional distress, three things need to be considered: what might be contributing to this behaviour; what a teacher might do when the behaviour is occurring; and what might support behavioural change over time (Roffey, 2019a, 2019b). Labelling a child with a disorder places the problem squarely within the child and the focus of intervention is for them to change. An interactional approach explores what needs to change in the environment. Contextual wellbeing (Street, 2018) moves away from the individual to the importance of connections, culture, and cohesiveness across a school. Relationships matter, words matter, the climate of the school matters, and therefore the values and vision of school leaders as well as the skills of educators. There are no quick fixes, but consistent small positive interventions can lead to big changes over time.

Whole-child, whole-school wellbeing

There are many excellent books on promoting school and student wellbeing (e.g. Bethune, 2018; Burke, 2020) and more coming on stream. But for brevity and clarity, here we summarise the aspects of positive education detailed above using the ASPIRE acronym (Roffey, 2017b) All these principles interact with each other and together provide a foundation for well-being and learning.

Agency: Healthy relationships are not about control. In schools, teachers need to be in charge of what happens in their class, clarify and reinforce expectations. This is not the same as controlling students. Giving students choices gives them responsibility. Similarly, teachers who are given autonomy by supportive senior leaders may feel their professionalism is respected. Teacher well-being is promoted both by this empowerment and also when initiatives are acknowledged.

Safety: Positive emotions open cognitive pathways, whereas fear, anxiety, and pressure can inhibit learning. All stakeholders in a school need to feel safe physically, emotionally, and psychologically. High social capital is the oppositive of a toxic culture where people are watching their back all the time. It is where trust, support, and kindness are expected and fostered. No-one speaks either to or about students, colleagues or families negatively.

Positivity: A healthy childhood is about experiencing the wonder of the new and having fun with people who care about you. Schools that recognise these important aspects of growth build positivity into everyday interactions. Students say they value teachers who are light-hearted and able to have fun with learning. Putting a life-sized drawing of a child on the window of a classroom and talking to this image about the class can result in attention, laughter, and reduced stress.

Inclusion: This means ensuring everyone feels they belong in school regardless of background or ability. This includes pupils seeing themselves as making progress and being invited to participate in both formal and informal activities. Inclusion is also demonstrated by how schools respond to the contexts of their communities. Inclusive belonging is promoted when people across the school are given activities that enable them to get to know each other and build the understanding that is the foundation for healthy supportive relationships.

Respect: Respect is about honouring the contexts in people's lives, not jumping to judgement but listening to diverse stories. Respect is demonstrated, however, not only in what is said in conversations but in all communications. These include non-verbal messages such as who sits where in a meeting, how meetings are conducted, and the ways in which people are either empowered or intimidated.

Equity: Treating everyone the same does not take account of people's circumstances, needs, or perspectives. Equality can therefore cause damage. Equity, on the other hand, takes account of differences and provides a bespoke approach where needed. This means that flexibility needs to be built into school policies and processes. This applies to teachers and communities as well as students.

As can be seen from this chapter, creating positive primary schools is not hard and has great benefits for all stakeholders, whatever their background. It just takes the vision, the will, the determination, and the emotional literacy to build a team and follow the evidence. It really is a no-brainer! No-one who has done this ever regrets it.

Discussion points

Inclusion: How can schools ensure that every child and every family feel welcome and experiences a sense of belonging? How would you know policy and practice is effective?

Behaviour: It is easy to jump to conclusions about children whose behaviour is challenging. What would a system for monitoring needs that sensitively involves families look like?

Friendship: This doesn't happen by chance for all students. Some need more help to establish positive connections with others. Regularly mixing students up for specific conversations/activities so they get to know each other helps as does giving the whole class responsibility for ensuring no one gets left out.

Understanding neurological development: Have all staff had the opportunity to learn about the impact of experience on learning, emotions, and behaviour and the importance of epigenetics – especially the quality of relationships?

Teacher wellbeing: Happy teachers are more effective educators. How can demands be decreased and resources increased to reduce toxic stress in school?

Suggested resources

- The following two chapters in Kern, P., & Wehmeyer, M. (2021). *The Palgrave Book of Positive Education*. All chapters are open access.
  - Louise Tidmand. "Building Positive Emotions and Playfulness."
  - Tom Brunzell. "Trauma Aware Practice and Positive Education."
- Peter Gray: TED Talk on the Decline of Play: https://www.youtube.com/watch?v=Bg-GEzM7iTk&t=4s
- Roffey, S., & Parry, J. (2014). *Special Needs in the Early Years: Supporting collaboration, communication and co-ordination* (3rd ed.). Routledge.
- Dowling, E., & Elliott, D. (2012). *Understanding children's needs when parents separate*. Speechmark Books.

- Deal, R., & Roffey, S. *Strengths in Circles: Building Groups that Flourish and Fly*. Set of cards for discussion that put the ASPIRE principles of Agency, Safety, Positivity, Inclusion, Respect and Equity into practice. Available digitally from St Luke's Innovative Resources.
- Sue Roffey TEDx Talk Schools as Family – aligning education with healthy child development. https://www.ted.com/talks/sue_roffey_school_as_family_education_aligned_with_healthy_child_development.
- Telesur English. (2019). *This is how a Palestinian teacher greets her students*. https://www.youtube.com/watch?v=bPeEIyHboWo.

References

Allen, K., Kern, M.L., Broderick, D., Hattie, J., & Waters, L. (2018). What schools need to know about fostering school belonging: A meta-analysis. *Educational Psychology Review, 30*(1), 1–34.

Baker, L., Falecki, D., & Green, S. (2017). Positive early childhood education: Expanding the reach of positive psychology into early childhood. *European Journal of Applied Positive Psychology, 1*(8), 1–12.

Bethune, A. (2018). *Wellbeing in the Primary Classroom: A practical guide to teaching happiness and positive mental health*. Bloomsbury.

Brunzell, T., & Norrish, J. (2021). *Creating trauma-informed strengths-based classrooms: Teacher strategies for nurturing students' healing, growth and learning*. Jessica Kingsley Publishers.

Brunzell, T., Stokes, H., & Waters, L. (2016). Trauma-informed positive education: Using positive psychology to strengthen vulnerable students. *Contemporary School Psychology, 20*, 63–83, https://doi.org/10.1007/s40688-015-0070-x.

Burke, J. (2020). *The ultimate guide to implementing wellbeing programmes for schools*. Routledge.

Dobia, B., Parada, R.H., Roffey, S., & Smith, M. (2019). Social and emotional learning: From individual skills to class cohesion. *Educational and Child Psychology, 36*(2), 78–90.

Dowling, E., & Elliott, D. (2012). *Understanding children's needs when parents separate*. Speechmark Books.

Durlak, J.A., Weissberg, R.P., Dymnicki, A.B., Taylor, R.D., & Schellinger, K.B. (2011). The impact of enhancing students' social and emotional learning: A meta-analysis of school based universal interventions. *Child Development, 82*(1), 405-432.

Dweck, C.S. (2006). Mindset: *The new psychology of success.* Random House.

Ginns, P., & Martin, A. (2018). Personal best: How setting PB goals can significantly improve student performance. *Australian Association for Research in Education*. https://www.aare.edu.au/blog/?p=3332.

Gray, P. (2011). The decline of play and the rise of psychopathology in children and adolescents. *The American Journal of Play, 3*(4), 443–463.

Howard, J., & Mcinnes, K. (2013). The impact of children's perception of an activity as play rather than not play on emotional well-being. *Child Care Health Development, 39*(5), 737–742.

Hromek, R., & Roffey, S. (2009) Games as a pedagogy to promote social and emotional learning: 'It's fun and we learn things'. *Simulation and Gaming, 40*(1).

Kuruvilla, A., & Jacob, K.S. (2007). Poverty, social stress and mental health. *Indian Journal of Medical Research, 126*, 273–278.

Northern Ireland Government. (n.d.). *Nurturing your child's mental health through play*. https://www.education-ni.gov.uk/sites/default/files/publications/education/play-matters-nurturing-your-childs-mental-health-through-play.pdf.

Noble, T., McGrath, H., Roffey, S., & Rowling, L. (2008). *A scoping study on student wellbeing*. Australian Government, Department of Education, Employment & Workplace Relations (DEEWR).

OECD. (2020). *Future of education and skills 2030*. https://www.oecd.org/education/2030-project/teaching-and-learning/learning.

Owen, P.M., & Gillentine, J. (2011). Please touch the children: Appropriate touch in the primary classroom. *Early Child Development and Care, 181*(6), 857–868. doi: 10.1080/03004430.2010.497207.

Quinlan, D.M., Swain, N., Cameron, C., & Vella-Brodrick, D.A. (2015). How 'other people matter' in a classroom-based strengths intervention: Exploring interpersonal strategies and classroom outcomes. *The Journal of Positive Psychology, 10*(1), 77–89, doi: 10.1080/17439760.2014.920407.

Quinlan, D., Swain, N., & Vella-Brodrick, D.A. (2012). Character strengths interventions: Building on what we know for improved outcomes. *Journal of Happiness Studies, 13*(6), 1145-1163.

Quinlan, D., & Roffey, S. (2021). Positive education with disadvantaged students. In M. Kern & M. Wehmeyer (Eds.), *The Palgrave Handbook of Positive Education*. Palgrave.

Roffey, S. (Ed.). (2002). *School behaviour and families: Frameworks for working together*. David Fulton Publishers.

Roffey, S. (2017a). Ordinary magic' needs ordinary magicians: The power and practice of positive relationships for building youth resilience and wellbeing. *Kognition und Paedagogik 103 March, Social Resiliens,* 38-57.

Roffey, S. (2017b). The ASPIRE principles and pedagogy for the implementation of social and emotional learning and the development of whole school wellbeing. *International Journal of Emotional Education, 9*(2), 54-70.

Roffey, S. (2018). *Children and Trauma*. http://growinggreatschoolsworldwide.com/wp-content/uploads/2018/01/Children-and-trauma.pdf.

Roffey, S. (2019a). *The primary behaviour cookbook: Strategies at your fingertips*. Routledge.

Roffey, S. (2019b). *The secondary behaviour cookbook: Strategies at your fingertips*. Routledge.

Roffey, S. (2020). *Circle solutions for student wellbeing*. Sage.

Roffey, S., & O'Reirdan, T. (2001). *Young children and classroom behaviour*. David Fulton Publishers.

Roffey, S., & Parry, J. (2014). *Special needs in the early years: Supporting collaboration, communication and co-ordination*. Routledge

Ryan, R.M., & Deci, E.L. (2017). *Self-determination theory: Basic psychological needs in motivation, development, and wellness*. The Guilford Press.

Schonfeld, D.J., Adams, R.E., Fredstrom, B.K., et al. (2015). Cluster-randomized trial demonstrating impact on academic achievement of elementary social-emotional learning. *School Psychology Quarterly, 30,* 406-420.

Seligman, M.E.P. (2011). *Flourish*. Nicholas Brealey Publishing.

Seligman, M.E.P., Ernst, R.M., Gillham, J., Reivich, K., & Linkins, M. (2009). Positive education, positive psychology and classroom interventions. *Oxford Review of Education, 35*(3), 293-311.

Shoshani, A., & Stone, M. (2017). Positive education for young children: Effects of a positive psychology intervention for pre-school children on subjective wellbeing and learning behaviours. *Frontiers in Psychology*. https://doi.org/10.3389/fpsyg.2017.01866.

Skiba, R., Reynolds, C.R., Graham, S., Sheras, P., Close Conely, J., & Garcia-Vasquez, E. (2006). *Are zero tolerance policies effective in the schools? An evidentiary review and recommendations*. Zero Tolerance Task Force Report for the American Psychological Association.

Street, H. (2018). *Contextual wellbeing: Creating positive schools from the inside out*. Wise Solutions Books.

UNESCO/MGIEP (2020). *Re-thinking learning: A review of Social and Emotional Learning in School Systems*. https://mgiep.unesco.org/rethinking-learning.

Werner, E., & Smith, R. (2001). *Journeys from childhood to the midlife: Risk, resilience, and recovery*. Cornell University Press.

Woods, D.M., & Chen, K.-C. (2010). Evaluation Techniques for Cooperative Learning. *International Journal of Management & Information Systems (IJMIS), 14*(1). https://doi.org/10.19030/ijmis.v14i1.815.

Yoshikawa, H., Aber, J.L., & Beardslee, W.R. (2012). The effects of poverty on the mental, emotional, and behavioral health of children and youth: Implications for prevention. *American Psychologist, 67*(4), 272-284. https://doi.org/10.1037/a0028015.

Part 2

Connecting with others

Connecting with others is one of the fundamental human needs (Deci & Ryan, 2012; Maslow, 1958). Even a brief connection with a stranger impacts significantly our mental and physical health (Fredrickson, 2013). Thus, most of the main theories of well-being comprise an element of connection or a sense of social support (Burke, 2021). Longitudinal studies identified it not only as a predictor of future well-being but also a critical element for developing empathy, helping young people adapt and contribute to the society as adults (Vaillant, 2003; Werner & Smith, 1996). It is no wonder that one of the first parts of this book focuses on this phenomenon.

In this part, human connection is discussed in the context of relationships (Chapter 3). Specifically, we introduce a model that students and teachers can use to develop positive relations in school. Chapter 4 discusses the importance of self-confidence and self-efficacy, which are one of the foundations for pro-social behaviour. Chapter 5 delves deeper into the characteristics that can help young people and teachers connect, by developing their strength of courage. Chapter 6 develops the idea of connection further, in the context of character strengths. Finally, Chapter 7 delves into the coaching conversations in school that enhance well-being.

As you read this part, you may reflect on the following:

- How can I use this to connect with my school community?
- What am I doing already to help me connect?
- What can I do more of to help me connect?

DOI: 10.4324/9781003228158-4

3 Positive relationships

Jolanta Burke

Positive relationships are a foundation for well-being. They are a cornerstone of positive education and physical and mental health. This chapter presents the rationale for the need for educators to take an active role in facilitating relationships with students and colleagues.

Introduction

People are one of the fundamental sources of well-being. A robust study traced individuals' happiness throughout the day and found that people were happiest when in the company of others and at their unhappiest when alone (Kahneman et al., 2007). Research in school confirmed these findings showing that relationships (teacher–student, student–student, and teacher–teacher) are the most significant source of well-being for both students and teachers (Powell et al., 2018). Moreover, it is essential for young people, whose friendships are a crucial stage of development that may affect their future lives (Meter & Card, 2016; Werner & Smith, 2001). Thus, focusing on helping the school community develop and maintain a relationship is one of the most crucial objectives for educators, which this chapter aims to address.

Theoretical foundations

Relationships are a complex domain, composite of various parts and including an array of topics that range from a romantic relationship to work-related and school-related relations and friendships. Many long-term friendships (student–student and teacher–teacher) are created in school and work, respectively (Hoggard, 2005). Friendships serve three primary purposes (Anderson & Fowers, 2020). For some, they hold a utility value. They help individuals feel supported, gain advice, valuable skills, or increase their popularity by allowing them to belong to a social group. For others, it is a pleasure of friendship, a mutual enjoyment that drives their relationship and helps it flourish.

Nevertheless, some have it all in the form of virtuous friendship, which includes the value of both pleasure and utility. Therefore, individuals who develop this type of friendship derive pleasure from each other's company and find their relationship helpful. These types

DOI: 10.4324/9781003228158-5

of friendships contribute to the school community's hedonic and eudaimonic well-being, not to mention that mere prioritising friendship is associated with better overall health (Lu et al., 2021).

The benefits of friendships are vast. They include an improvement of well-being, life satisfaction; also, young people's social relationships protect them or support them in coping with depression or prevent self-harm (Aggarwal et al., 2017; Filia et al., 2021). However, the benefits of friendship go beyond psychological. For example, relationships with others are a protective factor against ageing and the impairment of cognitive and physiological functioning (Blieszner et al., 2019; Holt-Lunstad et al., 2010). Moreover, they prevent students from dropping out of school (Carbonaro & Workman, 2013). Considering how valuable friendships are for children and adults, educators must encourage them in schools.

At the same time, friendships are not the only type of relationships that are helpful in organisations. For example, Dutton and Spreitzer (2014) argue that for employees to flourish at work, they need high-quality connection, which facilitates their physical and psychological health and allows teachers to display more learning behaviours, commitment, and engagement. High-quality connections refer to respectful interactions with colleagues that enable them to complete their job and are filled with mutual trust and play. Similarly, what students are looking for in a school is to help them maintain their well-being, feeling connected to others, having trusting relationships with adults and peers, feeling "noticed", supported when they feel stuck, and being able to walk away from bullies (Powell et al., 2018). These types of relationships are not based on friendships but on high-quality connections. Thus, maintaining high-quality connections filled with mutual respect may be beneficial to the school community, just as much as nourishing friendships.

Finally, friendships and high-quality connections enhance the school community's well-being, as momentary connections are often very beneficial (Fredrickson, 2013). These connections may happen between individuals who have developed a relationship (friendship or high-quality connection), alternatively between acquaintances or strangers. These brief moments happen when teachers share a joke when students and teachers look at each other after they both witnessed something entertaining, smile at each other when passing by, or when students grab the last bag of crisps sitting in a basket in the school canteen simultaneously, look at each other and burst out laughing. During these momentary experiences, individuals share positive emotions, express mutual care towards each other, and asynchrony occurs between their behaviours and physiological processes. Facilitating the experiences of these fleeting connections can help teachers improve the school community's well-being.

The mattering wheel

The need for connection is reflected in some of the main theories of motivation. For example, Maslow's hierarchy of needs included "belonging" as one of its core elements (Maslow, 1958); the Self-determination Theory considered the need for relatedness as one of the three psychological needs (Ryan & Deci, 2000). This need for connection is particularly salient with specific students, such as the third culture kids (TCK), of whom there are plenty in schools worldwide (Burke, 2021). TCKs are children brought up in a culture different from their parent's culture. They are the children of emigrants who continue to speak the language or practice the cultural traditions at home. Their children, however, need to negotiate between the culture they are exposed to at home, the culture in which they live, and create their own third culture, which is an amalgamation of various cultures. For TCK, belonging and connections at school are particularly important as often they feel disconnected from their external environment, report feeling rootless, and may have difficulties building their identity (Miller et al., 2020; Van Reken & Polllock, 1999). In an international environment that young people live, the need for connection and belonging is vital, as it can help young people feel like they matter.

Mattering is the perception that individuals play a significant role in the world around them (Prilleltensky & Prilleltensky, 2021). Mattering occurs when teachers feel that they are a crucial part of the school community, when students feel that their opinion is considered necessary, and when young people feel they matter in their family, circle of friends, or community. Research with over 2,000 adolescents connected young people's antisocial and self-destructing behaviours to not feeling that they mattered (Elliot et al., 2009). The author identified three ways in which people could matter to others: (1) awareness, meaning that others notice their presence; (2) importance, that they care and are concerned about them; (3) reliance, meaning that others rely on them to contribute with something meaningful. Applying these ways actively in school and work can enhance the school community's relationships and build young people's identity.

This model was further developed by Prilleltensky and Prilleltensky (2021), who created "The Mattering Wheel", according to which individuals need to *feel* valued and *add* value in various aspects of their lives, i.e. self, relationships with others, at work (if applicable), or in their community (e.g. school). This means that they need to feel they matter to themselves, they have people in their lives to whom they matter, and they both add value and are valued by people at work and in their community. Sometimes, when individuals feel they matter a lot in one area of their lives (e.g. work), they put all their energy towards it, resulting in a vicious cycle (e.g. workaholism), whereby they do not have enough bandwidth to devote to alternative aspects of their lives. Creating an equilibrium whereby they feel valued and add value to all four aspects of their lives is the ideal outcome, even though it may be difficult for some to accomplish. However, the school community can significantly add value to young people by allowing them to feel they matter in their community, which may have a knock-on effect on their self-image, thus helping them appreciate themselves and their lives more and other people communities in their lives.

Practice

"Try this" for educators

One way relationships and the perception that others matter can be built is by capitalisation (Gable et al., 2006). Positive events occur more frequently than negative, therefore offering an opportunity to strengthen relationships (Gable & Reis, 2010). This strengthening of relationship refers to the way individuals, in this case, teachers and peers, react to positive events. When good things happen, they have four options in which to respond (Gable et al., 2006):

1   Active-destructive: provides negative feedback to the joyous event, e.g. when a student received a good grade, active, destructive feedback would be telling them it must have been a mistake, as they are not smart enough for a grade like this.
2   Passive-destructive: provides no positive or negative feedback to the good news, e.g. when a student receives a good grade, ignores the good news, changes the subject.
3   Passive-constructive: provide positive feedback but point out the negative aspects of the good news, e.g. when a student receives a good mark, saying well done and adding that now they will need to try to reach this standard constantly.
4   Active-constructive: provide unconditional positive feedback, e.g. when a student received a good grade, congratulate wholeheartedly and celebrate their success.

The active-constructive response brings people closer together, enhances their positive effect, contributes to well-being, and boosts their mood (Lambert et al., 2013; Pagani et al., 2020). More importantly, it is done in a safe environment, as reacting to adverse events can be particularly risky for relationship development (Gables et al., 2012). Reacting in an active-constructive manner can help individuals build a relationship without testing it. Its benefits extend to both parties, those who share the good news and those who celebrate the news unconditionally with others (Peters et al., 2018). Therefore, educators may encourage this way of responding in a classroom.

"Try this" for students

The benefits of gratitude are often discussed in the actor's context, i.e. the person who practices gratitude (e.g. Bohlmeijer et al., 2021; Emmons & McCollough, 2003; Watkins et al., 2003; Wood et al., 2010). However, one of the most prominent benefits of expressing gratitude lies in its impact on the actor, the recipient. Recently, researchers also observed the beneficial effect of expressing gratitude on individuals who observe the exchange of gratitude, referred to as the witnessing effect (Algoe et al., 2020). Thus, expressing gratitude may help build multiple relationships and contribute significantly to people believing that they matter. Subsequently, students may be encouraged to express gratitude regularly in front of others, to enhance their relationships.

Case study

Mary refused to go to school. Since the beginning of the school year, she experienced such high levels of anxiety when going to school that eventually, the thought of going to school was too hard for her to take, and two months later, she refused to do it. Finally, after spending three weeks at home, she received a post parcel. Upon the teacher's suggestion, children in Mary's class created a scrapbook with good wishes, reflections, and pictures that described how much they missed her and what specific things she did that contributed to the class. Mary read and re-read the messages. Finally, after a few days, she found the courage to go back to school. While the process of returning to school continued to be difficult, the positive relationships she began to develop with her friends were helpful.

Discussion points

* Discuss examples from your life of people's behaviours when they believed that they were not valued or did not add value to others?
* What actions have you or others taken to help them realise that they mattered?
* What actions can you take to prevent students from feeling like they didn't matter?

Suggested reading

Cool teacher activities: https://www.coolcatteacher.com/happy-matteringmonday/.
Prilleltensky, I., & Prilleltensky, O. (2021). *How people matter: Why it affects health, happiness, love, work, and society*. Cambridge University Press.

References

Aggarwal, S., Patton, G., Reavley, N., Sreenivasan, S. A., & Berk, M. (2017). Youth self-harm in low- and middle-income countries: Systematic review of the risk and protective factors. *International Journal of Social Psychiatry*, 63(4), 359–375. https://doi-org.elib.tcd.ie/10.1177/0020764017700175

Algoe, S. B., Dwyer, P. C., Younge, A., & Oveis, C. (2020). A new perspective on the social functions of emotions: Gratitude and the witnessing effect. *Journal of Personality and Social Psychology*, 119(1), 40–74. https://doi-org.elib.tcd.ie/10.1037/pspi0000202.supp (Supplemental).

Anderson, A. R., & Fowers, B. J. (2020). An exploratory study of friendship characteristics and their relations with hedonic and eudaimonic well-being. *Journal of Social and Personal Relationships*, 37(1), 260–280. https://doi-org.elib.tcd.ie/10.1177/0265407519861152

Blieszner, R., Ogletree, A. M., & Adams, R. G. (2019). Friendship in later life: A research agenda. *Innovation in Aging*, 3(1), igz005. https://doi-org.elib.tcd.ie/10.1093/geroni/igz005

Bohlmeijer, E. T., Kraiss, J. T., Watkins, P., & Schotanus-Dijkstra, M. (2021). Promoting gratitude as a resource for sustainable mental health: Results of a 3-armed randomized controlled trial up to 6 months follow-up. *Journal of Happiness Studies*, 22(3), 1011–1032.

Burke, J. (2021). *The ultimate guide to implementing wellbeing programmes for school*. Routledge.

Carbonaro, W., & Workman, J. (2013). Dropping out of high school: Effects of close and distant friendships. *Social Science Research*, 42(5), 1254–1268. https://doi-org.elib.tcd.ie/10.1016/j.ssresearch.2013.05.003

Deci, E. L., & Ryan, R. M. (2012). Self-determination theory. In P. A. M. Van Lange, A. W. Kruglanski, & E. T. Higgins (Eds.), *Handbook of theories of social psychology* (pp. 416–436). Sage Publications Ltd. https://doi.org/10.4135/9781446249215.n21

Dutton, J. E., & Spreitzer, G. M. (2014). *How to be a positive leader: Small actions, big impact*. Berrett-Koehler Publishers.

Elliot, A. J., Maier, M. A., Binser, M. J., Friedman, R., & Pekrun, R. (2009). The effect of red on avoidance behavior in achievement contexts. *Personality and Social Psychology Bulletin*, 35(3), 365–375.

Emmons, R. A., & McCullough, M. E. (2003). Counting blessings versus burdens: An experimental investigation of gratitude and subjective well-being in daily life. *Journal of Personality and Social Psychology*, 84(2), 377–389. https://doi-org.elib.tcd.ie/10.1037/0022-3514.84.2.377

Filia, K., Eastwood, O., Herniman, S., & Badcock, P. (2021). Facilitating improvements in young people's social relationships to prevent or treat depression: A review of empirically supported interventions. *Translational Psychiatry*, 11(1), 305. https://doi-org.elib.tcd.ie/10.1038/s41398-021-01406-7

Fredrickson, B. L. (2013). *Love 2.0: how our supreme emotion affects everything we think, do, feel, and become*. Hudson Street Press.

Gable, S. L., Gonzaga, G. C., & Strachman, A. (2006). Will you be there for me when things go right? Supportive responses to positive event disclosures. *Journal of Personality and Social Psychology*, 91(5), 904–917. https://doi-org.elib.tcd.ie/10.1037/0022-3514.91.5.904

Gable, S. L., Gosnell, C. L., Maisel, N. C., & Strachman, A. (2012). Safely testing the alarm: Close others' responses to personal positive events. *Journal of Personality and Social Psychology*, 103(6), 963–981. https://doi.org/10.1037/a0029488

Gable, S. L., & Reis, H. T. (2010). Good news! Capitalizing on positive events in an interpersonal context. In M. P. Zanna (Ed.), *Advances in experimental social psychology* (Vol. 42., pp. 195–257). Academic Press. https://doi-org.elib.tcd.ie/10.1016/S0065-2601(10)42004-3

Hoggard, L. (2005). *How to be happy.* BBC Books.

Holt-Lunstad, J., Smith, T. B., & Layton, J. B. (2010). Social relationships and mortality risk: A meta-analytic review. *PLoS Medicine*, 7(7), 1–20. https://doi-org.elib.tcd.ie/10.1371/journal.pmed.1000316

Kahneman, D., Krueger, A. B., Schkade, D. A., Schwarz, N., & Stone, A. A. (2007). A survey method for characterizing daily life experience: The day reconstruction method. In S. Maital (Ed.), *Recent developments in behavioral economics* (pp. 105–109). Elgar Reference Collection. International Library of Critical Writings in Economics, vol. 204. Cheltenham, UK and Northampton, MA: Elgar.

Lambert, N. M., Gwinn, A. M., Baumeister, R. F., Strachman, A., Washburn, I. J., Gable, S. L., & Fincham, F. D. (2013). A boost of positive affect: The perks of sharing positive experiences. *Journal of Social and Personal Relationships*, 30(1), 24–43. https://doi-org.elib.tcd.ie/10.1177/0265407512449400

Lu, P., Oh, J., Leahy, K. E., & Chopik, W. J. (2021). Friendship importance around the world: Links to cultural factors, health, and well-being. *Frontiers in Psychology*, 11, 570839. https://doi-org.elib.tcd.ie/10.3389/fpsyg.2020.570839

Maslow, A. H. (1958). A dynamic theory of human motivation. In C. L. Stacey & M. DeMartino (Eds.), *Understanding human motivation* (pp. 26–47). Howard Allen Publishers. https://doi-org.elib.tcd.ie/10.1037/11305-004

Meter, D. J., & Card, N. A. (2016). Stability of children's and adolescents' friendships: A meta-analytic review. *Merrill-Palmer Quarterly*, 62(3), 252–284. https://doi-org.elib.tcd.ie/10.13110/merrpalmquar1982.62.3.0252

Miller, S. T., Wiggins, G. M., & Feather, K. A. (2020). Growing up globally: Third culture kids' experience with transition, identity, and well-being. *International Journal for the Advancement of Counselling*, 42(4), 414–423.

Pagani, A. F., Parise, M., Donato, S., Gable, S. L., & Schoebi, D. (2020). If you shared my happiness, you are part of me: Capitalization and the experience of couple identity. *Personality and Social Psychology Bulletin*, 46(2), 258–269. https://doi-org.elib.tcd.ie/10.1177/0146167219854449

Peters, B. J., Reis, H. T., & Gable, S. L. (2018). Making the good even better: A review and theoretical model of interpersonal capitalization. *Social & Personality Psychology Compass*, 12(7), 1. https://doi-org.elib.tcd.ie/10.1111/spc3.12407

Powell, M. A., Graham, A., Fitzgerald, R., Thomas, N., & White, N. E. (2018). Wellbeing in schools: What do students tell us? *Australian Educational Researcher*, 45(4), 515–531.

Prilleltensky, I., & Prilleltensky, O. (2021). *How people matter: Why it affects health, happiness, love, work, and society.* Cambridge University Press.

Ryan, R. M., & Deci, E. L. (2000). Intrinsic and extrinsic motivations: Classic definitions and new directions. *Contemporary Educational Psychology*, 25(1), 54–67. https://doi-org.elib.tcd.ie/10.1006/ceps.1999.1020

Isaacowitz, D. M., Vaillant, G. E., & Seligman, M. E. (2003). Strengths and satisfaction across the adult lifespan. *The International Journal of Aging and Human Development*, 57(2), 181–201.

Van Reken, R. E., & Pollock, D. C. (1999). *The third culture kid experience: Growing up among worlds.* Intercultural Pr.

Watkins, P. C., Woodward, K., Stone, T., & Kolts, R. L. (2003). Gratitude and happiness: Development of a measure of gratitude, and relationships with subjective well-being. *Social Behavior & Personality: An International Journal*, 31(5), 431–452. https://doi-org.elib.tcd.ie/10.2224/sbp.2003.31.5.431

Werner, E.E. & Smith, R.S. (1996). Journeys from childhood to midlife: Risk, resilience, and recovery. Ithaca & London: Cornell University Press.

Werner, E. E., & Smith, R. S. (2001). *Journeys from childhood to midlife: Risk, resilience and recovery.* Cornell University Press.

Wood, A. M., Froh, J. J., & Geraghty, A. W. A. (2010). Gratitude and well-being: A review and theoretical integration. *Clinical Psychology Review*, 30(7), 890–905. https://doi-org.elib.tcd.ie/10.1016/j.cpr.2010.03.005

4 Self-confidence and self-efficacy development in schools

Suzy Green, Daniela Falecki, and Clive Leach

This chapter provides an overview of the scientific literature relating to self-confidence and self-efficacy and in particular interventions that have evidence for their development. The chapter concludes with a case study highlighting the application of relevant science to the development of self-confidence in a school setting.

Introduction

Most people would acknowledge that self-confidence is key to success in life. While boundless articles exist in the broader public on the topic, particularly regarding how to develop it, psychological science holds a significant and growing body of evidence that helps us to define it, measure it, and develop it. This is particularly relevant in school settings as confidence has also been deemed important because of its predictive validity for academic achievement (Phan & Ngu, 2019; Artino, 2012). In addition, the related construct of self-efficacy, which is often used interchangeably or acts as a proxy for the measure of confidence in psychological science, has also been shown to be highly correlated with psychological well-being and positive mental health (Natovová & Chýlová, 2014; Caprara et al., 2006). As such, this chapter will focus on both self-confidence and self-efficacy.

As research continues to highlight the importance of "non-cognitive factors" such as confidence, it is becoming increasingly clear that both staff and students would greatly benefit from a knowledge of the underpinning science in order to enhance their own and others' achievement, well-being, resilience, and mental toughness. It is also suggested that self-confidence and self-efficacy are potentially malleable and, therefore, could become an important target of interventions to improve both academic achievement and well-being in line with the principles of Positive Education (Seligman., 2012). However, while evidence regarding the most effective techniques for self-confidence enhancement is lacking, there is a greater bank of research on self-efficacy. This chapter will provide an overview of the scientific literature relating to self-confidence and self-efficacy and, in particular, interventions that have evidence for their use in their development. The chapter will conclude with a case study highlighting the application of relevant science to the development of self-confidence and self-efficacy within a school setting.

DOI: 10.4324/9781003228158-6

Theoretical background

Self-confidence or self-efficacy?

Definitions abound in regard to "self-confidence". The Merriam-Webster Dictionary definition is "confidence in oneself and in one's powers and abilities". The Cambridge University Dictionary defines it as "the belief that you can do things well and that other people respect you". Within psychological science, a general definition holds that confidence reflects a degree of certainty about a perception, event, or outcome (e.g., Merkle & Zandt, 2006) and empirical investigations on confidence relate to judgements, events, or outcomes. While the construct of "confidence" has been investigated, theories have lacked uniformity (Cramer et al., 2009). Self-confidence has also been used interchangeably with 'self-efficacy' but may differ in definition, theoretical support, practical application, and construct composition (Cramer et al., 2009). While a review of the debate is beyond the scope of this chapter, a recent PsychInfo search from 2019 to 2021 utilising the term "confidence" found seven out of the first 20 publications utilise "self-efficacy" as the primary term and measurement within the study, demonstrating the relevance of "self-efficacy" as a primary approach to the study of confidence.

Another reason for this chapter's focus on "self-efficacy", is that it has a solid theoretical and empirical basis and is more relevant in an educational setting. Bandura (1997), a pioneer in the study of "self-efficacy", differentiated between self-confidence and self-efficacy. He noted that the term confidence lacks a target of certainty, whereas self-efficacy targets perceived competence in a given behaviour. In other words, self-efficacy represents both "affirmation of capability and strength of that belief" while confidence reflects only strength of certainty about a performance or perception (p. 382). Self-efficacy is therefore more dependent on action and recognised progress towards a goal or achievement.

Bandura defined "self-efficacy" as "a person's particular set of beliefs that determine how well one can execute a plan of action in prospective situations" (Bandura, 1977). Bandura's Social Cognitive Theory (1986) significantly influenced education, which was at the time grounded in behaviour principles of external punishment and reinforcement. Bandura challenged this notion citing social influences (external factors) and cognitive (internal factors) as significant influences on learning. While Bandura argued learning required more than a particular set of beliefs, he also identified how social and environmental factors could influence those beliefs. Self-efficacy as a construct of Social Cognitive Theory is considered an internal, cognitive factor.

Bandura (1977) identified that individuals develop their self-efficacy beliefs by interpreting information from four main sources of influence:

1   Mastery experiences – our direct experience of success when completing a task, e.g., did I complete the task successfully?
2   Level of arousal – our emotional and physical responses such as anxiety or excitement, e.g., how do I feel about completing the task?
3   Vicarious experiences – our observation of someone modelling the success of a task, e.g., how did someone else do the task?
4   Social persuasion – the feedback we receive from others, e.g., what are others saying about the task?

Mastery experiences are the most influential of these sources given that when individuals reflect on their success, a causal relationship appears between effort and reward (Tschannen-Moran & Woolfolk Hoy, 2007). When this success is shared, it can boost morale and motivation. Vicarious experiences are also powerful in building self-efficacy. When teachers or students see others performing well, expectations are generated that they too can respond positively to challenges. Social persuasion has the potential to influence efficacy when specific feedback is provided regularly with authenticity and trust. A word of caution is needed however in relation to emotional states of arousal, as high emotional states such as anxiety might undermine self-efficacy (Buonomo et al., 2019).

Outcomes and benefits of self-efficacy

Self-efficacy is closely linked with motivation and can affect individuals' task choices, effort, persistence, and achievement (Bandura, 1997). When self-efficacy is high, people are more likely to set high goals, be less afraid of failure and apply greater effort, particularly under stress and pressure (Artino, 2012). On the other hand, when self-efficacy is low, people may avoid tasks altogether or give up easily (Seligman, 2006). Both children and adults with high efficacy tend to be optimistic about the future and have higher levels of mental and physical health (Seligman, 2006). To ensure schools remain achievement arenas for adults and children, it is argued that self-efficacy must therefore be developed.

Consistent across different educational levels, there is clear evidence showing high levels of student self-efficacy as a predictor of academic performance (Phan & Ngu, 2019; Artino, 2012). When students set short-term goals, are taught learning strategies such as summarising, and receive rewards based on achievement, self-efficacy is increased (Graham & Weiner, 1996). Efficacy is very powerful as it guides students' actions and behaviours, including whether they will try to cope with challenging situations.

In keeping with the emphasis on beliefs, Teacher Efficacy refers to "a teacher's sense of competence - not some objective measure of actual competence" (Protheroe, 2008, p. 43). When teachers feel confident in their professional abilities, they feel more control over their daily tasks (Tschannen-Moran et al., 2007), are more motivated (Skaalvik & Skaalvik, 2007), and experience greater job satisfaction (Hoy & Davis, 2005). Teachers with high self-efficacy successfully meet the rising demands of students, are willing to stretch themselves and grow, persist in the face of challenges, foster learning autonomy, and convey high expectations (Donohoo, 2017). Efficacy beliefs drive teachers' focus which influences how teachers respond to student behaviour and learning. "If educators' realities are filtered through the belief that they can do very little to influence student achievement, then it is very likely these beliefs will be manifested into their practice" (Donohoo, 2017, p. 4).

More importantly, Collective Student Efficacy (CSE), students' beliefs that by working with other people they will learn more, and "Collective Teacher Efficacy" (CTE), the shared belief that teachers in a school make an educational difference to their students, have emerged as the key influences on student achievement (Hattie et al., 2016). The term CTE was originally coined by Bandura and later popularised when John Hattie named it as the 'new number one' at the annual Visible Learning Conference (2016). CTE had been shown previously by Goddard et al. (2000) who could demonstrate that differences of collective teacher efficacy between schools were more important in explaining student achievement than socio-economic status. Furthermore, individual teacher efficacy was influenced by CTE and vice versa (Hoy et al., 2002). When schools have a sense of collective teacher efficacy, students feel more supported and are more productive.

Mental toughness

The authors, on the basis of their work in many schools around the world, see close links between the constructs of self-efficacy and mental toughness. In an ever-changing environment, it is understood that resilience is a necessary skill for individuals to overcome and bounce back from adversity, to live a meaningful and happy life. Mental toughness, which includes confidence as one of its four core components, has emerged as a popular concept for teaching and developing resilience and positivity. A person who is confident in their ability to navigate challenges is more likely to be resilient and see such challenges as an opportunity rather than a threat.

Mental toughness is defined as "A personality trait which determines, in some part, how individuals respond mentally when exposed to stressors, pressure. opportunity and challenge irrespective of the prevailing situation" (Clough & Strycharczyk, 2021, p. 1). In simple terms, mental toughness is described as having a 'can-do' attitude, embracing challenge and opportunity alongside having the skills to be able to navigate successfully through change as it occurs.

Each of the four core components of Mental Toughness – confidence, control, commitment, and challenge (Figure 1) – aligns with some or all the sources for self-efficacy previously outlined:

- Control: the degree to which an individual believes they can control the things within and around them such as their emotions, dealing with anxiety and stress, and their locus of control (Mastery Experience & Level of Arousal)
- Commitment: the degree to which they can set, strive towards, and achieve goals and manage distractions along the way (Mastery Experience & Vicarious Experience)
- Confidence: the degree to which they believe in and feel positive about their strengths and capabilities, and ability to engage with those around them, including being able to ask for help and feedback when needed (Mastery Experience, Level of Arousal, Vicarious Experience & Social Persuasion)
- Challenge: the degree to which they can seek new learning experiences, tolerate failure, critical feedback, and respond to setbacks (Mastery & Vicarious Experience, Level of Arousal & Social Persuasion)

Mental toughness has been shown to correlate with coping self-efficacy (Nichols et al., 2011) and to be a strong non-cognitive predictor of academic achievement and has been compared with other psychological traits such as motivation and attitudes (Stankov, 2013; Stankov & Lee, 2014; Stankov et al., 2012, 2014). "Children who have higher perceptions of their competence or abilities have a greater preference to engage in challenging learning activities in particular" (Boggiano et al., 1988, p. 136). Mental toughness correlates positively with greater resilience, perseverance, confidence, and self-efficacy and correlates negatively with academic stress, test anxiety, and perceptions of bullying (McGeown et al., 2016). Studies have

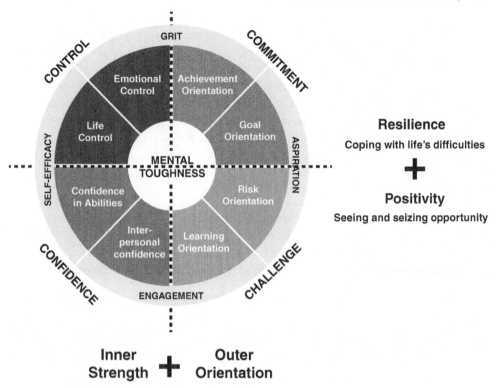

Figure 1 Clough et al. (2002) Developed the 4c Model of Mental Toughness (Image Used With Permission From AQR International Ltd).

also found that all 4Cs of mental toughness, including confidence, were strongly and inversely correlated with perceived stress and depressive symptoms of students in educational settings (St Clair-Thompson et al., 2015; Gerber et al., 2013). For adults, and particularly relevant to teachers, mental toughness has also been shown to buffer against anxiety, stress, and depression associated with job uncertainty and enhance their sense of control and self-efficacy in adapting to the changing work environments created by COVID-19 (Mojtahedi et al., 2020).

Mental toughness, and hence confidence or self-efficacy, can be developed in school staff and students through a range of interventions (Clough & Strycharczyk, 2021; St Clair-Thompson et al., 2015). These include:

- Positive Thinking – learned optimism, affirmations, thought stopping, self-talk.
- Visualisation – best future self, guided imaging.
- Anxiety Control – enhancing positive emotions, controlled breathing, relaxation, distraction.
- Attentional Control – dealing with interruptions, increasing attention span.
- Goal Setting – understanding and setting Specific, Measurable, Achievable, Relevant, Timely (SMART) goals.

We argue that all of these psychological interventions can positively impact on confidence. For example, learning controlled breathing as a portable anxiety management technique will enhance self-efficacy in situations such as delivering a presentation or speaking up on a matter. However, the range of these interventions also impact on the other components of mental toughness, i.e., challenge, control, and commitment. Therefore, we would argue that taking a multi-component intervention approach to the development of self-efficacy rather than one specific intervention may be more impactful. In fact, it has been suggested that multi-component positive psychology interventions (MPPIs) are more effective than single component (Carr et al., 2020). This is in alignment with the Synergistic Change Model (Rusk et al., 2018) which purports lasting positive change as a result of a positive psychology intervention (PPI) is most likely to occur when interventions are targeted at multiple domains of positive functioning.

Practice

Based on the research above, it would appear prudent for both educators and students to consciously and explicitly develop levels of individual and collective confidence and self-efficacy.

"Try this" for educators

For educators, strategies that build self-efficacy are closely linked to Bandura's four main sources:

1   Mastery experiences come from noticing the positive impact of planned strategies used by the teacher to connect and engage with students and are the most influential for building self-efficacy in teachers (Tschannen-Moran & Woolfolk Hoy, 2007). When teachers are able to reflect on their resourcefulness, they may feel a sense of accomplishment which acts as evidence of success. Improving teachers' abilities to notice and acknowledge positive impact strengthens their abilities to recognise personal attainments as professionals (Buonomo et al., 2019).
2   Vicarious experiences require teachers imagining themselves engaged in high-quality teacher practices. Observing a colleague model, effective teaching has been shown to be the second biggest influence on teacher self-efficacy (Palmer, 2006). By observing proficient peers or critiquing their own teaching on video, teachers can strengthen their belief in their capabilities (Gröschner et al., 2018).
3   Social persuasion involves effective and timely feedback from supportive leaders, colleagues, parents, or students. Mentoring and peer coaching have a long history in education as a model for reflection and improvement. Mentoring and coaching programmes increase teachers' readiness to experiment, innovate, and develop engaging lessons (Chong et al., 2012). Genuine and meaningful feedback and encouragement can help teachers grow from challenging experiences to persist in building mastery experiences (Clark & Newberry, 2019).
4   Levels of arousal are frequent in education where teachers recognise emotions can influence their goals, experience, and relationships with students (Buonomo et al., 2019). When teachers experience positive emotions towards their students or their role, these emotional states create a sense of pleasure and satisfaction which builds self-efficacy (Buonomo et al., 2019). Improving teachers' ability to notice and track positive emotional states can have an 'undoing effect' to restore psychological resources in the face of negative emotional states such as stress (Gloria et al., 2013).

While the self-efficacy of teachers is important for quality teaching, acknowledging teachers as part of a community and bigger system is equally important. For this reason, building Collective Teacher Efficacy must also be considered. Six enabling factors have been identified to create the conditions for Collective Teacher Efficacy (Donohoo, 2017). These include:

1   Advance teacher influence – when teachers can act as leaders with their own decision-making power on school improvement, they build efficacy (Hargreaves & Fullan, 2015).
2   Goal consensus – when leaders build consensus on goals, positive impacts can occur in school culture and teacher empowerment (Leithwood & Sun, 2009).
3   Teachers' knowledge about one another's work – celebrations of success build belief in competence (Escobedo, 2012).
4   Cohesive staff – the more cohesive staff are, the more they agree on the fundamentals of the organisation, the more likely they are to give in to social persuasion (Ross et al., 2004).
5   Responsiveness of leadership – when school leaders are able to respond to the needs of staff, they respond by working more diligently (Donohoo, 2017).
6   Effective system intervention – when effective systems of intervention and enrichment are in place, teachers' regard for their collective ability increases both self and collective efficacy (Donohoo, 2017).

Hattie is quick to add that CTE is not about making teachers feel good about what they do. Building internal beliefs about practice is more complex and requires ongoing professional learning with continuous reflection and feedback (Donohoo, 2017).

Strategies to enhance CTE include regular participation in teacher networks, collaborative inquiry, and peer coaching. Peer coaching reduces isolation while increasing opportunities for insight and collaboration. Through reflective questioning, individuals are able to question existing beliefs and internalise new practices. Collectively, vicarious sources of efficacy occur through observation of peers helping each other recognise success.

"Try this" for students

For students, this can be achieved in the following ways:

Goal setting

Mastery experiences can be gained by teachers helping students to visualise, articulate, and set SMART goals and assess their progress towards achieving them, including overcoming setbacks along the way (Artino, 2012). Critical to goal striving is the ongoing monitoring of progress towards them (which can be supported by utilising a coaching approach – see below). When students realise that they are achieving their goals, their self-efficacy increases.

Evidence-based coaching conversations

Studies suggest that evidence-based (solution-focused and cognitive behavioural) coaching conversations (Grant, 2003) in the form of teachers coaching students have positive outcomes for cognitive hardiness, well-being, hope, goal striving, and achievement and reduction of stress and depressive symptoms (Dulagil et al., 2016; Green et al., 2007). Coaching facilitates student awareness of strengths and resources and provides a safe space for individual reflection, strengths-based goal setting, action planning, and accountability (Green et al., 2021; Leach & Green, 2015; Madden et al., 2011).

Character strengths assessment and use

Hundreds of studies have demonstrated that positive outcomes arise for children, young people, teachers, and parents as they learn to recognise and use their character strengths (Peterson & Seligman 2004), including enhanced well-being, self-efficacy, resilience, engagement, academic attainment, and performance, as well as reductions in anxiety, stress, and depressive symptoms (Quinlan et al., 2019; Harzer et al., 2017; Waters & Sun, 2016). The Values in Action Character Strengths Survey (www.viacharacter.org) is recognised as an integral element of most positive education programmes.

Peer mentoring

Vicarious experiences can be created through peer mentoring programmes that recruit students who are doing well to help those lacking in confidence and model attitudes and behaviours that contribute to experience success (Artino, 2012). Matching those who may be struggling or at risk with peers who have coped previously with academic tasks or wider goals and who can help others to understand and develop coping strategies. This can build confidence in life and learning for those previously lacking efficacy.

Student assessment

There are a multitude of validated assessment tools and measures that can be applied to assess student self-confidence and self-efficacy specifically and in the wider context of student and whole-school well-being (Public Health England, 2021). These include the New General Self-efficacy Scale (Chen et al., 2001) and the Children's Self-efficacy Scale (Muris, 2001) alongside composite well-being measures such as the AWE (www.awewsomeschools.com), measures such as the MTQ48 Mental Toughness assessment (www.aqr.com) and apps that can record real-time student emotional experience such as EI Pulse (www.educatorimpact. com). These tools and assessments can inform strategic approaches to building self-efficacy, identify individual students at risk and in need of targeted prevention or early intervention, and ensure support is available to sustain and stretch further those who are doing well.

Case study

The British Secondary & High School Section of the Taipei European School (TES) embarked on a strategic approach in 2016, to enhance well-being and academic achievement within their school community.

Today, the heart of TES's mission is:

> To be a flourishing, multilingual and multicultural community of lifelong learners that embraces independence, curiosity and empathy to make a positive difference in local, national and global environments.

Arguably, at the core of the school's strategy has been to build and enhance the self-confidence and self-efficacy of students, staff, leaders, and the wider school community to navigate through the challenges and embrace the opportunities that life offers both within school and beyond. The school Well-being Framework has flourishing at its heart and encompasses the PERMAH model (positive emotions; engagement; relationships; meaning; accomplishment; health) and the Five Ways to Well-being (Figure 2). The TES strategy takes account of the individual needs of each student, facilitated through positive relationships and high-quality connections, and supported by an enabling environment that places equal focus on time and processes to ensure both academic outcomes and well-being (Figure 3).

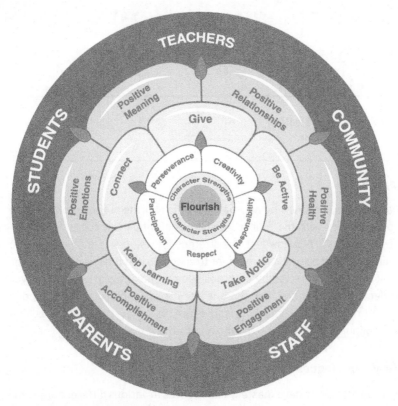

Figure 2 TES Well-being Framework.
Reprinted with permission from Taipei European School.

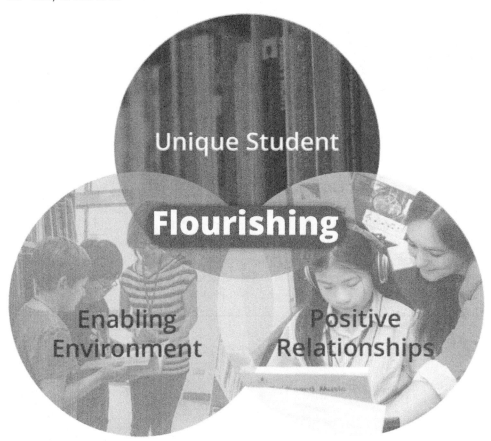

Figure 3 TES Well-being Strategy.
Reprinted with permission from Taipei European School.

The approach

TES has adopted the following approaches, which for the purposes of this case study have been aligned with the four main sources of influences for self-efficacy as defined by Bandura (1977). However, the strategy for well-being and Positive Education has been underpinned by a commitment to coaching and the creation of a school culture that has been informed by both positive psychology and coaching psychology. This reflects the recognition that 'no-one size fits all', and that an investment in time, space, and resources for coaching conversations is key to building resilience and mental toughness and sustaining ongoing positive change.

Mastery experiences

Students and teachers have mastery experiences in various different areas of school life, regularly engaging in structured goal-focused reflection practice about their own performance and growth. This includes protected time for teachers to engage in weekly professional reflection and a teacher professional development and review process that includes personal and professional goal setting and coaching.

For students, academic data is triangulated with well-being data gleaned from AWE (well-being) and MTQ48 (mental toughness) assessments to support each student. Through coaching conversations with Deans (year heads), students set goals taking into account academic aspirations and personal well-being. Interventions are individualised for the student and goal striving and progress regularly monitored.

Level of arousal

Emotional awareness and how to understand and manage emotions is a key theme and is widely incorporated into the school 'Core' well-being and mental toughness programme. This takes the form of learning about the important role of both positive and negative emotions; the language of emotions; learning about anxiety and stress and tools for emotional regulation. Interventions include a variety of mindfulness-based practices introduced across the school for staff and students ranging from 'mindful mocks' exam preparation to mindful moments in class time, and a specific focus on hope and optimism which can be features of the coaching conversations and their peer mentoring programme.

The EI Pulse App (www.educatorimpact.com) has been introduced to provide a weekly check on emotional well-being, safety, and positive identity. In addition, twice yearly well-being assessment using AWE alerts staff to students who may be struggling emotionally and lacking in confidence to seek support and also highlights potential derailing or safe-guarding issues.

Vicarious experiences

The school encourages and facilitates vicarious experiences, including the Senior Leadership Team accessing coaching to support their individual and collective well-being, and celebration of accomplishments through academic and values awards. For students, a peer mentoring programme allows students to share their coping strategies and steps taken towards successful outcomes.

In addition, the school has adopted a strengths-based approach across the community. All students and teachers take the VIA Character Strengths Assessment and regularly reflect upon and identify their strengths in action and show how they are applied in the service of their academic, professional, and personal goals. The school annually embraces World Character Day as a whole-school event sharing examples of how their own and each other's strengths contribute to individual, community, and societal well-being and achievement.

Social persuasion

TES seeks to ensure regular accountability and feedback is received on progress towards goals for staff. This includes through twice annual personal reflection with the headteacher, peer coaching, peer observations, and the establishment of Professional Learning Communities (PLCs) which provide a democratic, collaborative approach to professional learning, achieving professional targets, and building individual and collective teacher efficacy. In addition, the adoption of well-being champions provides continuous positive encouragement and reinforcement of the well-being agenda.

Similarly, students are provided for, through coaching and peer support, creating psychologically safe spaces within which to articulate their fears and aspirations, identify their strengths, try new things, evaluate progress, overcome obstacles and setbacks, and sustain their commitment to succeed.

The outcomes

TES sees a direct correlation between their focus on enhancing well-being, resilience, and mental toughness and the levels of self-confidence and self-efficacy demonstrated in their school community. There is a willingness of staff and students to engage in support and ask for help alongside the belief that they can succeed in their goals and aspirations and persevere in the face of challenges and setbacks. This is evidenced from action research into AWE data indicating a buffering effect against stress and challenge related to International General Certificate of Secondary Education (IGCSE) and International Baccalaureate (IB) exams which has contributed to the school achieving in 2021 its best ever exam results despite the additional impact of COVID-19 on the whole school community. They have also sustained high levels of collective teacher efficacy, well-being, workplace satisfaction, and retention of staff. The past five years have seen the TES create a thriving community that is achieving in terms of academic rigour, student destination, and pioneering in the world of Positive Education.

Discussion points

1   What strategies do you or your school currently utilise to build self-efficacy in students and staff?
2   What evidence-based strategies identified in this chapter could be easily implemented at your school?
3   What opportunities exist for staff to build collective teacher efficacy (CTE)?
4   How might coaching contribute to building mental toughness and self-efficacy in your students and staff?

Suggested resources

1   Collectiveƒ® Efficacy: How Educators' Beliefs Impact Student Learning, by Jenni Donohoo (2016), Corwin Press.
2   Collective Student Efficacy – Developing Independent and Inter-Dependent Learners, by John Hattie, Douglas Fisher, Nancy Frey, Shirley Clarke Available: 23rd June 2021.
3   Developing Mental Toughness in Young People, by Doug Strycharczyk, Peter Clough, Taylor & Francis, New Edition available: 3rd September 2021.
4   Palgrave Handbook of Positive Education by Margaret Kern, Michael Wehmeyer, Palgrave.

References

Artino, Jr., A. R. (2012). Academic self-efficacy: From educational theory to instructional practice. *Perspectives on Medical Education, 1*(2), 76–85. https://doi.org/10.1007/s40037-012-0012-5

Bandura, A. (1977). Self-efficacy: Toward a unifying theory of behavioural change. *Psychological Review, 84*(2), 191–215. https://doi.org/10.1037/0033-295X.84.2.191

Bandura, A. (1997). *Self-efficacy: The exercise of control.* Freeman.

Boggiano, A. K., Main, D. S., & Katz, P. A. (1988). Children's preference for challenge. *Journal of Personality and Social Psychology, 54*(1), 134–141. https://doi.org/10.1037/0022-3514.54.1.134

Buonomo, I., Fiorilli, C., & Benevene, P. (2019). The impact of emotions and hedonic balance on teachers' self-efficacy: Testing the bouncing back effect of positive emotions. *Frontiers in Psychology, 10,* 1670-1670. https://doi.org/10.3389/fpsyg.2019.01670

Caprara, G. V., Steca, P., Gerbino, M., Paciello, M., & Vecchio, G. M. (2006). Looking for adolescents' well-being: Self-efficacy beliefs as determinants of positive thinking and happiness. *Epidemiology and Psychiatric Sciences, 15*(1), 30–43.

Carr, A., Cullen, K., Keeney, C., Canning, C., Mooney, O., Chinseallaigh, E., & O'Dowd, A. (2020). Effectiveness of positive psychology interventions: A systematic review and meta-analysis. *The Journal of Positive Psychology, 1–21.* https://doi.org/10.1080/17439760.2020.1818807

Chen, G., Gully, S. M., & Eden, D. (2001). Validation of a new general self-efficacy scale. *Organizational Research Methods, 4*(1), 62–83. https://doi.org/10.1177/109442810141004

Chong, W. H., & Kong, C. A. (2012). Teacher collaborative learning and teacher self-efficacy: The case of lesson study. *The Journal of Experimental Education, 80*(3), 263–283. https://doi.org/10.1080/00220 973.2011.596854

Clark, S., & Newberry, M. (2019). Are we building preservice teacher self-efficacy? A large-scale study examining teacher education experiences. *Asia-Pacific Journal of Teacher Education, 47*(1), 32–47. https://doi.org/10.1080/1359866X.2018.1497772

Clough, P. J., Earle, K., & Sewell, D. (2002). Mental toughness: The concept and its measurement. In I. Cockerill (Ed.), *Solutions in sport psychology* (pp. 32–43). Thomson Publishing.

Clough, P., & Strycharczyk, D. (2021). *Developing mental toughness: Improving performance, wellbeing and positive behaviour in others.* Kogan Page Publishers.

Cramer, R. J., Neal, T. M. S., & Brodsky, S. L. (2009). Self-efficacy and confidence. *Consulting Psychology Journal, 61*(4), 319–334. https://doi.org/10.1037/a0017310

Donohoo, J. (2017). *Collective efficacy: How educators' beliefs impact student learning.* Corwin.

Dulagil, A., Green, S., & Ahern, M. (2016). Evidence-based coaching to enhance senior students' wellbeing and academic striving. *International Journal of Wellbeing, 6*(3), 131–149. https://doi.org/10.5502/ijw. v6i3.426

Escobedo, A. (2012). *Teacher perceptions of the effects of school celebrations of success on collective efficacy beliefs* [Unpublished doctoral dissertation]. University of Virginia.

Gloria, C. T., Faulk, K. E., & Steinhardt, M. A. (2013). Positive affectivity predicts successful and unsuccessful adaptation to stress. *Motivation and Emotion, 37*(1), 185–193. https://doi.org/10.1007/s11031-012-9291-8

Goddard, R. D., Hoy, W. K., & Hoy, A. W. (2000). Collective teacher efficacy: Its meaning, measure, and impact on student achievement. *American educational research journal, 37*(2), 479–507.

Graham, S., & Weiner, B. (1996). Theories and principles of motivation. In D. C. Berliner & R. C. Calfee (Eds.), *Handbook of educational psychology* (pp. 63–84). Macmillan.

Grant, A. M. (2003). The impact of life coaching on goal attainment, metacognition and mental health. *Social Behaviour and Personality, 31*(3), 253–263. https://doi.org/10.2224/sbp.2003.31.3.253

Green, S., Leach, C. J. C., & Falecki, D. (2021). Approaches to positive education. In M. L. Kern & M. L. Wehmeyer (Eds.), *Palgrave handbook of positive education* (pp. 21–48). Springer.

Green, S., Grant, A.M., & Rynsaardt, J. (2007). Evidence-based coaching for senior high school students: Building hardiness and hope. *International Coaching Psychology Review, 2*(1), 24–31.

Gröschner, A., Schindler, A. -K., Holzberger, D., Alles, M., & Seidel, T. (2018). How systematic video reflection in teacher professional development regarding classroom discourse contributes to teacher and student self-efficacy. *International Journal of Educational Research, 90*, 223–233. https://doi.org/10.1016/j.ijer.2018.02.003

Hargreaves, A., & Fullan, M. (2015). *Professional capital: Transforming teaching in every school.* Teachers College Press.

Harzer, C., Mubashar, T., & Dubreuil, P. (2017). Character strengths and strength-related person-job fit as predictors of work-related well-being, job performance, and workplace deviance. *Wirtschaftspsychologie, 19*(3), 23–38.

Hattie, J. (2016, July). Mindframes and Maximizers. 3rd Annual Visible Learning Conference held in Washington, DC.

Hattie, J., Fisher, D., Frey, N., Gojak, L. M., Moore, S. D., & Mellman, W. (2016). *Visible learning for mathematics, grades K-12: What works best to optimize student learning.* Corwin Press.

Hoy, A. W., & Davis, A. H. (2005). Teachers' sense of efficacy and adolescent achievement. *Adolescence and Education: Self-Efficacy Beliefs during Adolescence, 5*, 117–137.

Hoy, W. K., Sweetland, S. R., & Smith, P. A. (2002). Toward an organizational model of achievement in high schools: The significance of collective efficacy. *Educational Administration Quarterly, 38*(1), 77–93. https://doi.org/10.1177/0013161X02381004

Leach, C. J. C., & Green, S. (2015). The integration of positive psychology & coaching in education. In C. Van Nieuwerburgh (Ed.), *Coaching in professional contexts.* Sage Publications.

Leithwood, K., & Sun, J. P. (2009). Transformational school leadership effects on schools, teachers and students. *Research and Theory in Educational Administration, 8*, 1–22.

Madden, W. & Green, S., & Grant, A. (2011). A pilot study evaluating strengths-based coaching for primary school students: Enhancing engagement and hope. *International Coaching Psychology Review, 61*, 71–83.

McGeown, S. P., St Clair-Thompson, H., & Clough, P. (2016). The study of non-cognitive attributes in education: Proposing the mental toughness framework. *Educational Review, 68*(1), 96–113. https://doi.org/10.1080/00131911.2015.1008408

Merkle, E. C., & Zandt, T. V. (2006). An application of the poisson race model to confidence calibration. *Journal of Experimental Psychology, 135*(3), 391–408. https://doi.org/10.1037/0096-3445.135.3.391

Mojtahedi, D., Dagnall, N., Denovan, A., Clough, P., Hull, S., Canning, D., Lilley, C., & Papageorgiou, K. A. (2020). The relationship between mental toughness, job loss, and mental health issues during the COVID-19 pandemic. *Frontiers in Psychiatry, 11*, 607246–607246. https://doi.org/10.3389/fpsyt.2020.607246

Muris, P. (2001). A brief questionnaire for measuring self-efficacy in youths. *Journal of Psychopathology and Behavioural Assessment, 23*(3), 145–149. https://doi.org/10.1023/A:1010961119608

Natovová, L., & Chýlová, H. (2014). Is there a relationship between self-efficacy, wellbeing and behavioural markers in managing stress at University students? *Journal on Efficiency and Responsibility in Education and Science, 7* (1), 14–18. https://doi.org/10.7160/eriesj.2014.070103

Nicholls, A. R., Levy, A. R., Polman, R. C. J., & Crust, L. (2011). Mental toughness, coping self-efficacy, and coping effectiveness among athletes. *International Journal of Sport Psychology, 42*(6), 513–524.

Palmer, D. (2006). Durability of changes in self-efficacy of preservice primary teachers. *International Journal of Science Education, 28*(6), 655–671. https://doi.org/10.1080/09500690500404599

Peterson, C., & Seligman, M. E. (2004). *Character strengths and virtues: A handbook and classification* (Vol. 1). Oxford University Press.

Phan, H. P., & Ngu, B. H. (2019). *Teaching, learning and psychology.* Oxford University Press.

Protheroe, N. (2008). Teacher efficacy: What it is and does it matter? *Principal, 87*(5), 42–45.

Public Health England. (2021). *Measuring and Monitoring Children and Young People's Wellbeing: A Toolkit for Schools and Colleges.* Retrieved from: https://www.annafreud.org/media/4612/mwb-toolki-final-draft-4.pdf

Quinlan, D., Vella-Brodrick, D. A., Gray, A., & Swain, N. (2019). Teachers matter: Student outcomes following a strengths intervention are mediated by teacher strengths spotting. *Journal of Happiness Studies, 20*(8), 2507–2523. https://doi.org/10.1007/s10902-018-0051-7

Ross, J. A., Hogaboam-Gray, A., & Gray, P. (2004). Prior student achievement, collaborative school processes, and collective teacher efficacy. *Leadership and Policy in Schools*, *3*(3), 163-188. https://doi.org/10.1080/15700760490503689

Rusk, R. D., Vella-Brodrick, D. A., & Waters, L. (2018). A complex dynamic systems approach to lasting positive change: The synergistic change model. *The Journal of Positive Psychology*, *13*(4), 406-418. https://doi.org/10.1080/17439760.2017.1291853

Seligman, M. E. (2012). *Flourish: A visionary new understanding of happiness and well-being*. Simon and Schuster.

Seligman, M. E. P. (2006). *Learned optimism: how to change your mind and your life*. Vintage Books.

Skaalvik, E. M., & Skaalvik, S. (2007). Dimensions of teacher self-efficacy and relations with strain factors, perceived collective teacher efficacy, and teacher burnout. *Journal of Educational Psychology*, *99*(3), 611-625. https://doi.org/10.1037/0022-0663.99.3.611

Stankov, L. (2013). Noncognitive predictors of intelligence and academic achievement: An important role of confidence. *Personality and Individual Differences*, *55*(7), 727-732. https://doi.org/10.1016/j.paid.2013.07.006

Stankov, L., & Lee, J. (2014). Quest for the best non-cognitive predictor of academic achievement. *Educational Psychology*, *34*(1), 1-8. https://doi.org/10.1080/01443410.2013.858908

Stankov, L., Lee, J., Luo, W., & Hogan, D. J. (2012). Confidence: A better predictor of academic achievement than self-efficacy, self-concept and anxiety? *Learning and Individual Difference*, *22*(6), 747-758. https://doi.org/10.1016/j.lindif.2012.05.013

Stankov, L., Morony, S. & Lee, Y.P. (2014). *Confidence: The best non-cognitive predictor of academic achievement?*.Educational Psychology: An international journal of of Experimental Educational Psychology, 34:1, 9-28.

St Clair-Thompson, H., Bugler, M., Robinson, J., Clough, P., McGeown, S. P., & Perry, J. (2015). Mental toughness in education: Exploring relationships with attainment, attendance, behaviour and peer relationships. *Educational Psychology*, *35*(7), 886-907. https://doi.org/10.1080/01443410.2014.895294

Tschannen-Moran, M., & Hoy, A.W. (2007). The differential antecedents of self-efficacy beliefs of novice and experienced teachers. *Teaching and Teacher Education*, *23*(6), 944 -956. https://doi.org/10.1016/j.tate.2006.05.003

Waters, L., & Sun, J. (2016). Can a brief strength-based parenting intervention boost self-efficacy and positive emotions in parents? *International Journal of Applied Positive Psychology*, *1*(1-3), 41-56. https://doi.org/10.1007/s41042-017-0007-x

5 Courage in positive education

Cynthia L.S. Pury

Courage, defined here as taking a worthwhile risk, is one of the virtues that makes it possible for people to act despite risk or its common emotional consequence of fear. The chapter argues that it is important to consider the relative value of the objective of the action, which may be the key element that makes a risky action virtuous.

Introduction

Courage is a virtue that can be found in any setting where there are goals that are worth pursuing and risks to the individual. Not surprisingly, schools provide many different challenges and opportunities to students that can be met with courage. When I started doing research on courage in 2003, I was struck by how many of our participants mentioned an educational context for courageous actions. In our initial studies, we (Pury & Kowalski, 2007; Pury, Kowalski, & Spearman, 2007) asked undergraduate participants to describe a time they acted courageously. Many of these narratives described situations that happened in an educational setting, including narratives of being willing or at least able to upend one's life to move to a new school, standing up to bullying at school, and giving speeches or other public presentations.

In this chapter, I will review the two main theoretical accounts of courage in current psychological literature, different types of courage, different ways in which courage might be fostered, and cautions in doing so, before discussing potential specific applications to education.

Theoretical background

What is courage?

There are currently two main definitions of courage in the psychological literature. The first, standing up to fear, comes out of a clinical tradition. The original formulation, by exposure therapy pioneer Jack Rachman (1990, 2010), describes courage as a special exception to the usual three parts of the emotion of fear. Typically, a fear response to a stimulus involves a cognitive or subjective feeling of fear, a characteristic physiological response, and a specific action tendency to avoid or to flee the stimulus (Rachman, 1978). With courage, Rachman

DOI: 10.4324/9781003228158-7

proposed, individuals have either the cognitive/subjective component of fear and/or the physiological response of fear, but instead of avoiding or fleeing the feared stimulus they approach or confront it.

This model has been adapted by Peter Norton and his colleagues (Chockalingam & Norton, 2018; Norton & Weiss, 2009) into a related scale, which explicitly states in its instructions "Courage is defined as persistence or perseverance despite having fear. It takes courage to engage and persist in a terrifying activity. By definition, fear is necessary for someone to display courage" (Norton & Weiss, 2009, p. 214). This scale has been adapted for use with children (Muris, 2009; Muris, Mayer, & Schubert, 2010).

However, this particular definition of courage can raise multiple problems. First, in laboratory studies, individuals who have won awards for physical courage show a significantly lower physiological level of laboratory-induced fear than individuals who were not decorated for courage (Cox, Hallam, O'Connor, & Rachman, 1983; O'Connor, Hallam, & Rachman, 1985), although their subjective ratings of fear were similar. In our early studies of courage, we found that many of our participants retrospectively reported lower levels of fear during courageous actions; these participants were also more likely to say that the action they took would have been courageous for anyone to do (Pury et al., 2007). Thus, actions that might be particularly likely to be seen as courageous by others may not be characterised by extreme levels of fear.

Second, the children's version of Norton and Weiss's (2009) scale has a relatively high correlation (.63) with sensation-seeking (Muris et al., 2010). Matt Howard and colleagues (Howard & Alipour, 2014; Howard & Murry 2020) argue that Norton and Weiss's scale may be better characterised as measuring persistence despite fear rather than courage per se.

Finally, defining courage as taking action despite fear leads to multiple conceptual problems. The simplest one is nomenclature: if people who take actions seen as courageous by others are less afraid, are they less courageous? (See also Rachman, 1990). One possible way around this conundrum is to consider courage as a response to a risk, or the eliciting stimulus that often, but not always, produces fear. More on that below.

But there's a larger issue. Imagine two patients in a burn unit, equally injured when they ran into a burning house fire. Because this is a thought experiment, let's assume we have perfect knowledge, and we know each person was equally afraid when they ran into the fire. Patient A ran into the burning building to save a baby from the fire. A appears to most of us to have been extremely courageous, perhaps deserving of a medal. Patient B, on the other hand, ran into the burning building to film a short video clip of themselves surrounded by flames to post on social media. B's actions are unlikely to be seen as courageous and may even warrant a psych consult. So, why the person is taking the risk matters too.

Chris Rate and his colleagues (Rate, 2010; Rate, Clarke, Lindsay, & Sternberg, 2007) found that people's implicit theories of courage include three main components: intentionality or voluntariness, taken in pursuit of a noble or worthwhile goal, and taken despite personal risk to the actor. In my lab, we've shortened this to define courage as taking a worthwhile risk. This definition preserves Rate's three components while highlighting the relationship in magnitude between the risk and the goal. This allows us to look at several different observed features of courage.

First, there are multiple types of courage. The three most commonly described subtypes are physical courage, or the courage to take a physical risk usually to save another person from the same physical danger; moral courage, or the courage to risk social disapproval by standing up to others who are doing the wrong thing; and psychological courage, or the courage to risk one's own psychological stability in pursuit of something better for the self (Kelley et al., 2019; Lopez, O'Byrne, & Petersen, 2003; Pury et al., 2007; Putman, 2004). However, other types are also possible. Vital courage is the courage to get or to provide needed treatment (e.g., Finfgeld, 1999; Lopez et al., 2003). Workplace social courage, for example, has been defined as altruistic action on behalf of another that may damage the actor's reputation at work (Howard, Farr, Grandey, & Gutworth, 2016), while civil courage is defined as the courage to express displeasure to authorities or superiors (Greitemeyer, Fischer, Kastenmüller, & Frey, 2006).

However, not all courageous actions can be so neatly packaged. Blended courage, or taking the risks of one type of courage for the goals of another, is a possibility predicted by defining courage as taking a worthwhile risk and supported by empirical findings (Pury, Britt, Zinzow, & Raymond, 2014). Using this approach, the various types of courage are seen because of the way events typically unfold: if someone is in physical danger, typically a would-be rescuer needs to face that same danger themselves. Social wrongs are often correctable only if people are willing to face social disapproval by calling them out. And so on.

But this very definition suggests another typology: the distinction between process and accolade courage. Process courage is the mechanism by which someone faces a risk that is salient for them to reach a goal that is meaningful to them. Accolade courage, meanwhile, involves the properties of an action that leads an observer – including the actor themselves later on – to call an action courageous. With process courage, the lower the risk the more likely the action is to occur. But with accolade courage, the higher the risk the more likely the action is to be considered courageous (at least, up until the point at which the risk far surpasses the value of the goal) (Pury & Starkey, 2010).

We (Pury & Starkey, 2010) have argued that the action becomes foolish courage, or taking a much larger risk for a goal that isn't worth it. A similar, but more destructive type of courage is bad courage, when someone uses process courage to take an action that most observers would agree is not just not worth the risk, but is destructive or worse (Pury, Starkey, Kulik, Skjerning, & Sullivan, 2015). School shooters, for example, may believe that they are acting courageously and may even describe their own actions in terms that sound like courage.

Accolade courage also involves two additional perceptions: that the goal is worthwhile and that the actor faces a risk. To say that an action was courageous, in other words, we need to agree with the action and appreciate the risk. Instances in which one disagrees with the goal are rarely called courageous, and among courage researchers, we've all encountered situations in which the observer did not agree that a particular risk was present and thus the action was not courageous (Pury & Starkey, 2010).

One other way in which the observer or later self-judges an action high in accolade courage is if the action was successful in reaching the goal. This, I suspect, is one other way of judging the worthiness of the goal. Actions that are unsuccessful and even those that are only partially successful (e.g., saving some, but not all, of the ducklings attacked by a dog) are judged as less courageous than actions that are completely successful in attaining their goal (Pury & Hensel, 2010; Pury & Starkey, 2010).

Actions that are high in process courage and for which the individual faces unique risks because of their own specific characteristics would be personal courage - for example, the child with severe social anxiety who nonetheless gives a speech to their class (Pury et al., 2007). These actions are not likely to be seen as courageous except for those who know why this action was risky for that particular actor. The more clinically based definition of acting despite or standing up to fear seems to be centred squarely on these types of actions; moreover, within a clinical context, irrational fears should be stood up to as that is the point of most treatments for anxiety and related disorders - thus merely opposing it is pursuing a worthy goal.

Practice

Background

Much less research has been conducted on how to increase courage. Two notable examples come from clinical psychology and recent attempts to encourage high-fear participants to face their fear. Chockalingam and Norton (2018) found that paying participants to get closer to a feared spider resulted in greater approach of a spider - increasing the worthiness of the goal increased process courage. A more general version of this theme anecdotally is a process reported by many of our participants over the years to make themselves feel more courageous - reminding themselves of the goal and keeping focused on it helps.

Kramer and Zinbarg (2018) found that asking fearful participants to write narratives about a time they had successfully faced those fears led to greater approach-oriented cognition and to greater willingness to engage in the feared activity. Thus, providing a framework of a time in which one did take action meant one was more likely to see themselves as someone who could do so again.

In theory, courage can also be increased by decreasing the actual or perceived risk of the action. Paradoxically, that means that the action is more likely to be taken but less likely to be seen as courageous. However, if the end goal is to accomplish the action, then that's the desired outcome. It should also be able to be increased by actual and repeated practice of the action, beyond merely recalling a single instance of success in the past.

Any intervention to foster courage should be aware of the possibility of fostering bad courage; thus, the goals of the courageous action should be clear and positive.

"Try this" for educators

Next time, you are considering taking a risk, try explicitly thinking about the situation as a whole. Does the benefit of the goal outweigh the potential cost of the risk? If it does not, you might want to rethink: just taking a risk for a very trivial goal or even just for the sake of taking a risk isn't courage.

But if the value of the goal - to you - outweighs the potential cost of the risk, then it might be a good time to be courageous. One possible way to feel more courageous is to think deeply about what that goal means to you. When you find yourself feeling like you want to "chicken out", think about what it would mean to you to have that goal accomplished. If the action is on behalf of another person, why is it important to you to help them? If it is on behalf of yourself, what will you feel if you accomplish it?

And be gentle with yourself! Remember that the outcome you want isn't guaranteed. If the goal isn't accomplished, that doesn't mean it wasn't courageous to try. There's pretty good evidence that people discount the courage of attempts that don't succeed (Pury & Hensel, 2010).

"Try this" for students

Have students consider the "worthwhile" part of courage. Ask them to describe actions widely seen as courageous (firefighters who save people from burning buildings, Civil Rights leaders standing up for what's right, a local person who has received some sort of award for heroism, etc.) and describe not only the risks the person took but *why* they took that action. Why do we admire what they did?

Case study

Educational settings offer many opportunities for students to be courageous. Based on a re-analysis of the data from Pury et al. (2007) to include only the 37 (of the 250 total) narratives that specifically mentioned a school setting out of the most commonly reported types of courageous actions clearly involving school settings seem to be related to changing schools or attending a more challenging or less familiar next level of school. This was easily the most common type of education-related narrative, with 21 instances. Here's a sample narrative:

> I moved to a new high school in the middle of my high school career. I did not have any friends and I had moved from a place where I was raised and completely comfortable. It was courageous to walk in and talk to and become friends with a whole new school.

A similar theme of unfamiliar social risk was present for many students when selecting a college (recall that these were college student participants):

> I went to a college where I did not know one single soul. (Why was this action courageous?) Because I didn't go to school with the rest of my friends from high school. I branched out and went beyond my comfort zone.

Concerns about social rejection or exclusion were also present for students who stood up to school bullying or exclusion, present in eight narratives:

> Once, in high school, I overheard a girl in my class making fun of one of my friends. I turned around and asked her to stop and told her how hurtful making fun of people was. Standing up to someone for something that one believes in is not an easy thing to do. I was courageous because I stood up to her rather than allowing her to walk all over my friend.

> In high school, everybody was mean to this one guy who always sat by himself and did not talk to anyone. One day at lunch, I decided to go and sit with him and eat because he looked lonely and sad. As it turned out, he was a very nice guy. I believe it was courageous because I decided to take a stand against the majority of the school population. It takes a lot of courage to stand on your own and do something you believe is right when everyone else is saying that you are wrong.

While the predominant theme of the threat was emanating from fellow students, faculty may also sometimes be seen as a risk:

> A very intimidating teacher in my high school took a girl's necklace from her; because he said it wasn't part of the "dress code" (I went to a private high school). The necklace was her father's patron saint, who is in the military and works in DC. It was September 11th; one year anniversary; and the girl wore it as a sign for her dad to be safe on that day. So, I stood up to the teacher and told him he was wrong. I got the necklace back for her. (Why was this courageous?) Because I stood up to someone that scares everyone. The man is very intimidating and hard to deal with.

Another common theme of courage was the courage to give a public speech, particularly to large numbers of peers:

> When I was a freshman in high school; I had to get in front of the whole school and give a speech for student council. I am shy; and I don't like to speak in front of large groups of people. So, this was courageous because I had to put my fear aside.

Notably, all three narratives related to public speaking mentioned that the actor had fears of public speaking, making it personally courageous.

Other school-related instances of courage involved school sports teams (trying out for them and possibly failing, performing against a more difficult opponent than usual or working a more difficult routine than usual, and facing bullies on the team), taking a leave from schooling to obtain inpatient treatment, not panicking in bad weather on a field trip, saving a fellow student from physical injury during a school-sponsored outing, and donating blood at a school blood drive.

Although never particularly singled out by our participants as instances of courage, other likely targets might be retaking a failed class or simply showing up each day in a subject that one struggles in. This latter one in particular might not be seen by the student as courageous unless they can see the success of their actions (Pury & Hensel, 2010).

Discussion points

- Look for instances of the words "courage" and related terms (e.g., "brave", "hero") in news articles. How do the elements of accolade courage (agreeing there's a risk to the actor, agreeing that the goal is worthwhile, success of the outcome) fit or not fit with the labelling the action courageous?

- Think about times you've seen students to be courageous. Did you need to know anything specific about them to make that judgement? What was it?
- People don't always appreciate being called courageous, especially when it highlights a particular risk that's unique to them (as in high personal courage) or when they were not fully successful in reaching their goal. Considering this, what other types of praise can you give students who are behaving courageously who might not want to be told that particular term?

Suggested resources

Websites illustrating accolade courage:
https://www.carnegiehero.org/
https://www.iwmf.org/awards/courage-in-journalism-awards/
https://www.jfklibrary.org/events-and-awards/profile-in-courage-award

An outstanding book about the social science of courage:
Biswas-Diener, R. (2012). *The courage quotient: How science can make you braver*. Jossey-Bass. ISBN 978-0470917428.

References

Allen, K. -A., Kern, M. L., Vella-Brodrick, D., & Waters, L. (2017). School values: A comparison of academic motivation, mental health promotion, and school belonging with student achievement. *Educational and Developmental Psychologist, 34*(1), 31–47.

Burke, J. (2021). *The ultimate guide to implementing wellbeing programmes for school*. London: Routledge.

Chockalingam, M., & Norton, P. J. (2018). Facing fear-provoking stimuli: The role of courage and influence of task-importance. *The Journal of Positive Psychology*. doi:10.1080/17439760.2018.1497685

Cox, D., Hallam, R., O'Connor, K., & Rachman, S. (1983). An experimental analysis of fearlessness and courage. *British Journal of Psychology, 74*(1), 107–117. doi:10.1111/j.2044-8295.1983.tb01847.x

Deci, E. L., & Ryan, R. M. (2012). Self-determination theory. In P. A. M. Van Lange, A. W. Kruglanski, & E. T. Higgins (Eds.), *Handbook of theories of social psychology* (pp. 416–436). London: Sage.

Finfgeld, D. L. (1999). Courage as a process of pushing beyond the struggle. *Qualitative Health Research, 9*, 803–814.

Fredrickson, B. L. (2013). *Love 2.0: Finding happiness and health in moments of connection*. London, UK: Penguin Group.

Greitemeyer, T., Fischer, P., Kastenmüller, A., & Frey, D. (2006). Civil courage and helping behavior: Differences and similarities. *European Psychologist, 11*(2), 90–98. doi:10.1027/1016-9040.11.2.90

Harding, S., Morris, R., Gunnell, D., Ford, T., Hollingworth, W., Tilling, K., ... Kidger, J. (2019). Is teachers' mental health and wellbeing associated with students' mental health and wellbeing? *Journal of Affective Disorders, 253*, 460–466. doi:10.1016/j.jad.2019.03.046

Howard, M. C., & Alipour, K. K. (2014). Does the courage measure really measure courage? A theoretical and empirical evaluation. *The Journal of Positive Psychology, 9*(5), 449–459. doi:10.1080/17439760.2014.910828

Howard, M. C., Farr, J. L., Grandey, A. A., & Gutworth, M. B. (2016). The creation of the workplace social courage scale (wscs): An investigation of internal consistency, psychometric properties, validity, and utility. *Journal of Business and Psychology*. doi:10.1007/s10869-016-9463-8

Howard, M. C., & Murry, A. S. (2020). Does the courage measure (CM) measure persistence despite fear? *Testing, Psychometrics, Methodology in Applied Psychology, 27*(2), 271–277. doi:10.4473/TPM27.2.7

Kelley, K. L., Murphy, H. J., Breeden, C. R., Hardy, B. P., Lopez, S. J., O'Byrne, K. K., ... Courage, C. (2019). Conceptualizing courage. In M. W. Gallagher & S. J. Lopez (Eds.), *Positive psychological assessment: A handbook of models and measures* (2nd ed., pp. 157–176). Washington, DC: American Psychological Association.

Kramer, A., & Zinbarg, R. (2018). Recalling courage: An initial test of a brief writing intervention to activate a 'courageous mindset' and courageous behavior. *The Journal of Positive Psychology*, 1–10. doi:10.1080/17439760.2018.1484943

Lopez, S. J., O'Byrne, K. K., & Petersen, S. (2003). Profiling courage. In S. J. Lopez & C. R. Snyder (Eds.), *Positive psychological assessment: A handbook of models and measures* (pp. 185–197). Washington, DC: American Psychological Association.

Maslow, A. H. (1958). A dynamic theory of human motivation. In C. L. Stacey & M. DeMartino (Eds.), *Understanding human motivation* (pp. 26–47). Cleveland, OH: Howard Allen Publishers.

Muris, P. (2009). Fear and courage in children: Two sides of the same coin? *Journal of Child and Family Studies, 18*(4), 486–490. doi:10.1007/s10826-009-9271-0

Muris, P., Mayer, B., & Schubert, T. (2010). "You might belong in gryffindor": Children's courage and its relationships to anxiety symptoms, big five personality traits, and sex roles. *Child Psychiatry and Human Development, 41*(2), 204–213. doi:10.1007/s10578-009-0161-x

Norton, P. J., & Weiss, B. J. (2009). The role of courage on behavioral approach in a fear-eliciting situation: A proof-of-concept pilot study. *Journal of Anxiety Disorders, 23*(2), 212–217. doi:10.1016/j.janxdis.2008.07.002

O'Connor, K., Hallam, R. S., & Rachman, S. (1985). Fearlessness and courage: A replication experiment. *British Journal of Psychology, 76*(2), 187–197. doi:10.1111/j.2044-8295.1985.tb01942.x

Prilleltensky, I., & Prilleltensky, O. (2021). *How people matter: Why it affects health, happiness, love, work, and society.* Cambridge, UK: Cambridge University Press.

Pury, C. L. S., Britt, T. W., Zinzow, H. M., & Raymond, M. A. (2014). Blended courage: Moral and psychological courage elements in mental health treatment seeking by active duty military personnel. *The Journal of Positive Psychology, 9*, 30–41. doi:10.1080/17439760.2013.831466

Pury, C. L. S., & Hensel, A. D. (2010). Are courageous actions successful actions? *The Journal of Positive Psychology, 5*(1), 62–72. doi:10.1080/17439760903435224

Pury, C. L. S., & Kowalski, R. M. (2007). Human strengths, courageous actions, and general and personal courage. *The Journal of Positive Psychology, 2*(2), 120–128. doi:10.1080/17439760701228813

Pury, C. L. S., Kowalski, R. M., & Spearman, J. (2007). Distinctions between general and personal courage. *The Journal of Positive Psychology, 2*(2), 99–114. doi:10.1080/17439760701237962

Pury, C. L. S., & Starkey, C. B. (2010). Is courage an accolade or a process? A fundamental question for courage research. In C. L. S. Pury & S. J. Lopez (Eds.), *The psychology of courage: Modern research on an ancient virtue* (pp. 67–87). Washington, DC: American Psychological Association.

Pury, C. L. S., Starkey, C. B., Kulik, R. E., Skjerning, K. L., & Sullivan, E. A. (2015). Is courage always a virtue? Suicide, killing, and bad courage. *The Journal of Positive Psychology, 10*(5), 383–388. doi:10.1080/17439760.2015.1004552

Putman, D. (2004). *Psychological courage.* Dallas, TX: University Press of America.

Rachman, S. J. (1978). Human fears: A three systems analysis. *Scandinavian Journal of Behaviour Therapy, 7*(4), 237–245. doi:10.1080/16506077809456104

Rachman, S. J. (1990). *Fear and courage* (2nd ed.). New York, NY: W H Freeman/Times Books/ Henry Holt & Co.

Rachman, S. J. (2010). Courage: A psychological perspective. In C. L. S. Pury & S. J. Lopez (Eds.), *The psychology of courage: Modern research on an ancient virtue* (pp. 91–107). Washington, DC: American Psychological Association.

Rate, C. R. (2010). Defining the features of courage: A search for meaning. In C. L. S. Pury & S. J. Lopez (Eds.), *The psychology of courage: Modern research on an ancient virtue* (pp. 47–66). Washington, DC: American Psychological Association.

Rate, C. R., Clarke, J. A., Lindsay, D. R., & Sternberg, R. J. (2007). Implicit theories of courage. *The Journal of Positive Psychology, 2*(2), 80–98. doi:10.1080/17439760701228755

Vaillant, G. E. (2003). *Aging well: Surprising guideposts to a happier life.* New York: Little, Brown.

Werner, E. E. (1996). Vulnerable but invincible: High risk children from birth to adulthood. *European Child & Adolescent Psychiatry, 5*(Suppl 1), 47–51. doi:10.1007/BF00538544

6 Working with strengths in education

Why educators should strength spot in their students, and how students feel about this work

Denise Quinlan and Lucy Hone

There is increasing evidence about the positive effects of strengths programmes on well-being and academic achievement, and numerous programmes now exist to teach students about their strengths. Using insights and feedback from educators, students, and researchers, this chapter suggests strategies to embed a strengths focus in schools.

Introduction

Psychological strengths have been defined as a "pre-existing capacity for a particular way of behaving, thinking, or feeling that is authentic and energising to the user, and enables optimal functioning, development and performance" (Linley, 2008, p. 9) or as positive, malleable traits that contribute to optimal human development (Peterson & Seligman, 2004). Shown to benefit well-being and academic achievement, strengths programmes now feature in learning centres from preschool through primary and intermediate to high school. Founded on the notion that what is right and good about us is as real and as important as what goes wrong with us (Peterson & Seligman, 2004), strengths programmes in schools seek to enable students and their teachers to learn about strengths, identify their own (and others') strengths, and utilise them in their daily pursuits. What strengths programmes include, how they are working, and how they may be improved is the focus of this chapter.

Theoretical background

Strengths in schools: programmes and evidence

Although varied in delivery and style appropriate for age, culture, and context, most strengths programmes include the following elements:

Learning about strengths: programmes use a variety of strengths classifications and language. Popular classifications include Peterson and Seligman's VIA classification of character strengths (2004), Gallup's StrengthsFinder (Asplund et al., 2007; Rath, 2007), and Linley's Strengths Profile (formerly Realise2, 2008, 2010). Participants acquire a vocabulary of strengths, learning what strengths are and how to describe and recognise them.

DOI: 10.4324/9781003228158-8

Identifying one's strengths: a variety of tools, including card sorts and online inventories, exist to assist participants to identify their own strengths, and reflective and interactive classroom activities are used to encourage and explore daily strengths use.

Applying and developing one's strengths: most programmes encourage action to develop or use strengths, for example, in pursuit of personally meaningful goals, development of friendship, or to deal with challenge.

Noticing strengths in self and others (strengths spotting): as well as encouraging students to reflect on their own strengths use, many programmes now actively encourage students to notice strengths in others and the impact of their strengths use (Lavy, 2020).

From preschool to high school

Programmes now exist that support students from preschool ages through to senior high school. While a comprehensive review of strengths programmes is not within the scope of this chapter, we share brief examples of programmes for different school levels.

Early years/preschool

Lottman et al.'s (2017) approach to building strengths in very young students is based on strengths spotting. It places the work of building a common strengths language on educators and caregivers, through identifying strengths use and communicating its significance. Elaborating on the aware-explore-apply model (Niemiec, 2013) designed to promote mindful awareness of strengths, they suggest paying attention and reflecting back to young children the strengths use observed in them, the associated positive outcomes, and potential applications of the strengths in the future. The potential cumulative impact of this approach on a child's long-term development is evident:

Moment-making: catch them using their strengths and point them out.
Meaning-making: help a child reflect on an experience and describe its positive impact or the strengths use you see.
Memory-making: encourage them to reminisce about situations that involved strengths use.
Mindset-making: use feedback and conversation to reinforce a strengths mindset where children believe their strengths are alive within them and owned by them.

Primary/intermediate school

Many programmes for primary and intermediate schools embrace and support the collective nature of classroom learning. The Awesome Us programme engaged students in paired and group activities to discuss where and how they use their strengths, consider future strengths use, and practice strengths spotting in each other and the world around them (Quinlan et al., 2015). A whole-school approach adopted by Fox Eades in Celebrating Strengths (2008; Eades & Gray, 2017), encouraged schools to celebrate significant cultural events throughout the year, focusing on the strengths inherent in each occasion, e.g., harvest festival or Diwali, the festival of light.

Brownlee et al. (2012) have developed a whole-community, strengths-focused pro-gramme which emphasises discovering and discussing students' strengths with teachers and caregivers, using a specific strengths assessment inventory. Through the school year, students are encouraged to explore their strengths and expand them with the support of peers, caregivers, and teachers, and in the evolution phase, to reflect on changes achieved. The researchers note the important role of the teacher in initiating and encouraging strengths spotting amongst their students, noting strengths under a student's name on the class strengths wall. The strengths wall became part of classroom culture, "promoting students' self-reflection, self-esteem, and self-image" (Brownlee et al., 2012, p. 7).

High school

Programmes for high schools include Strengths Gym (Proctor et al., 2011; Proctor & Eades, 2019), Strengths Compass (Ledertoug, 2016), and Rashid et al.'s Strengths-Based Resil-ience programme (SBR, 2014, 2019). Most take a modular approach, providing lessons on each strength and exploring how it can be used, while others such as SBR offer teaching on strengths as part of a wider resilience training programme. The latter programme is one of the only positive psychology programmes we are aware of that explicitly addresses diversity and cultural fit, drawing attention to the need to ensure differences in strengths understand-ing and values can be identified and respectfully explored.

High schools have variously delivered strengths training in group time dedicated to pas-toral care, within English or Sports lessons, as part of student leadership (White & Waters, 2015), or in classroom teaching dedicated to well-being (Norrish & Seligman, 2015). We are aware of schools that have tried several modes of delivery for well-being programmes in an effort to increase effectiveness and reach (Quinlan & Hone, 2020).

Are strengths programmes working?

Research accumulating over the past two decades attests to the positive impact of strengths interventions and programmes on happiness, life satisfaction, academic self-efficacy and en-gagement, and achievement (Ghielen et al., 2018; Lavy, 2020; Proctor et al., 2011; Quinlan et al., 2012; Schutte et al., 2019; van Agteren et al., 2021). Programmes have also been shown to increase students' sense of relatedness to peers and teachers and enhance class cohesion (Quinlan et al., 2015). We now know that the classroom teacher's role may be pivotal, with stu-dent benefits from one strengths programme mediated (driven) in part by teacher strengths spotting (Quinlan et al., 2019). In other words, where teachers did not spot strengths in their students, the strengths programme was less effective. While strengths programmes can be effective, there is much to learn to ensure they are effective over the long term for all stu-dents in diverse populations.

Listening to the student and teacher voice

Although numerous studies have examined the effects of learning about or using strengths on performance and well-being in education (for a review, see Ghielen et al., 2018), few stud-ies have captured student and teacher voice on their experiences of working with strengths.

The students' perspective on strengths

Following a classroom-based strengths programme (details reported in Quinlan et al., 2015), students aged 8–12 years and their teachers shared their perspectives on strengths in focus groups and individual interviews. The four themes described below emerged from thematic analysis of the student data using an inductive approach (Thomas, 2006).

Owning and valuing strengths

Students were consistently able to define and describe strengths and demonstrated a clear sense of ownership of a number of strengths. They found learning about their strengths a valuable and positive experience, enabling a more favourable self-view and encouraging perseverance and continued strengths use:

> It was exciting knowing that I had strengths. More strengths than I thought I did. It means that I am capable of doing more than I do... I can keep on going and try, and not giving up on it.

The range of applications and benefits enumerated by students, for both positive and challenging times, went beyond those discussed in the strengths programme, representing adaptive use of strengths to assist their personal situations. A number of students described increased confidence or self-belief due to strengths and using strengths to control negative self-talk. Students valued the opportunity the strengths programme gave them to learn about themselves, but also, their classmates, whom they enjoyed seeing through a 'strengths lens'.

Automatic and unconscious strengths use

Unprompted, every student in the interview process and many in the focus groups described their strengths use as primarily automatic and unconscious. In their words, 'my strengths just come out'. Absorbed in their tasks, students were unaware of strengths used in the moment, didn't deliberately choose to use a strength, and only realised it on subsequent reflection, if at all. Deliberate strengths use often went awry. One student estimated only 30% of her strengths use was planned, and that half of that was unsuccessful. These 'backfires' of self-conscious strengths use were frustrating for students who were happier to rely on automatic use in the moment.

> Not really thinking about them - and doing it - makes it easier. Thinking about them really hard [makes it harder to use strengths], and just trying to do them.

Unconscious strengths use had implications for goal pursuit. Students found it helpful to think of strengths as resources that assist goal planning and boost morale, rather than in the moment, conscious strengths use.

> So you might think when you're planning a goal ... it will be really helpful if I use my kindness, or I use my love of learning... But then when the day happens you just do it.

Noticing and being noticed

All the students interviewed enjoyed noticing strengths in themselves, reporting feeling special, encouraged, or joyful. One student, with a challenging home life who reported being bullied in class, summed up the impact of noticing one's strengths:

> It really felt quite good. Just makes my hopes rise and stuff like that.

Virtually all students reported enjoying having their strengths noticed, with many observing that it prompted reciprocal strengths spotting in others. Commenting on strengths in others (strengths spotting) also felt good to students enabling them to feel helpful and closer to another person.

Even allowing for differences in awareness, it was clear that experiences of having their strengths noticed varied widely between students. For some, they were the only one noticing their strengths, and for others, friends and family featured. No student spontaneously mentioned their teachers, and when asked directly, only three out of ten said their teachers ever noticed their strengths. Students said teachers could use strengths spotting to 'get to know me better' and to help learning.

Despite enjoying practising and receiving strengths spotting, students did not always find it easy to do. Context mattered: students needed to feel safe, comfortable using the language of strengths, to know that the comment would be well received even if their observation was incorrect. Not knowing how to express a comment was the main obstacle discouraging students from making a strengths comment.

Understanding and interpreting

As would be expected in any group of students, understanding and application of strengths varied widely, from a basic categoric labelling of strengths use and literal interpretation of strengths and where they could be applied, through to a more sophisticated understanding, characterised by greater self-awareness and ability to apply strengths to their own life challenges. The latter group was more likely to display metacognition about strengths: considering the range of strengths applicable to a given situation, and identifying gaps in the strength classification or problems with its use.

The teacher perspective on strengths

Overall, the strengths programme was described by teachers as a positive experience for the students, whom they observed to be more enthusiastic and engaged with the programme than is usual with other class content. Using the same analytical approach as for students, three themes were identified from the teacher data.

Noticing changes in students, class, and self

Teachers noticed an increased willingness by many students to speak up in class, to be more open and accepting of students whose differences had previously led to them being isolated or teased, and a greater sense of class unity and togetherness. They observed the strongest effects on more reserved, less confident, or negative children, and those with low self-esteem or a problematic home life. Those who benefitted least include those who lacked empathy, were not comfortable with social contact, or had low literacy levels. Teachers suggested that these children might benefit from a small group programme format tailored to their needs.

Using more strengths language, noticing a broader range of strengths more frequently in students, and using a strengths focus to problem solve with students were amongst the changes teachers observed in themselves. Others described using strengths to praise and provide corrective feedback.

Adapting and applying strengths

Within three months of taking part in the strengths programme, participating teachers had applied strengths in a wide variety of ways, demonstrating their perceived relevance and benefits in the classroom. Strengths had been used in religious education, health, oral and written language, social studies, Circle Time (a social and emotional learning practice), and physical education. Teachers linked the character strengths to other schema familiar to students, such as learning strengths and critical thinking skills. They used strengths to manage classroom conflicts, provide specific student guidance, and even included strengths comments in their students' school reports.

Teachers had a clear sense of what pace and style of programme delivery would work for them and their students. Some planned to break activities down to smaller component parts or repeat them to support student learning. Some intended to drip feed the concepts to students slowly over time while others chose to focus on integrating strengths into health, art, or religious education programmes.

Not all strengths received equal attention in the classroom. Teacher and school preferences influenced frequency of use, as did perceived relevance to student and classroom challenges, and how well a strengths construct was understood by students. The most frequently used strengths across the participating classes were interpersonal strengths such as kindness, friendship, teamwork, and honesty and strengths that helped deal with adversity such as persistence and courage. Frequently mentioned strengths were often used to address classroom behavioural problems, or linked to school values, and were used to provide examples of how values could be implemented. The strengths which teachers reported were mentioned least in the classroom were spirituality, humility, prudence, perspective, and gratitude. The reasons for this included that a strength was difficult to explain, that students did not have a clear understanding of it, or that it was not the teacher's strength, and they were not comfortable discussing it.

Concerns about strengths in the classroom

Teachers' concerns centred on enabling students to develop a deeper understanding of strengths. To achieve this, they suggested follow-up activities, delivering strengths information within other subjects, adopting the strengths language across the whole school, and making it an integral part of teacher communications. The appropriateness of an international strengths classification for New Zealand schools was questioned, with one teacher advocating for the development instead of a local strengths language reflecting New Zealand's bi-cultural treaty commitment and values.

Student and teacher voice from Denmark

The findings from this New Zealand population aligns closely with results reported by Ledertoug (2016) from a Danish sample, where students and educators also described identifying with and taking ownership of their strengths. Similarly, Ledertoug reported that the majority of students demonstrated superficial rather than in-depth understanding of strengths. While students and teachers found the use of their strengths fun and energising, they found the application of strengths in schoolwork challenging, with students reporting that strengths are not used in teaching and are therefore somewhat forgotten. It is precisely to this challenge of embedding strengths in schools that we turn next.

Embedding strengths in schools

Learning they possess strengths is a valuable experience that encourages students to learn, explore, and persevere in the face of challenge. On this evidence alone, strengths deserve a place in schools. That strengths programmes support well-being and academic achievement further strengthens the case. However, although strengths interventions can be effective, this often ceases at the end of the intervention. "Strengths interventions, it appears are like medicines; they only work when you take them" (Quinlan et al., 2012, p. 1158). The challenge remains to embed a strengths focus within school culture so that these effects are durable. That will require further learning on how to create 'strengths supportive cultures' in schools. Student, teacher, and researcher insights and feedback suggest the following strategies may help embed strengths in schools.

Build a shared language of strengths

The establishment and use of a shared language of strengths fulfils several functions. Students and staff can become familiar with strengths, learning more about their own and others' strengths. Seeing strengths on visual reminders around the school and hearing them mentioned in school assemblies and events enables development of a shared language of strengths. For this shared language to really take root however, strengths language must be used in everyday discussion in the staffroom and classroom, in resolving conflict and difficulty, as well as in appreciating people. At its heart, the goal of a shared strengths language is to facilitate the 'noticing and being noticed' that breathes life into a strengths programme.

Develop a culture of strengths spotting

Teachers' strengths spotting is what students reported was the most significant factor influencing their ability to strengths spot in each other. Without the role modelling of teachers and influential students, the potential impact of strengths spotting between students is likely to be greatly diminished. Where students, teachers, and administrative and support staff are encouraged to model the practice of strengths spotting, a genuine strengths focus can take root in the school.

To develop a culture of strengths spotting in a school requires more than development of a shared language. It requires a culture of appreciation and recognition of the value of others, including those whose strengths don't match our own or are not part of the school's values. One challenge at the heart of strengths work in schools is to equip teachers with the skills and language to be able to notice strengths in each student. A school with a culture of strengths spotting will be able to act as a strengths mirror for all students, reflecting back strengths seen in every student. The school staff and systems will encourage and provide opportunities to notice strengths in all students, formally and informally, and strengths spotting will be used as a deliberate tool to build connection and engagement for learning.

Find permanent places for strengths in school life

As many teachers can verify, students can lose interest and engagement after repeated strengths learning activities. Schools require a variety of age and context appropriate approaches to embed strengths in school life. Some schools have elevated the place of strengths in their schools by giving strengths a permanent place in annual awards, school assemblies, student reports, and teacher performance reviews.

Linking strengths to the twenty-first-century competencies for thriving in life and work (Lavy, 2020) may encourage greater use by teachers. We have observed a similar approach over the past decade where leaders promoted strengths integration in their school by mapping strengths onto school vision, values, and learner competencies. Teachers may use strengths more readily when they view strengths as a pathway to values or competencies they endorse.

Younger students particularly may benefit from strategies that promote awareness of strengths use, such as time for planning and reflecting on strengths use in their day-to-day school activities. Classrooms are places where students regularly plan and reflect on learning. Adding a strengths-focused question to planning or reflection teaching resources may build strengths awareness and ownership with minimal change to teaching.

Educators may find ideas and inspiration from those who have collated strengths interventions and activities, notably Niemiec's comprehensive field guide for practitioners (2017). Holmgren et al. (2019) offer a range of strengths-focused activities for teachers to use to make their lessons more engaging and to combat the problem of boredom in schools (2019). Their premise is that by applying well-being and engagement strategies, such as use of students' strengths, teachers can create engaging lessons that facilitate greater learning and alleviate the significant problem of boredom and disengagement in education.

Conclusion

Students need support to identify and own their strengths, others to spot their strengths, support to plan and reflect on strengths use, role models of strengths spotting and reminders of strengths language. Fortunately for students, the people best placed to create authentic, meaningful, and educationally purposeful applications of strengths are their teachers.

Working closely with schools over the past decade reminds us that, given the necessary training and support, teachers are the right people for this job. We look forward to the next generation of strengths programmes, incorporating the best of research-based evidence, teacher-led innovation, and student voice.

Practice

Learn more about strengths

"Try this" for educators

- Find someone with whose top strength is amongst your lowest. Ask them how they use this strength, what it means to them, and the role it plays in their life. Use your new understanding to engage with students with similar strengths.
- In a conflict or when dealing with someone you find 'difficult', ask yourself, 'what strengths does this person have?' You don't have to like the ways in which they use the strength. Consider how you could use their strengths (and yours) to resolve or improve the situation.

"Try this" for students

- Start a discussion with, 'if your favourite strength had a superpower, what would it be, and why?'
- Faced with a challenging task, ask students which of their strengths they will dial up or down to help them.
- Ask a student, 'which of your strengths would you most like people to be aware of?'.

Discussion points

- Do you know your own strengths? How do you bring them to your teaching, meeting the needs of challenging students, resolving conflict, or supporting your own well-being?
- Do you know the strengths of the students you currently teach? What approaches could you use to learn more about their strengths, e.g., through direct discussion, observation, discuss with their peers, or reflective activities?
- Which student of yours might benefit most from having their strengths seen and valued?
- Which strengths get more 'airtime' than others in your school or classroom?
- How will you connect with and value the students with the strengths you notice or value least? Is there a connection between the strengths you notice and your own strengths?

Acknowledgements

We dedicate this chapter to our colleagues around the world whose work on strengths in education continues to advance this field.

Denise acknowledges the contribution and guidance of Dr Nicola Swain and Dr Dianne Vella-Brodrick in the Awesome Us strengths programme research study, and Jill Caldwell's contribution to the qualitative study described in this chapter.

Suggested resources

Holmgren, N., Ledertoug, M., Paarup, N., & Tidmand, L. (2019). *The battle against boredom in schools*. Strength Academy.

Niemiec, R. M. (2017). *Character strengths interventions: A field guide for practitioners*. Hogrefe Publishing.

Quinlan, D. (2019). *NZIWR podcast, bringing wellbeing to life: How strengths-based approaches support wellbeing*. Available from Apple podcasts, or nziwr.co.nz/podcasts.

Quinlan, D. (2020). *NZIWR podcast, bringing wellbeing to life: Strengths-based resilience*. Interview with Dr T. Rashid. Available from Apple podcasts, or nziwr.co.nz/podcasts.

Quinlan & Hone. (2020). *The educators' guide to whole-school wellbeing*. Routledge.

References

Asplund, J., Lopez, S. J., Hodges, T., & Harter, J. (2007). *The Clifton StrengthsFinder 2.0 technical report: Development and validation*. Gallup Inc.

Brownlee, K., Rawana, E. P., & MacArthur, J. (2012). Implementation of a strengths-based approach to teaching in an elementary school. *Journal of Teaching and Learning, 8*(1). https://doi.org/10.22329/JTL.V8I1.3069

Eades, J. F., & Gray, J. (2017). Applying positive psychology in the primary school: Celebrating strengths, a UK well-being project. In Proctor (Ed.), *Positive psychology interventions in practice* (pp. 107–121). Springer, Cham.

Fox Eades, J. (2008). *Celebrating strengths: Building strengths-based schools*. CAPP Press.

Ghielen, S. T. S., van Woerkom, M., & Christina Meyers, M. (2018). Promoting positive outcomes through strengths interventions: A literature review. *The Journal of Positive Psychology, 13*(6), 573–585.

Holmgren, N., Ledertoug, M., Paarup, N., & Tidmand, L. (2019). *The battle against boredom in schools*. Strengths Academy.

Lavy, S. (2020). A review of character strengths interventions in twenty-first-century schools: Their importance and how they can be fostered. *Applied Research in Quality of Life, 15*(2), 573–596.

Ledertoug, M. (2016). *Strengths-based learning – Children's character strengths as a means to their learning potential* (PhD thesis). Submitted to DPU/Aarhus University, Denmark.

Linley, P. A. (2008). *Average to A+: Realising strengths in yourself and others*. CAPP Press.

Linley, P. A. (2010). *Realise2: Technical report*. CAPP Press.

Lottman, T. J., Zawaly, S., & Niemiec, R. (2017). Well-being and well-doing: Bringing mindfulness and character strengths to the early childhood classroom and home. In C. Proctor (Ed.), *Positive psychology interventions in practice* (pp. 83–105). Springer.

Niemiec, R. M. (2013). VIA character strengths: Research and practice (The first 10 years). In H. Knoop & A. Delle Fave (Eds.), *Well-being and cultures: Perspectives on positive psychology* (pp. 11–29). Springer.

Niemiec, R. M. (2017). *Character strengths interventions: A field guide for practitioners*. Hogrefe.

Norrish, J. M., & Seligman, M. E. (2015). *Positive education: The Geelong grammar school journey*. Oxford Positive Psychology Series.

Peterson, C., & Seligman, M. E. (2004). *Character strengths and virtues: A handbook and classification* (Vol. 1). Oxford University Press.

Proctor, C., & Eades, J. F. (2019). *Strengths Gym®: Build and exercise your strengths!* Positive Psychology Research Centre.

Proctor, C., Tsukayama, E., Wood, A. M., Maltby, J., Eades, J. F., & Linley, P. A. (2011). Strengths gym: The impact of a character strengths-based intervention on the life satisfaction and well-being of adolescents. *The Journal of Positive Psychology, 6*(5), 377–388.

Quinlan, D., & Hone, L. (2020). *The educators' guide to whole-school wellbeing: A practical guide to getting started, best-practice process and effective implementation*. Routledge.

Quinlan, D. M., Swain, N., Cameron, C., & Vella-Brodrick, D. A. (2015). How 'other people matter' in a classroom-based strengths intervention: Exploring interpersonal strategies and classroom outcomes. *The Journal of Positive Psychology, 10*(1), 77–89.

Quinlan, D., Swain, N., & Vella-Brodrick, D. A. (2012). Character strengths interventions: Building on what we know for improved outcomes. *Journal of Happiness Studies, 13*(6), 1145–1163.

Quinlan, D., Vella-Brodrick, D. A., Gray, A., & Swain, N. (2019). Teachers matter: Student outcomes following a strengths intervention are mediated by teacher strengths spotting. *Journal of Happiness Studies, 20*(8), 2507-2523.

Rashid, T., Anjum, A., Chu, R., Stevanovski, S., Zanjani, A., & Lennox, C. (2014). Strength based resilience: Integrating risk and resources towards holistic well-being. In G. A. Fava & C. Ruini (Eds.), *Increasing psychological well-being in clinical and educational settings* (pp. 153-176). Springer.

Rath, T. (2007). *StrengthsFinder 2.0*. Simon and Schuster.

Schutte, N. S., & Malouff, J. M. (2019). The impact of signature character strengths interventions: A meta-analysis. *Journal of Happiness Studies, 20*(4), 1179-1196.

Thomas, D. R. (2006). A general inductive approach for analyzing qualitative evaluation data. *American Journal of Evaluation, 27*(2), 237-246.

van Agteren, J., Iasiello, M., Lo, L., Bartholomaeus, J., Kopsaftis, Z., Carey, M., & Kyrios, M. (2021). A systematic review and meta-analysis of psychological interventions to improve mental wellbeing. *Nature Human Behaviour, 5*(5), 631-652.

White, M. A., & Waters, L. E. (2015). A case study of 'The Good School': Examples of the use of Peterson's strengths-based approach with students. *The Journal of Positive Psychology, 10*(1), 69-76.

7 Coaching conversations to enhance well-being

Andrea Giraldez-Hayes

Over the last decade, there has been a growing interest to promote the whole-school well-being through the integration of positive psychology and coaching in schools. This chapter examines the use of coaching to promote well-being and enhance and amplify the effect of positive psychology interventions.

Introduction

How many hours a day do teachers, students, and other school community members spend engaging in conversations? As far as I know, there are no reliable statistics in schools. However, research studies in the workplace suggest that between "50% and 80% of the workday is spent in communicating, two-thirds of that in talking" (Klemmer & Snyder, 1972). We can argue that education is basically a process of communication and that the quality of communication between teachers and students, parents and children, colleagues, or different school community members does matter. Quality conversations strengthen relationships, impact people's thinking, and enhance learning, performance, and well-being (Grant, 2017; Mehl et al., 2010). Coaching-like conversations (Cheliotes & Reilly, 2010) have also proved an excellent resource in different contexts, including schools. Therefore, it is worth investing in learning and developing skills to improve our conversations. This chapter is an invitation to consider coaching, and more explicitly coaching skills, as a helpful positive education tool to facilitate learning and well-being.

Positive psychology and coaching

Positive psychology and coaching have been defined as complementary fields (Green, 2014), both aiming to cultivate optimal functioning and well-being. Burke and Passmore (2019) and Lomas (2019) have suggested that, when focusing on well-being, coaching could be considered as a positive psychology intervention, that is "treatment methods or intentional activities aimed at cultivating positive feelings, positive behaviours, or positive cognitions [and] enhance wellbeing" (Sin & Lyubomirsky, 2009, p. 467). Others have explored the use

DOI: 10.4324/9781003228158-9

of coaching to sustain or amplify the well-being gains experienced in the use of Positive Psychology Interventions (PPIs) (Green & Palmer, 2018; Panagiota & Burke, 2021).

These perspectives can be observed in the implementation of positive education and coaching in schools. Some schools invest in positive education only and create programmes based on the use of PPIs. Others consider coaching as a tool to develop leadership skills or improve teaching and learning performance but do not necessarily contemplate positive education or use PPIs. Finally, others, and that has been the case for many in the last few years, may decide to provide training in positive education using a range of PPIs (acts of kindness, gratitude, etc.) and draw on coaching to ensure sustainability. The last option is the focus of this chapter. We argue that the best approach to implementing positive education should consider cultivating quality coaching conversations across the school to create a coaching culture.

What is coaching?

One of the most popular definitions of coaching is Whitmore's (2009): "Unlocking a person's potential to maximise their performance. It is about helping them to learn rather than teaching them" (p. 126). Although the kind of coaching we consider in this chapter does not focus only on performance but mainly on well-being, the definition is still useful. It helps us understand that coaching conversations can unlock a person's potential (for example, helping them identify and use their strengths or developing a growth mindset). Also, to consider that, unlike teaching or mentoring, coaching is not about giving advice or telling people what to do but about helping them find their options and make their own decisions. Using Freire's words, it is about assisting them in becoming active agents of their own development and creating their lives (Freire, 2000).

Coaching is a one-to-one or one-to-many (as in group coaching) conversation. A skilled coach will listen and ask questions to respectfully challenge their conversational partner's thinking to help them to raise their self-awareness and set and achieve meaningful goals. In a coaching conversation, the coach is not an expert but a facilitator of learning. Hook (2015) describes coaching as a powerful learning experience that helps people to feel valued and listened, think more clearly, recognise their strengths, skills, and resources, identify desired goals or outcomes, as well as a wide range of options to achieve them and feel more confident and positive about change.

Although there are many coaching models, it has been argued that coaching is a solution-focused conversation (Grant et al., 2010). That means that the coaching conversation does not focus on the problem but the solution, helping the conversational partner consider what change they want to make, why they want the difference, and how they can achieve it.

Coaching skills

Coaching conversations differ from other conversations in schools because they are based on the use of a set of skills, including rapport, active listening, and effective questioning. Besides, most coaching conversations work within a framework or structure.

While teachers have developed and use these skills in their teaching, there is always a potential for improvement. Besides, teachers should help students to develop these skills to move towards a coaching culture.

The first step in every conversation is building **rapport and trust**. Rapport forms the basis of meaningful connectivity, allowing people to communicate openly and honestly and, in turn, helping to build trust. Although some people are skilled at building rapport and do it intuitively, others will need some practice. For example, think about a person you connect with easily. The chances are that the person is present in the conversation. They listen and demonstrate this by not interrupting, reflecting, summarising or asking questions related to your narrative, not judging you, using body language to encourage the development of your ideas, keeping confidentiality, and making the time for the conversation.

Active listening is getting out of your own thoughts and trying to understand the other person without judging. When you listen actively, you listen to what is being said and what is not being said. You are listening to the feelings and emotions behind the words. Besides, when you really listen, you are 'telling' the other person I see you; you are important to me. Rogers and Farson (1957) coined the term active listening. They consider it as a strategy to increase empathy. When you listen actively, you ask open-ended questions, reflect on another's feelings, and clarify and summarise what you have heard. Listening is one of the fundamental principles of coaching. A rule of thumb in coaching conversations is that the coach should listen 80% of the time, using the other 20% to summarise, paraphrase, offer feedback, and, essentially, ask questions.

Questions are the backbone of coaching conversations. As teachers, we ask students questions to see if they remember or understand, to seek information, or to gain agreement, among others. These questions, however, are pretty shallow as they do not require much thinking on the part of the learning. In coaching conversations, we aim to ask thought-provoking questions, that is, questions at a deeper level, inviting people to think for themselves. Coaching questions are open, and therefore there is no correct answer. Most will start with 'what', and some will begin with 'how', 'when', or 'which'. Because the intention is to challenge the other person to consider ideas from different or unusual perspectives, if you find that the initial responses are superficial, you can encourage the conversation partner to expand and develop the answers. To achieve this, you can use prompts like 'I am curious about...', 'What else...?', 'How did you do that?', 'What do you think/feel?'.

All these coaching skills can be learned and developed by teachers, students, and other school community members. Just developing and using these skills would improve your conversations. However, a good coaching conversation will also have a structure that gives direction to the process. There are many different coaching models, and all of them should be used with flexibility. One of these models, used in solution-focused coaching, is OSKAR (McKergow & Jackson, 2002). That is a five-part model:

- Outcome or objective. What do you want to achieve?
- Scale. Using a 1–10 scale to measure how close the person you are coaching is to achieving the desired Outcome.
- Know-How. Skills, knowledge, experience, or attributes that will help the person you are coaching to move forward.

- Affirm + Action. After praising the other person's skills, knowledge, experience, or attributes, you ask questions for them to focus on the actions they need to take to progress towards achieving the goal.
- Review usually takes place at the beginning of each coaching conversation – if you have a series – to review the actions the other person has taken, consider what has improved and what is needed to keep moving forward.

Coaching conversations in schools

The support and resources to apply coaching in schools have increased over the last decade, primarily aiming to enhance professional practice by supporting teachers (Leat et al., 2012) or leaders (Crow, 2012) or students coaching students (Eriksen et al., 2020). In addition, many books and peer-reviewed papers support the benefits of using some form of coaching in schools (Green et al., 2021).

Each school and each teacher should consider how coaching could be implemented in their organisation. It could be a formal process, hiring a professional coach or creating coaching training and practice opportunities for the staff. Eventually, the training could be aimed at students to also engage in peer coaching conversations. Another option could be to take part in some coaching training to learn and develop essential skills to improve school conversations using a coaching-like approach. Coaching could be used regularly or in on-off conversations related to teachers' and students' well-being. An example of coaching conversations combined with the use of PPIs can be found in Trom and Burke (2021). The authors observed the effect of a one-week-long randomised controlled trial in which one group of students completed a gratitude intervention and a second one engaged in a gratitude-and-coaching intervention. The results suggested that coaching can magnify the effect of PPIs. As suggested, coaching can also be considered as a PPI by itself. In a pilot study conducted by Madden et al. (2011), primary school boys participated in a strengths-based coaching programme and received eight group coaching sessions over two school terms. Students took the Values in Action-Youth assessment (Park & Peterson, 2006) to identify their strengths. The coaching conversations helped them set meaningful goals, be persistent to achieve them, and use their signature strengths in different ways. Students also engaged in another PPI, a "letter from the future", writing about themselves at their best. The results suggested an increase in students' self-reported levels of engagement and hope.

Case study

Bullying has become a problem in many schools. According to a recent study completed in the United States of America (National Center for Educational Statistics, 2019), one out of every five (20.2% students) report being bullied, and school-based prevention programmes decrease bullying by 25% (McCallion & Feder, 2013). To reduce the number of bullying cases in a public secondary school in Madrid, a group of teachers designed a two-week programme that included different positive psychology interventions and peer coaching conversations among students. The interventions used were the 'loving-kindness meditation' and the 'counting kindness' intervention.

As founded by Fredrickson et al. (2008), teachers expected that the 'loving-kind-ness meditation', practised three minutes five times a week, could increase positive emotions and, in turn, personal resources like social support. When suggesting the 'counting kindness' intervention, the idea was to invite people to savour the good things they had done for others. According to Otake et al. (2006), the intervention aimed to encourage students to keep track of their acts of kindness (e.g., helping a friend, sharing a sandwich, holding a door open) and compute a daily count of these actions for a week. Teachers allocated space to create a 'kindness mural'. They painted the wall with chalkboard paint, and chalks were available for students to describe their act of kindness before leaving school briefly.

The peer coaching conversations, one at the beginning of the programme, the second one at the end of the first week, and the last one at the end of the programme, aimed to help students to raise their self-awareness, define what kindness meant for them, and set goals related to the topic.

Although the experience was not part of formal research, teachers kept an observation record and organised students' forums to discuss the results. Most of them found the experience meaningful and recognised that the coaching conversations helped them reflect on themselves and keep their commitment throughout the project.

Discussion points

- What strategies does your school currently use to have better 'coaching-like' conversations?
- What opportunities exist for staff and students to develop coaching skills?
- What evidence-based strategies identified in this chapter could be easily implemented in your school?
- How might coaching contribute to support and amplify the effect of positive psychology interventions used by students and staff?

Suggested resources

Australian Institute for Teaching and School Leadership. Coaching Resources https://www.aitsl.edu.au/lead-develop/develop-others/coach-others/coaching-resources

British Educational Research Association. Coaching https://www.bera.ac.uk/search/coaching

Green, S., Leach, C., & Falecki, D. (2021). Approaches to positive education. In M. Kern & M. Wehmeyer (Eds.), *The Palgrave handbook of positive education* (pp. 21–48). Palgrave. This chapter considers and discuss the integration of positive psychology and coaching in schools.

Ippolito, J. (2019). *Want to transform schools & yourself? Think like a coach!* https://www.youtube.com/watch?v=qAW1E6iq7AU

Tschannen-Moran, B., & Tschannen-Moran, M. (2010). *Evocative coaching: Transforming schools one conversation at a time.* John Wiley & Sons. Appendix B: Practice Exercises, include a good range of ideas to practice and develop coaching skills.

References

Burke, J., & Passmore, J. (2019). Strengths based coaching–A positive psychology intervention. In L. Van Zyl & Sr. S. Rothmann (Eds.), *Theoretical approaches to multi-cultural positive psychological interventions* (pp. 473–475). Springer. https://doi.org/10.1007/978-3-030-20583-6_21

Cheliotes, L. M. G., & Reilly, M. F. (2010). *Coaching conversations: Transforming your school one conversation at a time*. Corwin Press.

Crow, G. M. (2012). A critical-constructive perspective of coaching for leadership. In S. Fletcher & C. Mullen (Eds.), *Sage handbook of mentoring and coaching in education* (pp. 228–240). Sage.

Eriksen, M., Collins, S., Finocchio, B., & Oakley, J. (2020). Developing students' coaching ability through peer coaching. *Journal of Management Education, 44*(1), 9–38.

Fredrickson, B. L., Cohn, M. A., Coffey, K. A., Pek, J., & Finkel, S. M. (2008). Open hearts build lives: Positive emotions induced through loving-kindness mediation build consequential personal resources. *Journal of Personal and Social Psychology, 95*(5), 1045–1062.

Freire, P. (2000). *Pedagogy of freedom: Ethics, democracy, and civic courage*. Rowman & Littlefield Publishers.

Grant, A. (2017). The third 'generation' of workplace coaching: Creating a culture of quality conversations. *Coaching: An International Journal of Theory, Research and Practice, 10*(1), 37–53. DOI: 10.1080/17521882.2016.1266005

Grant, A. M., Passmore, J., Cavanagh, M. J. & Parker, H. M. (2010). The state of play in coaching today: A comprehensive review of the field. In G. P. Hodgkinson & J. K. Ford (Eds.), *International review of industrial and organizational psychology 2010* (pp. 125–167). Wiley-Blackwell.

Green, S. (2014). Positive education: An Australian perspective. In M. J. Furlong, R. Gilman, & E. S. Huebner (Eds.), *Handbook of positive psychology in schools* (2nd ed.) (pp. 401–415). Taylor & Francis.

Green, S., & Palmer, S. (2018). Positive psychology coaching. Science into practice. In S. Green & S. Palmer (Eds.), *Positive psychology coaching in practice*. Routledge.

Green, S., Leach, C., & Falecki, D. (2021). Approaches to positive education. In M. Kern & M. Wehmeyer (Eds.), *The Palgrave handbook of positive education* (pp. 21–48). Palgrave.

Hook, P. (2015). *Coaching & reflecting pocketbook*. Management Pocketbooks.

Klemmer, E. T., & Snyder, F. W. (1972). Measurement of time spent communicating. *Journal of Communication, 22*(2), 142–158.

Leat, D., Lofthouse, R., & Towler, C. (2012). Improving coaching by and for school teachers. In Fletcher & C. Mullen (Eds.), *Sage handbook of mentoring and coaching in education* (pp. 43–58). *The Sage handbook of mentoring and coaching in education*. Sage.

Lomas, T. (2019). Is coaching a positive psychology intervention? Exploring the relationships between positive psychology, applied positive psychology, coaching psychology, and coaching. In L. Van Zyl & Sr. S. Rothmann (Eds.), *Theoretical approaches to multi-cultural positive psychological interventions* (pp. 371–389). Springer. https://doi.org/10.1007/978-3-030-20583-6_16

Madden, W., Green, S., & Grant, A. (2011). A pilot study evaluating strengths-based coaching for primary school students: Enhancing engagement and hope. *International Coaching Psychology Review, 61*(1), 71–83.

McCallion, G., & Feder, J. (2013). Student bullying: Overview of research, federal initiatives, and legal issues. *CRS Report*. https://sgp.fas.org/crs/misc/R43254.pdf

McKergow, P., & Jackson, M. (2002). *The solutions focus. Making coaching & change SIMPLE*. Nicholas Brealey.

Mehl, M. R., Vazire, S., Holleran, S. E., & Clark, C. S. (2010). Eavesdropping on happiness: Well-being is related to having less small talk and more substantive conversations. *Psychological Science, 21*(4), 539–541.

National Center for Education Statistics. (2019). *Student reports of bullying: Results from the 2017 school crime supplement to the national crime victimization survey*. https://nces.ed.gov/pubs2019/2019054.pdf

Otake, K., Shimai, S., Tanaka-Matsumi, J., Otsui, K., & Fredrickson, B. L. (2006). Happy people become happier through kindness: A counting kindnesses intervention. *Journal of Happiness Studies, 7*(3), 361–375.

Park, N., & Peterson, C. (2006). Character strengths and happiness among young children: Content analysis of parental descriptions. *Journal of Happiness Studies, 7*(3), 323-341.

Rogers, C., & Farson, R. (2021). *Active listening*. Mockingbird Press LLC.

Sin, N., & Lyubomirsky, S. (2009). Enhancing well-being and alleviating depressive symptoms with positive psychology interventions: A practice-friendly meta-analysis. *Journal of Clinical Psychology, 65*(5), 467-487. https://doi.org/10.1002/jclp.20593

Trom, P., & Burke, J. (2021). Positive psychology intervention (PPI) coaching: an experimental application of coaching to improve the effectiveness of a gratitude intervention. *Coaching: An International Journal of Theory, Research and Practice*, 1-12.

Whitmore, J. (2009). *Coaching for performance*. Nicholas Brealey.

Part 3

Connecting with self

Contemporary education faces critical issues related to the challenges of living in an uncertain, ever-changing, hyperconnected, and fast-paced world, and mental health is one of the most pressing issues. A significant number of students (NHS Digital, 2020; Pew Research Center, 2019) and teachers (Nuffield Foundation, 2020) are stressed out and experience anxiety, depression, and other symptoms. The potential impact of connecting with self – or self-connection – on well-being should be considered in this context. Klussman et al. (2020a) define self-connection as "(1) an awareness of oneself, (2) an acceptance of oneself based on this awareness, and (3) an alignment of one's behaviour with this awareness" (p. 1) and suggest that self-connection gives people a sense of stability and connection between desires and behaviours and acceptance of those desires, which in turns boosts well-being. Considering the vital link between self-connection, health, and well-being (Klussman et al., 2020a, 2020b), the authors contributing to this section offer three different options and perspectives to ignite and cultivate self-connection.

In Chapter 8, the author provides a framework of life meaning in schools by reviewing research and practices to cultivate young people's sense of meaning and purpose. Chapter 9 discusses the possibility of cultivating compassion in schools and suggests that teachers, students, and the wider community engage in compassion-based initiatives (CBIs), as they help them understand the nature of their minds and others. Chapter 13 invites students, teachers, and parents to embrace meditation considering its benefits for health and well-being. Finally, Chapter 14 reviews a list of strength-based interventions to connect to selves in school. All authors offer an overview of the most recent research on their topics and tips to introduce these practices in the schools.

As you read this part, you may reflect on the following:

- What would be the advantages of connecting with your inner self?
- How can you help students and others in the school community to connect with themselves?
- How could your school embrace a compassionate approach?

DOI: 10.4324/9781003228158-10

References

Klussman, K., Nichols, A. L., Langer, J., & Curtin, N. (2020a). Does positive affect lead to perceptions of meaning in life? The moderating role of self-connection. *European Journal of Applied Positive Psychology, 4*(3), 1–11.

Klussman, K., Nichols, A. L., Langer, J., & Curtin, N. (2020b). Connection and disconnection as predictors of mental health and wellbeing. *International Journal of Wellbeing, 10*(2), 89–100.

NHS Digital. (2020). Mental health of children and young people in England. *NHS*. https://files.digital.nhs.uk/CB/C41981/mhcyp_2020_rep.pdf

Nuffield Foundation. (2020). More teachers reporting mental health problems than ever. *Nuffield Foundation*. https://www.nuffieldfoundation.org/news/more-teachers-reporting-mental-health-problems-than-ever

Pew Research Center. (2019). Most U.S. teens see anxiety and depression as a major problem among their peers. *PRC*. https://www.pewresearch.org/social-trends/wp-content/uploads/sites/3/2019/02/Pew-Research-Center_Teens-report_full-2.pdf

8 Has life no meaning? Cultivating youth life meaning in schools

Gökmen Arslan and Murat Yıldırım

This chapter emphasises the importance of promoting life meaning of young people in school settings and designing meaning-based intervention services to foster youth academic functioning, psychosocial health, and flourishing.

Introduction

With cognitive development, which enables individuals to think in abstract terms and explain future possibilities, young people frequently ask questions about life meaning and purpose (Shek, 2012). Given the lifespan development perspective, these questions help young people to establish a stable identity, be productive, develop close relationships, and build social and career roles (Erikson, 1968; Steger et al., 2009). During adolescence, individuals also spend more time at school, and schools do not only provide a venue for improving their academic functioning but also are a setting where they can develop their emotional, behavioural, and social skills (Arslan et al., 2021). Therefore, developing school-based strategies for enhancing youths' life meaning is essential to design and implement school-based prevention and intervention services to foster youth academic functioning, mental health, and well-being.

Although academic-based outcomes are identified as one of the main purposes of education, questions on life meaning and purpose are central to debates about what optimal education should be in schools. Schools are therefore a unique setting for cultivating student flourishing, and there is a need to emphasise the deeper purposes of education organised not only around youths' academic functioning but also their mental health and well-being (Heng et al., 2020). The purpose of this chapter is to form a better understanding of meaning in life and provide ways of the promotion of this concept in schools. The chapter thus provides a framework of meaning in life in young people by reviewing research and practices to cultivate their sense of meaning and purpose in life in the school context.

DOI: 10.4324/9781003228158-11

Theoretical background

Life meaning has become a popular topic in research and practice, particularly with the emergence of positive psychology. Positive psychology is the science of positive individual traits and experiences. It emphasises improving the psychosocial and emotional well-being and preventing psychopathology that arises when life is barren and meaningless. Similar to existential perspectives, positive psychology emphasises the ability of people to establish meaning. Life meaning is individuals' positive regard of their life and is related to beliefs that give meaning in life. People have an essential role in developing meaning in their life, and every person can find meaning and purpose in life (Frankl, 2000). This construct refers to making sense or coherence out of individuals' existence and having a purpose in which they can strive to achieve their aims (Reker et al., 1987). Life meaning is also identified as one of the main components of flourishing, reflecting belonging to, and serving something that individuals believe is bigger than the self (Seligman, 2011).

More recently, meaning in life has been characterised by motivational (goal or purpose), cognitive (coherence), and emotional (that one's life matters) components (Wong, 2012; see Figure 4). Frankl (2000), the founder of logotherapy, has identified meaning in life as an essential and universal human motive, and the searching for meaning is a primary force in people's life. Frankl (2000) has also emphasised that people can discover meaning in life through three avenues: doing a deed or creating a work, experiencing something or encountering someone, and facing unavoidable suffering in our lives. Accordingly, life incudes suffering, and people can discover meaning by searching and finding their unique role in life.

Wong (2012) has highlighted a four-facet definition of meaning in life in terms of *purpose, understanding, responsibility, and enjoyment*, called as the PURE model. According to this framework of meaning, meaningful living is a balanced life resulting from

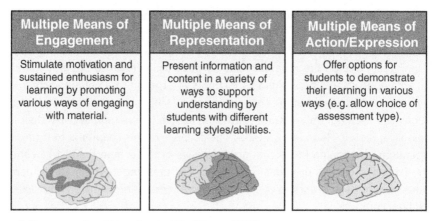

Figure 4 Components of Meaning in Life (Wong, 1997).

the dynamic interaction between positive and negative forces and managing a balance among different sources of meaning, between achievement and accepting one's limitation (Wong, 2012b). The key to meaning in life is an individual's ability to navigate between these opposite forces to accomplish an optimal balance (Yıldırım et al., 2021). Based on this framework, Arslan and Yıldırım (2021b) conceptualised life meaning in the school context as young people's appraisal of their life, referring to acknowledging the intrinsic value of life, meaningful relationships, and achievement in school. Although there are some differences in the definitions of meaning in life, researchers seem to agree on the main facets of meaning in life, such as value and purpose. Thereby, life meaning is a life-image reflecting that one's life is significant, responsible, enjoyable, purposeful, and meaningful.

Some scholars have emphasised that meaning in life is cognitive in nature (Ho et al., 2010) and help individuals to organise and interpret their experiences as well as having a purpose in which they can motive to achieve long-term goals (Li et al., 2018). The questions about life meaning and purpose widely begin in adolescence, and the exploration of life meaning during this developmental period is essential to establish a stable identity and social roles (Erikson, 1968; Steger et al., 2009). This also contributes to young people's psychological health and well-being in later development stages (Arslan & Yıldırım, 2021b). A strong sense of life meaning, for example, helps young people to create and sustain long-term goals (Morgan & Robinson, 2013), which can influence their mental health and adjustment. Further, during adolescence, people experience a variety of cognitive changes, such as thinking about abstract ideas, the process of thinking itself (i.e., metacognition), and what is possible (Oogarah-Pratap et al., 2020). With cognitive development, young people start to ask various questions about school life to search meaning and purpose before transitioning from adolescence to adulthood.

People are capable of searching for meaning in life irrespective of some characteristics, such as age, gender, IQ, and educational background (Frankl, 2000), and the need for meaning exists for all age groups, including young people. Meaning in life can hence be assumed an essential and universal need in all ages. Life meaning is individually constructed (Frankl, 2000) and identified through individuals' values and worldview that help them to search and find purpose and meaning in their life (Wong, 2012b). Developmentally, adolescence is a critical developmental stage to establish and sustain a deep understanding of meaning in life because of developmental tasks and various biological and psychosocial changes. Additionally, young people do not only experience developmental suffering during this period but also are a vulnerable group who may face various adverse circumstances (e.g., maltreatment, peer pressure, risky behaviour, and violence). Given Frankl's perspective on the ways of discovering meaning in life (Frankl, 2000), young people are able to search for life meaning, and this searching for meaning might influence their mental health and well-being not only in adolescence but also in adulthood (Arslan et al., 2021). Recently, some research has supported this notion indicating that young people report higher levels of the search for meaning in life than older age groups (Steger et al., 2009), and having a sense of meaning significantly contributes to people's later mental health and well-being in face of adverse life experiences (Arslan & Yıldırım, 2021b; Yıldırım et al., 2020). Therefore, developing a sense of meaning in life during adolescence can be an important source of resilience and serves as a protective factor for successfully coping with adverse circumstances and mental health problems.

Practice

"Try this" for students

We often hear the following statements and questions "Does life has a purpose? What kind of life is worth living? I don't know what I want to do in my life" from young people. Although having a sense of life meaning is essential across the lifespan, it is especially important during adolescence that is a relatively sensitive time for the development of a healthy functioning and stable identity. Having a strong sense of life meaning help young people to develop a healthy personal identity and worldview (Erikson, 1968), and the absence of life meaning is associated with poor physical health, lower well-being (e.g., life satisfaction, positive affect), and greater psychosocial and behavioural challenges among adolescents (Arslan & Yıldırım, 2021a; Heng et al., 2020; Yıldırım & Arslan, 2021). Therefore, adolescence is proposed as an optimal developmental stage to explore and promote youth's meaning and purpose in life (Cotton Bronk et al., 2009).

Empirical evidence has documented that meaning in life is positively associated with subjective and psychological well-being (Arslan & Allen, 2021; Heng et al., 2020) and is negatively related to anxiety, stress, and depressive symptoms (Arslan et al., 2020) and risky behaviours (Lin & Shek, 2019) among young people. For example, young people with depressive symptoms reported lower levels of meaning in life than those without these symptoms (Kleftaras & Psarra, 2012), and people committed to exploring life meaning and purpose during adolescence were also more positive, hopeful, and adaptive, and they are able to effectively deal with challenges (Burrow et al., 2010). Hence, meaning and purpose in life might help young people to protect their mental health in face of adversities and well-being and serve as a resilience factor to promote youth-valued outcomes (Arslan & Allen, 2021; Arslan & Yıldırım, 2021a). A systematic review by Lim and Kang (2018) documented that the meaning-centred approach was an effective intervention strategy for exploring life meaning and promoting positive youth outcomes both in young people with problems (e.g., cancer, adjustment problems) and in healthy adolescents. Overall, using meaning-centred prevention and intervention services in schools may be useful to improve well-being and the quality of life and reduce psychosocial challenges among young people.

"Try this" for educators

Logotherapy is a meaning-based approach to improve meaning and purpose in life and provides a unique contribution of healing in times of suffering. Unlike traditional therapeutic approaches, which often focus on mental health symptoms, logotherapy emphasises people's strengths and their searching for purpose and meaning in life. Thereby, logotherapy provides an essential therapeutic strategy for healing through life meaning. Although there is evidence supporting the effectiveness of logotherapeutic strategies and interventions on mental health and well-being, very few studies have focused on youth-valued outcomes, specifically, in school settings. Applying logotherapeutic strategies by educators promote young people to establish meaning and purpose in life, which in turn contributes to developing self-awareness that benefits to improve their capacity to select the appropriate choices which contribute to fostering their healthy development and well-being. Hanna and Minton (2021) have offered logotherapy-based school approach for responsible decision-making to provide mental health services and to achieve educational objectives.

With the application of this framework in school settings, young people can understand their own feelings and thoughts about their life situation; the choices open to them, and the consequences of their choices. Additionally, the logotherapeutic approach might help young people to contribute something to their life through school tasks and works, experience something or new relationships, and choose a courageous attitude toward unexpected adversities in their lives (Frankl, 2000; Wong, 2012). Logotherapy-based group intervention was empirically found an effective strategy to reduce psychological distress and addictive behaviours (e.g., depression, anxiety) and improve effective coping strategies in the face of adversities among young people (Liu et al., 2021). School counsellors or educators can use logotherapy-based strategies to help students to be aware of the overriding goal of their life and improve their academic performance, motivation, and engagement with school activities.

Based on Frankl's logotherapy, Wong (2012) has proposed a meaning-centred approach that is a hybrid model of existential traditions and cognitive–behavioural strategies and informed by existential positive psychology (i.e., second wave positive psychology [PP 2.0]). Meaning-centred approach is based on the PURE model (Wong & Wong, 2012) that presents strategies and practices for building a healthier and happier life.

Given a large part of young people life is school, it follows that evidence relevant to the benefits of meaning-centered approach is most likely practicable to young people's school life. For example, Wong (2012) has emphasised some typical strategies of how mental health providers can use the PURE framework in meaning-centered interventions as follows:

1 Explore young people's stated purpose and motivations for change and their preferred future without their problems,
2 Help young people gain new understanding and insight of their own difficulties,
3 Lead young people to embrace their freedom and responsibility to implement actions based on their self-efficacy beliefs, personal strengths, and available resources, and
4 Guide young people to experiment with whether their actions would bring about positive change; If not, then, they need to either modify their actions or goals.

Taken together, meaning-centered approach provides a flexible framework of positive-based interventions to promote mental health and well-being through meaning in life. Therefore, school counsellors and educators could develop strategies (e.g., modelling, workshops, and coaching) to teach and improve the PURE components in young people. Meaning-centered interventions could help youths to develop realistic and measurable action strategies, deal with challenges, and link their school goals to life goals. Meaning-centered intervention strategies could also be useful to improve youths' sense of meaning and purpose in life at schools, which in turn enhance their resilience and positive coping strategies to foster their mental health and flourishing.

Case study

Ayşe struggles with a history of depression; she is a 14-year-old adolescent female living with her parents and two younger siblings. Her family is looking for a new school because of her failing in school and problems getting along with her peers. She was suffering from the following symptoms: frequent sadness and crying, diminished interest in daily activities, losing weight, low self-concept, guilt, anxiety, irritability, insomnia, feelings of worthless, and difficulty concentrating. Furthermore, she experienced problems in her interpersonal relationships, persistent negative thoughts about her scholastic abilities. Logotherapy is introduced to her to discover her life's purposes and motivates her to break the chain of the depression symptoms that she is experiencing. With techniques of logotherapy, she was assisted to find the reasons to live with full of purpose and engagement in life and school despite the miseries, pain, and suffering he is going through. At the end of therapy sessions, she had some basic skills to cope with depression and meaning in life without paying attention to sufferings. This process helps her to create a new life-image reflecting that her life is significant, responsible, enjoyable, purposeful, and meaningful.

Discussion points

- What really matters in your life?
- What are the ingredients of meaning in life?
- How can you improve youth sense of meaning in life at school settings?
- How can meaning-centered strategies be used in school settings?

Suggested resources

- Frankl, V. (2000). *Man's search for ultimate meaning*. MJF Books.
- Hanna, S. A., & Minton, S. J. (2021). A meaning-centred, whole-school approach for responsible decision-making: The logotherapeutic framework. *Irish Educational Studies*, 1–18. https://doi.org/10.1080/03323315.2021.1899017
- Wong, P. (2012). From logotherapy to meaning-centered counseling and therapy. In P. T. P. Wong (Ed.), *The human quest for meaning: Theories, research, and applications, 2nd ed.* (pp. 619–647). Routledge/Taylor & Francis Group.

References

Arslan, G., & Allen, K. -A. (2021). Exploring the association between coronavirus stress, meaning in life, psychological flexibility, and subjective well-being. *Psychology, Health and Medicine*. https://doi.org/10.1080/13548506.2021.1876892

Arslan, G., & Yıldırım, M. (2021a). Coronavirus stress, meaningful living, optimism, and depressive symptoms: A study of moderated mediation model. *Australian Journal of Psychology*, 1–12. https://doi.org/10.1080/00049530.2021.1882273

Arslan, G., & Yıldırım, M. (2021b). A longitudinal examination of the association between meaning in life, resilience, and mental well-being in times of coronavirus pandemic. *Frontiers in Psychology, 12*. https://doi.org/10.3389/fpsyg.2021.645597

Arslan, G., Yıldırım, M., Karatas, Z., Kabasakal, Z., & Kılınc, M. (2020). Meaningful living to promote complete mental health among university students in the context of the COVID-19 pandemic. *International Journal of Mental Health and Addiction*. https://doi.org/10.1007/s11469-020-00416-8

Arslan, G., Yıldırım, M., & Leung, M. M. (2021). Mediating effect of personal meaning in the prediction of life satisfaction and mental health problems based on coronavirus suffering. *Frontiers in Psychology, 12*, 537. https://doi.org/10.3389/fpsyg.2021.638379

Burrow, A. L., O'Dell, A. C., & Hill, P. L. (2010). Profiles of a developmental asset: Youth purpose as a context for hope and well-being. *Journal of Youth and Adolescence, 39*(11), 1265-1273. https://doi.org/10.1007/s10964-009-9481-1

Cotton Bronk, K., Hill, P. L., Lapsley, D. K., Talib, T. L., & Finch, H. (2009). Purpose, hope, and life satisfaction in three age groups. *The Journal of Positive Psychology, 4*(6), 500-510. https://doi.org/10.1080/17439760903271439

Erikson, E. H. (1968). Identity: Youth and crisis. In *Identity: Youth and crisis*. Norton & Co.

Frankl, V. (2000). *Man's search for ultimate meaning*. MJF Books.

Hanna, S. A., & Minton, S. J. (2021). A meaning-centred, whole-school approach for responsible decision-making: The logotherapeutic framework. *Irish Educational Studies*, 1-18. https://doi.org/10.1080/03323315.2021.1899017

Heng, M. A., Fulmer, G. W., Blau, I., & Pereira, A. (2020). Youth purpose, meaning in life, social support and life satisfaction among adolescents in Singapore and Israel. *Journal of Educational Change, 21*(2), 299-322. https://doi.org/10.1007/s10833-020-09381-4

Ho, M. Y., Cheung, F. M., & Cheung, S. F. (2010). The role of meaning in life and optimism in promoting well-being. *Personality and Individual Differences, 48*(5), 658-663. https://doi.org/10.1016/j.paid.2010.01.008

Kleftaras, G., & Psarra, E. (2012). Meaning in life, psychological well-being and depressive symptomatology: A comparative study. *Psychology, 3*(4), 337-345. https://doi.org/10.4236/psych.2012.34048

Li, M., Fan, W., Cheung, F. M., & Wang, Q. (2018). Could meaning in life contribute to adolescents' vocational commitment and identity? A longitudinal analysis in different chinese cultures. *Journal of Pacific Rim Psychology, 12*, e36. https://doi.org/10.1017/prp.2018.24

Lim, Y. S., & Kang, K. A. (2018). Systematic review of meaning-centered interventions for adolescents. *Child Health Nursing Research, 24*(3), 263-273. https://doi.org/10.4094/chnr.2018.24.3.263

Lin, L., & Shek, D. T. L. (2019). The influence of meaning in life on adolescents' hedonic well-being and risk behaviour: Implications for social work. *The British Journal of Social Work, 49*(1), 5-24. https://doi.org/10.1093/bjsw/bcy029

Liu, X., Jiang, J., & Zhang, Y. (2021). Effects of logotherapy-based mindfulness intervention on internet addiction among adolescents during the COVID-19 pandemic. *Iranian Journal of Public Health*. https://doi.org/10.18502/ijph.v50i4.6005

Morgan, J., & Robinson, O. (2013). Intrinsic aspirations and personal meaning across adulthood: Conceptual interrelations and age/sex differences. *Developmental Psychology, 49*(5), 999-1010. https://doi.org/10.1037/a0029237

Oogarah-Pratap, B., Bholoa, A., & Ramma, Y. (2020) Stage theory of cognitive development–Jean piaget. In B. Akpan & T. J. Kennedy (Eds.), *Science education in theory and practice*. Springer Texts in Education. Springer, Cham.

Reker, G. T., Peacock, E. J., & Wong, P. T. P. (1987). Meaning and purpose in life and well-being: A life-span perspective. *Journal of Gerontology, 42*(1), 44-49. https://doi.org/10.1093/geronj/42.1.44

Seligman, M. E. P. (2011). *Flourish: A visionary new understanding of happiness and well-being*. Free Press.

Shek, D. T. L. (2012). Life meaning and purpose in life among Chinese adolescents: What can we learn from Chinese studies in Hong Kong? In P. T. P. Wong (Ed.), *The human quest for meaning: Theories, research, and applications, 2nd ed.* (pp. 335-355). Routledge/Taylor & Francis Group.

Steger, M. F., Kawabata, Y., Shimai, S., & Otake, K. (2008). The meaningful life in Japan and the United States: Levels and correlates of meaning in life. *Journal of Research in Personality, 42*(3), 660-678. https://doi.org/10.1016/j.jrp.2007.09.003

Steger, M. F., Oishi, S., & Kashdan, T. B. (2009). Meaning in life across the life span: Levels and correlates of meaning in life from emerging adulthood to older adulthood. *The Journal of Positive Psychology, 4*(1), 43-52. https://doi.org/10.1080/17439760802303127

Wong, P. T. P. (1998). Meaning-centered counseling. In P. T. P. Wong (Ed.), *The human quest for meaning: A handbook of psychological research and clinical applications* (pp. 395-435). Lawrence Erlbaum Associates Publishers.

Wong, P. (2012a). From logotherapy to meaning-centered counseling and therapy. In P. T. P. Wong (Ed.), *The human quest for meaning: Theories, research, and applications, 2nd ed.* (pp. 619–647). Routledge/ Taylor & Francis Group.

Wong, P. T. P. (2012b). Toward a dual-systems model of what makes life worth living. In P. T. P. Wong (Ed.), *The human quest for meaning: Theories, research, and applications, 2nd ed.* (pp. 3–22). Routledge/ Taylor & Francis Group.

Wong, P. T. P. (2016). Meaning centered positive group intervention. In *Clinical perspectives on meaning: Positive and existential psychotherapy* (pp. 423–445). Springer International Publishing. https://doi. org/10.1007/978-3-319-41397-6_21

Wong, P. T. P., & Wong, L. C. J. (2012). A meaning-centered approach to building youth resilience. In P. T. P. Wong (Ed.), *The human quest for meaning: Theories, research, and applications, 2nd ed.* (pp. 585–617). Routledge/Taylor & Francis Group.

Yıldırım, M., & Arslan, G. (2021). A moderated mediation effect of stress-related growth and meaning in life in the association between coronavirus suffering and satisfaction with life: Development of the stress-related growth measure. *Frontiers in Psychology, 12*, 529. https://doi.org/10.3389/fpsyg. 2021.648236

Yıldırım, M., Arslan, G., & Aziz, I. A. (2020). Why do people high in COVID-19 worry have more mental health disorders? The roles of resilience and meaning in life. *Psychiatria Danubina, 32*(3–4), 505–512.

Yıldırım, M., Arslan, G., & Wong, P. T. P. (2021). Meaningful living, resilience, affective balance, and psychological health problems among Turkish young adults during coronavirus pandemic. *Current Psychology.* https://doi.org/10.1007/s12144-020-01244-8

9 Embedding compassion in schools

The what's, the why's, and the how's

Frances A. Maratos, Julie Hurst, Caroline Harvey, and Paul Gilbert

There is growing evidence that the cultivation of compassion-focused motives and emotions has profound effects on mental health and well-being. This chapter outlines the importance of embedding compassion in school and educational settings for pupils/students, those who teach them, and for the contextual organisation of education.

Introduction

There is considerable evidence that being motivated to be caring and compassionate to self and others has a range of psychophysiological effects that support physical and mental health, and pro-social behaviour (Booker et al., 2019; Di Bello et al., 2020; Kim et al., 2020; Seppala et al., 2017). Although compassion awareness and compassion training are not currently part of educational curricula, given their impact on general well-being, there are increasing calls for compassionate approaches to be embraced within the education sector (Coles & Gent, 2021; Kohler-Evans & Barnes, 2015; Maratos et al., 2019a; Peterson, 2017). Indeed, schools are becoming ever-more stressful environments for teachers. Carmichael (2017) reported that 30% of UK teachers leave the profession within the first five years of qualifying, citing excessive workload and bureaucracy. Moreover, Ofsted (2019) found that 76% of teachers reported their job had a negative impact on their mental health, with occupational well-being and general life satisfaction low, and teachers generally disappointed with the profession. Added to this, one in ten primary aged children, and one in seven secondary aged pupils are reported to suffer from a mental disorder, and this number is increasing (NHS Digital, 2018). Countering this, compassion-based initiatives (CBI's): provide children with emotional coping skills; address bullying; allow for safe space creation; enable collaboration; increase resilience; support the development of ethical behaviour; and promotion of prosociality – which all culminate in encouraging positive and supportive learning environments (Coles, 2015; Goleman & Davidson, 2017; Lavelle, 2017; McAdam & Lang, 2009; Peterson, 2017; Roeser et al., 2018; Welford & Langmead, 2015). Moreover, for teachers and educators, CBIs enhance socio-emotional competencies, well-being and reduce distress (Maratos et al., 2019b). Hence, embracing compassion across educational sectors has utility to improve the mental health of educators and students alike.

DOI: 10.4324/9781003228158-12

Theoretical background

What is compassion?

The value of cultivating compassion for prosocial behaviour and well-being has been recognised for thousands of years (Ricard, 2015). Exact definitions of compassion vary (Gilbert, 2017; Mascaro et al., 2020). Some seek to define it in terms of attributes (Strauss et al., 2016), whereas others have sought an evolutionary approach that identifies the underlying motives of caring behaviour and its derivative, 'compassion' (Gilbert, 2020; Goetz et al., 2010). Although the evolution of caring behaviour has a number of different roots, a pivotal major evolutionary challenge was care of offspring. The evolution of parental caring behaviour generated motives to be sensitive and attentive to the distress and needs of an infant and address them appropriately. The evolution of feature detectors for 'distress and need' that trigger appropriate caring behaviour evolved with a range of physiological systems that are now known to be linked to caring behaviour. These include alterations to the autonomic nervous system, particularly the vagus nerve (Di Bello et al., 2020; Porges, 2017), a range of neurocircuits (Vrtička et al., 2017) and hormonal changes (Carter et al., 2017). Importantly, compassion training can influence these physiological processes (Singer & Engert, 2019).

Caring behaviours include how to alleviate distress by protecting, feeding, comforting or rescuing (Mayseless, 2016). In attachment theory (Cassidy & Shaver, 2018), caring also involves providing the young with a secure base to learn how to face life tasks. In humans, this involves enabling the child to feel valued, cared for, and encouraged and rewarded in developmental achievements. The verbal and non-verbal behaviour of a caring parent stimulates physiological infrastructures that give rise not only to brain maturation, but also a positive sense of self and confidence. A second function of attachment and caring behaviour is to offer a safe haven; the offer of a soothing and calming immediate environment when the child is distressed. The study of adverse childhood experiences demonstrates the many and varied harmful effects a lack of such care can result in (see Hughes et al., 2017 for review). Importantly, schools can serve as a basis through which caring attitudes and behaviours can be nurtured and, leading on from this, a platform through which compassionate behaviours and a compassionate ethos can be developed.

While animals also provide care for their offspring, caring and compassion are different. Compassion is a derivative of caring that requires more complex cognitive abilities. About 2 million years ago our ancestors began to evolve three new types of cognitive competency. One was forms of reasoning using symbols and language that enabled us to create complex representations of the relationships between processes. Bryne (2016) called this insight. The second was enhanced complex competencies for mentalisation, empathy and theory of mind. To expand, it would be difficult to be compassionate unless we had some insight into the causes of people's suffering and difficulties and, then, what would be helpful in these instances (Luyten et al., 2020). The third competency was a new type of conscious awareness; 'meta-cognition' and where we became conscious of being conscious. Siegel (2018) calls it 'awareness of awareness'. It gives rise to capacities for mindfulness and the ability to observe our own minds in action (Manuello et al., 2016). Together these combined competencies give rise to knowing intentionality. These competencies allow for us to develop, unlike animals, hierarchical goal (e.g., healthy behaviours to promote better mental health and longevity; something a lion would never understand). Thus, these competencies allowed us to develop intentionally, including intentionality to be thoughtful, empathic and caring (i.e., compassionate).

In addition, compassion as defined by Gilbert (2014) as well as others (e.g., Goetz et al., 2010) requires an understanding of the nature of suffering as a conscious experience. For example, we can care for our gardens, houses or prized possessions, but we wouldn't have compassion if our garden flooded. We would have compassion for our friend whose prized garden had flooded because we recognise: (1) the meaning of the garden to our friend; and (2) their experience of suffering the loss of something they prized. Compassion is therefore unique to humans and involves (a) deliberately, intentionally and knowingly focusing on the suffering and needs of self and others; and (b) deliberately and intentionally trying to work out what would be helpful. Importantly, individuals who struggle with these competencies can struggle with compassion. Hence part of compassion training is to build these competencies, to encourage, develop and promote relationships with caring motives.

Here, motives underpin life tasks – avoiding harm, acquiring resources, securing status, developing friendships, joining groups, finding sexual partners, caring for children. Via evolutionary processes, these motives are underpinned by stimulus-response algorithms of the type: if A occurs, is felt or noticed … then do B. For example: if threat … then activate sympathetic nervous system (fear) and run or hide; if sexual opportunity … then activate sympathetic nervous system (sexual arousal), approach and engage; if hungry… then activates sympathetic nervous system (drive) and go search for food (see here Maratos & Pessoa, 2019). Whereas some reflect basic hierarchical needs, others are much more complex and reflect the complex challenges of human life:

For example – if one's house is on fire, then there is a need to escape which activates threat, but if the house has additional occupants that will perish if not rescued, then drive and compassion are also activated.

So, once we understand compassion is an evolved motivational system growing from mammalian caring (Gilbert, 2014), we can understand why compassion involves not only a sensitivity to suffering in self and others but, additionally, a commitment to try to alleviate and prevent this suffering. As part of this, the introduction of CBIs in education should include focus on the flows of compassion. These are compassion for self, compassion for others and the acceptance of compassion from others (although for an alternative approach see Neff, 2003).

In summary, humans have a startling array of recently evolved cognitive competencies; far too many to explore here. Among the most salient, however, are our capacities for self-awareness, knowing awareness, knowing intentionality, capacities for systemic thinking and reasoning, thinking in time (i.e., we can reflect on the past and imagine a future), various forms of metacognition (such as the ability to worry about worrying), theory of mind and empathy, and capacities for self-observation that underpin processes such as mindfulness (see Gilbert, 2019). These competencies can alter many forms of motivation, including caring and compassion. However, as we have seen through human history, knowing intentionality can also motivate sadism, torture and mass murder, etc. It is this intentional knowing – behind our harming behaviours – that makes aspects of human behaviour cruel and sadistic. In the case of Felidae for example, we would not regard the suffering a lion causes its prey as cruel or sadistic. This is because we understand that the lion has no insight or intention as to the suffering it causes; rather it is a basic algorithm of 'need food to survive; kill prey'. The ethos of compassion is to recognise the evolved/developed competencies of humans and our knowing intentionality; and therefore, harness within ourselves and others, the propensity for good (or at the very least 'do no harm') vs. bad. Crucially, when we knowingly and intentionally engage in suffering, with efforts to be helpful and not harmful, that is 'compassion' – whether for the self, for others, or being able to accept such from others (Gilbert, 2017, 2018).

Practice

Schools can provide a major place where knowing intentionality and our multiple and varied motivational systems, complex competencies and biological underpinnings, can become choreographed and played out. Schools are not only places where we learn core academic subjects (e.g., Maths, English, Science and beyond), but schools also provide a context for personal maturation via the development of relational networks between peers and authority (Coles, 2015; Peterson, 2017). In modern day society, schools provide a foundation for children and adolescents to learn how to cooperate or compete, to support or bully, to respect authority or have contempt for it; all aspects of knowing intentionality. Importantly, numerous reports highlight that schools should be a source for children to learn how to communicate, develop the motivation to share and care, acquire empathy skills, develop ethical values and respect; compared with an ethos of being fearfully deferential or submissive to authority (see also Yeager et al., 2018). To this end, a number of grassroots movements have emerged in the UK that support such former principles, this not only includes our own Compassion in Schools movement (e.g., www.cmtschools.org), but also Mindfulness in Education (www.mindfulnessinschools.org/; www.themindfulnessinitiative.org/) and Schools in Mind (www.annafreud.org/schools-and-colleges/), to name but a few.

   The movement of bringing CBIs into schools and the education sector more generally has been championed by many (e.g., Coles, 2015; Lavelle et al., 2017; Maratos et al., 2019b; Peterson, 2017a; Roeser et al., 2018), but must include guarding against naïveté in the specific compassion training. In the model we champion, a central tenet is to recognise that compassion needs to address the dark side of humanity as well as promoting well-being through, as described above, knowing intentionality (Gilbert, 2009, 2018; Marsh, 2019). To recap, humans, as a species have inflicted intense suffering with our wars, holocausts, tortures, history of slavery, and countless other atrocities and cruelties; yet we can also show extraordinary motives and capacity to be helpful to others, even at a cost to ourselves (Preston, 2013). Those within education can learn from these examples and, thus, educational settings can be a pivotal place of psychoeducation. Indeed, the core content of any compassion-focused curriculum should include: (i) how we have the propensity for both bad and good; and (ii) reflection as to which 'seeds' of thoughts and behaviours we would wish to nurture and grow. This includes not only in respect to others, but also in respect to oneself. That is, in this context, not only compassion for others but also compassion for the self and receiving compassion from others (i.e., the flow of compassion).

In educational settings where this flow of compassion ethos has been embedded, compassion-based approaches have been found to offer a potential means of increasing psychological well-being for students, staff, parents and the wider community. This includes increasing parental engagement and decreasing low-level disruptive behaviour and fixed-term exclusions, while at the same time upholding the education priorities of the school (Welford & Langmead, 2015). Most recently, Maratos et al. (2019b), Maratos et al. (2020) and Matos et al. (submitted) have found embedding compassionate mind training (CMT) in teaching and school staff CPD is feasible, well-received and improves both physiological and psychological well-being. Whilst detailed in Maratos et al. (2020) this specific 6-module curriculum core content covers: what compassion is, the nature of our tricky brains, the three circles model of emotion (threat, drive and soothing), compassionate and mindful practices, multiple selves, embracing a compassionate compared with critical self, and compassionate communication. Now trialled with circa 600–700 educators across the UK and Portugal, this specific CMT programme leads to improvements in self-compassion, compassion towards others and improved positive affect, as well as reductions in fears of compassion anxiety and depression (Maratos et al., 2019b; Matos et al., submitted). Qualitative analyses have further revealed benefits of the CMT curriculum for dealing with emotional difficulties (Maratos et al., 2019b). Physiological analyses have further revealed beneficial effects of the specific CMT on heart-rate variability, blood pressure and cardiovascular reactivity; all indicators of bodily stress responses (Matos et al. submitted; Maratos, Sheffield et al. submitted). Such results offer much promise when considering 67% of UK educational professionals working in primary, secondary or further education described themselves as stressed by their work (Educational Support Partnership, 2018) and that educators across many countries and sectors are reporting high levels of burnout (Gray et al., 2017).

Whilst less well researched, early benefits of employing compassion-based practices with school pupils include improvements in environmental mastery, greater personal growth, decreased negative affect, increased life satisfaction, self-acceptance, autonomy and purpose in life (Bach & Guse, 2015). Karr et al. (2019) further report that a compassion-based group intervention with five fourth-grade children (i.e., aged 9–10) resulted in those children gaining familiarity with affiliative states and emotion-regulation strategies and can decrease feelings of anxiety and depression. Most recently, Maratos and colleagues have developed a six-module compassion-based Personal, Social, Health and Economic Education (PSHE) curriculum for pupils transitioning from primary to secondary school. This curriculum includes a focus on understanding the three emotion systems of the mind/body (Lesson 1), with each system and its triggers a focus of Lessons 2–4 (drive in Session 2, threat in Session 3 and compassion in Session 4). Practices are also introduced from session 2 onwards, beginning with regal walking and calm place imagery in Lesson 2 and soothing and/or hand breathing in Lesson 3. Compassion-based practices and imagery are introduced in Session 4, with the flow of compassion introduced in Sessions 4–6. Specifically, practicing compassion for others following Session 4, practicing compassion for the self-following Session 5, and practicing the three flows of compassion (i.e., including accepting compassion from others) in Session 6 and beyond. Therefore, our specific compassion PSHE is focused on knowing intentionality, in a child-friendly manner, through understanding the emotion systems of the mind and how compassion can allow for balance to be achieved within these systems both within ourselves and others. Preliminary analyses of this curriculum, using a robust randomised control trial design, reveals the specific compassion-based PSHE, as compared to standard PSHE, results in reductions in socially prescribed perfectionism, negative self-compassion and the maintenance of stable trait anxiety (whilst this increased in the control group). In addition, thematic analysis revealed children found the lessons positively impacted management of their own well-being, emotions and behaviour, as well as positively impacted upon class behaviour (Maratos, Wood et al., submitted).

Finally, in higher education, Maratos et al. (2019a) have argued that the introduction of compassion into teaching pedagogy can promote the health and well-being of HE staff and the student body. Leading on from this, Harvey et al. (2020) have recently trialled a 'light touch' CBI in the higher education sector. This curriculum focuses on compassionate communication in group work and specifically the 'micro skills of compassionate communication' (MSCC). HE Students are introduced to the concept of compassionate communication in relation to group work, with a focus on identifying both helpful and unhelpful group behaviours (i.e., knowing intentionality). Students are then encouraged to embody helpful group behaviours during seminar and group activities to support the functioning of the group, and to recognise and take action to address any unhelpful behaviours as they occur. Regarding this HE curriculum, preliminary focus groups conducted with both staff and students revealed promising results with some students noting that, in addition to employing these new skills within the HE learning environment, they had also put them into practice in other interactions outside of university. Specifically, thematic analysis revealed three benefits of the MSCC approach in HE. These are its use in (i) addressing unhelpful group behaviours; (ii) employing helpful group behaviours; and (iii) enhancing inclusivity. A final theme emphasised support for the roll out of this approach more widely across the HE sector, and work to progress this is currently underway. Thus, the research of Harvey et al. (2020) reveals that supporting students to develop micro skills of compassionate communication has the potential to bring benefits not only within HE settings but also within sider society, as students trained in these techniques have opportunity to embed them into numerous further settings, e.g., personal and social interactions; the workplace, etc.

To sum, applying CBI's within education settings has many benefits. For teachers, educators and school-staff, utilising CBIs may address the unprecedented retention and mental health crisis noted across educational sectors worldwide, with compassion practices leading to increased positive indicators of mental and physiological health and decreased negative indicators of mental health. These results accord with more general meta-analyses of the benefits of CBIs across a range of differing adult populations (e.g., Kirby et al., 2017). Additionally, whilst less well researched, early evidence of the benefits of employing CBI's with school pupils points to the introduction of such having very real and beneficial effects on their mental-health and well-being. This is of more importance now than ever, especially when considering COVID-19 has exacerbated mental health issues. For example, a startling 39% of children aged 11-16 have reported that the UK 2020 Covid lockdown made their lives worse, with this number increasing to 54% for those with a probable mental disorder (NHS Digital, 2020). Finally, whilst in its infancy, the application of CBI's in higher education shows promise as a way of enhancing feelings of inclusivity. This not only provides students with a more rewarding experience during group work, but as compassionate communication skills are transferable, the implementation of these across further HE learning contexts and beyond (e.g., home life), to positive effect.

"Try this" for educators

In this section, we offer three practices that Educators can practise to better develop their emotion regulation skills and their compassionate self. Two are taken from our evaluated CMT curricula with educators and the third is taken from Salzberg, who is also a prominent practitioner in the field of compassion research and applied practice.

Soothing rhythm breathing

DIFFICULTY: EASY TO MEDIUM

In our version of soothing rhythm breathing, we embrace an embodied cognition approach and educate individuals (e.g., teachers) as to 'what is in the mind is in the body, and what is in the body is in the mind'. You can find male and female audios of our soothing rhythm breathing practice at www.cmtschools.org but below is an overview. This practice should take you about 7-8 minutes.

First, sit comfortably with your feet flat on the floor, about a shoulder width apart, and your back straight and head in line. Your posture is comfortable but up right because the idea is to become relaxed but also to stay alert rather than to become sleepy. This can happen if your head drops forward. Gently close your eyes or look down at the floor or allow your gaze to be unfocused if you prefer.

PAUSE

Create a gentle facial expression, an expression of friendliness as if you are with somebody you like. Try relaxing your facial muscles by letting your jaw drop slightly and then letting your mouth turn up into a slight smile. Increase the smile to the point that it is comfortable for you and gives you that feeling of friendliness.

PAUSE

Now we are going to focus on your breathing. Notice the air coming in through your nose, down into your diaphragm, staying a short while and then moving back out through your nose. Notice how your diaphragm moves gently as you breathe in and out. For the development of soothing rhythm breathing, we will be breathing slightly slower and slightly deeper than we would normally. To give you a guide, the in-breath is often about 3 seconds with a gentle hold, and then 3 seconds for the out-breath with a gentle hold. You might try to breathe a little faster and then a little slower until you find a breathing rhythm that is comfortable for you, is a gentle rhythm and gives you the feeling of 'slowing down'. Also, focus particularly on the outbreath, and the air leaving your nose with a steady rhythm. Try to ensure that the in-breath and the out-breath are even, or that the out-breath is slightly longer, but don't rush them.

PAUSE

As you develop your rhythm, notice and focus on the feeling of inner slowing with each out breath. Notice how your body responds to your breathing, as if you are linking up with a rhythm within your body, this is soothing and calming to you. Notice how this links to your friendly facial expression. Practice this for 30 seconds.

PAUSE

Now we can just 'ground ourselves for a moment'. Sensing the weight of your body resting on the chair and the floor underneath you. Allow yourself to feel held and supported

PAUSE

...coming to rest in the present moment
...staying alert with good body posture.

PAUSE

Remember that it is perfectly ok for your mind to wander. Simply notice it happening and then gently guide your attention back to an awareness of your body and breathing steadily in and out, just sensing the flow of air coming in and out of your nostrils. If it helps, you can use the internal mantra 'mind slowing down' on one outbreath and 'body slowing down' on the next outbreath.

PAUSE

...just gently observe your breathing.
...gently allowing things to be as they are.
...feeling your body slowing down.

PAUSE

So now, once again, check on your friendly facial expression, the gentle smile and then continue to experience your soothing rhythm breathing. Feel the feeling of slowing down gently. Stay with this now for the next 2 minutes or so, just breathing slightly deeper and slightly longer than you would normally. Try and stay alert and just focus on your practice and if it helps the internal mantra of 'mind slowing down' on one outbreath and 'body slowing down' on the next outbreath in a kind, warm and friendly voice tone.

PAUSE

Now when you are ready, open your eyes or refocus and look about you. Increase your smile slightly for a moment or two, and then take a stretch, moving your body.

Soothing rhythm breathing can be practised at any time. For example, whilst waiting for a bus, sitting on a train, the moment you arrive home from work in your car; before you enter your home (e.g., to the chaos of your partner and children) or even when taking a bath.

The more you practise noticing how breathing affects your body and your mind, the more familiar you will become with allowing yourself to slow down. Sometimes it's good just to remind ourselves to slow down with our breathing, even if we can only do it for 30 seconds or a minute. The more we practise, the more we will become familiar with helping our mind and body, but also keeping our mind alert.

Compassionate other imagery

DIFFICULTY: MEDIUM

In this practice, we teach individuals (e.g., teachers) to cultivate self-compassion by imagining a compassionate other. This is a further practice taken from our CMT for Teachers programme (www.cmtschools.org) but this particular exercise has also been shown to be useful in helping individuals cope with pain (see Maratos & Sheffield, 2020). Again, this practice should take you around 7–8 minutes.

To begin this practice, choose a moment when you are unlikely to be disturbed for a while and sit comfortably. Now take a straight posture and focus on your soothing rhythm breathing, with the air coming in through your nose and down gently into your diaphragm, then out through your nose again. Notice the feeling of your body slowing down. Adopt a friendly facial expression and voice tone. Remember as we go through the exercise that you may find your mind wandering. Do not worry about this, just gently and kindly bring it back onto the task we are doing.

PAUSE

In this imagery, we are going to ask you to play with a fantasy where you imagine yourself to be the focus of another mind that cares about you. Just like we can imagine our ideal holiday or meal, that has everything we want of it, you can create an ideal compassionate image. It can be beyond human failing or inconsistencies and be exactly as you need it to be. Some people find that having a visual image of this compassionate other helps them to feel like the recipient of compassion. People have had images of other humans, animals, the sea or sun or an energy, while others do not get clear images, but just a 'hazy sense of something or someone'... Remember any images of a compassionate source that you create will probably be more like daydreaming and they don't need to be clear visual pictures in your mind.

PAUSE

Whatever form your imagery takes we would like you to imagine that this ideal compassionate mind has certain qualities. These are superhuman - complete and perfect compassionate qualities that are there for you to experience.

They include;

- A deep commitment to you - to help you find strength, and take joy in your happiness.
- Wisdom gained through experience and maturity.
- It truly understands you and the struggles we go through in life.

- Strength of mind - it cannot become overwhelmed by our pain or distress, but remains present, enduring it with us.
- Warmth is conveyed by kindness, gentleness, care and openness.
- Acceptance - it is never judgemental.

PAUSE

Please don't worry about remembering all of these qualities and emotions just focus on the ones that you can.

Now, take a moment to think about this other mind that is so deeply committed to helping you cope and to your happiness and well-being...

Pause (and between each of the below, to allow focus on each separate quality)

Focus on the sense of wisdom and the understanding that are there for you...

Imagine the strength and dependability of this other being ...

Focus on the great warmth and kindness that permeates the whole image and is directed at you...

Imagine feeling understood and completely accepted...

Focus on the kindness that is there for you...

Imagine feelings of care and concern that are there for you ...

Imagine the gentle warmth of this compassion flowing toward you ...

Pause

Now, when you feel ready, let the image of your compassionate other fade. Spend a moment or two reflecting on the feelings that have arisen in you. Notice how that feels in your body.

For a few moments just be, without paying attention to anything in particular and when you feel ready, you can open your eyes and gently stretch your body (and finish the practice).

Circle of Love meditation

Difficulty: medium

This is an exercise from meditation teacher and compassion practitioner Sharon Salzberg (https://www.sharonsalzberg.com). It helps develop the three flows of compassion: from us to others, from others to us and towards ourselves. It is best done with eyes closed and either sitting or lying down quietly. This exercise can also be used with children from pre-teen upwards, initially for quite short amounts of time, and then longer as they become more proficient in the stages.

To begin the meditation, choose a moment and a place where you feel safe, comfortable and are unlikely to be disturbed for a while. As you close your eyes, just very lightly notice your breathing. There is no need to try to change it, just gently rest your attention on it. Allow yourself to just be with your breath, not doing anything.

Next picture yourself in the centre of a circle made up of the most loving, kind and compassionate beings you can imagine. They may be family, friends, neighbours or even pets. There may be some people in your circle who you've never met but have been inspired by. Maybe they exist now, or they've existed historically, or even in fiction. Equally they may be people you see almost every day. Whoever comes to mind for you is fine.

They are all sending you kindness, love and compassion. All you need to do is receive the love of those who love you. Allow yourself to receive the love, attention, compassion, care and kindness of everyone in your circle of love.

Don't question whether you deserve it or not, just allow it all to flow towards you.

Notice how you feel when you receive this love. You may feel gratitude and awe, or you might feel shy. Whatever emotion may arise, you just let it wash through you. Open yourself up to receiving love.

Imagine that it is flowing into the centre of your chest near your heart. Feel yourself receiving and storing it there. There's nothing special that you need to do to deserve this kind of care. It's simply because you exist. Allow yourself to fill with the feelings.

Now send loving care to the people in your circle.

You can allow the loving kindness and compassion you feel coming towards you to flow back to them and then from them towards all people everywhere. You can give out the care and kindness in the same way it flowed to you.

You can also send it to yourself whenever you need it. It is stored inside you, so it is part of you.

When you have spent whatever amount of time you choose on the practice, allow your circle to gently fade away and reflect for a moment or two on how the flow of compassion felt for you and when you are ready to end the practice. It is also interesting to note how you feel going about your typical daily routine after you've completed this exercise a few times.

This can take a little practice before the flow of compassion feels easy, so do not worry if you need to spend some time on this before it feels like a natural response.

"Try this" for students

In this section, we offer three practices that pupils and/or students can practice to better develop their emotion regulation skills and their compassionate communication skills. Two are taken from our CMT PSHE curriculum with pupils aged 10-12 (Maratos, Wood et al., submitted) and the third is taken from our HE curriculum with pupils/students aged 18+ (Harvey et al., 2020).

In our CMT PSHE pupil curriculum, we further use simplified versions of soothing rhythm breathing and compassionate other (described above), but for the purposes of demonstrating more of our practices, below we outline regal walking and calm place imagery (for school pupils), and then also identifying and addressing a monopoliser in a group (for HE students/ older pupils).

Regal walking

DIFFICULTY LEVEL: EASY

In this practice, the key is to introduce some of the qualities of compassionate imagery, whilst also allowing children to understand 'what is in the body is in the mind, and what is in the mind is in the body'. In school settings, we ask teachers and classroom assistants to join in and often take the children to an outside space to practise this practice. Teachers have informed us that they use this practice to bring calm to their classrooms (e.g., after children come in from morning, lunch or afternoon break). An overview of this exercise can also be found at www.cmtschools.org

1   Imagination

Imagine that you are a king or a queen. Open your chest. Shoulders back. Make a slight curve in your back. Imagine you are a CONFIDENT, PROUD and CALM individual.

2   Slowing the body down

Imagine that you are a king or queen, WALK SLOWLY and use slower, calm movements. Take DEEPER BREATHS, make your breaths come from your tummy and BREATHE MORE SLOWLY than you normally would.

3   Face

Walk around CALMLY and with PRIDE

Hold your head up high and with a slight or GENTLE SMILE on your face.

In this exercise, we further tell the children to hold the gentle smile if they look at others and perhaps say hello in a calm, kind voice tone – but the emphasis is on imaging themselves as a king or queen who is confident, proud and calm, and walks and breathes slowly and with pride.

Calming space imagery

DIFFICULTY LEVEL: MEDIUM

In this practice, the key is to introduce children to experimenting with imagery, whilst also using the imagery to allow children to develop a calming, contented, positive space. Some individuals may mistakenly refer to this as 'safe space' imagery. However, we never use the words 'safe space or safe place' imagery with children in a classroom setting, as this imagery is designed for just that i.e., classroom settings (and not clinical or therapeutic settings, where unsafe places may be a focus of therapeutic intervention). Additionally, in our work, as we introduce compassion as a general tool for all to improve well-being, we aim for calming space imagery to be associated with low-level positive emotions and therefore also the soothing system (which we first introduce in Module 1). We introduce the practice of calming imagery in Module 2, but it forms the basis of our compassionate other practice in Module 4 and compassionate self-practice in module 5.

Prior to engaging in the imagery, we show and discuss with children, various images, including which to them represents a sense of calm. We then get the children to focus on their posture (e.g., straight back in chair, feet flat on the floor) and breathing (e.g., deeper/slower), before taking the children/entire class through the below:

Use your imagination

Bring to mind an image of a calming, positive, place (real, imagined or a combination of both). This is a place where you would feel calm and safe. Try to focus on different senses whilst imagining this.

1   Visual – what images do you associate with that space (sea, woodlands, open fields…)?
2   Sound – what can you hear when bringing that image to mind (waves crashing, birds singing, music playing…)?
3   Feelings – how do you feel when you are imagining being in that space (calm, relaxed, happy, content…any other feelings…)?

Take a few moments to do whatever feels comfortable and good in that scene …relax, explore… whatever you like.

When you are ready just gently refocus on the here and now.

We sometimes find that children can struggle with this exercise at first when in a class setting and are aware of the distracting presence of others. So, we ask children to remember their own body bubble and space, and to close their eyes when engaging with the imagery (i.e., when we take them through the practice). With particularly excitable children or classes, it is permissible for children to put their heads on their desks (i.e., on their arms) to allow full focus on the imagery practices. In those particular instances, we get the children when first slowing down (i.e., grounding) to focus on the weight of their heads on their arms.

Identifying and addressing a monopoliser

DIFFICULTY LEVEL: MEDIUM

This exercise forms part of our HE student (and Teacher) curriculum, but would also be appropriate for older children (e.g., teens). Below we present an overview from the perspective of using with HE students:

One of the unhelpful behaviours that can often occur in group settings is when a single person dominates the conversation. We will refer to this dominant person as a 'monopoliser'. Other people might try to join in the conversation, but the monopoliser quickly shuts them down and continues to espouse their viewpoint. Many of you will recognise situations where this has occurred - it can happen in class discussions, during family gatherings, in social groups with friends, and in the workplace; indeed in any group setting or conversation. So, one thing we do is to encourage students to notice when someone might be monopolising a conversation, and then to practice ways in which they might address this type of behaviour.

Step 1:   Encourage students to notice when someone might be monopolizinging a conversation

Ask students to think about a time when someone dominated a conversation or a time when they were in a group and were unable to make their point of view heard. This could be during a seminar or workshop or other classroom activity, or it could be during social settings, or at work.

Ask them if they are ever aware of doing this themselves during conversations

Note that there might be differences in when they act as a monopoliser depending on who they are interacting with.

Step 2:   Explore the consequences of monopolizinging

Ask students to reflect on how they felt when someone else monopolizied a conversation:

What were the consequences for them?

Encourage students to reflect how this situation put them in a position of disadvantage (noticing disadvantage or distress in yourself or others is the first part of the definition of compassion we work to)

Ask students what they believe the consequences were for the monopoliser, did the monopoliser miss out on other valuable points of view? Did they remain unchallenged, and therefore might think others were happy with them taking the lead etc.?

Step 3:   Show students the video of a Monopoliser*

Use the following link to show students an example of a monopoliser:
https://www.youtube.com/watch?v=HLVcL6So3I8

This provides an example of a student monopolizinging a group discussion and highlights some of the consequences.

Step 4:   Identify how the behaviour of the monopoliser might be addressed

Start by reminding students that when practicing the micro skills of compassionate communication, it is everyone's responsibility to address the unhelpful behaviour, so both the monopoliser and the other group members can all take steps to address this.

Step 5:   Discuss what action the monopoliser can take

Ask students what the monopoliser could do to help the situation.

Encourage students to think about self-monitoring – the monopoliser should monitor their own contribution to ensure they are not dominating the conversation.

...The monopoliser could recognise that they have been dominating the discussion and invite opinions from others.

...They could make sure that everyone else in the group is asked if they want to contribute.

Ask students what kind of body language the monopoliser could use to encourage others to join the discussion.

Step 6:   Discuss what action other group members might take

Ask students what other group members could do to help address the behaviour of the monopoliser.

Encourage students to think about how they might use their body language or eye contact to indicate to the monopoliser that other people want to talk. This could involve sliding a hand across a table in front of the monopoliser to gain their attention, it could be a hand raised, or direct eye contact with the speaker, and/or them moving their gaze to others in the group.

Other options could be to verbally interject, to suggest that others would like to share their views, or to be very direct and to say something like '...it's been great to hear all your ideas about this, but I think other people would also like to contribute...'

Recognise that many students could find this quite challenging, so encourage students to be assertive in taking action to help address situations such as this.

Step 7:   Show students the video Addressing a Monopoliser*

Use the following link to show students an example of addressing a monopoliser:
https://www.youtube.com/watch?v=w2XNwfC4S4w

This provides examples of how the monopoliser might engage in self-monitoring to address the situation, and also how other group members might take some action to address the monopoliser. Importantly, this is an example of how the behaviour of a monopoliser might be addressed in a compassionate manner. Because all the students in the group have been introduced to the concept of the MSCC, they are more attuned to, and accepting of others commenting on aspects of their communication style and the group dynamic. This also means that the group tutor/teacher is able to observe various helpful and unhelpful behaviours during group discussions and discuss these with the students directly. This can really help students become more attuned to their own role and communication style/s within group settings.

Final thoughts

This example helps students to understand the impact of a monopoliser on a group discussion and to become more aware of how they might help to address this. This could be from the perspective of increased self-monitoring in the case of the monopoliser, and through identifying ways in which they might take action to ensure other members of the group, including themselves, can have their voices heard.

*The video resources identified within this example form part of the work by Harvey et al. (2020).

Case studies

In recent times, during partial lifting of COVID-19 restrictions, we have been working with classes in Year 6 and Year 7. Each week, from week 3 onwards, we ask the children and teacher to reflect upon their use of the practices we have introduced in the classroom and their daily lives. The below represents examples of what the children and teacher of one Year 6 class have shared with us as to the applied use of the practices to improve their well-being. All names are, of course, pseudonyms.

Case 1

Philip struggles with anxiety, he stated to us that any techniques focused on breathing do not help and make him feel uncomfortable as he finds it draws too much attention to what is going on in his body and focusing on his breathing can introduce panic. [This is one reason why we do not introduce Soothing Rhythm Breathing with children early on in our PSHE curriculum]. On introducing calming place imagery, Philip was able to use this practice to develop an image in which he is surrounded, or embedded within, a hazy blue light. He explained that he was able to use this image when in class to induce a feeling of calmness and peacefulness – emotions his teacher said he struggled with a great deal. Philip also reported using the calming place imagery when his father was suddenly taken very ill at home. In the face of this alarming event, he used the imagery to help himself cope with his anxiety. He found the blue light provided him with a sense of comfort during this difficult time. This was an important development for Philp, who, until he developed the blue light imagery, had seemed somewhat reticent about participating fully in the lessons. Using the techniques at home marked a turning point. A little time later, when his father had returned home, Philip described how the class discussions of compassion prompted him to think of how he might help his father during his recuperation. Philp resolved to provide glasses of water for his father so he would not go thirsty until he was recovered enough to do so for himself.

Case 2

Jas has struggled with being in crowded places (i.e., agoraphobia) since COVID-19, and noted this as partly a consequence of the various UK lockdowns that have been progressed and then the easing of restrictions. She explained to us how she had recently been to the cinema with her family, an event that has not been possible for the past circa 18 months. On entering the cinema foyer, Jas explained how she began to get very worried and anxious as it was too crowded for her. She explained to us, and the class, how she was able to use hand breathing and regal walking to calm herself down, and then go on to utilise calming place imagery to distract herself from the busy environment. She explained that this really helped her to stay calm and that when they entered the cinema she was in a relaxed and calm state that helped her to focus on (and therefore enjoy) the film.

Case 3

In week 3 of the PSHE, we entered the classroom prior to our PSHE session to a very calm and serene class, I commented that I would be able to hear a pin drop. Miss Leaves explained to us that prior to our visit she had taken the children out to practice regal walking, with herself, the class and the teaching assistant all engaging in regal walking in the playground. She added that she had found this technique a useful practice to ensure the children were in a manner ready for learning, especially as in the class a number of children seem to struggle with anxiety, ADHD or autism.

In another instance, Miss Leaves further described how one child became upset in a lesson and so she had taken the child outside of the classroom (into the main corridor). She then asked the teaching assistant to find the relevant support worked for the child, whilst she (Miss Leaves) continued to teach the class their lesson as per usual. When the teaching assistant returned with the relevant support worker, the child had very much calmed down. The child explained to those adults present that they had been able to use soothing rhythm breathing to calm themselves down to reduce their distress. This is in accord with the definition of compassion we use across all our curriculum which is: (i) noticing that someone, or ourselves, are struggling or in distress; and (ii) doing something about it to help ourselves or others.

Discussion points

1   To embrace a compassionate ethos across school settings, to what extent do you think it is important for all school employees or otherwise, including perhaps the senior leadership team and non-teaching staff (e.g., midday supervisors), to understand and embrace a compassionate approach? What about at the level of class settings can a compassionate ethos be introduced in specific classes, without wider support for the approach across the school/school employees?

2   In our approach to compassion, we emphasise that compassion involves not only 'compassion to self', but also the flows of 'compassion to others' and being accepting of 'compassion from others'. Why are all aspects important? Can one truly be compassionate if not embracing all three aspects? Which aspect or aspects, do you think, you or others working in your profession, perhaps struggle with most?

3   In the practice section above, we reflect on one particular unhelpful behaviour that can often occur in group settings. This is when a single person dominates the conversation, which we call a 'monopoliser'. We also stress that it is the responsibility of the entire group to address such behaviours. Reflect on your own communication style...do you have a tendency to monopolise group conversations...or is the reverse true? In either case, how could you address such behaviours for the benefit of a group (be it your fellow colleagues or others)?

Suggested resources

For further information about Compassion in the Classroom and the work of Dr Maratos and colleagues please visit https://cmtschools.org/. This website contains free resources including audios of the Soothing Rhythm Breathing exercises, hand breathing and regal walking. It further contains video resources to support the development of compassionate communication in Higher Education and references/access to our publications across the field of Compassion in Education.

In respect to compassion more generally, further audio and video resources can be found as follows:

For more information on the work of Paul Gilbert and the Compassionate Mind foundation (including audio and video resources) visit https://www.compassionatemind.co.uk

For information on compassion-based meditation practices from Sharon Salzberg visit https://www.sharonsalzberg.com

From information the work of Kristen Neff, including audio and video recordings visit https://self-compassion.org

References

Bach, J. M., & Guse, T. (2015). The effect of contemplation and meditation on "great compassion" on the psychological well-being of adolescents. *The Journal of Positive Psychology, 10*(4), 359-369.

Booker, C., Mazzarelli, A., & Trzeciak, S. (2019). *Compassionomics: The revolutionary scientific evidence that caring makes a difference.* Fire Starter Publishing. https://books.google.co.uk/books?id=uQrdvAEACAAJ

Byrne, R. W. (2016). *Evolving insight.* Oxford University Press. https://books.google.co.uk/books?id=1Ds6CwAAQBAJ

Carmichael, N. (2017). *Recruitment and retention of teachers*. House of Commons, 32. https://publications. parliament.uk/pa/cm201617/cmselect/cmeduc/199/199.pdf%0Ahttp://search.ebscohost.com/login. aspx?direct=true&db=aph&AN=103682153&site=ehost-live&scope=site

Carter, C. S., Bartal, I. B.-A., & Porges, E. C. (2017). The roots of compassion: An evolutionary and neuro-biological perspective. In E. M. Seppala, E. Simon-Thomas, S. L. Brown, M. C. Worline, C. D. Cameron, & J. R. Doty (Eds.), *The Oxford handbook of compassion science* (pp. 173–184). United States: Oxford University Press.

Cassidy, J., & Shaver, P. R. (2018). *Handbook of attachment, third edition: Theory, research, and clinical applications*. Guilford Publications. https://books.google.co.uk/books?id=WhIKDwAAQBAJ

Coles, M. I. (Ed.). (2015). *Towards the compassionate school: From golden rule to golden thread*. Stoke on Trent: Trentham Books.

Coles, M. I., & Gent, B. (2021). *Education for survival: The pedagogy of compassion*. Institute of Education Press (IOE Press). https://books.google.co.uk/books?id=1ZSQzQEACAAJ

Di Bello, M., Carnevali, L., Petrocchi, N., Thayer, J. F., Gilbert, P., & Ottaviani, C. (2020). The compassionate vagus: A meta-analysis on the connection between compassion and heart rate variability. *Neuroscience & Biobehavioral Reviews, 116*, 21–30. https://doi.org/10.1016/j.neubiorev.2020.06.016

Education Support Partnership. (2018). *Teacher wellbeing index 2018*. https://www.educationsupport. org.uk/resources/research-reports/teacher-wellbeing-index-2018.

Gilbert, P. (2009). *The compassionate mind*. Little, Brown Book Group.

Gilbert, P. (2014). The origins and nature of compassion focused therapy. *British Journal of Clinical Psychology, 53*(1), 6–41. https://doi.org/10.1111/bjc.12043

Gilbert, P. (Ed.). (2017). *Compassion*. Routledge. https://doi.org/10.4324/9781315564296

Gilbert, P. (2018). *Living like crazy*. Annwyn House. http://hdl.handle.net/10545/622177

Gilbert, P. (2019). Explorations into the nature and function of compassion. *Current Opinion in Psychology, 28*, 108–114. https://doi.org/10.1016/j.copsyc.2018.12.002

Gilbert, P. (2020). Compassion: From its evolution to a psychotherapy. *Frontiers in Psychology, 11*(December). https://doi.org/10.3389/fpsyg.2020.586161

Goetz, J. L., Keltner, D., & Simon-Thomas, E. (2010). Compassion: An evolutionary analysis and empirical review. *Psychological Bulletin, 136*(3), 351–374. https://doi.org/10.1037/a0018807

Goleman, D., & Davidson, R. J. (2017). *Altered traits*. United States: Avery Publishing.

Gray, C., Wilcox, G., & Nordstokke, D. (2017). Teacher mental health, school climate, inclusive education and student learning: A review. *Canadian Psychology/Psychologie Canadienne, 58*(3), 203–210.

Harvey, C., Maratos, F. A., Montague, J., Gale, M., Clarke, K., & Gilbert, T. (2020). Embedding compassionate micro skills of communication in higher education: Implementation with psychology undergraduates. *Psychology of Education Review, 44*(2), 68–72.

Hughes, K., Bellis, M. A., Hardcastle, K. A., Sethi, D., Butchart, A., Mikton, C., … Dunne, M. P. (2017). The effect of multiple adverse childhood experiences on health: A systematic review and meta-analysis. *The Lancet Public Health, 2*(8), e356–e366. https://doi.org/10.1016/S2468-2667(17)30118-4

Karr, J., Roberson, C., & Tiura, M. (2019). Kind warriors: A qualitative study of a compassion-based intervention for children. *Counselling and Psychotherapy Research, 20*(1), 39–45. https://doi.org/10.1002/capr.12266

Kim, J. J., Cunnington, R., & Kirby, J. N. (2020). The neurophysiological basis of compassion: An fMRI meta-analysis of compassion and its related neural processes. *Neuroscience & Biobehavioral Reviews, 108*, 112–123. https://doi.org/10.1016/j.neubiorev.2019.10.023

Kirby, J. N., Tellegen, C. L., & Steindl, S. R. (2017). A meta-analysis of compassion-based interventions: Current state of knowledge and future directions. *Behavior Therapy, 48*(6), 778–792. https://doi.org/10.1016/j.beth.2017.06.003

Kohler-Evans, P., & Barnes, C. D. (2015). Compassion: How do you teach it? *Journal of Education and Practice, 6*(11), 33–36 (5 Seiten). https://eric.ed.gov/?id=EJ1081717

Lavelle, B. D. (2017). Compassion in context: Tracing the buddhist roots of secular, compassion-based contemplative programs. In E. M. Seppala, E. Simon-Thomas, S. L. Brown, M. C. Worline, C. D. Cameron, & J. R. Doty (Eds.), *Oxford handbook of compassion science* (p. 701). Oxford University Press.

Lavelle, B. D., Flook, L., & Ghahremani, D. G. (2017). A call for compassion and care in education: toward a more comprehensive prosocial framework for the field. In E. M. Seppala, E. Simon-Thomas, S. L. Brown, M. C. Worline, C. D. Cameron, & J. R. Doty (Eds.), *The Oxford handbook of positive psychology* (2nd ed.). *Compassion Science* (p. 701). Oxford: Oxford University Press.

Luyten, P., Campbell, C., Allison, E., & Fonagy, P. (2020). The mentalizing approach to psychopathology: State of the art and future directions. *Annual Review of Clinical Psychology, 16*. https://doi.org/10.1146/annurev-clinpsy-071919-015355

Manuello, J., Vercelli, U., Nani, A., Costa, T., & Cauda, F. (2016). Mindfulness meditation and consciousness: An integrative neuroscientific perspective. *Consciousness and Cognition, 40*, 67–78. https://doi.org/10.1016/j.concog.2015.12.005

Maratos, F. A, & Pessoa, L. (2019). What drives prioritized visual processing? A motivational relevance account. *Progress in Brain Progress, 247*, 111–148. https://doi.org/10.1016/bs.pbr.2019.03.028

Maratos, F.A., Sheffield, D. (2020). Brief Compassion-Focused Imagery Dampens Physiological Pain Responses. *Mindfulness, 11*, 2730–2740. https://doi.org/10.1007/s12671-020-01485-5

Maratos, F. A, Gilbert, P., & Gilbert, T. (2019a). Improving well-being in higher education: Adopting a compassionate approach. In P. Gibbs, J. Jameson, & A. Elwick (Eds.), *Values of the university in a time of uncertainty* (pp. 261–278). Cham: Springer International Publishing. https://doi.org/10.1007/978-3-030-15970-2_18

Maratos, F. A., Montague, J., Ashra, H., Welford, M., Wood, W., Barnes, C., ... Gilbert, P. (2019b). Evaluation of a compassionate mind training intervention with school teachers and support staff. *Mindfulness, 10*(11), 2245–2258. https://doi.org/10.1007/s12671-019-01185-9

Maratos, F. A., Matos, M., Albuquerque, I., Wood, W., Palmeira, L., Cunha, M., Lima, M., & Gilbert, P. (2020). Exploring the international utility of progressing compassionate mind training in school settings: A comparison of implementation effectiveness of the same curricula in the UK and Portugal. *Psychology of Education Review, 44*(2), 73–82.

Maratos, F. A., Sheffield, D., Wood., W., McEwan., K., Matos, M., & Gilbert, P. (submitted) The physiological effects of a compassionate mind training course with school teachers and support staff.

Maratos, F. A., Wood, W., Cahill., R., Hernandez, Y., & Gilbert, P. (submitted). Investing in pupil wellbeing: A randomised control study of a compassion-based PSHE pupil curriculum.

Marsh, A. A. (2019). The caring continuum: Evolved hormonal and proximal mechanisms explain prosocial and antisocial extremes. *Annual Review of Psychology, 70*(1), 347–371. https://doi.org/10.1146/annurev-psych-010418-103010

Mascaro, J. S., Florian, M. P., Ash, M. J., Palmer, P. K., Frazier, T., Condon, P., & Raison, C. (2020). Ways of knowing compassion: How do we come to know, understand, and measure compassion when we see it? *Frontiers in Psychology, 11*. https://doi.org/10.3389/fpsyg.2020.547241

Matos, M., Albuquerque, I., Galhardo, A., Cunha, M., Lima, M., Palmeira, L., Petrocchi, N.

Mayseless, O. (2016). *The caring motivation*. Oxford University Press. https://doi.org/10.1093/acprof:oso/9780199913619.001.0001

McAdam, E., & Lang, P. (2009). *Appreciative work in schools: Generating future communities*. Kingsham Press. https://books.google.co.uk/books?id=LZUIcgAACAAJ

Neff, K. (2003). Self-compassion: An alternative conceptualization of a healthyattitudetoward oneself. *Self and Identity, 2*(August 2002), 85–101. https://doi.org/10.1080/15298860390129863

NHS Digital. (2018). *Mental health of children and young people in England, 2017* (Vol. 0819). https://digital.nhs.uk/data-and-information/publications/statistical/mental-health-of-children-and-young-people-in-england/2017/2017#key-facts

NHS Digital. (2020). *Mental health of children and young people in England, 2020: Wave 1 follow up to the 2017 survey*. https://digital.nhs.uk/data-and-information/publications/statistical/mental-health-of-children-and-young-people-in-england/2020-wave-1-follow-up

Ofsted. (2019). Teacher well-being at work in schools and further education providers. *Ofsted*, 4–45. https://assets.publishing.service.gov.uk/government/uploads/system/uploads/attachment_data/file/819314/Teacher_well-being_report_110719F.pdf

Peterson, A. (2017). *Compassion and the Self*. In *Compassion and education: Cultivating compassionate children, schools and communities* (pp. 91–109). London: Palgrave Macmillan UK. https://doi.org/10.1057/978-1-137-54838-2_5

Porges, S. W. (2017). Vagal pathways: Portals to compassion. In E. M. Seppälä, E. Simon-Thomas, S. L. Brown, M. C. Worline, C. D. Cameron, & J. R. Doty (Eds.), *Oxford library of psychology. The Oxford handbook of compassion science* (pp. 189–202). Oxford University Press.

Preston, S. D. (2013). The origins of altruism in offspring care. *Psychological Bulletin, 139*(6), 1305–1341. https://doi.org/10.1037/a0031755

Ricard, M. (2015). *Altruism: The power of compassion to change yourself and the world*. Atlantic Books. https://books.google.co.uk/books?id=qH28BwAAQBAJ

Roeser, R. W., Colaianne, B. A., & Greenberg, M. A. (2018). Compassion and human development: Current approaches and future directions. *Research in Human Development, 15*(3-4), 238-251. https://doi.org/10.1080/15427609.2018.1495002

Seppala, E., Simon-Thomas, E., Brown, S. L., Worline, M. C., Cameron, C. D., & Doty, J. R. (2017). In E. Seppala, E. Simon-Thomas, S. L. Brown, M. C. Worline, C. D. Cameron, & J. R. Doty (Eds.), *Oxford handbook of compassion science* (1st ed.). New York: Oxford University Press.

Siegel, D. (2018). Aware: *The science and practice of presence–The groundbreaking meditation practice.* Penguin Publishing Group. https://books.google.co.uk/books?id=X1NADwAAQBAJ

Singer, T., & Engert, V. (2019). It matters what you practice: Differential training effects on subjective experience, behavior, brain and body in the ReSource Project. *Current Opinion in Psychology, 28*, 151-158. https://doi.org/10.1016/j.copsyc.2018.12.005

Strauss, C., Lever Taylor, B., Gu, J., Kuyken, W., Baer, R., Jones, F., & Cavanagh, K. (2016). What is compassion and how can we measure it? A review of definitions and measures. *Clinical Psychology Review, 47*, 15-27. https://doi.org/10.1016/j.cpr.2016.05.004

Vrtička, P., Favre, P., & Singer, T. (2017). *Compassion.* In P. Gilbert (Ed.), *Compassion: Concepts, research and applications.* Oxon: Routledge. https://doi.org/10.4324/9781315564296

Welford, M., & Langmead, K. (2015). Compassion-based initiatives in educational settings. *Educational and Child Psychology, 32*(1), 71-80. https://www.researchgate.net/publication/320584562

Yeager, D. S., Dahl, R. E., & Dweck, C. S. (2018). Why interventions to influence adolescent behavior often fail but could succeed. *Perspectives on Psychological Science, 13*(1), 101-122. https://doi.org/10.1177/1745691617722620

10 Meditation-based tools for balance, focus, and health

Padraic J. Dunne

Many of the problems we face as human beings have their origin in thought and how we perceive the world around us. Meditation practice can be part of the solution here, not just for mitigating symptoms but also for promoting flourishing and well-being. This chapter presents the evidence-based meditation practice of Attention-Based Training (ABT) to help educators and students cultivate health within and outside of the classroom.

Introduction

If you want to be a better educator or student - meditate. If you want to be a better parent - meditate. If you want to be a better colleague or friend - meditate. The basic practice is simple, does not require hours of daily practice but it does require commitment and a touch of discipline. The benefits and positive impacts can be far reaching and last a lifetime. Meditation, when practiced by educators and students alike can enhance the teaching alliance and enrich life within and beyond the classroom (Ackerman, 2021; Li, 2021; Waters, Barsky, Ridd, & Allen, 2015). The variety and number of meditation exercises seem to be growing daily, making it difficult for educators and students to choose the most impactful routine (Matko & Sedlmeier, 2019). I recommend a bespoke approach that matches the needs, skills and interest of both parties. Sometimes, specific events call for specific meditation practices, for example when cultivating compassion for an ill classmate or managing exam-related anxiety. More often, students require a consistent daily practice to help develop and cultivate focus and attention. The educator can subsequently encourage regular practice in the classroom that can help students (and educators) to develop a home routine. Educators and students should collaborate to develop a manual and plan of action for the academic year. In this chapter, I will endeavour to highlight the principal types of meditation practices and how they can be deployed for specific issues as well as to help cultivate the health and well-being (psychological and physical) of all concerned. I will end by describing a case study conducted between our Centre and students in an Irish secondary school.

DOI: 10.4324/9781003228158-13

Theoretical background

Meditation – the myths

It is important to dispel some myths surrounding meditation practice. First, meditation is not about stopping thinking. No matter how tranquil you feel in the body and how calm your mind is at any given time, there will always be thoughts, sensations, emotions and memories emerging from your mind, brain and body (Delorme & Brandmeyer, 2019). This is especially the case at the start of meditation practice and for those new to sitting still, without doing. It is the nature of the mind to be constantly active. The goal is not to stop thinking or sensing; usually, the goal is to disengage, move around, beyond and above thoughts, sensations, emotions and memories (Delorme & Brandmeyer, 2019). In fact, we sometimes acquire greater benefits from turbulent practice; you will not build muscle in the gym by lifting feathers. In other types of practices, we might have a specific goal; for example, cultivating compassion using specific imagery (Ribeiro, 2021).

Secondly, you do not need to practice for hours each day to receive any benefit from meditation practice. Our research (Dunne et al., 2019) shows that positive effects emerge after only 5 minutes of practice, twice daily for four weeks. Finally, although meditation practice is a core aspect of Buddhism and many religions around the world, including early Christianity (Chow, 2021), you do not have to be religious to gain the benefits. The atheist's brain can gain the same rewards from regular practice as the devout religious one. These core practices are thousands of years old with clear guidelines and benefits that science is now beginning to confirm.

Modern stress and the thinking process

You are not your thoughts (Aurelius, 2002). This is a very important statement; one that many of us forget from time to time. This concept is especially important during times of accumulating stress and anxiety, which can often have negative effects on mental and physical health. Your brain will respond in the same manner to a paper tiger or a real one, if you tell it that both represent a significant threat (Sapolsky, 2004). In the face of either threat, your perception and thinking processes will combine to activate the brain and nervous system, resulting in a cascade of stress hormones, including adrenaline (Sapolsky, 2004). The consequences are, accelerated heart rate and increased blood pressure, increased oxygen intake, decreased digestion, enhanced energy consumption, sweating, dilated pupils and tunnel vision. Additionally, activity in the logical/cognitive part of the brain decreases, as the brain's emotional and reactive centre takes control. This is all very fine and necessary, if you need to run from the real tiger. However, it is not very helpful if you are sitting in a busy classroom, feeling frustrated with your students, educator or classmates. Furthermore, while these necessary stress responses help us in the heat of battle, they can have serious negative impacts on our body, if activated over long periods. The outcome can be burnout and chronic anxiety, associated with heart, gut, loss of immune system function, as well as fatigue-related issues.

If the thinking process is the problem (in many instances), it is also the source of the solution. Remember, you are not your thoughts; you have a choice whether to attribute meaning to these collection of words that emerge in your mindscape. You can choose whether to engage these thoughts or not. More often than not, when we engage these first (often-negative) thoughts, they initiate a domino effect that can lead to narratives of thinking, which can be catastrophic in nature, as they project into the future. As I mentioned at the beginning, you cannot stop your thinking process. However, you can disengage from these initial thoughts, thereby stopping this cascade of negative and threatening thinking processes. We can use meditation to help us practice this disengagement on a moment-by-moment basis. Eventually and over time, we learn how much choice we actually have in relation to engaging thoughts, memories, sensations and emotions. We cannot stop thoughts, memories, sensations and emotions but we can choose how we react (or not) to them. Meditation limits these engagements, stops the development of catastrophic narratives and reduces the perceived threat. This can only be a good thing and is, in essence, the first and central aim of meditation practice.

Meditation – the proven benefits

We have experienced a tsunami of information on the proposed benefits of meditation over the past two decades, with words like mindfulness entering the common lexicon. The US National Library of Medicine (PubMed) database shows that 5,979 scientific and medical research articles and reviews were published between 2000 and 2020, with the word meditation in the title or abstract. Admittedly, not all of these peer-reviewed, published manuscripts are of stellar quality. However, the point remains that research is booming in this field, with interested parties from a wide range of multi-disciplinary fields, including neuroscience, medicine, psychology, behavioural science and sociology, among many others.

Meditation practice consistently seems to have a positive impact on mental health (Keng, Smoski, & Robins, 2011), especially anxiety, stress and burnout (Dunne et al., 2019) as well as on sleep (Black, O'Reilly, Olmstead, Breen, & Irwin, 2015; Shallcross, Visvanathan, Sperber, & Duberstein, 2019), the immune (Black & Slavich, 2016), and cardiovascular systems (Levine et al., 2017), as well as on brain structure and function (Ricard, Lutz, & Davidson, 2014). In short, meditation can retrofit the brain, allowing for greater focus, attention (Dunne et al., 2019) and cognitive control as well as emotional regulation (Tang, Hölzel, & Posner, 2015). For more information, I would recommend a 2018 special edition of *Scientific American Mind* (Gawrylewski, 2018).

Are all meditations the same?

The short answer is no. Broadly speaking, basic meditation falls into three types of practices, with three central aims:

1   Metacognition (thinking about thinking), associated with the development of self- and other-awareness; mindfulness (Kabat-Zinn, 1990) falls into this category;
2   Concentration-based meditation, which employs an anchor such as the breath or a chosen phrase (mantra) to develop a focus and attention that ultimately serves to transcend

Table 1 The Three Categories of Meditation Practice as Defined by Singer and Engert (2019)

Issue	*Meditation practice type*
Anxiety, physical discomfort, and pain	Mindfulness
Loss of focus and inability to pay attention	Attention-based training (ABT)
Poor empathic skills, problems with perspective	Loving-kindness meditation

      turbulent thought and emotion – examples include Attention-based Training (ABT) (Dunne et al., 2019), mantra and Zazen (Japanese) sitting meditation (Suzuki & Dixon, 2020);

3   Meditation focused on cultivating compassion and gratitude (Lama, 2012) for self and others – e.g. loving-kindness meditation.

German researchers based at the Max Plank Neuroscience Lab in Berlin, have conducted a large study (ReSource Project) on these three different types of meditations and their impact on the mind and body (Singer & Engert, 2019). Study participants experienced three different types of meditative practices over nine months that affected the brain, body and behaviour in different ways. Their conclusion? If you want to use meditation practice as a tool to help with specific issues, then you have to use the right instrument (or meditation practice) for the right job (Table 1).

Meditation, mindfulness and positive psychology

Positive Psychology is the study of human strengths and virtues leading to the development of activities and ways of being that promote human flourishing (Seligman, 2013). To date, much of meditation (including mindfulness)-based research has focused on a deficit-based approach to research and interventions, with a specific attention on alleviating human dis-ease in clinical settings. Although often successful in this regard (by mitigating disease symptoms), Ivtzan and Lomas have argued that mindfulness-based research (in particular) since the late 1970s, has failed to realise the full potential of this meditation practice (Ivtzan & Lomas, 2016). The same authors propose that Mindfulness-based programmes such as Mindfulness-based Stress Reduction (Kabat-Zinn et al., 1998) and Mindfulness-based Cognitive Therapy (Barnhofer et al., 2009) do not have a specific focus on promoting human flourishing through the cultivation of positive emotions, relationships, meaning, purpose, gratitude, signature strengths, optimism and a sense of accomplishment.

    As a result, three principle positive psychology-based mindfulness practices have emerged that have been designed to cultivate human flourishing, as measured by well-being outcomes such as gratitude, self-compassion, self-efficacy, meaning and autonomy. These practices and programmes include the Positive Mindfulness Programme (PMP) developed by Ivtzan et al. (2016), Mindful Self-Compassion (MSC) by Germer and Neff (2013) and the Mindfulness-based Strengths Practice (MBSP) developed by Niemiec and Lissing (2016). Although more research is needed, these new Positive Psychology-led approaches to meditation show promise in their capacity to promote flourishing and well-being, not just symptom mitigation.

Based on our experience and research, we recommend a blended approach to meditation practice in the classroom and at home, that tackles the common problems of reduced focus, increased fatigue, and anxiety but also cultivate compassion, acceptance and positive self-regard. This programme includes basic ABT practice, grounded in simple breathing exercises, coupled with the Body Scan meditation.

Practice

Attention-based training (ABT)

ABT is based on mantra meditation practice (Freeman, 2014; Main, 2006), whereby, we choose an anchor such as a chosen phrase or the breath, to help ground us in the present moment. We return to this anchor on a moment-by-moment basis, each time we become distracted by thoughts, memories, sensations, images or emotions. At the RCSI Centre for Positive Psychology and Health, we offer a free 8-week ABT programme (Dunne, 2021a), however, the basic practice is enough to begin with.

Many traditions use specific chosen phrases or mantras for cultural and religious reasons (Main, 2006). However, in ABT, any phrase can be used to start. For example, I sometimes use the phrase, *I am here now*. The phrase can be said (internally or aloud) all at once when inhaling and then again upon exhalation. Alternatively, the phrase can be split in two: *I am* during inhalation; *here now* upon exhalation. It might take some practice to find which version suits each person best.

An alternative anchor to the chosen phrase is the use the breath itself. Personally, this is my favourite; however, it is up to you as educator and your class of students as to what suits you best. You can spend some time practicing each one but once you chose, stick with that; do not flip-flop between the two. Flip-flopping will interfere with the generation of a sustainable practice.

When using the breath as an anchor, try to keep it low, slow and deep to begin with. The perfect cycle of breathing is usually 6 per minute – 5 seconds in and 5 seconds out (McKeown, 2021). Try to keep the transition between inhalation and exhalation as smooth as possible. Each time you become distracted by thoughts, memories, sensations and emotions, simply return to your breath.

During practice, it is normal to drift off into a daydream, only realising the fact, after 20 seconds or more. This is perfectly normal. Each time you return to your anchor, you strengthen the capacity of your mind and brain to stay focused and present. Remember, you cannot stop thinking, feeling or having an itchy foot. Be kind to yourself. Each time you become distracted, return to your anchor. Examples of how to use each anchor can be found on our website (Dunne, 2021b).

The basic ABT practice (Figure 5):

- Practice for 2 minutes during class and at home for at least 66 days:
- Sit in a gentle upright position; feet on the floor, hands on your lap
- Set a timer for 2 minutes

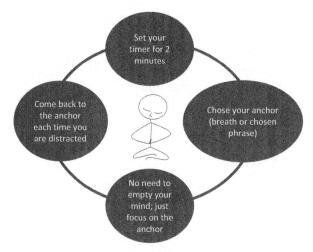

Attention-based Training (ABT)

- Disengage from thought, emotions,
sensations & memories by simply returning
to your anchor, on a moment by moment
basis

Figure 5 The Basics of ABT Practice.

- Close your eyes if possible; if you don't want to close your eyes, you can pick a focal point in front of you, such as a picture on the wall
- Choose your anchor
- Remember to breathe normally throughout
- Each time you become distracted by memory, thoughts, sensations and emotions, disengage and return to your anchor
- When your timer goes off, open your eyes and enjoy the feeling of being present.

Meditation practice is not easy. Therefore, we recommend starting slow and building from there. Begin with 2 minutes, twice daily (classroom and at home) for the first two weeks of practice. Go at your own pace; be gentle with yourself as educator and with your students. If you can and if everyone agrees, add 1 minute each week until you reach 10 minutes of practice at least once daily.

The body scan

Sometimes we are too agitated, restless, angry or upset to engage the basic ABT practice. In such instances, we can use the body scan meditation, (a form of mindfulness) to help calm the body prior to the main practice. There are many guided body scan practices online that can be accessed freely (FMP, 2021). A 10-minute version can be found on our website (Dunne, 2021).
  You can also guide your own body scan by using the following steps:

- The body scan can be conducted lying down or upright in the usual position. However, it is probably best to avoid the horizontal position, if you are tired.

- Close your eyes, take a low, slow and deep breath and bring your conscious awareness down into the toes of your left foot.
- Can you sense your individual toes? Don't worry if you cannot.
- Move slowly up through your foot, sole, heel, ankle, lower leg and calf, before stopping for a moment at the left knee.
- From your knee, move into your left thigh muscle and consciously relax it.
- Be on the lookout for tense or sore joints, tendons, ligaments and muscles.
- Bring your attention to your left hip, move slowly across your pelvis and down into the topes of your right foot.
- Can you sense your big toe?
- Move as before, slowly up your right leg until you reach your right hip.
- Get a sense of the weight of your body as you sit.
- Next, move your attention to the base of your back.
- Move slowly up either side of your spine, gently relaxing the muscle as you move.
- Pause for a moment as you reach between your shoulder blades.
- Move next into the muscles of your left shoulder.
- Relax this muscle.
- Bring your attention down to the fingers of your left hand.
- Move gently up through your whole hand, wrist, upper arm, elbow and relax the muscle of your upper arm.
- From your left shoulder, move across to your right one and relax as before.
- Bring your attention down to the tips of your right hand and move back up slowly through your right arm until you reach your shoulder again.
- Bring your conscious awareness to the back of your neck.
- Feel the weight of your head as it rests on your neck.
- Next, move around to your throat and your jaw.
- Relax your jaw muscles and your tongue.
- Move slowly up either side of your face, your cheekbones and temples.
- Smooth out your forehead and relax the muscles around your eyes.
- Move around to the back of your head and slowly toward your scalp at the top.
- Breathe into your whole head.
- Take a final low, slow and deep breath.
- Open your eyes or begin a 2-minute ABT practice.

The body scan can be used to help with tension headaches, stomach aches, insomnia as well as general aches and pains. It can also be applied to resisting urges and cravings (to over eat for example).

Combining the basic ABT practice with the body scan

You can alternate between either practice in the classroom, combine them both on a daily basis, or use the body scan when agitated or restless, and prior to the main ABT practice.

Making your meditation practice stick

It is very important to apply some basic principles of behaviour change science, in order to help students and educators develop sustainable meditation practices. We are all time-poor, with busy lives. Therefore, we should not leave the development of a new practice to chance. Research from University College London shows that it takes on average, 66 days to form a new habit (Lally, van Jaarsveld, Potts, & Wardle, 2010). Have this number in mind when you discuss this new practice with students. Encourage each student to make a plan to maintain his or her new meditation practice. This requires a plan for the school week (in school and at home), as well as a practice plan for the weekend. Each student (including the educator) should put pen to paper, in order to make their own personal practice plans.

Purpose and motivation

The practice needs to have a purpose or meaning that fuels the motivation to sustain itself; we need strong reasons to help us stay the course. The reasons why we want to practice can emerge from an initial classroom survey, e.g. students want to alleviate anxiety and improve focus; become better on the sport field; regulate emotions. It can also be important to show your students that many of their role models practice meditation, as do global leaders and successful entrepreneurs. Conduct a simple Google search for individuals in the public eye, who practice meditation in your country or region, whom the students admire. For example, young men often believe that meditation is a soft practice with no relevance to them. However, professional athletes, soccer and rugby players practice meditation for focus and health, as do professional military units (Dube, 2019).

Track change

It helps if we can monitor and track improvement. Encourage students to make private daily scores related to anxiety and focus during the school week (if anxiety and focus represent challenges that they wish to tackle). A subjective scoring system between 1 and 10 can be set up in a notebook, with 1 implying poor focus and 10 indicating perfect attention. The educator can also survey the class for how they feel as a group, on a daily basis.

Make time for practice and keep it consistent

A policy of same time and position helps sustain new habits. If the class time remains the same each week, develop a routine, where educator and students adopt the same posture at the same time and in the same way, each session. If this is a school-led process, then it will help to have a daily practice routine. Do the same for home practice. Remember to write everything down in a practice notebook.

Make it easy

Try not to schedule practice during busy and noisy times. If practicing at home, be mindful of where you practice; quiet rooms, free of distraction are best.

Reward the brain for a job well done

This is especially important for home practice. Develop short, medium and long-term rewards. Write them down in your practice notebook. For example, a short-term reward might be a favourite TV show in the evening once you finish practicing. Long-term rewards could mean a free class in school to watch a movie.

"Try this" for educators

Practice what you preach

Spend some time developing your own practice, prior to beginning any programme with students. Experiment with timing, develop a detailed practice plan and remember to document any change that might occur (physically, socially and emotionally).

Be compassionate

We all fail. Meditation is hard. Life is busy. It can be easy to develop unrealistic expectations about your practice. If you forget or simply do not feel like practicing for a few days, that is OK. Vow to start again the following day. Remember that there is no such thing as a good or bad meditation practice. In fact, turbulent practice sessions can be more valuable than tranquil ones. Accept everything that happens in the present moment, without judgement. Apply this same compassion to students and ensure that they adopt the same approach to their own practice.

The core ABT practice is not easy for everyone

Finally, remember that you and your students will be at different stages in relation to the personal capacity to meditate. Meditation might be harder for some than for others. This is OK. At the time of writing, there are no guidelines about how long students should meditate for. Since meditation can be difficult for many people (adults and students alike), I recommend starting with just 60 seconds and building from there. Some students might experience dark images and memories from the past, during practice. Advise these students to stick with the body scan, for the time being.

Some caveats

Is meditation suitable for students diagnosed with Attention Deficit Hyperactivity Disorder (ADHD)? In short, the jury is still out. There is some evidence to suggest that mindfulness practice can be beneficial for ADHD (Sweet, 2021; van der Oord, 2012). Likewise, students who have experienced recent trauma of any kind, including bereavement are not advised to engage in meditation practice; enhancing internal awareness might lead to re-traumatisation. Finally, some students simply might not like meditation practice and therefore should be allowed to sit out these sessions as they occur in the classroom. Educators should exercise their own judgement on a case-by-case basis; this will also depend on available resources.

"Try this" for students

Survey the classroom to identify which practice suits best

I believe that like all good researchers, educators should conduct a short survey of their students in order to address the specific needs and abilities of the class. It is also important for students to feel that they have co-ownership of the process.

For example, an open discussion regarding the common issues faced by students can help foster a collaborative approach to developing a class manual for meditation practice. Many secondary school students have issues staying focused in class or when studying class material. In such cases, it can be very helpful to start a programme of concentration-based meditation practices such as ABT (sitting, focused meditation).

Anxiety is also a common issue experienced by students, the sources of which can be many and varied: social pressures, home-life issues, competition, performance pressures (sports, examinations, etc.). Although anxiety begins in the mind, it can have deleterious knock-on effects, leading to recurrent infections, muscle aches and pains, gastrointestinal issues, and persistent headaches, among others. The body scan can enhance awareness of these physical issues, encourage us to accept discomfort in the present moment, which can ultimately lead to a reduction in symptom severity.

Demonstrate to each other that these practices are for everyday issues in the real world

Have regular conversations with students about applying their practice in the real world. Have a weekly check-in and try to have as many different situations as possible. For example, cultivating tolerance with a younger sibling, managing exam stress in the moment, managing anxiety in a social environment, enhancing sport performance and cultivating creative pursuits.

Case study

The RCSI winter school

Background

Part of the newly established (November 2019) RCSI Centre for Positive Psychology and Health's remit is to develop and promote freely accessible educational material for the public, related to flourishing and well-being.

The RCSI University of Medicine and Health Sciences, Centre for Positive Psychology and Health developed and delivered a ten-week online programme (October to December 2020) to 22 transition year students (co-education) based at Athy College, a secondary school based in Athy, Co. Kildare, Ireland (population = 8,218 in 2020). Transition Year (TY) is an optional one-year school programme taken in the year after the Junior Certificate (year 3 of high school) in Ireland. TY provides students with access to programmes designed to cultivate life skills that incorporate work experience. The Centre received police clearance from Irish Police (Garda) and ethical approval from the RCSI Research Ethics Committee to conduct this project.

Course content

The RCSI Winter School contained information on positive psychology and ABT practice. Positive psychology elements included:

- Positive psychology basics (happiness and well-being, optimism and gratitude)
- Growth mindsets
- Signature strengths

A full attention-based training programme was developed specifically for this age group (15-16 years old), which contains the following subjects:

- Introduction meditation practices and the basic practice (ABT 2 minute and the body scan)
- How to make sustainable habits
- Urge surfing and managing cravings
- Cultivating acceptance
- Cultivating compassion
- Managing self-judgement
- Total health – the importance of mind and body practices
- Biofeedback technologies to support meditation practice

Each online session took the format of two classes – 2 × 40-minute classes with a 5-minute break in between. The first class of each week began with a 40-minute discussion on meditation practice (technique and application), followed by a second 40 minutes on positive psychology-related topics. Students practiced the body scan meditation daily at home and in the class for 10 minutes each time, in conjunction with their TY head. The basic ABT practice was left to the student's discretion at home.

The Assistant Principle Guidance Counsellor for the school facilitated the weekly online sessions that were co-delivered between three members of RCSI Centre for Positive Psychology and Health staff. Students were subsequently given weekly home-work practice and discussed the sessions during the week with their TY head educator.

Quantitative assessment

Students completed the EPOCH (measuring engagement, perseverance, optimism, connectedness and happiness) positive psychology scale for adolescents (Kern, Benson, Steinberg, & Steinberg, 2021) and the Perceived Stress Scale(Cohen, 2021) before and after the programme (weeks 1 and 11). There was a non-statistically significant trend towards an improvement in perceived stress (n = 22; time point 1 score = 20.2; time point 2 score = 16.8; paired student t-test p = 0.07) but no change in the EPOCH measurements.

Qualitative assessment

Educators and the school principal were very pleased with the programme as were the students. Student interviews were conducted at the end of the academic year by the

Assistant Principle Guidance Counsellor, with a representative cohort of TY students. During these interviews, students revealed that they used the meditation techniques learned in the programme to help with emotional regulation and manage exam-related stress. Growth mindsets in relation to failure as well as an understanding of the nature of thoughts were also very helpful for overall well-being during the academic year.

Summary conclusion

The RCSI Winter School will begin again in October 2021 with an improved curriculum based on feedback from students and educators. Students requested specific advice and practices to help manage exam stress, further develop focus and assist with fatigue.

Discussion points

Does modern society lead to the development of human beings who are more comfortable with doing than being? What are the advantages to being still? What is the difference between being still and being bored? Is there a difference?

If you are not your thoughts, then what is the nature of thinking? Are there two versions of you? One that thinks and one that watches you thinking?

Suggested resources

Documentary series

- Headspace guide to meditation. Netflix 9 December 2020 (https://www.netflix.com/title/81280926)

Books

- Kabat-Zinn, J. (2013). *Full catastrophe living: Using the wisdom of your body and mind to face stress, pain, and illness*. New York, NY: Bantam Books.
- Williams, M., & Penman, D. (2011). *Mindfulness: An eight-week plan for finding peace in a frantic world*. Emmaus, PA: Rodale Books.
- Hanson, R., & Mendius, R. (2009). *Buddha's brain: The practical neuroscience of happiness, love & wisdom*. Oakland, CA: New Harbinger Publications.

Website

- RCSI Centre for Positive Psychology and Health – free resources. www.rcsi.com/dublin/about/faculty-of-medicine-and-health-sciences/centre-for-positive-psychology-and-health/public-engagement

References

Ackerman, C. E. (2021). Mindfulness in education: 31+ ways of teaching mindfulness in schools. Retrieved from https://positivepsychology.com/mindfulness-education/

Aurelius, M. (2002). *The meditations*. New York: Random House.

Barnhofer, T., Crane, C., Hargus, E., Amarasinghe, M., Winder, R., & Williams, J. M. (2009). Mindfulness-based cognitive therapy as a treatment for chronic depression: A preliminary study. *Behaviour Research and Therapy, 47*(5), 366-373. doi:S0005-7967(09)00033-3 [pii]10.1016/j.brat.2009.01.019

Black, D. S., O'Reilly, G. A., Olmstead, R., Breen, E. C., & Irwin, M. R. (2015). Mindfulness meditation and improvement in sleep quality and daytime impairment among older adults with sleep disturbances: A randomized clinical trial. *JAMA Internal Medicine, 175*(4), 494–501. doi:10.1001/jamainternmed.2014.8081

Black, D. S., & Slavich, G. M. (2016). Mindfulness meditation and the immune system: A systematic review of randomized controlled trials. *Annals of the New York Academy of Sciences, 1373*(1), 13–24. doi:10.1111/nyas.12998

Chow, S. (2021). Meditation spirituality and religion. Retrieved from https://www.news-medical.net/health/Meditation-Spirituality-and-Religion.aspx

Cohen, S. (2021, 10th August 2021). Perceived stress scale. Retrieved from https://www.mindgarden.com/documents/PerceivedStressScale.pdf

Delorme, A., & Brandmeyer, T. (2019). When the meditating mind wanders. *Current Opinion in Psychology, 28*, 133–137. doi:10.1016/j.copsyc.2018.12.006

Dube, R. (2019). How this Elite Navy seal found strength and success through mindfulness. *FORBES.* Retrieved from https://www.forbes.com/sites/robdube/2019/06/24/how-this-elite-navy-seal-found-strength-and-success-through-mindfulness/?sh=7150807013bf

Dunne, P. J. (2021a). 8-Week attention-based training prgramme. Retrieved from http://www.tinyurl.com/axvfys7u

Dunne, P. J. (2021b). The body scan meditation. Retrieved from https://www.youtube.com/watch?v=XSw-WLmooWg

Dunne, P. J. (2021c). Choosing an anchor for your meditation practice. Retrieved from https://www.youtube.com/watch?v=7w3G_Dist84&list=PL6DbJmB3fDQp_vwTqepv7LDjx3UqB2Ht5&index=3

Dunne, P. J., Lynch, J., Prihodova, L., O'Leary, C., Ghoreyshi, A., Basdeo, S. A., … White, B. (2019). Burnout in the emergency department: Randomized controlled trial of an attention-based training program. *Journal of Integrative Medicine, 17*(3), 173–180. doi:10.1016/j.joim.2019.03.009

FMP. (2021). Free resources. Retrieved from https://www.freemindfulness.org/download

Freeman, L. (2014). *Fully alive: The daily path of christian meditation.* United States: Orbis Books.

Gawrylewski, A. (2018). Be a better you (smart, happy, relaxed). *Scientific American Mind, 27*, 1–112.

Germer, C. K., & Neff, K. D. (2013). Self-compassion in clinical practice. *Journal of Clinical Psychology, 69*(8), 856–867. doi:10.1002/jclp.22021

Ivtzan, I., & Lomas, T. (Eds.). (2016). *Mindfulness in positive psychology. The science of meditation and wellbeing.* London: Routledge.

Ivtzan, I., Young, T., Martman, J., Jeffrey, A., Lomas, T., Hart, R., & Eiroa-Orosa, F. J. (2016). Integrating mindfulness into positive psychology: A randomised controlled trial of an online positive mindfulness program. *Mindfulness, 7*(6), 1396–1407. doi:10.1007/s12671-016-0581-1

Kabat-Zinn, J. (1990). *Full catastrophe living: Using the wisdom of your body and mind to face stress, pain and illness* (1st ed.). United States: Delta.

Kabat-Zinn, J., Wheeler, E., Light, T., Skillings, A., Scharf, M. J., Cropley, T. G., … Bernhard, J. D. (1998). Influence of a mindfulness meditation-based stress reduction intervention on rates of skin clearing in patients with moderate to severe psoriasis undergoing phototherapy (UVB) and photochemotherapy (PUVA). *Psychosomatic Medicine, 60*(5), 625–632. doi:10.1097/00006842-199809000-00020

Keng, S. L., Smoski, M. J., & Robins, C. J. (2011). Effects of mindfulness on psychological health: A review of empirical studies. *Clinical Psychology Review, 31*(6), 1041–1056. doi:10.1016/j.cpr.2011.04.006

Kern, M. L., Benson, L., Steinberg, E., & Steinberg, L. (2021). The EPOCH measure of adolescent well-being. Retrieved from https://www.peggykern.org/uploads/5/6/6/7/56678211/epoch_measure_of_adolescent_well-being_102014.pdf

Lally, P., van Jaarsveld, C. H. M., Potts, H. W. W., & Wardle, J. (2010). How are habits formed: Modelling habit formation in the real world. *European Journal of Social Psychology, 40*(6), 998–1009. doi:10.1002/ejsp.674

Lama, D. (2012). How to be compassionate: A handbook for creating inner peace and a happier world. London: Ebury Publishing.

Levine, G. N., Lange, R. A., Bairey-Merz, C. N., Davidson, R. J., Jamerson, K., Mehta, P. K., … Smith, S. C., Jr. (2017). Meditation and cardiovascular risk reduction: A scientific statement from the American Heart Association. *Journal of the American Heart Association, 6*(10). doi:10.1161/jaha.117.002218

Li, S. (2021). Psychological wellbeing, mindfulness, and immunity of teachers in second or foreign language education: A theoretical review. *Frontiers in Psychology, 12*(2739). doi:10.3389/fpsyg.2021.720340

Main, J. (2006). *Door to silence: An anthology for meditation.* Norwich: Canterbury Press.

Matko, K., & Sedlmeier, P. (2019). What is meditation? Proposing an empirically derived classification system. *Frontiers in Psychology*, 10, 2276-2276. doi:10.3389/fpsyg.2019.02276

McKeown, P. (2021). *The breathing cure: Exercises to develop new breathing habits for a healthier, happier and longer life*. Ireland: OxyAtBooks.

Niemiec, R. M., & Lissing, J. (2016). Mindfulness-based strengths practice (MBSP) for enhancing well-being, managing problems, and boosting positive relationships. In I. Ivtzan & T. Lomas (Eds.), *Mindfulness in positive psychology: The science of meditation and wellbeing* (pp. 15-36). London: Routledge/Taylor & Francis Group.

Ribeiro, M. (2021). What is compassion meditation? (+ mantras and scripts). *Meditation*. Retrieved from https://positivepsychology.com/compassion-meditation/

Ricard, M., Lutz, A., & Davidson, R. J. (2014). Mind of the meditator. *Scientific American, 311*(5), 38-45. doi:10.1038/scientificamerican1114-38

Sapolsky, R. M. (2004). *Why zebras don't get ulcers*. New York: Times Books.

Seligman, M. E. P. (2013). *Flourish: A visionary new understanding of happiness and well-being*. New York: Atria Paperback.

Shallcross, A. J., Visvanathan, P. D., Sperber, S. H., & Duberstein, Z. T. (2019). Waking up to the problem of sleep: Can mindfulness help? A review of theory and evidence for the effects of mindfulness for sleep. *Current Opinion in Psychology, 28*, 37-41. doi:10.1016/j.copsyc.2018.10.005

Singer, T., & Engert, V. (2019). It matters what you practice: Differential training effects on subjective experience, behavior, brain and body in the ReSource Project. *Current Opinion in Psychology, 28*, 151-158. doi:10.1016/j.copsyc.2018.12.005

Suzuki, S., & Dixon, T. (2020). *Zen mind, beginner's mind: 50th anniversary edition*. Boulder: Shambhala.

Sweet J. Exercise and Meditation Help Kids With ADHD in Just 10 Minutes: Very Well Mind; 2021 [Available from: https://www.verywellmind.com/exercise-and-meditation-helps-kids-with-adhd-study-says-5195016

Tang, Y. Y., Hölzel, B. K., & Posner, M. I. (2015). The neuroscience of mindfulness meditation. *Nature Reviews Neuroscience, 16*(4), 213-225. doi:10.1038/nrn3916

Van der Oord S, Bögels SM, Peijnenburg D. The Effectiveness of Mindfulness Training for Children with ADHD and Mindful Parenting for their Parents. J Child Fam Stud. 2012;21(1):139-47.

Waters, L., Barsky, A., Ridd, A., & Allen, K. (2015). Contemplative education: A systematic, evidence-based review of the effect of meditation interventions in schools. *Educational Psychology Review, 27*(1), 103-134. doi:10.1007/s10648-014-9258-2

11 Strengths-based interventions for students and staff

Christian van Nieuwerburgh and Ashley Green

Character strengths are now widely understood to be the positive aspects of personality which can impact optimal functioning and well-being. This chapter focuses on the use of strengths-identification and strengths-spotting in educational settings.

Introduction

The use of positive psychology in education has controversially been dubbed "positive education" (Seligman, 2002). It is argued that the aim of positive education is to "develop the skills of well-being, flourishing and optimal functioning in children, teenagers and students, as well as parents and educational institutions" (Boniwell & Tunariu, 2019, p. 247). Green et al. argue that the use of positive psychology in education facilitates "student, staff, and whole school wellbeing" (2012, p. 115). We prefer the term "positive psychology in education" because identifying this work as "positive education" may convey the impression that education as a whole is not positive. We argue that education, with its focus on learning and growth, is inherently positive. Positive psychology adds to this endeavour by adding a wealth of recent research and practices that can support educational organisations to strengthen their focus on well-being and personal development. In parallel, there has been a surge in interest about "character education" and "values education" as ways of improving attainment and enhanced well-being (Arthur, 2010, p. 1).

With character strengths being described as capacities for thinking, feeling, and behaving (Park et al., 2004) and as positive traits that are core to our being (Niemiec, 2014), it is understandable for strengths to be heralded in schools which are endeavouring to implement positive psychology in education to enhance the well-being provision for their community. Burke (2021) suggests that strengths interventions could become a fundamental component of a school's well-being strategy due to the benefits these interventions can procure, some of which will be outlined in this chapter.

While positive psychology in education has two broad applications: the teaching of positive psychology concepts (such as well-being, resilience, and positive emotions), and the use of positive psychology activities and interventions to improve outcomes and enhance

DOI: 10.4324/9781003228158-14

well-being, this chapter will be considering the latter application, focusing specifically on the use of character strengths in educational settings.

Theoretical background

What are character strengths?

With mounting research in the area of strengths, there are many definitions and viewpoints surrounding the topic. For the purposes of this chapter, the authors have drawn on the Values-In-Action (VIA) model (Peterson & Seligman, 2004). These 24-character strengths are categorised under six virtues. This classification is presented as 'psychological ingredients' that collectively attribute to what is 'right' with us as human beings, helping people to display virtues and goodness.

VIA (values in action inventory)

The VIA was designed in the early 2000s to counterbalance the so-called Diagnostic and Statistical Manual (DSM) of Mental Disorders. At the time, a main limitation transpired to be the lack of language, or scientific research, into the best qualities in people: much was available to support the diagnosis of what could be 'wrong'. The DSM is the most influential document used by psychologists for the diagnosis and the classification of mental disorders. Arguing that psychology has tended to focus on human weakness and mental illness, Peterson and Seligman embarked on a three-year project, enlisting the expertise of 55 scientists to carry out extensive research, which contributed to the creation of the VIA Classification of character strengths and virtues (Peterson & Seligman, 2004). The systematic approach started with the analysis of literature where virtues and strengths had been discussed, including Buddhist text dating back 2,500 years, ancient philosophy, and books of various religions. With six main themes emerging (courage, humanity, justice, temperance, transcendence, and wisdom), the six virtue categories were set. Further research into global cultures, language, and countries added to the refinement of characters strengths to be included under the virtue categories, with some researchers visiting remote tribes across the world, as well as groups in western societies. With the final 24 character strengths being inclusive of those who differed in a variety of areas, for example, in geography or spiritual practices, gender or age, the establishment of the categorisation was then validated with a measurement tool, known as the VIA Survey outlined below. A complete list of character strengths and their descriptions can be accessed in Peterson and Seligman (2004) or by visiting www.viacharacter.org.

VIA Survey of character strengths

With strengths being seen as the "active ingredients for positive living" (Snyder & Lopez, 2009, p. 73), there are numerous psychometric measures that identify strengths, most notably Values in Action Inventory of Strengths (VIA-IS), Gallup (commonly used in organizational contexts for a fee) and the Strengths Profile, which includes the identification of weaknesses. These measures have been validated as reliable in identifying a person's strengths (Snyder & Lopez, 2009). More recently, it has been argued that there may also be advantages to people's self-identifying strengths (Fouracres & van Nieuwerburgh, 2020). In this chapter, we will be referring to the VIA-IS throughout as it is widely accessible online and free to complete (viacharacter.org). Since it was launched, over 13 million people have completed the survey (according to viacharacter.org), making it one of the most robust, efficacious strength measurement tools. A popular and well-known survey, it was chosen as the most appropriate for this chapter which aims to promote the use of strengths in education, where financial budgets can be stretched or limited. However, the ideas and strategies discussed below can be implemented using any recognised strengths inventory.

Upon completion of the psychological survey, the participant is issued with a report that orders the strengths from 1 to 24 with the first strength being the participant's "top strength". The identification of a person's top five strengths, which are called "signature strengths", can be an interesting experience for participants who have not taken an inventory of their strengths, some of which may not have previously differentiated between innate personal strengths and talents.

Benefits of strengths

Knowing one's strengths and using them more frequently and more broadly in life is considered a positive psychology intervention (PPI). In other words, acknowledging one's strengths and finding ways to use them regularly can enhance well-being (Govindji & Linley, 2007; Park et al., 2009). Recent research is encouraging, showing how strengths use can decrease stress (Wood et al., 2011), boost happiness (Seligman et al., 2005), increase engagement (Madden et al., 2011), and make it more likely to achieve goals (Linley et al., 2010). More currently, a study in Spain during the COVID-19 lockdown (Martinez-Marti et al., 2020) interpreted data to suggest fostering character strengths during a time of adversity can increase mental health and positive emotions. Hone et al. (2005) reported that participants who were aware of their strengths were nine times more likely to psychologically flourish than those who were unaware of their strengths, while those who reported using their strengths at work were 18 times more likely to psychologically flourish than their colleagues who did not employ strengths in the workplace.

There have been a variety of studies carried out in which strength-based interventions have been applied in school settings to research well-being outcomes for students. Increases in positive affect and life satisfaction were evident in adolescent participants in Proctor et al.'s (2011) *Strengths Gym* intervention, which is based on the VIA Character Strengths framework. Interestingly, after an 18-month follow up, students who participated in a five-week hope intervention (Marques et al., 2011) had maintained their increased levels of life satisfaction and self-worth, highlighting that well-being can be improved for students over a period of time when their focus is directed to one character strength specifically. It is important to note that this study did not find any direct correlation between improved academic achievement and the character strength interventions.

It is valuable to also be aware of the overuse and underuse of character strengths, sometimes referred to as "strengths blindness" (Niemiec, 2014). For example, a person who has curiosity as their top strength could be perceived as nosey when overusing this strength in a situation or during a personal conversation. An underuse of appreciation of beauty and excellence could mean someone undervaluing the skill of another or missing out on the joy of nature that surrounds them on their commute to work.

Practice

"Try this" for educators

When offered new ideas or concepts within the realm of 'well-being', teachers often instinctively consider how these can be introduced effectively to the students. However, educators must be given the space to learn about the scientific underpinnings of the concept being introduced, then time to actively experience or practice the concepts themselves, in order to enrich the opportunities they provide for the students; character strengths are no different.

When considering how positive psychology can be applied in educational settings, it is important to develop strategies that include achievable milestones that have been agreed between management teams and those responsible for growing positive psychology initiatives or well-being programmes in an educational setting. Character strengths are an ideal starting point for schools to begin their journey towards flourishing. It might be helpful to integrate the global initiative 'Character Day' (Shlain, n.d.) into the school well-being strategy. The event normally takes place in September and could provide an opportunity to launch character strengths within school communities for the students and parents, where school staff have had ample time to familiarise themselves with the strengths beforehand. Sufficient time for staff can be mapped out accordingly within school well-being strategies. It is possible for strengths to be the theme for the first term, giving the whole community time to embed character strengths language into the daily ecology of their schools.

There are many resources available when bringing character strengths into a new context, which can be enjoyable for staff and students alike! Character strength cards are a tangible resource that school staff can explore for themselves before taking them to the classroom. When all school staff are together on a school training day, they can be introduced to character strengths through a workshop-style session. Staff can sit in small groups with a set of character strength cards per table and begin to explore the strengths language through the cards. Very soon, staff will be discussing the language together – more often than not, sharing which strength words they perceive themselves to lack! Staff can then choose a card that resonates with them as their 'top' strength and share this with their group. It is valuable to give staff time to reflect on what it felt like to talk about their top strength to others; there can be a wide variety of feelings experienced and this is something to be mindful of when asking students to take part in similar activities. Another useful task is to ask staff to 'gift' a card to a colleague within the group. This can be called 'strength spotting', where one person spots one of the strengths in another and shares this with them. For example, "I see the strength of kindness in you because you always give so much of your time to others when they need support".

Following on from the workshop activities, all staff can be asked to complete the free online VIA Character Strength survey which can be set up for an organisation on the website. On completion of the survey, staff will receive a free report where their strengths are ordered from 1 to 24. The first five strengths on the report are what Niemiec (2018) refers to as the "signature strengths" (p. 18), these can vary for a person over time but have shown to be most intrinsically linked to who the person is at the core (Seligman, 2002). Another useful element of the survey is that the data can be collated as an organisation (from consenting participants), analysed, and considered when moving forward with strategy. For example, it could be discovered that gratitude is one of the most frequent signature strengths amongst staff within the school. This could be shared with staff after the data has been analysed and celebrated as a positive overall attribute of the team that can be utilised more frequently. As the understanding of strengths deepens, staff can choose which strengths they wish to employ, both personally and professionally, on a day-to-day basis by perhaps using this strength in a different way each day or simply having it at the forefront of their mind in a variety of situations. Going further, staff could begin to learn about the signature strengths of colleagues by strength spotting and bringing strengths into professional conversations. During professional review meetings, both leaders and teaching staff could bring strengths into the conversation in order to positively construct steps and goals moving forward. For example, during a discussion about a possible promotion, a leader might ask a staff member "How might you utilise your top strength of appreciation of beauty and excellence when considering this new position?". The staff member might then reflect or have a discussion with someone who they admire and already perceive to demonstrate excellence in a similar role to the one they are applying for.

"Try this" for students

Once school staff have experienced strengths for themselves, both personally and professionally, many ideas and opportunities for the students will become apparent. When asked to discuss their 'strengths', students very often begin to describe their interests, talents, or aptitudes. For example, a young child may describe themselves as good at reading or at football. However, without immersion in character strengths education, they may not realise that their strength of love of learning could be instrumental in their joy of reading about new things or characters. The strength of perseverance could be at play for a keen footballer who never misses an opportunity to train and improve their skills. Knowing about these strengths innately can encourage students to apply these strengths to other areas of their lives. What about those children we come across, who are unduly hard on themselves? Giving them a set of strength words provides these students with vocabulary to articulate positive thoughts about themselves. Also, this shared strengths language enables educators to share the strengths they have spotted in students, particularly those who lack confidence or put pressure on themselves academically.

Many of the practical suggestions outlined in the "Try This" for educators section can be replicated for students. Introducing the character strengths language through a resource, such as the aforementioned cards, can be an exploratory session for students of all ages. Even very young children can begin the journey of acquiring the language of strengths through discussions of words already familiar to them, such as love or teamwork. Although exposure to all 24-character strengths and six virtue categories is valuable, specific strengths can be allocated to year groups as part of the positive psychology in education or well-being strategy, so that a child moving through the school is sure to experience in-depth learning about each strength at a suitable developmental stage; the strengths of prudence or perspective could be too abstract for a child in foundation stage without language being adapted appropriately. Strengths can be discussed in weekly assemblies as a focal point or with relevance to current events. Perhaps children can be awarded at assembly for a particular demonstration of a strength which was spotted by their teacher. Classes can choose a strength of the week to consider daily and students can spend time spotting strengths in others, not only in their friends but story characters and real-life people they meet during their daily lessons. Teachers who fully embed character strengths as part of their positive psychology in education provision will naturally begin to include opportunities to utilise character strengths within their planning for the lessons to be delivered to students.

Case study

In 2019, co-author Ashley Green worked alongside fellow well-being leaders Rosemin Guerrero and Niamh Moore with their school director in JESS Dubai, United Arab Emirates, to introduce character strengths to a staff of approximately 350 people. Hosting workshops where everyone was introduced the science of character strengths, before experiencing activities using character strength cards, enabled everyone to familiarise themselves with the classification of strengths. All staff were asked to complete the survey and discuss different ways they could utilise their strengths both personally and professionally. Staff were provided with various case studies during the workshops to begin considering the vast range of opportunities to employ strengths day-to-day both in situations that could arise at home or in the workplace with colleagues and students. Only after ample time was spent encouraging staff to focus on their own strengths, did training move towards considering how strengths could be introduced to students. Strengths have been embedded into the schools' strategy for enhancing well-being and positive psychology provision for the community. Staff often draw on many of the suggestions outlined previously in this chapter. According to Seligman, "greater wellbeing enhances learning, the traditional goal of education. Positive mood produces broader attention, more creative thinking and more holistic thinking" (2011, p. 80).

Another encouraging case study sharing best practice is from Rolleston College in New Zealand. Here, teachers devised a 'Check and Connect' initiative where students and staff are catered for through a suite of well-being activities designed to foster a relationship-based approach to enhancing well-being. Characters strengths cards are included in the offerings; learners randomly pick a strength and consider how they might use that strength in the week (Quinlan & Hone, 2020, p. 141).

Conclusion

In this chapter, we have presented a case and some ideas for using strengths in school with both staff and students. We believe that strengths identification, strengths spotting, and strengths use in schools can have an immediate positive and uplifting effect on the educational community. Further, when staff, students, and parents are more aware of their strengths and resources, they are likely to apply these in the educational setting, enhancing their everyday experience and leading to improved outcomes.

Discussion points

- Have you considered your character strengths before? Do this before completing the online survey. If you have already taken the survey, perhaps you can reflect on your signature strengths and how you are going to use them day-to-day.
- How do you envisage character strengths in your school? Do they align with your well-being strategy?

References

Arthur, J. (2010). *Of Good Character; Exploration of Virtues and Values in 3-25 Year-Olds.* Exeter: Imprint Academic.

Boniwell, I., & Tunariu, A. (2019). *Positive Psychology: Theory, Research and Applications* (2nd ed.). London: Open University Press.

Burke, J. (2021). *The Ultimate Guide to Implementing Wellbeing Programmes for School.* London: Routledge.

Fouracres, A., & van Nieuwerburgh, C. (2020). The lived experience of self-identifying character strengths through coaching: An interpretative phenomenological analysis. *International Journal of Evidence Based Coaching and Mentoring, 18*(1): 43-56.

Govindji, R., & Linley, A. (2007). Strengths use, self-concordance and well-being: Implications for strengths coaching and coaching psychologists. *International Coaching Psychology Review, 2*: 143-53.

Green, L. S., Oades, L. G., & Robinson, P. L. (2012). Positive education programmes: Integrating coaching and positive psychology in schools. In: C. van Nieuwerburgh (Ed.), *Coaching in Education: Getting Better Results for Students, Educators and Parents* (pp. 115-132). London: Routledge.

Hone, L.C., Jarden, A., Duncan, S. & Schofield, G.M. (2005). Flourishing in New Zealand workers: Associations with lifestyle behaviors, physical health, psychosocial, and work-related indicators. *Journal of Occupational and Environmental Medicine, 57*(9): 973-983.

Linley, P. A., Nielsen, K. M., Gillett, R., & Biswas-Diener, R. (2010). Using signature strengths in pursuit of goals: Effects on goal progress, need satisfaction, and well-being, aand implications for coaching psychologists. *International Coaching Psychology Review, 5*: 6-15.

Madden, W., Green, S., & Grant, A. M. (2011). A plot study evaluating strengths-based coaching for primary school students: Enhancing engagement and hope. *International Coaching Psychology Review, 6*: 71-83.

Marques, S. C., Lopez, S. J., & Pais-Ribeiro, J. L. (2011). Building hope for the future: A program to foster strengths in middle-school students. *Journal of Happiness Studies, 12*(1): 139-152.

Martinez-Marti, M. L., Theirs, C. I., Pascual, D., & Corradi, G. (2020). Character strengths predict an increase in mental health and subjective well-being over a one-month period during the COVID-19 pandemic lockdown. *Frontiers in Psychology, 11*: 584567.

Niemiec, R. M. (2014). *Mindfulness and Character Strengths: A Practical Guide to Flourishing.* Boston, MA: Hogrefe.

Niemiec, R. M. (2018). *Character Strengths Interventions: A Field Guide for Practitioners.* Massachusetts: Hogrefe Publishing.

Park, N., Peterson, C., & Ruch, W. (2009). Orientations to happiness and life satisfaction in twenty-seven nations. *The Journal of Positive Psychology, 4*: 273-9.

Park, N., Peterson, C., & Seligman, M. E. P. (2004). Strengths of character and well-being. *Journal of Social and Clinical Psychology, 23*(5): 603-619.

Peterson, C., & Seligman, M. E. P. (2004). *Character Strengths and Virtues: A Handbook and Classification.* Washington, DC: American Psychological Association Press.

Proctor, C., Tsukayama, E., Wood, A. M., Maltby, J., Eades, J. F., & Linley, P. A. (2011). Strengths gym: The impact of a character strengths-based intervention on the life satisfaction and wellbeing of adolescents. *The Journal of Positive Psychology, 6*(5): 377-388.

Quinlan, D. M., & Hone, L. C. (2020). *The Educators' Guide to Whole-School Wellbeing: A Practical Guide to Getting Started, Best-Practice Process and Effective Implementation.* New York, NY: Routledge.

Seligman, M. (2002). *Authentic Happiness.* New York, NY: Free Press.

Seligman, M. (2011). *Flourish.* New York, NY: Free Press.

Seligman, M., Steen, T., Park, N., & Peterson, C. (2005). Positive psychology progress: Empirical validation of interventions. *American Psychologist, 55*: 5-14.

Shlain, T. (n.d.). *Character Day*. Retrieved May 12, 2021 from, https://www.letitripple.org/characterday

Snyder, C. R., & Lopez, S. J. (2009). *Handbook of Positive Psychology* (2nd ed.). Oxford: Oxford University Press.

Wood, A. M., Linley, P. A., Maltby, J., Kashdan, T. B., & Hurling, R. (2011). Using personal and psychological strengths leads to increases in well-being over time: A longitudinal study and the development of the strengths use questionnaire. *Personality and Individual Differences, 50*: 15-19.

Part 4

Creativity in schools: Arts, playing, and language

Although there is much debate on the role of arts, playing, and creativity in our society, several studies in the fields of education, psychology, and more recently, positive psychology have highlighted their contribution to human flourishing (Clark, 2017; Clift & Camit, 2016; Gillam, 2018; Lomas, 2016; Nakamura & Csikszentmihalyi, 2003). Furthermore, as suggested in a report by the American Academy of Arts & Sciences (2013, cited by Tay et al., 2018), "the arts and humanities ... are critical to our pursuit of life, liberty, and happiness" (p. 13).

With this in mind, we could assert that schools should promote arts and creativity, although that is not always the case. Many readers would probably remember Robinson's provocative TED Talk, Do schools kill creativity? Robinson (2016) suggested that "creativity now is as important in education as literacy [although] we should treat it with the same status".

Considering the relevance of arts and creativity to well-being, we thought the topic could contribute to the literature in positive psychology in schools. Therefore, Chapter 12 considers the role of arts in schools and the approaches that may better promote well-being. Chapter 13 brings the perspective of music and technology and their role in well-being. Chapter 14 explores the role of play in young people's development and well-being for both students and teachers. Finally, Chapter 15 explores the role of language and its influence on how people perceive, experience, and understand the world.

As you read this part, you may reflect on the following:

- Why are arts, play, and creativity important in schools?
- How do you engage with arts, play, and creativity?
- How could arts, play, and creative approaches be embedded in the school curriculum?

References

American Academy of Arts & Sciences. (2013). *Humanities report card*. https://www.amacad.org/binaries/hum_report_card.pdf

Clark, C. (Ed.). (2017). *Play and wellbeing*. Routledge.

Clift, S., & Camic, P. M. (Eds.). (2016). *Oxford textbook of creative arts, health, and wellbeing: International perspectives on practice, policy, and research*. Oxford Textbooks in Public Health.

Gillam, T. (2018). *Creativity, wellbeing and mental health practice*. Springer.

DOI: 10.4324/9781003228158-15

Lomas, T. (2016). Positive art: Artistic expression and appreciation as an exemplary vehicle for flourish-ing. *Review of General Psychology, 20*(2), 171–182.

Nakamura, J., & Csikszentmihalyi, M. (2003). The motivational sources of creativity as viewed from the paradigm of positive psychology. In L. G. Aspinwall & U. M. Staudinger (Eds.), *A psychology of hu-man strengths: Fundamental questions and future directions for a positive psychology* (pp. 257–269). American Psychological Association. https://doi.org/10.1037/10566-018

Robinson, K. (2006). *Ken Robinson: Do schools kill creativity?* [Video file]. http://www.Ted.Com/Talks/Ken_robinson_says_schools_kill_creativity

Tay, L., Pawelski, J. O., & Keith, M. G. (2018). The role of the arts and humanities in human flourishing: A conceptual model. *The Journal of Positive Psychology, 13*(3), 215–225.

12 Arts and well-being

Andrea Giraldez-Hayes

Art plays an essential role in human life. Children and young people engage in and socialise through narratives, songs, roleplaying, stories, dance, photography, and other art forms in interaction with their daily experience. This chapter aims to raise awareness of the benefits that arts can bring to students' emotional development, mental health, and well-being.

Introduction

Can you imagine life without art? Stop and think for a few minutes. Then, try to recall the many opportunities you engage with some form of art as an observer, a creator, or a performer in your daily life. You have probably identified many examples, as the truth is that literally, from the cradle to the grave, different forms of art play an essential role in our lives. We live immersed in art, and we become so used to it that sometimes we do not notice it is there. Broadly, art can be defined as any human activity – and the products thereof – that allows people to express their thoughts and emotions, interact, and communicate. That integrates different fields that have evolved throughout the history of humankind, such as sculpture, dance, painting, poetry, craftwork, cinema, theatre, play, photography, or storytelling. These are all activities common to humans in every culture despite having received formal education or not. In fact, as John Dewey believed, "every person is capable of being an artist, living an artful life of social interaction that benefits and thereby beautifies the world […] Art functions as experience. Processes of inquiry, looking and finding meaning are transformative" (Goldblatt, 2006, p. 17).

The life-enhancing power of art has not only been recognised since ancient times but also in numerous research studies, some related to positive psychology (Chilton & Wilkinson, 2009; Hampshire & Matthijsse, 2010; Wilkinson & Chilton, 2031). Research has confirmed the power of art to mobilise people's strengths (Cadell et al., 2005), change narratives and induce positive emotions (Chilton, 2014), build self-esteem and confidence (Hui & Stickley, 2010), engage in positive relationships (Brouillette, 2009; Gauntlett, 2011), keep on flowing (Csikszentmihalyi, 2013), find meaning (Steger et al., 2014), develop resilience (Macpherson et al., 2016), build hope (Stacey & Stickley, 2010), or have a sense of accomplishment (Brouillette, 2009).

DOI: 10.4324/9781003228158-16

Considering the benefits of art for people's emotional development, health, mental health, and well-being, the question is how we can make sure that we engage and help others to take part in art activities regularly and, more specifically, how we do it in schools.

Art and well-being in schools

We have a tiny minority of people calling themselves artists. I am recommending that everyone should be an artist. I am not recommending it in a spirit of dilettantism, but as the only preventive of a vast neurosis which will overcome a wholly mechanised and rationalised civilisation (Read, 1955).

The power of art and its substantial contribution to health and well-being have been extensively researched (Camic, 2008; Gallant et al., 2017; Jensen & Bonde, 2018; Leckey, 2011) and, among others, a comprehensive report, Creative Health: The Arts for Health and Wellbeing (APPG, 2017), shows the impact of arts in different age groups, from childhood to the end of life, offering a wide range of examples.

In the realm of positive psychology, arts have been deemed positive psychological interventions, that is, "treatment methods or intentional activities aimed at cultivating positive feelings, positive behaviours, or positive cognitions–enhance well-being and ameliorate depressive symptoms" (Sin & Lyubomirsky, 2009, p. 467). Darewych and Riedel Bowers (2018) and Louis et al. (2017), among others, observe how arts and humanities boost human flourishing, and *The Wiley Blackwell Handbook of Positive Psychological Interventions* (Parks & Schueller, 2014) includes a chapter on creativity considered as a new and emerging area of intervention.

The potential of arts and its impact on the elements of the PERMA well-being model (Seligman, 2018) have also been researched. For example, it has been suggested that music promotes positive emotions (Lamont, 2012), engagement (O'Neill, 1999), relationships (Boer & Abubakar, 2014), meaning (Rudd, 2009), and accomplishment (Southgate & Roscigno, 2009). In the context of education, Giraldez-Hayes et al. (in press), Croom (2014), and Lee et al. (2017) observed how participation in music programmes in schools was beneficial for the development of the five components of the PERMA model (Seligman, 2018). However, a word of caution is needed as the benefits of music and other art forms do not happen in a vacuum. Art programmes and the integration of arts in other school subjects should be for all students, not only for the talented ones. It is essential to understand that although genius can probably not be taught, skills can. In some cultures, especially the Western ones, there is a belief that only those who are gifted or possess special artistic abilities can participate in art-making activities. That is an unfounded belief that stops students or moves teachers to exclude them from engaging in art projects that would benefit their well-being. Actually, the discussion between nature and nurture, that is, if artistic talent is innate or learned, has been in the centre of the debate for a long time (Michael, 1991; Upitis, 2011), and although it is not the purpose of this chapter to engage in that debate, as an author, I need to declare my ontological assumptions: drawing from research and practice evidence, I believe that artistic talent is learned and that anyone can engage in art activities in schools and communities. The primary purpose of these activities is not to train artists, although eventually, some will end up being professional sculptors, actors,

or musicians. The aim is to offer equal opportunities inviting everyone to engage and celebrate the transformational role of arts in people's life.

Research has also suggested that participating in arts experiences aids the development
of a broad range of skills, including problem solving and critical thinking (Lampert, 2006),
effective communication and social development (Brouillette, 2009), resilience (Kim, 2015),
or conflict resolution (Bang, 2006) which in turn has an impact on children's confidence and
self-esteem. As Bob Bates, founder of Inner-City Arts in Los Angeles, claims,

> Making art requires thinking and decision: what colour will I use, how can I make this
> stand up, how can I make this stronger, quieter, brighter, more bendable. As [children]
> make art, and solve these problems, they begin to believe in themselves. The confidence
> helps them in everything they do.
>
> (London Training for Excellence, n.d.)

Furthermore, arts provide a way out for those who find it difficult to speak up or share their
thoughts and feelings but can express them by drawing, sculpting, singing, dancing, or writing. As suggested by Mattaraso (2019),

> Art helps us accept the dangerous, unstable things we avoid in everyday life … It allows
> us to … give our fears, anger, desires, hatred and love the space to breathe safely, speak
> freely, dream and fantasise, imitate; to discover what we like, feel and don't know we feel
> and like; to fall down without getting hurt, to strike out and not hurt others.
>
> (p. 43)

Although the obvious way to provide opportunities to all students would be protecting art
subjects in schools – and we must do it – we invite readers to take a holistic view by considering participatory and community art projects and a cross-curricular perspective to integrate
art activities in other school subjects and activities, both options that have been proved to
be effective.

Participatory and community art

A wide range of terms (e.g., participatory art, socially engaged art, community art, dialogic
art, relational art, activist art) define different approaches to art projects that have something in common: using the arts to facilitate dialogue and interaction within a group. For the
sake of clarity, in this chapter, we will refer to two of these modalities, namely participatory
and community art, without making a clear-cut distinction. However, it seems appropriate to
start by defining both concepts.

Participatory art has been defined as that "created through the participation of people
in addition to the artist or art collective. In participatory art, people, referred to as citizens,
regular folks, community members, or non-artists interact with professional artists to create
the works" (Finkelpearl, 2014). It is a wide and diverse field of artistic practice that integrates
community art, a human rights-based approach that evolved from cultural democracy and
has been described as an "artistic activity that is based in a community setting, characterised
by interaction or dialogue with the community and often involving a professional artist col-
laborating with people who may not otherwise engage in the arts" (Tate, 2017).

Participatory and community art projects in schools can be an excellent approach and resource for students, teachers, parents, and the wider community to enhance and celebrate human relationships. In these projects, art becomes an invitation to learn about ourselves and others, and the result of these collective actions creates the conditions for exchange, communication, and well-being.

Arts integration

An exemplary approach to arts integration is the one developed by The Kennedy Center since 1976. Their system helps educators understand the different ways in which the arts can find their ways in schools – arts as curriculum, arts-enhanced curriculum, and arts-integrated curriculum – and highlights that all three are essential, needed, and defensible (The Kennedy Center, 1990–2021). All three are equally important. However, for this chapter, it is worth considering an arts-integrated curriculum, which is when "the arts become the approach to teaching and the vehicle for learning" (The Kennedy Center, 1990–2021). A few examples of this approach in which arts have been used to enhance students' well-being and to foster social participation are a development of the Targeted Mental Health in Schools project using arts in five schools in Nottinghamshire (City Arts, n.d.), Magic Me (see https://magicme.co.uk), or Partners in the arts (see https://spcs.richmond.edu/professional-education/areas/teaching-instruction/partners-arts).

The approach to arts-based education has also been successfully used and researched in positive education projects, such as the one developed by Seligman in Geelong Grammar School in Australia (Seligman et al., 2009). The project integrated the Penn Resiliency Program (PRP) to increase students' ability to handle stressors and everyday problems among teenagers by teaching them assertiveness, decision-making, creative brainstorming, relaxation, and other coping mechanisms to adopt a realistic and flexible approach to the problems they encounter. As part of a randomised control evaluation, year 9 students were assigned to two language arts classes. One contained a positive psychology curriculum to help students identify their signature character strengths and use them in day-to-day life, and the other one did not. For the first group, the programme increased engagement in learning, enjoyment of school, and achievement, and improved social skills. However, it did not improve other outcomes such as reported anxiety and depression symptoms. Therefore, the authors conclude that more intensive interventions or a combination of the Penn Resilience Programme and other positive psychology programmes should be considered.

Chemi (2015) has also developed and explored the emotional outputs of integrated-arts projects in Danish schools. She suggests that the positive emotions and cognitive intensity experienced in artistic activities had positive consequences for students' learning, development, and well-being. A significant number of integrated-arts projects in schools, not explicitly linked to the positive psychology perspective, had similar results. For example, studying hope and gratitude in the English curriculum as topics during the analysis of characters, reading uplifting texts such as *Invictus* by Henley, exploring mindfulness and meditation in the Cultural and Religious curriculum, or analysing the difference in happiness across continents in Geography.

"Try this" for educators

Throughout my career, I have developed many participatory and community art programmes to promote well-being. As part of my role, I had the opportunity to work with hundreds of teachers to whom, like a mantra, I used to repeat: "It is not possible to teach arts without enjoying arts". Considering the many benefits of arts as positive psychology interventions, teachers should observe how they embrace art-based activities in their daily lives. They should also think about how they could engage in art activities by themselves or, even better, with others, and how those activities help them have a more balanced and fulfilling life. It is this first-hand experience that will not only contribute to their well-being but also provide ideas to develop arts-integrated projects in schools. Indeed, as suggested by Beghetto (2021), "unless teachers believe they can support student creativity [and engagement in arts activities], have some idea of how to do so, and are willing to try then it is unlikely that [they will offer] systematic opportunities" (p. 480).

"Try this" for students

Years ago, working in a secondary school, I asked students how many times they had engaged in arts-related activities during the last three months. The numbers were disheartening. Some students mentioned those activities were expensive and they did not have enough money. As a result of that conversation, we created a calendar of free art activities that students could join, from concerts, movies, or exhibitions to opportunities to sign in choirs or participate in an improv group. By doing that, we were promoting arts as activities they could enjoy in their free time. The results were encouraging as, three months later, they had all engaged in one or more actions, and arts and the benefits they were experiencing became part of their conversations.

Participatory and community art projects developed in schools can also be unique opportunities to promote positive effects such as immersion, embeddedness, socialisation, and reflectiveness. A good example is the Magic me (already mentioned in this chapter https://magicme.co.uk), an arts charity that creates art projects in partnership with schools to bring generations together and build stronger and safer communities. Dancers, musicians, photographers, or actors design arts-based projects to stimulate conversation and exchange ideas among people diverse in culture and faith and age group.

The best source for teachers to create their own participatory and community art projects is not the ones being developed in schools but the ones that take place out of educational settings and can provide the ideas and inspiration to create new projects in schools. Therefore, we suggest that the reader familiarise themselves with these projects or, even better, take part in them to learn and bring new ideas to their schools. The "Suggested resources" section includes some useful links.

Case study

LOVA, Opera as a Learning Vehicle, is a paradigmatic example of an arts-integrated curriculum promoting well-being. When teachers develop the project, their class becomes a company that devotes an entire course to creating and launching their own opera. The project takes place during school hours, and students are empowered to adopt different roles and work through the tasks by themselves. The ownership of learning shifts from teacher to student. Establishing an authentic learning environment fosters and improves academic, social, and emotional skills necessary to flourish and thrive.

Mary Ruth McGinn, a primary school teacher in Maryland, after training in the Creating Original Opera programme at the New York Metropolitan, applied the project in her classroom for several years and trained hundreds of teachers in partnership with Peter Hoyle (USA), Pedro Sarmiento, and Miguel Gil (Spain). As a result of this partnership, teachers in different countries, including Spain and Mexico (see Soliveres et al., 2021) have implemented the project in their schools.

McGinn explains that this is not an arts programme, but the opera is the vehicle to develop socioemotional skills.

> The programme starts the first day of school because everything we do academically informs the opera process, just as the opera process informs the curriculum. For instance, the kids have an authentic context through which they can apply math and science to build the sets and footlights from scratch, whereas in a traditional format math and science and other subjects are taught in isolation.
>
> (Dormady Eisenberg, 2007)

See McGhinn's TEDx Talk and LOVA, referenced in the suggested resources section, to learn more about this project.

Discussion points

1   How do you engage in arts?

In this chapter, we have argued that whether it is listening to music, sewing, doodling, dancing, singing, or appreciating architecture or nature outdoors, art activities are beneficial for your mind and body (APPG, 2017). We have also suggested that the first step to "teach art" or to integrate arts in your curriculum is for teachers to engage and enjoy art-based activities. Finally, remember that you do not need to be an artist with a capital A and that you can create the habit of engaging in arts in the same way that you create habits for eating well or exercising. With this in mind, reflect on your current engagement with arts in your daily life and consider new opportunities. The following questions may help.

o   What artistic practices do you enjoy the most?

o   Is there something that you always wanted to try - singing in a choir, painting, acting, etc.- and you never did?

o   What opportunities are available?

2   Learning *in* the arts, *about* the arts, or *through* the arts

Upitis (2011) suggests that teachers have a fundamental contribution to make to arts education. In a literature review, she identified three approaches: learning in, about, and through the arts. After reading this chapter, is one of these approaches more adequate to promote students' well-being through arts? Why? Why not?

Suggested resources

All Change Arts. *World class art made by, with and for communities.* https://www.allchangearts.org
A Restless Arts. *How participation won and why it matters.* https://arestlessart.com/resources/community-art-in-britain
Empathy Museum. https://www.empathymuseum.com
LOVA. https://proyectolova.es/en/
Mary Ruth McGhinn. *Authentic learning as a vehicle for change.* https://www.youtube.com/watch?v=ggYL9gQeVEk

References

APPG. (2017). *Creative health: The arts for health and wellbeing.* https://www.culturehealthandwellbeing.org.uk/appg-inquiry/Publications/Creative_Health_Inquiry_Report_2017_-_Second_Edition.pdf
Bang, A. H. (2016). The restorative and transformative power of the arts in conflict resolution. *Journal of Transformative Education, 14*(4), 355–376.
Beghetto, R. (2021). Creative learning in education. In M. Kern & M. Wehmeyer (Eds.), *The Palgrave handbook of positive education* (pp. 473–493). Palgrave Macmillan.
Boer, D., & Abubakar, A. (2014). Music listening in families and peer groups: Benefits for young people's social cohesion and emotional well-being across four cultures. *Frontiers in Psychology, 5.* https://doi.org/10.3389/fpsyg.2014.00392
Brouillette, L. (2009). How the arts help children to create healthy social scripts: Exploring the perceptions of elementary teachers. *Arts Education Policy Review, 111*(1), 16–24.
Cadell, S., et al. (2005). The use of the arts and the strengths perspective: The example of a course assignment. *Social Work Education, 24*(1), 137–146.
Camic, P. (2008). Playing in the mud: Health psychology, the arts and creative approaches to health care. *Journal of Health Psychology, 13*(2), 287–298. https://doi.org/10.1177/1359105307086698
Chemi, T. (2015). Learning through the arts in Denmark: A positive psychology qualitative approach. *Journal for Learning through the Arts, 11*(1), 6.
Chilton, G. C. (2014). *An arts-based study of the dynamics of expressing positive emotions within the intersubjective art making process.* Drexel University ProQuest Dissertations Publishing.
Chilton, G., & Wilkinson, R. (2009). Positive art therapy: Envisioning the intersection of art therapy and positive psychology. *Australia and New Zealand Journal of Art Therapy, 4*(1), 27–35.
City Arts. (n.d.). *Art works. Using the arts to promote emotional health and wellbeing in schools.* https://city-arts.org.uk/wp-content/uploads/2013/03/Art-Works.pdf
Croom, A. M. (2014). Music practice and participation for psychological well-being: A review of how music influences positive emotion, engagement, relationships, meaning, and accomplishment. *Musicae Scientiae, 19*(1), 44–64. https://doi.org/10.1177/1029864914561709
Csikszentmihalyi, M. (2013). *Flow: The psychology of happiness.* Random House.
Darewych, O. H., & Riedel Bowers, N. (2018). Positive arts interventions: Creative clinical tools promoting psychological well-being. *International Journal of Art Therapy, 23*(2), 62–69.
Dormady Eisenberg, S. (2017). A Maryland teacher changes lives by creating opera in the classroom. *Huffpost.* https://www.huffpost.com/entry/maryland-elementary-school-opera_b_3194823
Finkelpearl, T. (2014). Participatory art. In M. Kelly (Ed.), *Encyclopaedia of aesthetics.* Oxford University Press.
Gallant, K., Hamilton-Hinch, B., White, K., Litwiller, F., Lauckner, H. (2017). Removing the thorns": The role of the arts in recovery for people with mental health challenges. *Arts & Health, 11*(1), 1–14. https://doi.org/10.1080/17533015.2017.1413397

Gauntlett, D. (2011). *Making is connecting: The social meaning of creativity*. Polity Press.

Giraldez-Hayes, A., et al. (in press). A veces lloro, pero son lágrimas de alegría: Percepciones de bienestar psicológico a partir de la práctica musical compartida. *Encuentros: Revista de Ciencias Humanas, Teoría Social y Pensamiento Crítico*.

Goldblatt, P. (2006). How John Dewey's theories underpin art and art education. *Education and Culture, 22*(1), 17-34.

Hampshire, K. R., & Matthijsse, M. (2010). Can arts projects improve young people's wellbeing? A social capital approach. *Social Science & Medicine, 71*(4), 708-716.

Hui, A., & Stickley, T. (2010). Artistic activities can improve patients' self-esteem. *Mental Health Practice, 14*, 30-32.

Jensen, A., & Bonde, L. O. (2018). The use of arts interventions for mental health and wellbeing in health settings. *Perspectives in Public Health, 138*(4), 209-214. https://doi.org/10.1177/1757913918772602

Kim, H. (2015). Community and art: Creative education fostering resilience through art. *Asia Pacific Education Review, 16*(2), 193-201.

Lamont, A. (2012). Emotion, engagement and meaning in strong experiences of music performance. *Psychology of Music, 40*(5), 574-594.

Lampert, N. (2006). Critical thinking dispositions as an outcome of art education. *Studies in Art Education, 47*(3), 215-228.

Leckey, J. (2011). The therapeutic effectiveness of creative activities on mental well-being: A systematic review of the literature. *Psychiatric and Mental Health, 18*(6), 501-509. https://doi.org/10.1111/j.1365-2850.2011.01693.x

Lee, J., Krause, A., & Davidson, J. (2017). The PERMA well-being model and music facilitation practice: Preliminary documentation for well-being through music provision in Australian schools. *Research Studies in Music Education, 39*(1), 73-89.

London Training for Excellence. (n.d.). Art that builds problem-solving skills. *London Training for Excellence*. https://www.londontfe.com/blog/Art-That-Builds-Problem-Solving-Skills

Louis, T., Pawelski, J., & Keith, M. (2017). The role of the arts and humanities in human flourishing: A conceptual model. *The Journal of Positive Psychology, 13*(3), 215-225. https://doi.org/10.1080/17439760.2017.1279207

Matarasso, F. (2019). A restless art. How participation won, and why it matters. *Calouste Gulbenkian Foundation*. https://arestlessart.files.wordpress.com/2019/03/2019-a-restless-art.pdf

Macpherson, H., Hart, A., & Heaver, B. (2016). Building resilience through group visual arts activities: Findings from a scoping study with young people who experience mental health complexities and/or learning difficulties. Journal of Social Work, 16(5), 541-560.

Michael, J. (1991). Art education: Nurture or nature—Where's the pendulum now? *Art Education, 44*(4), 16-23. https://doi.org/10.1080/00043125.1991.11652884

O'Neill, S. A. (1999). Flow theory and the development of musical performance skills. *Bulletin of the Council for Research in Music Education, 141*, 129-134.

Parks, A., & Schueller, S. (2014). *The Wiley Blackwell handbook of positive psychological interventions*. Wiley Blackwell.

Read, H. (1955). Education through art—A revolutionary policy. *Art Education, 8*(7), 3-17.

Rudd, E. (2009). Music and the quality of life. *Nordisk Tidsskrift for Musikkterapi, 6*(2), 86-97.

Seligman, M. (2018). PERMA and the building blocks of well-being. *The Journal of Positive Psychology, 13*(4), 333-335.

Seligman, M. E., Ernst, R. M., Gillham, J., Reivich, K., & Linkins, M. (2009). Positive education: Positive psychology and classroom interventions. *Oxford Review of Education, 35*(3), 293-311.

Sin, N., & Lyubomirsky, S. (2009). Enhancing well-being and alleviating depressive symptoms with positive psychology interventions: A practice-friendly meta-analysis. *Journal of Clinical Psychology, 65*(5), 467-487. https://doi.org/10.1002/jclp.20593

Soliveres, R., Giraldez-Hayes, A., & Parejo, J. L. (2021). Opera in primary education for the development of social and emotional skills: A case study from Mexico City. *British Journal of Music Education, 38*(3), 234-248. https://doi.org/10.1017/S0265051721000103

Southgate, D. E., & Roscigno, V. J. (2009). The impact of music on childhood and adolescent achievement. *Social Science Quarterly, 90*(1), 4-21.

Stacey, G., & Stickley, T. (2010). The meaning of art to people who use mental health services. *Perspectives in Public Health, 130*, 70-77.

Steger, M. F., et al. (2014). Through the windows of the soul: A pilot study using photography to enhance meaning in life. *Journal of Contextual Behavioral Science, 3*(1), 27–30.

Tate. (2017). Community art, art term. *Tate.* https://www.tate.org.uk/art/art-terms/c/community-art

The Kennedy Center. (1990–2021). What is arts integration? Explore the Kennedy Center's comprehensive definition. *The Kennedy Center.* https://www.kennedy-center.org/education/resources-for-educators/classroom-resources/articles-and-how-tos/articles/collections/arts-integration-resources/what-is-arts-integration

Upitis, R. (2011). *Arts education for the development of the whole child.* Elementary Teachers' Federation of Ontario.

Wilkinson, R. A., & Chilton, G. (2013). Positive art therapy: Linking positive psychology to art therapy theory, practice, and research. *Art Therapy, 30*(1), 4–11.

13 Music, technology, and well-being

Evangelos Himonides

This chapter suggests that the arts - particularly music - often in tandem with technology, can foster greater development and a more positive lifelong learning experience. Different examples illustrate the fundamental role that music plays in our lives and echo the importance of fostering musical development, engagement, and praxis throughout the lifespan.

Introduction

Music is generally accepted as a universal human phenomenon; some would even argue, a solely human phenomenon and the very celebration of humanity. We have access to robust scientific evidence suggesting that humans were purposely making sophisticated instruments with the intent to make and/or perform music about 50,000 years ago (e.g. the Aurignacian period flute). One could safely assume that we were using our voices as instruments and also use primitive percussion instruments way before we were making flutes (Himonides, 2019). Some scholars go as far as to argue that music precedes language (Mithen, 2007), and that it is our very innate musicality that was catalytic to the development of early languages. Empirical musicologist Adam Ockelford (Perkins & Service, 2013) very graphically argues:

> ... no, I think music is part of being human. There's no such thing as an unmusical human being. And music is a sort of social glue that holds us all together right from the very early stages mums and babies bond critical pieces of music like a gurgles in fact they grasp the tunes before the words if you listen to a baby as they start to sing a nursery rhyme, you'll get the contour of the melody before the words are properly formed. So you've already got this sort of clothesline of music, on which the pegs of words are strung later on.

There are different arguments about music's evolutionary functions and why music has become important; mate selection is one of these. There is also recently published evidence about how music is used in attracting people of the opposite sex. Music has been found to play a major role in the process of mating but also social cohesion, group effort (e.g. like

DOI: 10.4324/9781003228158-17

working together in time, going to battle, engaging in sports, and physical challenges). Music plays an important role in sexual development, motor scale, conflict reduction, where hopefully people will through music, fight less, and save time passing, which means that if you're sharing time with other human beings, with music, you won't be doing something else which might be dangerous. It is therefore somewhat sensible to infer the congenital relationship between music and well-being and, furthermore, the pursuit of happiness. Consequently, it is perhaps natural to see how music interweaves with the core principles of the somewhat young field of positive psychology.

Background

It is very interesting to witness modern-day ethe and attitudes towards the understanding of whether there is value, meaning, 'effectiveness', necessity, purpose, usefulness, scope, and reason for engaging in specific activities. One could hypothesise that much policy, research, funding, and political discourse are driven by the new revolution of metrics and 'robust' evidence. This, on the surface, sounds like a very noble – if not necessary – standpoint, but it harbours dangers and can lead to confusion and disastrous decision-making. How can this be? Like with many approaches and enquiry, the methodological approach is key. Therefore, 'how' we ask a question, 'what questions we ask', and 'what is our analytical approach' in answering those are of vital importance. Music and the arts in general, even though perhaps the most universal phenomena of humanity, have not been able to escape this pitfall. A number of studies have sprouted over the last decade, claiming to have employed 'systematic' approaches, concluding that music has no positive impact on health and well-being. To some, this reverse engineered approach in trying to gauge the effectiveness of something that is an integral part of humanity itself is simply unnecessary; to others, perhaps it is frivolous. If music was not important, it would have become a vestige and followed an evolutionary path towards extinction. So even if this author is known to be a passionate supporter of the need for musicians and music enthusiasts to stop being apologetic for their love and dedication to music, and equally passionate for people under the overarching field to stop feeling obliged to advocate for music because of its other-than-musical benefits (i.e. instead of the fulfilment, joy, satisfaction, eudemonia, and pleasure in musicking), it would be important to celebrate the immense power of music holistically, in the fashion of a summary of key points raised by Susan Hallam (2015) and augmented by Hallam and Himonides (2022).

Most importantly, we shall try to stress the importance of what music *can* do, not what music *will* do. This distinction might appear to be confusing, but it is actually crucial in helping us become liberated from the tyranny of causality and move towards positive potential, opportunity, flexibility, and freedom. Causality in itself is almost certainly not 'tyrannical'; quite contrarily so, it is absolutely vital to pursue causal pathways in many aspects of life and enquiry, often to protect ourselves and loved ones, and to stay alive. Challenges, though, exist when we try to do this with everything, especially when that is complex, context-specific, dynamic, ever evolving, and as unique as every single human being that lives and has ever lived! Interestingly, this discourse about what music *can* do versus what music *will* do can be interwoven with and supported by the evolution of the notion of *well-being*. Research in health and well-being has usually been centred on either jeopardy (i.e. when health and well-being are under threat) or pathology (i.e. when health and well-being had already been affected). This naturally led to the need for conducting intervention-type research in order to explore how these pathologies could be cured, reversed, or rectified. This is the mainstream way in which we conduct medical research.

With the development of modern society, the continual increase of socio-economic status globally, the increase in wealth, health, access to education, and sense of life satisfaction and well-being, we started augmenting our scope of enquiry and began looking at health and well-being in a more holistic way. We started looking at comfort, health, and happiness as part of everyday life and no longer as variables 'of problem' inside a researcher's lab. This has naturally introduced the need for employing different methodological approaches, often highly qualitative, human-centric, and often focusing on making sense of discourse and reported lived experiences. Unfortunately, policymakers, politicians, and funding bodies continue to require 'hard evidence' in order to support societal and educational initiatives and, even more unfortunately, 'hard evidence' is often misunderstood or misinterpreted as evidence that comes from research that followed very specific methodological and analytical frameworks, mainly the paradigm of randomised controlled trials (RCTs), which are the golden standard of research in medicine and related fields. Furthermore, in order for advocates for music and the arts to engage with 'the game' of hard evidence mining and provision, they have conducted and/or participated in research that tried to employ components from the medical research paradigm. This has led to a number of studies that introduced independent variables such as "musician" and "non musician"; "musical" and "amusic"; "formally trained" and "informally educated" and, even more worryingly, interventions that were presented or treated as deterministic, such as "received tuition"; "engaged with music technology"; "participated in choral singing"; "played in a djembe drum circle"; "used the iPad"; "collaborated online". One might wonder, how do we classify someone as *non musician?*, or even who is an *actual musician?*, how do we measure the levels of musicianship?, can somebody be exclusively formally trained?, what happens to that very person after they've watched *n* videos on YouTube? Similarly, we might have some questions about whatever was presented as the actual intervention: is the offering of *x* number of hours of lessons on subject/topic *y* for *z* number of sessions a compiled, deterministic, standardised, and identical experience for all students that participated? To a scientist in a laboratory, it often appears to be; to any person that has ever taught in their lives, the answer is likely to be a very passionate *no*, if they decide to take the question seriously. There are simply too many confounding factors at play and it is fairly impossible to look at direct impact of music on a specific outcome. Consequently, if someone wanted to assess education, learning, and development by distilling findings from enquiry that employed foreign (i.e. non fit-for-purpose) methodological approaches, they would probably lead themselves to misunderstanding, confusion, and misconception. What if, for example, we wanted to measure the effectiveness of a COVID-19 new vaccine by interviewing people? What if we wanted to do the same thing by observing them in the street? Both are valid methodological approaches; they are just not appropriate for what we aim to research.

Gladly, the majority of people that understand education, learning, and development are also conducting appropriately designed research and are sensitised in their analyses of the datasets and the interpretation of their findings.

In assessing the evidence-base in a more inclusive way, Hallam and Himonides (2022) present the following summary of findings regarding the power of music:

Music *can* have a positive impact on many different areas in our lives. In a social context, music *can* play a major role in fostering cohesion (but it can also be catalytic in conflict). It *can* support cohesion within subgroups, while at the same time, it can be used for intensifying bias against other groups.

For the individual, music *can*:

- promote aural perception, leading to enhanced language and literacy skills;
- support the development of spatial reasoning and subsequently some elements of mathematics;
- support memory functions, executive functioning, intellectual development, creativity, and academic attainment;
- enhance the performance of fine and gross motor skills; and
- support personal and social development.

It can have a positive impact on well-being, although in some circumstances, the impact can be negative. Finally, music can support physical and mental health, particularly when used in conjunction with other treatments.

Practice

The power of music is celebrated hereafter in two quite diverse 'vignettes' with which this author has had the opportunity to be involved. They are presented here as a reminder of how important music and musicking are, both at a societal, but also at a personal level.

Safeguarding Afghan musical heritage

It is often said that the first thing that a totalitarian regime, dictatorship, or autocracy do the moment they assume power is to try to control (or even completely ban) the arts, and particularly music. Regretfully, a somewhat 'milder' manifestation of this is also evident in democratic countries that are governed by deeply conservative and right-wing ideologies, with the ostracisation of Arts subjects in education and the reduction of funding throughout the artistic sectors.

Such an unfortunate example is that of the rich musical heritage of Afghanistan. Since the 1978 coup d'etat and the assumption of power by the Taliban, music was targeted and banned. Ethnomusicologist John Baily, a scholar who has dedicated his professional life in studying Afghan music says:

… it has been impossible for anyone to do the kind of research we did–freely attending and recording musical events like outdoor picnics, weddings and concerts. In any case, public music-making on that scale closed down. Even after the fall of the Taliban regime in 2001, the status of music remained highly contested.

In 2012, this author developed a free online resource (accessible openly at https://oart.eu) that aimed to offer information about the Rubab, the national musical instrument of Afghanistan.

The technology introduces visitors to the Rubab's tuning and playing, using notation, audio recordings, photographic material, and a large number of multi-angle instructional videos that feature John Baily himself playing the Rubab. Since its launch, and at the time of writing, the Online Afghan Rubab Tutor (OART) has received over three 3 million visits. What is very powerful, though, is that although there is a very good number of visits from the Afghan diaspora and enthusiasts around the world, the majority of interactions and the majority of comments and e-reactions to the video content originated from within Afghanistan. There are numerous messages of gratitude and appreciation, often prayers, from Afghan people offering thanks for teaching them and safeguarding their musics. It is very disheartening to see all the hard work that has been conducted since 2001, particularly that within the Afghanistan National Institute of Music (ANIM), founded and directed by Dr Ahmad Sarmast, being demolished within one week of the Taliban resuming power in the summer of 2021. ANIM was annexed; musical instruments were destroyed; music was banned, once again. Technology, though, continues to play a crucial role in safeguarding the cultural heritage of Afghanistan. OART and numerous other resources shall remain unsilenced, regardless of the daily attacks that they receive. The opening paragraph of the OART leads to a powerful verse from Maulana Jalaluddin Rumi:

> Do you know what the voice of the rubab is saying?
> "Come follow in my steps and find the way;
> Since through error you'll discover what's right,
> Since through questions you'll end up with answers."

Singing without a voice box

In the numerous decades of this author's professional involvement with music, no other para-digm of the power of participating in group musical activity comes close to that of the world's first alaryngeal choir, founded and supported by the British charity Shout at Cancer. Laryn-gectomy is the surgical procedure of the complete removal of the laryngeal assembly (aka the voice box). This is predominantly performed onto individuals in advanced stages of throat cancer. This is a highly invasive procedure that results in massive anatomical and functional changes in the body. After laryngectomy, patients no longer breathe from the mouth and nose, but through an opening in the neck. Patients' mouths become directly connected to their gullet and stomach. With the removal of the laryngeal assembly, which also includes the vocal folds (formerly known as vocal cords), patients lose their ability to 'phonate' (i.e. pro-duce a voice) normally and have to spend a long time in copious rehabilitation and training in order to develop new ways of communicating. There are four main ways with which this can be achieved but, currently, what is considered to be the norm is 'tracheoesophageal speech', where a surgical puncture allows the placement of a replaceable unidirectional valve that diverts air from the trachea into the esophagus. By blocking the external stoma (i.e. the hole) and applying pressure that has been measured to between seven and eight times the amount of pressure that is required for normal phonation, laryngectomees learn to divert air to the installed unidirectional valve towards their newly developed pharynx and introduce vibrations that can be articulated as sounds. These sounds are the laryngectomees' "new voice". This new alaryngeal voice is quite variable amongst individuals, has a limited frequency range, and is of much less energy and more limited range, compared to what we call a normal voice. This, on top of the actual trauma, agony, pain, and discomfort that the operation and consecutive treatments have on the laryngectomee, introduces an incredibly challenging new reality where individuals have to develop a new identity through this new instrument for communication. One simply has to think of the general aversion that most of us have to hearing our own recorded voice… Imagine hearing a completely different voice…; a different and also quite 'abnormal' one. Now imagine trying to use this voice in order to perform basic, everyday, tasks, like call somebody on the phone, ask for something over the counter in a pharmacy, perhaps report a stolen credit card to your bank. It is possible that we walk past and/or interact with numerous people that suffer all kinds of ailments daily, and outside our awareness. Laryngectomees cannot 'hide'… the moment they wish to perform one of the most basic human functions – to communicate – curious heads start to turn. This is perhaps one of the reasons why incidents of depression and social isolation are particularly frequent within throat cancer patients. The charity Shout at Cancer was founded in 2015, by medical doctor Thomas Moors. Dr Moors aspired to develop activities and interventions that would help throat cancer patients to deal with rehabilitation past laryngectomy and to regain confidence in finding their 'new voice'. One of the numerous things that he'd achieved is the creation of the world's first alaryngeal choir; a choir of people without voice boxes. Few examples could be more powerful than that of a group of people without voice boxes who still wish to sing and, furthermore, perform in front of audiences. The choir comprises people with different backgrounds, a small number used to be professional musicians, some used to love participating in musical activities, and some had never done so; singing as laryngectomees was their first ever performing experience. The choir has engaged in different projects, with different artistic directions: some performances involved jazz and poetry, some involved classical music, some festive music, some even involved beatboxing (Moors et al., 2020). The alaryngeal choir members have been reporting their experiences and offering feedback continually. Overwhelmingly, the feedback has been positive; but not always… Music *can* cause this!

Sara, an active member of the Shout at Cancer choir testifies:

> *I used to love to sing, and I never thought it would be possible, but I did sing We Are The Champions by Queen in front of them all…*

Another choir member says:

> *From having NO VOICE, just silent cries, I now speak again and sing in a choir.*

In 2021, Shout at Cancer received *The Queen's Award for Voluntary Service; this* is the highest award given to volunteer groups across the United Kingdom.

Sounds of Iintent

A final example of the powerful synergy of music and technology in fostering the development of children and young people with complex needs is the *Sounds of Intent* project (https://soundsofintent.org). The Sounds of Intent research project was set up in 2002 jointly by the Institute of Education (now UCL Institute of Education), Roehampton University, and the Royal National Institute of the Blind. The research team had developed a framework of musical development that covers the whole range of ability from profound and multiple learning difficulties (PMLD) to those with autism, with or without exceptional musical abilities (so-called savants). This framework led to the development, by this author, of the world's first and still the only free online portal that allows parents, carers, and practitioners to access valuable resources for supporting their pupils. The online resource, launched officially in 2012, is freely available to anyone who wishes to use it, and works on all platforms, though it is particularly well suited to touchscreen technology, such as tablets and smartphones. The software enables ideas for promoting children's engagement with music to be viewed and downloaded, and for individual children to be assessed.

Teachers, therapists, other practitioners, and parents can register to assess their children's development online. Assessments can be made as a one-off or over a period of time. The results can be printed out as numbers or in graphical form. This unique resource is not just helping registered practitioners; all of the available audio-visual materials, assessment guidelines, musical materials, and other information are openly available to teachers, carers, and practitioners without the need for registration. Since its launch in 2012 and to the time of writing, the Sounds of Intent portal has received over 12 million visits and different resources have been downloaded in excess of 4 million times. Nearly 8,000 individual pupils are being assessed formally on the site, by nearly 900 registered practitioners, representing approximately 400 schools around the world. Sounds of intent is not just a remarkable exemplar of how technology can support the musical development and well-being of people in need; it is also perhaps one of the very few examples, globally, where research and practice within the bodymind diverse world (e.g. profound and multiple learning difficulties-PMLD; severe learning difficulties-SLD; moderate learning difficulties-MLD, under the general umbrella of special educational needs and disability) is informing mainstream practice (Himonides et al., 2017). Since the establishment of Sounds of Intent, there has been a successful launch of Sounds of Intent in the Early Years (https://eysoi.org) and the possibility of adopting the original framework for use in research and practice within the later years is currently being researched by colleagues in Canada (Professor Andrea Creech's work called Creative Later Years).

Epilogue

It is somewhat of an impossible task to unpack the power of music within such a short body of text. Nevertheless, it is hoped that the rehearsed summary of evidence, in tandem with the diverse vignettes, succeeded in offering a brief celebration and can perhaps support the argument for a continued – and inclusive – dialogue about music's role in health and well-being throughout the lifespan. It comes as relatively surprising that this discourse is quite sparse within positive psychology nomenclature. The role of technology is also an important part of this discourse. Technology has so much to offer outside of the stereotypical perception as a sterile 'tool'. The global pandemic has led to some claiming a 'paradigm shift'. This author is not particularly convinced that the paradigm has 'shifted'; it seems that life during the pandemic has 'amplified' the role of technology, be it to keep learning going, to keep us in contact with loved ones, to share video clips on social media of people singing from their balconies in Italy, to the sprouting of countless virtual choirs, to sharing the guitar licks of astronauts in space, in order to uphold morale. The technological humanity and the musical humanity have been in tandem from the beginning. So, perhaps it doesn't matter how many spoonfuls of music help the medicine go down... perhaps what matters is how important music is to humans and the preservation of their humanity.

Discussion points

1   The English Baccalaureate, or EBacc, excludes creative, artistic, and technical subjects from counting in school league tables. Do you think that this undermines creativity, and to what extent? What do you think is the impact of this onto future generations?
2   How does the "future classroom" look, in your opinion, and why so? What is the role of the arts, and music specifically, in that future classroom?
3   Can you think of other examples where the arts and music have been (or are being) controlled by totalitarian regimes? What parallels can be drawn between those?

Suggested resources

1   The Online Afghan Rubab Tutor (OART): https://oart.eu
2   Shout at Cancer: https://www.shoutatcancer.org
3   Sounds of Intent: https://soundsofintent.org
4   Inspire-Music: https://inspire-music.org
5   The Impact of Music on Human Development and Well-Being: https://www.frontiersin.org/research-topics/7467

References

Hallam, S. (2015). *The power of music: A research synthesis of the impact of actively making music on the intellectual, social and personal development of children and young people*. International Music Education Research Centre (iMerc) Press.

Hallam, S., & Himonides, E. (2022). *The power of music: An exploration of the evidence*. Open Book Publishers.

Himonides, E., Ockelford, A., & Vogiajolu, A. (2017). Technology, SEN and EY. In A. King, E. Himonides, & A. Ruthmann (Eds.), *The Routledge companion to music, technology, and education*. Routledge, Taylor & Francis Group.

Himonides, E. (2019). The misunderstanding of music-technology-education: A meta perspective. In G. E. McPherson & G. F. Welch (Eds.), *The Oxford handbook of music education*, Volume 2 (pp. 432–456). Oxford University Press. https://doi.org/10.1093/oxfordhb/9780199928019.013.0029_update_001

Mithen, S. (2007). *The singing Neanderthals: The origins of music, language, mind and body* Harvard University Press.

Moors, T., Silva, S., Maraschin, D., Young, D., Quinn, J. M., de Carpentier, J., Allouche, J., & Himonides, E. (2020). Using beatboxing for creative rehabilitation after laryngectomy: Experiences from a public engagement project. *Frontiers in Psychology, 10*, 2854. https://doi.org/10.3389/fpsyg.2019.02854

Perkins, S., & Service, T. (2013, February 18). The story of music question time. In *Music and the Brain*. BBC Radio 3. https://www.bbc.co.uk/programmes/b01qqfm8

14 Playing and thriving in school

Trudy Meehan

This chapter offers a brief case study of a Play Club where free play is given a space in the school day. Practice activities that encourage play, strengths, and a growth mindset are outlined, and educators are directed to valuable resources.

Introduction

Peter Gray (2011) advocates for more free play (freedom to explore, with trust but not structure from the adults). As we shall see in the following chapter, he is not alone in calling for more play opportunities. Play is where children learn that they are in control, can solve their problems, see other people's points of view, and experience joy, competency, and creativity. Gray states that play supports an internal locus of control, arguing that reduced internal locus of control sets children up to experience depression and anxiety in later life. Gray makes a case for a correlation between a decline in opportunities for free play and an increase in depression and anxiety in young people. It is difficult to experimentally test the hypothesis that a decrease in play will increase mental distress. However, the change in young people's mental health is theoretically congruent with a decrease in play opportunities.

In this chapter, we will assume Gray's (2009, 2013) definition of play as a self-directed activity chosen by the child; intrinsically motivated; guided by mental rules mostly implicit; recruits the imagination, and is conducted in an active but not stressed state of mind.

Schools, particularly those using a positive education framework, can play a pivotal role in providing space for free play in the lives of children.

Theoretical background

Theorists of play, regardless of their background, agree that play is central to children's social and emotional development and has importance in physical and cognitive development. One of the most common theories of play is the psychoanalytic theory which sees play as a way for children to process complex emotional experiences and achieve emotional balance. Arousal theory proposes that children use play to modulate the levels of arousal in their

DOI: 10.4324/9781003228158-18

nervous system. Cognitive theorists of play argue that children's cognitive capacities develop in play through interaction, imagination, and recreation of events. Vygotsky and Bruner argue for a socio-constructivist theory of play whereby the child's development is scaffolded by the play interactions with sensitive adults and peers. Piaget argues that the child's cognitive development occurs independently of this scaffolding interaction. Postmodern theories of play have questioned the role of culture in understanding play and problematized earlier generalizing theories such as Piaget's work. They argue for a consideration of the interaction of the child and their cultural environment.

Experimental work in the psychoneurobiology of play from theorists and researchers like Panksepp (2007) and Brown (1998, 2009) has affirmed the essential role of play in the lives of children and adults. Panksepp's work (Panksepp, 2007; Scott & Panskepp, 2003; Panksepp et al., 1984) argues that play is one of seven essential human survival drives, including, seeking, rage, fear, lust, care, and panic. The function of play is to build pro-social brains that know how to interact with others in positive ways (Panksepp, 2008). We play to learn to be social, but we also play for the joy of playing as an activity in its own right. Stuart Brown (2009) documents the devastating impact of the lack of play during childhood. His work looks at the play histories of violent murders, and he argues that lack of play may be a predictor of the inability to inhibit or modify violent impulses. Both Brown and Panksepp and psychologist Peter Gray (2011) argue for the essential nature of play for our survival and well-being in mammals and humans, both children and adults.

> The PLAY affective system, aptly named by Panksepp, is more deeply rooted in the mammalian brain than many other higher-level processes. To thrive, however, play is a phenomenon that must be cultivated and harvested continuously, I believe, for the health and long-term survival of our species. Play is so deeply rooted in mammalian brain systems that it has been shown to be a fundamental drive, as are the drives for food, sleep and sex.
>
> (Brown & Eberle, 2017, pp. 47-48)

Play is essential for our ability to develop the skills for survival, social interaction, and flourishing.

Positive psychology describes elements of the experience of play (positive emotions, relationship, engagement, flow) but does not often deal directly with play. Csikszentmihalyi (2014) comes closest to understanding play in his description of flow, but he is careful to stress that while they share many features, "play is not synonymous with flow" (p. 137). However, we can link the work of Peter Grey with some key theorists in Positive Psychology to deepen our understanding of play in this positive context. Carol Dweck's work on Growth Mindsets (2012) tells us that children need to dare to fail to build resilience and for their brain development. Her work reveals that one's abilities are not fixed and that we can grow our brains with challenges. Growth Mindsets and play are related in important ways. Play encourages exploration and experimentation, requires failure and mistakes, makes them possible, and lowers the stakes. Free play allows for even more mistakes and fluidity.

Additionally, play is a way to develop a tolerance for fear, which is essential to be daring enough to take the challenges required for a Growth Mindset. Children learn how to experience risk, decide how much risk to take, and learn to tolerate fearful situations. The strengths work of Lea Waters (2017) tells us that we function best when we are working from our strengths. Children who can engage in free play will naturally gravitate to using their strengths in their exploration and play. Positive education argues that we need to educate for happiness and academic ability (Seligman et al., 2009). Positive education sees the value of playfulness as a positive emotion and the need to focus on flourishing, well-being, and resilience. If we draw on the work of Peter Gray, we can understand why play is central to many aspects of positive education and positive psychology.

Recently, the British Psychological Society (2021) has written a position paper called Time to Play where they argue for an increase in the amount of time for children to play in the school day. Similarly, in collaboration with American Association for the Child's Right to Play (IPA/USA) and the Alliance for Childhood, the US Play Coalition authored a 2019 position paper titled "A Research-Based Case for Recess". A 2019 report by Baines and Blatchford reviews the only systematically collected data on the timing of breaks in primary and secondary schools in the United Kingdom over 30 years. Their report documents between 65 minutes (for children aged 11-16) and 45 minutes (for children aged 5-7) less break time per week. The study also reports a notable decline in the amount of time children spend meeting up with friends in person outside of the school setting. Up to 47% of children in 2017 reported seeing their friends only at the weekend or less than once per week. The relevance of this finding is that it highlights the value of playtime in the school day in children's social lives.

If we are serious about positive education and human flourishing, we cannot ignore the essential role of play for both children and adults in the school setting. Given the general decline in free play for children in our society, the school holds fantastic promise as a place where more space can be made for free play. Research is starting to show that increasing time to play will improve well-being and overall student performance.

Practice

Play is firmly established as essential to learning for young children. We see this with the advances in play-based learning embedded in our Early Childhood Education Curriculums and our early primary curriculums. Despite this, we need to do more. We need to expand the time for play within the school day as recommended by Baines and Blatchford (2019) and campaigns in the United Kingdom and United States advocating for an increase in free playtime in the school day. Importantly, not only is play essential for children, but it is also essential and rewarding in the lives of adults, especially teachers. Current ongoing research investigates the value of play for teachers in schools (National Institute for Play, 2021). Researchers at the National Institute of Play argue the importance of providing teachers with space and the tools to play, stating that "play-based learning with playful teachers heightens overall long-term performance". What can we do in our school settings to support play?

Try this for educators and students

Clay model - inspired by the work of Lea Waters (2017)

Materials needed - piece of modelling clay

1   Make a clay model of yourself, include the whole body and head. Keep the activity time limited to 20 minutes to avoid perfectionism or a focus on getting it right.
2   Ask those who made the model (educators and students) to stop and look at their model and consider what they notice first.
3   Ask them if they noticed the mistakes and the bits that look wrong or out of proportion first or if they noticed the good bits first?
4   Most people notice the mistakes and bad bits first because of negativity bias. This is an opportunity to reflect on this cognitive habit of noticing the bad first. It highlights the importance of deliberately focusing on strengths and the good bits.
5   Discuss how parents/carers and teachers might also sometimes notice the bad things a student does before they notice the good things.

Learn to wince, instead of pounce - inspired by Julie Lythcott-Haims (2015)

Materials - none

1   When you notice students about to make a mistake or take a risk, avoid jumping in immediately.
2   The goal is to manage hazards but allow reasonable risk and the potential for failure and mistakes.
3   The educator needs to tolerate the discomfort of seeing the failure occur and avoid jumping in too early before the child has a chance to learn how the mistake happened.
4   "Allowing freedom within limits to try and fail and get better is the only way children (or anyone) will ever learn how to do things for themselves. Perfectionism is not only the enemy of the good; it is the enemy of adulthood" (Lythcott-Haims, 2015, p. 174).

Failure day - inspired by the work of Carol Dweck (2012)

Materials - anything you use to create rewards/certificates of reward for the students
    The goal of this day is to inspire a Growth Mindset by demystifying failure and making it a rewarding experience and also to model failure and tolerance of failure for our students.

1   Set up a day where the students get rewarded not for their successes but for their failures.
2   Have a reward system in place that is similar to the usual classroom rewards for success.
3   Have some phrases ready like "well done Sue I love how you nearly did x, you failed but you had to try to make it to the fail so let's celebrate that fail today"; "who will be the most daring to try to fail today? Oh look I failed right here I think I deserve a dare to fail reward"
4   Ensure you model failure as an educator and live the Grown Mindset path yourself!

Spaghetti marshmallow tower challenge – inspired by the work of Carol Dweck (2012)

The goal of this activity is to foster design thinking which supports a Growth Mindset. In design thinking, trial and error practice and the inevitable fails are important in accomplishing a task. The students are encouraged to practice design thinking principles of thinking, doing, protyping, and iteration.

Materials – Lots of sticks of dry spaghetti, balls of string, rolls of tape, and one large marshmallow per group.

1   Give supplies to each team (each team should have the materials needed to build a tower each).
2   Set time limit for building of 18 minutes.
3   Give the instruction, "build the tallest tower possible that will support the marshmallow, you have 18 minutes".
4   Set a timer for 18 minutes and allow the students to use their imagination and to fail many times and do not intervene with ideas or suggestions.
5   Verbally reward and encourage failure and iteration.
6   For more ideas on design thinking type playful tasks, visit https://tinkerlab.com/spaghetti-tower-marshmallow-challenge/

Laughter – inspired by the work of Panksepp (2007)

The goal of this activity is to encourage laughter in the classroom. Ultimately, childhood laughter and shrieking are indicators of the quality of natural play, an emotional process evident in humans (Scott & Panksepp, 2003) and certain other animals (Panksepp, 2007).

Materials – imagination and sense of humour

1   Decide on an activity that will bring laughter into the classroom.
2   Engage in the activity and allow the noise of the laughter to fill the room.
3   Example activities that can encourage laughter include: learning to juggle, students finding jokes; learning to beatbox. Learning a novel activity like Beatboxing provides opportunities for students to laugh at themselves and at their educators as the educators try and fail. Students will tend to be better at Beatboxing than educators so it can be a very playful and funny activity.
4   You can find Beatbox tutorials on YouTube that you can practice with your students.

Let it grow project – inspired by the work of Peter Gray (2009, 2011, 2013)

Materials – access to the internet to sign up at https://letgrow.org/program/the-let-grow-project/

The aim of this project is to encourage independence and resourcefulness in young people's lives.

1   Sign up for the project or modify the project to suit your school.
2   Look at the resources on the Let it Grow website to decide on a parent/carer information letter to go home before setting the homework.

3   Set your students homework "go home and do something new, on your own. Climb a tree, do a household job, make a meal...".

4   Build time into the school day to reflect on these homework tasks.

In schools where Play Club has been instituted (before the COVID-19 pandemic when mixing between children was possible), positive outcomes are reported. One of which is young people initiating playing together outside of the school day. There are reports that parents/carers and teachers learned a lot about the students' abilities to problem solve that surprised them and gave them confidence in allowing more free play and self-directed activities. Children are reported to be better at resolving conflict and there are some schools where children who were isolated because of bullying type behaviour were able to find friendships in the free play setting.

Case study - Play Club

The goal of Play Club is to encourage confidence, problem solving, social skills, creativity, and resourcefulness in young people. The aim is to provide students with an opportunity for free play where they can engage in self-directed activities.

   This intervention is focused on Primary School children (all classes, all ages). It requires one hour a week time commitment from the whole school. It is important to have buy-in from the Board of Management and the Principal of the school as well as from parents/carers and teachers. The task is to introduce one hour of free play into the school environment. There are a few key features of this hour of free play.

1)   It is free play: This means that it is self-directed and self-selected by the students. They can choose to be part of it or not and they get to design and direct the type of play.

2)   Low-level adult intervention: Since it is free play, it needs to be child led and to have adults take a background role. The role of the adults is to provide the space and to remove any obvious hazards and to only intervene when there is a clear need based on the assessment of the danger.

3)   All ages: Children of all ages and from all classes play and are allowed to play together and mix age cohorts.

4) Limited by clear rules: The rule for educators is "do not intervene unless there are clear hazards". The rules for the students are "do not deliberately hit or physically hurt another child"; "get permission to leave the grounds"; and "listen to the adults who will intervene only when they must".

5)   Equipment: Some loose items can help inspire creativity and play. Things like hula hoops, old household objects/toys; tires, tree branches, traffic cones, boxes, blankets/sheets.

6)   Communication: Communication with parents and carers is important so that they understand the reasons for and the activity of play club.

7)   Resources - for full details of how to implement Play Club in your school, log onto https://letgrow.org/program/play-club/

Discussion points

1 Play is conducted in an alert, active, but relatively non-stressed frame of mind.
2 What tasks do children need to accomplish in order to successfully maintain a relatively non-stressed frame of mind while playing?
3 What institutional practices and policies stand in the way of play in the lives of students and educators?
4 What key points from this chapter would you like parents and carers to know and what difference would it make to your educational practice if parents and carers knew this information?

Suggested resources

https://www.gov.ie/en/campaigns/lets-play-ireland/

National Government of Ireland campaign to remind children and adults of the value of play. It suggests resources for play during the Covid-19 pandemic. http://www.nifplay.org/

National Institute of Play an NGO dedicated to the science of human play

https://tinkerlab.com/

Provides online resources for activities that encourage free play, creativity and design thinking.

https://letgrow.org/

An online resource and project that you can sign up to that encourages independence, exploration and resourcefulness in young people.

https://www.youtube.com/watch?v=hrw68eID4Zk

Stuart Brown on The Neuroscience of Play

https://www.youtube.com/watch?v=Bg-GEzM7iTk

Peter Gray on The Decline of Play

https://files.eric.ed.gov/fulltext/EJ985541.pdf

Gray, P. (2011). The decline of play and the rise of psychopathology in children and adolescents. *American Journal of Play, 3*(4), 443–463.

https://usplaycoalition.org/partnersforplay

US Play Coalition website that is a platform for sharing resources on the value of play.

References

Baines, E., & Blatchford, P. (2019). *School break and lunch times and young people's social lives: A follow-up national study.* Nuffield Foundation. https://www.nuffieldfoundation.org/wp-content/uploads/2019/11/Baines204240220BreaktimeSurvey20-20Main20public20report20May19-Final1.pdf

British Psychological Society. (2021). *Time to play: Position paper and call for ten minutes more play time in the school day for all students.* https://www.bps.org.uk/time-to-play

Brown, S. (1998). Play as an organizing principle: Clinical evidence and personal observations. In M. Bekoff & J. A. Beyer (Eds.), *Animal play: Evolutionary, comparative, and ecological perspectives* (pp. 242–251). Cambridge University Press.

Brown, S. L. (2009). *Play: How it shapes the brain, opens the imagination, and invigorates the soul.* Penguin.

Brown, S., & Eberle, M. (2017). A closer look at play. In T. Marks-Tarlow, M. Solomon, & D. J. Siegel (Eds.), *Play and creativity in psychotherapy* (pp. 38–58). Norton.

Csíkszentmihályi, M. (2014). *Flow and the foundations of positive psychology. The collected works of Mihaly Csikszentmihalyi*. Springer.

Dweck, C. S. (2012). *Mindset*. Robinson.

Gray, P. (2009). Play as a foundation for hunter-gatherer social existence. *American Journal of Play, 1,* 476–522.

Gray, P. (2011). The decline of play and the rise of psychopathology in children and adolescents. *American Journal of Play, 3*(4), 443–463.

Gray, P. (2013). *Free to learn: Why unleashing the instinct to play will make our children happier, more self-reliant, and better prepared for life*. Basic Books.

Lythcott-Haims, J. (2015). *How to raise an adult*. Macmillan.

National Institute for Play. (2021). Ongoing research. http://www.nifplay.org/opportunities/education/

Panksepp J. (2007). Neuroevolutionary sources of laughter and social joy: Modelling primal human laughter in laboratory rats. *Behavioral Brain Research, 182*(2), 231–44. doi: 10.1016/j.bbr.2007.02.015

Panksepp, J. (2008). Play, ADHD, and the construction of the social brain: Should the first class each day be recess?. *American Journal of Play, 1*(1), 55–79.

Panksepp, J., Siviy, S., & Normansell, L. (1984). The psychobiology of play: Theoretical and methodological perspectives. *Neuroscience & Biobehavioral Reviews, 8*(4), 465–492.

Scott, E., & Panksepp, J. (2003). Rough-and-tumble play in human children. *Aggressive Behavior, 29,* 539–551. https://doi.org/10.1002/ab.10062

Seligman, M. E. P., Ernst, R. M., Gillham, J., Reivich, K., & Linkins, M. (2009). Positive education: Positive psychology and classroom interventions. *Oxford Review of Education, 35,* 293–311.

US Play Coalition in collaboration with American Association for the Child's Right to Play (IPA/USA) and the Alliance for Childhood. (2019). *A research-based case for recess: Position paper*. https://usplaycoalition.org/wp-content/uploads/2019/08/Need-for-Recess-2019-FINAL-for-web.pdf

Waters, L. (2017). *The strengths switch: How the new science of strength based parenting can help your child and your teen to flourish*. Avery Publishing Group.

15 Well-being lexicon in schools

Tim Lomas

Language has a powerful influence on how people perceive, experience, and understand the world. One way to influence outcomes like well-being is to help people refine and enrich their conceptual tool kit, such as providing a more detailed lexicon for them to process and understand their emotions. A potentially new avenue of exploration involves engaging with the intriguing phenomenon of untranslatable words.

Introduction

At its best, education helps people develop and flourish in all aspects of life, not only intellectually, but psychologically, socially, even spiritually. In that respect, a key area of development is around emotions, as reflected in paradigms such as Social and Emotional Learning (Weissberg et al., 2015). Such learning can take many forms, but among the most prominent is the cultivation of emotional granularity (EG) - sometimes also called emotional differentiation - which describes the "ability to make fine-grained, nuanced distinctions between similar emotions" (Smidt & Suvak, 2015, p. 48). Crucially, this capacity is not merely a fixed trait, but a skill amenable to training (Kashdan et al., 2015).

Indeed, school interventions have been developed to help children cultivate EG, expanding their knowledge and use of emotion words (Brackett et al., 2012). Such learning is not only valuable for its own sake (i.e., teaching children about emotions) but is associated with a host of beneficial outcomes, such as improved well-being, behaviour, and academic performance (Lennarz et al., 2018). It has been argued, for instance, that EG training helps people better identity, understand, and regulate their emotions, which in turn facilitates these kinds of positive outcomes (Fogarty et al., 2015). In that respect, this chapter offers an intriguing and novel possibility for further enhancing EG, namely by engaging with 'untranslatable' words from other cultures.

Theoretical background

The central thesis of this chapter is that untranslatable words have the potential to promote social and emotional learning and to enhance students' development more generally.

DOI: 10.4324/9781003228158-19

At present, this is merely a hypothesis: to my knowledge, it has not yet been explored empirically. However, it is supported by a good deal of relevant research and theorizing, as I've reviewed in detail elsewhere (Lomas, 2018a, 2018c, 2021b). The relevant work spans a wide range of topics and disciplines, which are beyond our scope to consider here, so I shall just briefly mention three areas of literature that are particularly salient: emotional granularity, linguistic relativity, and untranslatability.

The idea of EG is associated in particular with Lisa Feldman Barrett (2006). Her conceptual-act model skilfully interweaves what until recently have been the two main perspectives on emotions in the literature: naturalistic and constructivist. The former tends to regard emotions in an essentialist way as 'natural kinds' (i.e., universal affective responses): Russell's (1980) circumplex model, for instance, positions affective states as the product of two independent neurophysiological systems, valence (pleasant vs. unpleasant) and arousal (active vs. passive); relatedly, the basic emotions paradigm associated with Ekman (2016) holds that all people experience six basic emotions (anger, disgust, fear, sadness, surprise, and enjoyment). By contrast, constructivist theories suggest that emotions are not universally available inner states but are products of social interaction and of the broader cultural context in which this interaction occurs (Harré, 1986).

Intriguingly though, Barrett's model manages to incorporate insights from both perspectives. As per naturalistic theories, she proposes that humans experience momentary states of 'core affect' that may be relatively universal. However, the interpretation and conceptualisation of such states depend on people's linguistic-conceptual schemas, which thus incorporates the kind of insights found in constructivist theorising. A similar dynamic is found in Matsumoto and Hwang's (2012) notion of culturally driven emotion regulation: this proposed that humans inherit "a set of biologically innate emotions that are produced by a core emotion system", but how these emotions are felt, interpreted, and reacted to is culturally "calibrated" (p. 92). Thus, in these models, people's culture and language play significant roles in their experience and understanding of emotions.

This latter point links to the second main area of work relevant here, the linguistic relativity hypothesis (LRH), also known as the Sapir-Whorf Hypothesis, acknowledging the theorists most closely linked to this idea, the anthropologists Sapir (1929) *and* Whorf (1940). Essentially, the LHR is an all-encompassing label for the contention that culture, via language, shapes people's psychological processes and experiences. This vision was summarised by Whorf: "We dissect nature along lines laid out by our native languages... The world is presented as a kaleidoscopic flux of impressions which has to be organized... largely by the linguistic systems in our minds" (pp. 213-214). In the decades since, a wealth of research has corroborated these insights, although there are of course significant ongoing debates (for instance, around the extent to which language influences our experience).

Among this literature is work pertaining to emotions, which is of course relevant to theories like Barrett's (2006) conceptual-act model. From the perspective of the LRH, people's experience and conceptualisation of emotions are strongly shaped by their cultural context, mediated and influenced in particular by their language. Indeed, work in this area suggests that certain emotional states may only be experienced by people from particular cultures – depending on factors such as their values, norms, and traditions – as for instance reflected in research into 'culture-bound' psychiatric illnesses (Simons & Hughes, 2012). Conversely, other anthropological research has focused on the way some seemingly common emotions appear to not be widely experienced in certain cultures, or might be felt and interpreted in ways that diverge from their manifestations in Western contexts (Beatty, 2013).

A particularly interesting and generative way into considering cross-cultural differences in emotions is through our third main area of literature: untranslatable words. While untranslatability is a contested phenomenon, it commonly refers to a word that lacks an exact equivalent in one's own language. Essentially, then, such words can be seen as signifying phenomena which one's culture has overlooked or undervalued – perhaps because it is not common or salient enough to have been granted the distinction of having its own label – but which another culture has noticed, valued, and named. So, from the perspective of the LRH, the value of such words is manifold.

To begin with, they can assist us in understanding other cultures, offering insights into their values, traditions, and ways of being (Wierzbicka, 1989). Then, beyond being informative vis-à-vis the culture that created a given word, they enrich other lexica. Indeed, cultures 'borrowing' words are central to language development, and of the more than 600,000 lexemes in the Oxford English Dictionary, the percentage of such loanwords is estimated to be as high as 41% (Tadmor, 2009). One of the main reasons is to help fill a 'semantic gap' in the borrowing language, i.e., "the lack of a convenient word to express what [one] wants to speak about" (Lehrer, 1974, p. 105). Thus, words get borrowed if they allow people to articulate phenomena in ways that they struggled to with their existing lexicon.

Such considerations apply to all areas of life, including – most relevantly here – emotions. In that respect, over recent years, I have been engaged in an ongoing project to create a lexicography of untranslatable words pertaining to well-being, with a central aim of enriching our conceptual lexicon in this area (Lomas, 2016, 2018a, 2021b). Well-being scholarship has been critiqued as Western-centric, as has psychology more generally, with much of its work involving scholars and participants described by Henrich et al. (2010) as WEIRD (belonging to societies that are Western, Educated, Industrialised, Rich, and Democratic). Thus, a central premise of my project is that untranslatable words can enrich the nomological network in psychology (and English more broadly). Indeed, such words already have enhanced the field, including loanwords from languages such as Greek (e.g., psyche), Latin (e.g., id), and German (e.g., Gestalt).

So far, I have collected over 1,800 words from over 150 languages. My approach has been to analyse these thematically using an adapted form of Grounded Theory (a qualitative methodology which allows theory to emerge inductively from data). In that respect, I have currently identified 12 main thematic categories, each of which comprises numerous themes and subthemes, and have so far published analyses focusing on eight of these. The categories themselves can be further aggregated into three meta-categories. The first meta-category is qualia, encompassing positive feelings (Lomas, 2017a), ambivalent feelings (Lomas, 2017b), cognition, and embodiment. The second is relationships, featuring love (Lomas, 2018b), prosociality (Lomas, 2021a), eco-connection (Lomas, 2019b), and aesthetics (Lomas, 2022). And the third is personal development, including character (Lomas, 2019c), spirituality (Lomas, 2019a), competence, and understanding. I believe that these analyses can help expand our conception and understanding of well-being, and – most relevantly here – potentially increase people's EG, as the next section elucidates.

Practice

Given the discussion above, I would suggest that untranslatable words have significant potential for enriching learning. This includes, most prominently, social and emotional learning, and in particular, enhancing EG. Beyond that, they have the potential to expand students' horizons in other ways, such as fostering their awareness, appreciation, and understanding of other cultures. This latter potential is particularly valuable in terms of recent moves towards encouraging diversity and inclusion in the classroom, particularly in the context of multicultural societies (Bartz & Bartz, 2018), and relatedly in discussions around 'decolonising' the curriculum, aiming to make learning less Western-centric and more inclusive of other cultural perspectives (Meighan, 2019).

However, despite the potential value of untranslatable words in relation to these interlinked goals, there appear to be few published studies attesting to their use. Of the handful I could locate, these tend to be just in the context of language education specifically. Metcalf (1998), for instance, discusses their value in the context of German language classes, while Ardi (2012) mentions their role in building language students' translation competencies. Relatedly, in terms of educating teachers themselves, Lovtsevich (2005) and Sarigul and Ashton-Hay (2005) articulate the value of such words in raising cultural awareness in the context of language teaching. However, more recently, Loinaz (2019) suggested they could play a role in social and educational learning, particularly in exploring cross-cultural differences around which specific social and emotional skills are likely to be valued or promoted in a given pedagogical setting. In that spirit, here are some other suggestions for engaging with untranslatable words in the classroom. These can be grouped into two main types of activities: identifying words; engaging with words.

"Try this" for educators

I would encourage teachers to *themselves* engage in the activities that I suggest for students (outlined below). I particularly recommend the first type of activity (identifying relevant words), but educators might also get value from engaging in the second type of activity (engaging proactively with words). Furthermore, while such activities would be productive even if done independently, I would also encourage the educator to share their *own* learning journey with the class (e.g., talking about words that are meaningful to them). Besides offering a good role model for this kind of engagement, it also allows opportunities for bonding and connection between the educator and their students.

"Try this" for students

The first type of activity involves students identifying or encountering relevant words, which is the precondition for the second type of activity below. The simplest option for this first type could just involve students perusing my lexicography (www.drtimlomas.com/lexicography). They could be guided to do so in various ways, including selecting words that the student: (a) just finds interesting for some reason; (b) has actually experienced in some way; (c) have not experienced but would like to; or (d) have not experienced and would not like to. Alternatively, though, if possible, students could be invited to share their own words, which would likely be a more engaging and enriching experience. Many classes will be multicultural, featuring students from diverse backgrounds and speaking a range of languages. As such, in the spirit of encouraging diversity and inclusion, students could be invited to introduce words and ideas from their own culture and language to the class.

Such words could specifically pertain to emotions – and so may potentially help students to cultivate EG, as per the hypothesis of this chapter – or alternatively could relate to anything at all, if one wanted a broader focus. In setting instructions and guidance for these tasks, it will be important to calibrate these according to students' capacities. Older students may potentially be able to grasp the notion of untranslatability, and so could be invited to share words they (or other people) deem to be untranslatable. The concept may be trickier for younger students, who could simply be invited – if they speak a language other than English – to share relevant words, regardless of whether these are untranslatable. Some students may only speak English, of course, and may not have another language to draw on. In such cases, these students could be invited to share instances of dialect or terminology that might not be widely used in English but which are meaningful to the student and their family or friends. Such exercises would then create a list of relevant words which can then be used in the second type of activity.

This second type features activities to encourage students to actually engage productively with words that resonate with them. One could harness various creative approaches to this end. In each case, students could be asked to pick a favourite word, one that especially resonated with them for some reason. They could then explore this resonance or appeal in myriad ways, with the details depending of course on their age and competencies. In terms of visual arts, they could draw or paint a picture to capture the meaning of the word and its personal significance to them, with this activity potentially amenable to students of all ages. In a musical context, students could be asked to write a piece of music or even just a simple melody that likewise expresses the word's meaning and appeal, or – if that is beyond their capacities – just to choose a song they already know that captures its sense. Similarly, they could harness movement and posture to create a dance sequence, or even just a simple gesture, that embodies it.

Moving into a discursive space, there are many potential activities to help students explore the meaning of words and their connection to them. Students could be invited to write a short fiction story centred around the word in some way; alternatively, the story could be non-fiction and focus on actual events and experiences in their lives. Similarly, they could write a poem that expresses the nature and qualities of the word and brings it poetically to life. Some activities could be even more involved and harness forms of experiential learning. In that respect, for instance, students could be invited to spend some short period of time (e.g., a week) reflecting on the word, and being open to how it manifests or appears in their lives during that time, and to keep a journal in relation to this. Really, the possibilities are extensive, and engagement with such words could potentially be brought into almost any kind of classroom activity.

Discussion points

- As educators, perhaps reflect on how your own language shapes and limits your ability to conceptualise and articulate your emotions (and your experiences more broadly). Have you had feelings or sensations, for instance, that you've been unable to express for want of an appropriate word?

- Similarly, if you have students who speak other languages to yours, consider how these different linguistic backgrounds may impact your respective emotional and broader life experiences. What might such students be able to share with and teach you, based on their own particular cultural and linguistic expertise?
- Just as students may benefit from engaging in the activities suggested above, these might also enrich and deepen your own EG and expand your conceptual horizons. If inviting students to try the activities, you could also participate in them and explore your emotional and learning journey together with the students.

Suggested resources

- The lexicography itself, together with various papers, articles, and presentations, is publicly available at www.drtimlomas.com/lexicography.
- The Lost Words is another beautiful project on the value of language, which has been widely embraced in educational circles: https://www.thelostwords.org/lostwordsbook. It began as a book by Robert MacFarlane and Jackie Morris, exploring nature-related words from among the languages and dialects of the British Isles. It has since led to related projects, such as an album and various educational initiatives.
- John Koenig's Dictionary of Obscure Sorrows is a fascinating project, in which he creates neologisms to represent subtle states of mind – spanning all kinds of feelings – for which English lacks a word: https://www.dictionaryofobscuresorrows.com/. This may encourage students to be creative in inventing their own words.
- Paul Ekman's Atlas of Emotions is an interaction tool that allows people to explore and identify their emotions: http://atlasofemotions.org/. It is not about language per se, but in capturing a cartographic process of mapping experiential states is very much in keeping with the spirit of the lexicography.

References

Ardi, H. (2012). Is theory of translation needed to build students' translation competence? *International Conference on Languages and Arts*, 320–328.

Barrett, L. F. (2006). Are emotions natural kinds? *Perspectives on Psychological Science*, 1(1), 28–58.

Bartz, J., & Bartz, T. (2018). Recognizing and acknowledging worldview diversity in the inclusive classroom. *Education Sciences*, 8(4), 196.

Beatty, A. (2013). Current emotion research in anthropology: Reporting the field. *Emotion Review*, 5(4), 414–422.

Brackett, M. A., Rivers, S. E., Reyes, M. R., & Salovey, P. (2012). Enhancing academic performance and social and emotional competence with the RULER feeling words curriculum. *Learning and Individual Differences*, 22(2), 218–224.

Ekman, P. (2016). What scientists who study emotion agree about. *Perspectives on Psychological Science*, 11(1), 31–34.

Fogarty, F. A., Lu, L. M., Sollers, J. J., Krivoschekov, S. G., Booth, R. J., & Consedine, N. S. (2015). Why it pays to be mindful: Trait mindfulness predicts physiological recovery from emotional stress and greater differentiation among negative emotions. *Mindfulness*, 6(2), 175–185.

Harré, R. (1986). *The Social Construction of Emotions*. Oxford: Blackwell.

Henrich, J., Heine, S. J., & Norenzayan, A. (2010, July 1). Most people are not WEIRD. *Nature*, 466, 29.

Kashdan, T. B., Barrett, L. F., & McKnight, P. E. (2015). Unpacking emotion differentiation: Transforming unpleasant experience by perceiving distinctions in negativity. *Current Directions in Psychological Science*, 24(1), 10–16.

Lehrer, A. (1974). *Semantic Fields and Lexical Structures*. Amsterdam: North-Holland Publishing Co.

Lennarz, H. K., Lichtwarck-Aschoff, A., Timmerman, M. E., & Granic, I. (2018). Emotion differentiation and its relation with emotional well-being in adolescents. *Cognition and Emotion*, 32(3), 651–657.

Loinaz, E. S. (2019). Teachers' perceptions and practice of social and emotional education in Greece, Spain, Sweden and the United Kingdom. *International Journal of Emotional Education*, 11(1), 31-48.

Lomas, T. (2016). Towards a positive cross-cultural lexicography: Enriching our emotional landscape through 216 'untranslatable' words pertaining to well-being. *Journal of Positive Psychology*, 11(5), 546-558.

Lomas, T. (2017a). The spectrum of positive affect: A cross-cultural lexical analysis. *International Journal of Wellbeing*, 7(3), 1-18.

Lomas, T. (2017b). The value of ambivalent emotions: A cross-cultural lexical analysis. *Qualitative Research in Psychology*. https://doi.org/10.1080/14780887.2017.1400143

Lomas, T. (2018a). Experiential cartography and the significance of "untranslatable" words. *Theory and Psychology*, 28(4), 476-495.

Lomas, T. (2018b). The flavours of love: A cross-cultural lexical analysis. *Journal for the Theory of Social Behaviour*, 48(1), 134-152.

Lomas, T. (2018c). *Translating Happiness: Enriching our Experience and Understanding of Wellbeing through Untranslatable Words*. Boston, MA: MIT Press.

Lomas, T. (2019a). The dynamics of spirituality: A cross-cultural lexical analysis. *Psychology of Religion and Spirituality*, 11(2), 131-140.

Lomas, T. (2019b). The elements of eco-connection: A cross-cultural lexical enquiry. *International Journal of Environmental Research and Public Health*, 16(24), 5120.

Lomas, T. (2019c). The roots of virtue: A cross-cultural lexical analysis. *Journal of Happiness Studies*, 20(4), 1259-1279.

Lomas, T. (2021a). The dimensions of prosociality: A cross-cultural lexical analysis. *Current Psychology*, 40, 1336-1347.

Lomas, T. (2021b). Towards a cross-cultural lexical map of wellbeing. *The Journal of Positive Psychology*, 16(5), 622-639. https://doi.org/10.1080/17439760.2020.1791944

Lomas, T. (2022). The appeal of aesthetics: A cross-cultural lexical analysis. *Psychology of Aesthetics, Creativity, and the Arts*. https://doi.org/10.1037/aca0000484

Lovtsevich, G. N. (2005). Language teachers through the looking glass: Expanding Circle teachers' discourse. *World Englishes*, 24(4), 461-469.

Matsumoto, D., & Hwang, H. S. (2012). Culture and emotion: The integration of biological and cultural contributions. *Journal of Cross-Cultural Psychology*, 43(1), 91-118.

Meighan, P. J. (2019). An "educator's" perspective: How heritage language pedagogy and technology can decolonize the English classroom. *TESOL Journal*, 11(2), 1-5.

Metcalf, E. -M. (1998). *Children's and Young Adult Books in the Intermediate and Advanced German Class: Two Projects*. Die Unterrichtspraxis/Teaching German, 148-153.

Russell, J. A. (1980). A circumplex model of affect. *Journal of Personality and Social Psychology*, 39(6), 1161.

Sapir, E. (1929). The status of linguistics as a science. *Language*, 5(4), 207.

Sarigul, E., & Ashton-Hay, S. (2005). Culture and English language teaching: Raising awareness. In *Proceedings 9th International INGED (Turkish English Education Association) Conference*. Ankara Turkey: Economics and Technical University.

Simons, R. C., & Hughes, C. C. (2012). *The Culture-Bound Syndromes: Folk Illnesses of Psychiatric and Anthropological Interest*. London: Springer Science & Business Media.

Smidt, K. E., & Suvak, M. K. (2015, June 1). A brief, but nuanced, review of emotional granularity and emotion differentiation research. *Current Opinion in Psychology*, 3, 48-51.

Tadmor, U. (2009). Loanwords in the world's languages: Findings and results. In M. Haspelmath & U. Tadmor (Eds.), *Loanwords in the World's Languages: A Comparative Handbook* (pp. 55-75). Berlin: De Gruyter Martin.

Weissberg, R. P., Durlak, J. A., Domitrovich, C. E., & Gullotta, T. P. (Eds.). (2015). Social and emotional learning: Past, present, and future. In *Handbook of Social and Emotional Learning: Research and Practice* (pp. 3-19). New York: The Guilford Press.

Whorf, B. L. (1940). *Science and Linguistics*. Indianapolis: Bobbs-Merrill.

Wierzbicka, A. (1989). Soul and mind: Linguistic evidence for ethnopsychology and cultural history. *American Anthropologist*, 91(1), 41-58.

Part 5

Inclusion

We all want to feel we matter (Prilleltensky & Prilleltensky, 2021). As children, we want our family to look after us and acknowledge that we matter; when we go to school, we want to feel that we are noticed, appreciated, and ultimately that we matter; when we become adults, we want to feel we matter to our friends and family, and know that what we do every day matters. The consequences of not feeling that we matter are dire, and usually result in negative and sometimes catastrophic outcomes, such as increased aggression, isolation, and bullying. This is why, helping others feel that they are fully included, that they belong, is of upmost importance to us all.

In this chapter, we delve into various aspects of inclusion. We consider it from the school belonging perspective (Chapter 16) and identify evidence-based ways that teachers and students can use to help everyone feel included. We also consider it from the school bullying perspective (Chapter 17) and identify ways in which positive psychology can be applied to reduce and prevent bullying. Chapter 18 discusses the use of positive psychology and strength-based approaches in the context of disability. Finally, Chapter 19, proposes a framework that will help students and teachers fully embrace inclusion in their school community.

As you read this part, you may reflect on the following:

– What inclusion activities does my school engage with already that work?
– What additional activities can be implemented to help everyone feel they matter?
– What can I personally do to make a difference?

Reference

Prilleltensky, I., & Prilleltensky, O. (2021). *How people matter: Why it affects health, happiness, love, work, and society.* Cambridge, UK: Cambridge University Press.

DOI: 10.4324/9781003228158-20

16 School belonging as an essential component of positive psychology in schools

Kelly-Ann Allen, Christopher Boyle, Denise Wong, Rebecca G. Johnson, and Fiona May

Research on school belonging applies the well-established understanding that we have a fundamental need to belong, to gain knowledge that students are a part of an adaptive, ephemeral, and complex school environment. This chapter sets out the fundamentals of school belonging and its link to positive school psychology.

Introduction

Why belonging matters

Individuals with a strong sense of belonging are happier, healthier, and achieve more than those without it (Jose et al., 2012; Marraccini & Brier, 2017; Neel & Fuligni, 2013). Conversely, people with unmet belonging needs are more likely to experience mental health problems (Parr et al., 2020), physical health problems (Begen & Turner-Cobb, 2015; Richard et al., 2017), suicidal ideation (McClelland et al., 2020), and early mortality (Holt-Lunstad et al., 2015; Rico-Uribe et al., 2018). These differences clearly indicate the importance of developing a sense of belonging in one's life. Moreover, when comparing the psychological pain of not belonging with physical pain from injury, brain imaging studies have found that recovering from the psychological pain of rejection is more difficult than recovering from physical pain (Eisenberger, 2012; Kawamoto et al., 2015). This may be because the experience of social rejection can be mentally relived repeatedly, whereas broken bones heal in time (Sebastian et al., 2011). It is clear that empirical evidence supports the view that having a sense of belonging is a protective factor for mental and physical well-being (Walton & Brady, 2017).

Belonging in adolescence

While having a sense of belonging is important for everyone across the lifespan, it is especially important during adolescence (Davis-Alldritt, 2012; Jose et al., 2012). When a need for belonging is thwarted during this period, the pain of rejection is experienced more intensely than at any other developmental period due to the stronger need to belong

DOI: 10.4324/9781003228158-21

outside the family unit (compared with younger children) and the diminished capacity to regulate emotions (Pfeifer & Blakemore, 2012; Sebastian et al., 2011). This may explain why adolescents' needs for belonging can be unfulfilled, they are more likely to abuse drugs and alcohol, report higher rates of suicidal ideation, experience more symptoms of depression and anxiety, and underachieve academically (Boen et al., 2020; Neel & Fuligni, 2013; Parr et al., 2020).

The above implications of a lack of belonging are likely due to the pivotal role belonging plays in achieving the key adolescent developmental task of identity formation (Brechwald & Prinstein, 2011; Tanti et al., 2011). That is, an individual's identity is shaped not only by personal beliefs and interests which change and evolve through exploration but also by their relationships and sense of belongingness with significant others (Abbassi, 2016; Albarello et al., 2018). Achieving this developmental task has been found to be critical for adolescent psychosocial adjustment and transitioning into adulthood (Erikson, 1994; World Health Organization, 2014). However, despite the developmental drive to belong, an adolescent's ability to do so may be hindered by two primary changes that occur during adolescence. First, developmental changes in the social region of the brain during this time mean adolescents are more vulnerable to social rejection than younger children and adults (Blakemore, 2012). This is because they are not only more reactive to emotional cues, but they are also still learning how to accurately interpret facial emotions (Arain et al., 2013, Burnett et al., 2011; Wang et al., 2008). Second, changes in the school structure from primary to secondary school mean even though adolescents need more regular contact with non-parental adults, the transition to secondary school results in less regular contact with teachers compared with primary school (García-Moya, 2020).

The distinct developmental vulnerability to social rejection and the mismatch between adolescents' developmental needs and the secondary school structure may explain why adolescence is the peak period in which disconnection from school occurs (O'Brennan & Furlong, 2010; Organisation for Economic Co-operation and Development, 2017) and when most mental health disorders emerge (Kessler et al., 2007; Patel et al., 2007). Given the consequences of a low sense of belonging and the important socialisation context schools provide (Allen & Bowles, 2012; Allen et al., 2018a), it is no surprise belonging in school has attracted significant research attention over the last three decades (Anderman, 2003; Slaten et al., 2016; Uslu & Gizir, 2017) and generated appeals for secondary schools to prioritise building students' sense of school belonging (Allen & Bowles, 2012; Allen et al., 2018).

Theoretical background

What is school belonging?

Schools are recognised as being especially influential contexts for students' development and psychosocial adjustment (Bronfenbrenner, 1979; Meece & Schaefer, 2010) and important places for fostering a sense of belonging. School belonging has been described in various ways in the literature – as school bonding, engagement, attachment, community, and connectedness, for example. However, there is even less consistency in these descriptions than in definitions of school belonging. Students who report not having a sense of belonging to school also use a variety of terms, such as alienated, disengaged, socially isolated, or disaffected (Willms, 2003). Terminology is often used interchangeably (Anderman, 2002; Rowe & Stewart, 2009), and a given term's meaning in a particular context might depend upon the individual author using it (Libbey, 2007). Some theorists have even suggested that belonging is a component of school connectedness (McNeely & Falci, 2004). The discrepancies in terminology arguably dilute the potency of the research drawn from the field and muddy the implications for schools.

Overall, there are a number of high-quality research studies which have been conducted on the long-term outcomes of school belonging (e.g., O'Connor et al., 2011; Steiner et al., 2019), but there is still considerable room for further research such as, for example, to extend the age groups of the adult cohorts examined and to explore other potential outcomes of school belonging not already examined in the literature (e.g., relationship quality and post-school pathways). While the link between school belonging and positive outcome is well established, the converse is also true. Indeed, a low sense of belonging is also strongly associated with anti-social behaviour and school misconduct, including risk-taking behaviour related to substance and tobacco use (Goodenow, 1993). For this purpose, different theoretical frameworks have been developed, in order to better understand the concept of school belonging so that it could be better promoted in educational institutions and one such widely accepted framework is Bronfenbrenner's socioecological model of school belonging.

Given the important outcomes stemming from school belonging, there is a need to find meaningful ways of prioritising and fostering school belonging in schools. Investigating the ways in which school belonging is defined and represented in schools and understanding the unique themes that may influence school belonging from a systems perspective is important because, according to Bronfenbrenner (1979), schools offer the second most important set of relationships available to students aside from family. Moreover, as previously discussed, a sense of belonging is a vital need for normal adolescent development, particularly in respect to fostering identity, psychosocial adjustment, and social supports (Allen et al., 2014). It also plays an important role for academic outcomes, well-being, and prosocial school behaviour (Demanet & van Houtte, 2012; Jose et al., 2012; Sari, 2012).

Socioecological model of school belonging

Bronfenbrenner's socioecological framework (1977, 1979) can be employed to demonstrate that the factors associated with school belonging operate at different levels. On a personal or individual level, individuals hold a sense of their cultural identity, whether it be racial, ethnic, or religious (Bronfenbrenner, 1979; Faircloth & Hamm, 2005; Neville et al., 2014). On a micro level, adolescents have immediate interactions with their parents and teachers which become places of belonging and support for the individual (Bronfenbrenner, 1977). Allen et al. (2016) highlight that from Bronfenbrenner's point of view (1977), families are the first place of belonging for individuals when they are children. As they develop into adolescents, teachers become important to students' belonging as high school students spend the majority of their time at school (Allen et al., 2016; Chhuon & Wallace, 2014).

Although the microsystem, being the closest in proximity to the individual, is the system that has the most influence on an individual's development (Wang & Eccles, 2012), little is known about the macrosystem's effect on the individual (Allen et al., 2018b). The macrosystem, in the context of school belonging, can refer not only to legislation and national education initiatives, but broader cultural and social norms (Allen et al., 2016). As such, broader culture may influence the ways in which students are taught to interact with the world.

A strength of the socioecological perspective is that the multi-dimensional nature of school belonging can be demonstrated rather than narrowly focusing on the classroom's role in belonging (Allen et al., 2016). For this purpose, this chapter seeks to examine, on the basis of the socioecological framework, how measures can be implemented at the different levels within the framework in order to foster school belonging. This will be carried out through a quick review of literature to identify commonly cited practices which are recognised as being effective in improving a sense of belonging. In doing so, the main objectives of this chapter would be to:

1   Describe and provide an overview of belonging as an important construct in positive psychology and school belonging in positive education
2   To present summary findings of a rapid review that demonstrate the main drivers for school belonging.

Practice

Rapid confirmatory literature review

A rapid review of the literature was conducted for the purpose of this chapter as a way to summarise practices that influence school belonging at the classroom and school level. The authors used the following databases: OVID Medline, PSYCINFO, ERIC and Cochrane Library. Search terms included: (school belonging OR school connectedness OR school membership OR school bonding) AND (teacher support OR teacher relationship OR teacher OR school support OR social support OR fairness OR extracurricular activities OR groups OR inclusion OR diversity OR equity OR peer support OR friends OR policy OR procedures OR strategic plan OR practices), focusing on students in secondary education. Additionally, the meta-analysis of Allen et al. (2018) and the systematic review of Greenwood and Kelly (2019) were referred to for additional papers by screening the reference lists.

Evidence-base to support implementation in schools

Tables 2 and 3 provide a summary of the results of the review process used to identify the evidence-base of school belonging practices, and the processes that schools might use to enact these practices.

"Try this" for educators

Table 2 Literature Review: School Belonging Practices Evidence-Base (Teacher-Level Factors)

Student-identified school belonging practices	Source/s in published literature	Processes to support implementation in schools
Teacher-level factors		
Emotional Support		
Approachable and understanding	Allen et al. (2018) Bowen et al. (1998) Brewster and Bowen (2004) Reschly et al. (2008) van Ryzin et al. (2009) Sakiz (2012) Shochet et al. (2007) Waters et al. (2010)	• Supporting teachers to build positive relationships with students through consistency, a positive approach, persistence and rapport building, and ensuring teachers have time to get to know and understand their students (e.g., Anderman, 2003; Bowen et al., 1998; Chapman et al., 2014; Garcia-Reid, 2007; Garcia-Reid et al., 2005; Reschly et al., 2008; Shochet et al., 2007, 2011; Waters et al., 2010; Zimmer-Gembeck et al., 2006).
Positive regard	Garcia-Reed et al. (2005) Garcia-Reed (2007) Hallinan (2008)	• Connecting students with additional support or counselling or psychological support services when necessary (Biag 2016; Bower et al., 2015; Greenwood & Kelly, 2019) and normalising access to this support by students (Anderson et al., 2006).
Social Support		
Connections with peers	Wang and Eccles (2012) Wentzel (1998)	• Providing opportunities for students to become involved in both school-based activities such as sports and house activities (e.g., Jennings, 2003; Shochet et al., 2011; Whitlock, 2007, Zimmer-Gembeck et al., 2006) in addition to activities in the local community that foster a sense of belonging to the broader networks surrounding students (e.g., Bower et al., 2015; Greenwood & Kelly, 2019).
Support to become involved in school events/activities	Allen et al. (2018) Wang and Eccles (2012) Wentzel (1998) Zimmer-Gembeck et al. (2006)	
		• Supporting teachers to promote school belonging by facilitating positive connections with peers through awareness of peer-group interactions and creating opportunities for students to get to know each other (e.g., Allen et al., 2016; Hamm et al., 2011).
		• Exploring buddy systems, peer support or peer mentoring programs within the school (e.g., Allen et al., 2016; Goodenow & Grady, 1993; Reschly et al., 2008; Shochet et al., 2011; van Ryzin et al., 2009; Whitlock, 2007; Zimmer-Gembeck et al., 2006).
Respect and inclusion		

(Continued)

Student-identified school belonging practices	Source/s in published literature*	Processes to support implementation in schools
Acknowledge diversity/ inclusive practices	Goodenow and Grady (1993) Holt and Espelage (2003) Reschly et al. (2008) Sakiz (2012)	• Establishing a school culture that values diversity and is respectful, inclusive and tolerant (Goodenow & Grady, 1993; Reschly et al., 2008). • Ensuring teachers and staff model respectful and inclusive behaviours in all of their interactions and that they use fair practices and consistent, agreed upon approaches to disciplinary issues (e.g., Allen et al., 2016; Garcia-Reid et al., 2005; Hawkins et al., 1991; Sakiz, 2012; Whitlock; 2007).
Respect and equity	Anderman (2003) Chapman et al. (2014) Hallinan (2008) Sakiz (2012)	

"Try this" for students

Table 3 Rapid Literature Review: School Belonging Practices Evidence-Base (School-Level Factors)

School-level factors		
Social and emotional support	Allen et al. (2018) Wang and Eccles (2012) Wentzel (1998)	• Fostering a school culture which emphasises respectful and supportive relationships across all levels of the school community; that reminds students of their value; and that maintains an enduring positive regard for all students (e.g., Anderson et al., 2006; Greenwood & Kelly, 2019). • Prioritising the emotional well-being of both students and staff and the importance of the student-teacher relationship alongside academic indicators of effectiveness in school strategic planning processes (e.g., Allen et al., 2018; Hattie, 2009; Stirling & Emery, 2016). • Supporting teachers to provide general pastoral support to students in addition to academic support and providing the conditions to facilitate this, such as time and resources (e.g., Allen et al., 2016; Biag, 2016; Greenwood & Kelly, 2019).
Activities and opportunities for social connection	Blomfield and Barber (2010) Dotterer et al. (2007) Knifsend and Graham (2012) Shochet et al. (2007) Waters et al. (2010)	• At a school-level, ensuring students have multiple opportunities for social connection through extra-curricular and group activities (e.g., Allen et al., 2016; Blomfield & Barber, 2010; Dotterer et al., 2007; Flitcroft & Kelly, 2016; Greenwood & Kelly, 2019; Shochet et al., 2007). • Allocating time in the curriculum to teach social and emotional learning to students (e.g., Allen et al., 2016; Frydenberg et al., 2009; Schonert-Reichl & Lawlor, 2010; Wyn et al., 2000).

(Continued)

School-level factors

Respect, equity, and diversity	Chapman et al. (2014) Holt and Espelage (2003) Sakiz (2012)	• Involving students and the broader school community in the development of whole school policies and procedures that ensure fairness, student safety and consistent disciplinary practices and ensuring these are implemented consistently by all school staff (e.g., Allen et al., 2016; Garcia-Reid et al., 2005; Greenwood & Kelly, 2019; Hawkins et al., 1991; Whitlock, 2007). • Creating school cultures that value diversity and support the inclusion of all students (e.g., Bower et al., 2015).
Positive school culture	Battistich et al. (1996) Cunningham (2007) Osterman (2000) Shochet et al. (2007)	• Establishing a school-wide vision and mission that prioritises school belonging (e.g., Allen et al., 2016; Bryson, 2004; Legters et al., 2002; Owings & Kaplan, 2003; Stemler et al., 2011; Teddlie & Reynolds, 2000). • Creating policies and procedures to ensure a positive, safe, nurturing and inclusive environment for all students (Biag, 2016; Chapman et al., 2014). • Having high expectations for the learning of all students (e.g., Biag, 2016). • Nurturing strong connections between staff, enabling collegial support (e.g., Bower et al., 2015). • Strong leadership that values and models practices that support school belonging (e.g., Anderson et al., 2006). • Creating a positive school identity to encourage student sense of belonging to their school (e.g., Flitcroft & Kelly, 2016).
Supportive and effective teachers	Allen et al. (2018) Garcia-Reid et al. (2005) Garcia-Reid (2007) van Ryzin et al. (2009) Wentzel (1998)	• At the school level, ensuring staff well-being and connectedness is prioritised at a policy and practice level (e.g., Allen et al., 2018; Bower et al., 2015; Noble & McGrath, 2008).
Environment/safety	Allen et al. (2018) Garcia-Reid et al. (2005) Hallinan (2008) Samdal et al. (1998) Whitlock (2007)	• Establishing a safe environment for all students (including zero-tolerance bullying procedures) (e.g., Biag, 2016; Cunningham, 2007; Garcia-Reid et al., 2005; Shochet et al., 2007).
Student voice/choice	Zimmer-Gembeck et al. (2006)	• Ensuring opportunities for student voice and choice making are embedded within the school culture (e.g., Anderson et al., 2006; Greenwood & Kelly, 2019; Sakiz, 2012; Stirling & Emery, 2016).

An overview of the results indicates that, irrespective of the level of intervention, teachers remain a central point of focus when considering best practices for fostering school belonging. Indeed, as has been evidenced in both Tables 2 and 3, teachers heavily influence school belonging mainly through a supportive pastoral role. The success of this role is first determined through school-level factors by, for example, establishing policies which would encourage the well-being of the students and especially potentially vulnerable students such as Sam. An additional, but less obvious requirement, would also be the school's recruitment process which would ensure that teachers must be conversant with the principles of positive school belonging and thus able to directly contribute to that concept. These two approaches help to ensure that mainly supportive and positive teachers are available to interact and support students. Moreover, teachers should not be expected to be inherently cognisant of all the principles of belonging and/or positive psychology and it would be prudent to provide appropriate training in this regard thus strengthening the notion that good belonging is good teaching. As is clear from the case study, Sam needs support – at least at the beginning of her new school life – and a teacher trained to recognise the level of support is key to ensuring an effective culture of belonging. In this case, as reflected in the results, the role of teachers as a supportive figure encompasses emotional support, social support as well as other additional support in learning which may be required. The authors of this chapter have also noted that the process of developing close connections with students is dependent on the teachers' characteristic personality in terms of whether they have the ability to build and maintain positive relations while devoting time to understanding individual students.

In addition to practices which involve teachers, adopting measures that specifically target students has been found to be a commonly cited approach for promoting school belonging. In this context, the schools' core mission should be such that it promotes school belonging by, for example, having a school culture where diversity and respect are valued while ensuring that such values are instilled and adopted by all students. Furthermore, both the school system and the teachers should aim to create a particular school environment where student well-being is important. Moreover, such an environment should not only encourage them to develop positive relationships but also provide them with the opportunities to do so. The fact that these measures are widely cited by various researchers provides evidence that they are recognised as effective practices which can help in fostering school belonging.

Case study

Sam is 13 years old and had just transferred to an urban high school after moving with her family from a more rural setting. Beginning at a new school is always difficult but in Sam's particular situation this is exacerbated by the size of the new school and the difference in culture that exists between urban and rural lifestyles. By having to make new friends and join new groups the facilitation of this through school structures and with teachers who are cognisant of the importance of creating an atmosphere of positive school belonging has been invaluable.

Conclusion

Bronfenbrenner's (1979) ecological framework for human development serves as a reminder that within any school setting, each student is a part of a greater whole influenced by formal and informal groupings and overarching systems that are common and typically represented within all schools. In this chapter, a rapid review of literature was undertaken to identify commonly cited measures which are considered to contribute to a sense of belonging within school settings. The results supported Bronfenbrenner's ecological framework in that the practices identified were not only limited to students but also involved surrounding factors such as the school systems, policies and teachers which, altogether, exert some degree of influence on students. Hence, it can be concluded that measures which can be adopted for improving school belonging should not be limited in focus but instead should include all the different levels encompassed with the framework. In addition, this text makes an original contribution to the field of psychology and education through the use of a socio-ecological framework to better understand the relevant themes that influence school belonging within a secondary school system.

Discussion points

What were some of the pivotal moments at school that influenced your sense of belonging to school (either positive or negative)?

Think about your favourite teacher at school. What attributes did they have? What did they do that made you like them? What did they say? What strategies could you adopt in your own teaching that could be inspired by them?

If you work in a school today, what are your own feelings about your workplace? Would you say you had a high, moderate, or low sense of school belonging to your school? What are some of the facilitators and barriers to your belonging?

Think about the last time you felt like you 'did not belong' somewhere? What strategies did you put in place to overcome those feelings?

Suggested resources

1   Allen, K. A. (2020). *Psychology of belonging*. UK: Routledge (Taylor and Francis Group).
2   Allen, K. A., & Kern, P. (2019). *Boosting school belonging in adolescents: Interventions for teachers and mental health professionals*. Routledge.
3   Allen, K. A., & Kern, M. L. (2017). *School belonging in adolescents: Theory, research, and practice*. Springer Social Sciences. ISBN 978-981-10-5996-4
4   Allen, K. A., Jamshidi, N., Berger, E., Reupert, A., Wurf, G., & May, F. (2021). Effective school-based interventions for building school belonging in adolescence: A systematic review. *Educational Psychology Review*, 1–29. https://doi.org/10.1007/s10648-021-09621-w
5   Allen, K. A., Reupert, A. E., & Oades, L. G. (Eds.) (2021). *Building better schools with evidence-based policy: Adaptable policy guidelines for teachers and school leaders* (1st ed., pp. 1–369). Routledge. ISBN: 9780367458898. Free to download here: https://www.taylorfrancis.com/books/oa-edit/10.4324/9781003025955/building-better-schools-evidence-based-policy-kelly-ann-allen-andrea-reupert-lindsay-oades

References

Abbasi, N. (2016). Adolescent Identity Formation and the School Environment. In K. Fisher (Ed.), *The Translational Design of Schools*. SensePublishers. https://doi.org/10.1007/978-94-6300-364-3_4

Albarello, F., Crocetti, E., & Rubini, M. (2018). I and Us: A Longitudinal Study on the Interplay of Personal and Social Identity in Adolescence. *Journal of Youth and Adolescence*, 47(4). https://doi.org/10.1007/s10964-017-0791-4

Allen, K. -A., & Bowles, T. (2012). Belonging as a Guiding Principle in the Education of Adolescents. *Australian Journal of Educational and Developmental Psychology*, 12, 108–119.

Allen, K., Kern, M. L., Vella-Brodrick, D., Hattie, J., & Waters, L. (2018a). What Schools Need to Know About Fostering School Belonging: A Meta-Analysis. *Educational Psychology Review*, 30(1). https://doi.org/10.1007/s10648-016-9389-8

Allen, K. -A., Kern, M. L., Vella-Brodrick, D., & Waters, L. (2018b). Understanding the Priorities of Australian Secondary Schools Through an Analysis of Their Mission and Vision Statements. *Educational Administration Quarterly*, 54(2). https://doi.org/10.1177/0013161X18758655

Allen, J. P., Pianta, R. C., Gregory, A., Mikami, A. Y., & Lun, J. (2011). An Interaction-Based Approach to Enhancing Secondary School Instruction and Student Achievement. *Science*, 333(6045). https://doi.org/10.1126/science.1207998

Allen, K. A., Ryan, T., Gray, D. L., McInerney, D. M., & Waters, L. (2014). Social Media Use and Social Connectedness in Adolescents: The Positives and the Potential Pitfalls. *The Australian Educational and Developmental Psychologist*, 31(1). https://doi.org/10.1017/edp.2014.2

Allen, K. -A., Vella-Brodrick, D., & Waters, L. (2016). Fostering School Belonging in Secondary Schools Using a Socio-Ecological Framework. *The Educational and Developmental Psychologist*, 33(1). https://doi.org/10.1017/edp.2016.5

Anderman, E. M. (2002). School Effects on Psychological Outcomes During Adolescence. *Journal of Educational Psychology*, 94(4). https://doi.org/10.1037/0022-0663.94.4.795

Anderman, L. H. (2003). Academic and Social Perceptions as Predictors of Change in Middle School Students' Sense of School Belonging. *The Journal of Experimental Education*, 72(1). https://doi.org/10.1080/00220970309600877

Arain, M., Haque, M., Johal, L., Mathur, P., Nel, W., Rais, A., Sandhu, R., & Sharma, S. (2013). Maturation of the Adolescent Brain. *Neuropsychiatric Disease and Treatment*, 9, 449–461. https://doi.org/10.2147/NDT.S39776

Battistich, V., Schaps, E., Watson, M., & Solomon, D. (1996). Prevention Effects of the Child Development Project. *Journal of Adolescent Research*, 11(1). https://doi.org/10.1177/0743554896111003

Begen, F. M., & Turner-Cobb, J. M. (2015). Benefits of Belonging: Experimental Manipulation of Social Inclusion to Enhance Psychological and Physiological Health Parameters. *Psychology & Health*, 30(5). https://doi.org/10.1080/08870446.2014.991734

Biag, M. (2016). A Descriptive Analysis of School Connectedness: The Views of School Personnel. *Urban Education*, 51(1), 32–59.

Blakemore, S. -J. (2012). Development of the Social Brain in Adolescence. *Journal of the Royal Society of Medicine*, 105(3). https://doi.org/10.1258/jrsm.2011.110221

Blomfield, C. J., & Barber, B. L. (2010). Australian Adolescents' Extracurricular Activity Participation and Positive Development: Is the Relationship Mediated by Peer Attributes? *Australian Journal of Educational & Developmental Psychology*, 10, 114–128.

Boen, C. E., Kozlowski, K., & Tyson, K. D. (2020). "Toxic" Schools? How School Exposures during Adolescence Influence Trajectories of Health through Young Adulthood. *SSM - Population Health*, 11. https://doi.org/10.1016/j.ssmph.2020.100623

Bowen, G. L., Richman, J. M., Brewster, A., & Bowen, N. (1998). Sense of School Coherence, Perceptions of Danger at School, and Teacher Support among Youth at Risk of School Failure. *Child and Adolescent Social Work Journal*, 15(4). https://doi.org/10.1023/A:1025159811181

Bower, J., van Kraayenoord, C., & Carroll, A. (2015). Building Social Connectedness in Schools: Australian Teachers' Perspectives. *International Journal of Educational Research*, 70, 101–109.

Brechwald, W. A., & Prinstein, M. J. (2011). Beyond Homophily: A Decade of Advances in Understanding Peer Influence Processes. *Journal of Research on Adolescence*, 21(1). https://doi.org/10.1111/j.1532-7795.2010.00721.x

Brewster, A. B., & Bowen, G. L. (2004). Teacher Support and the School Engagement of Latino Middle and High School Students at Risk of School Failure. *Child and Adolescent Social Work Journal*, 21(1). https://doi.org/10.1023/B:CASW.0000012348.83939.6b

Bronfenbrenner, U. (1977). Toward an Experimental Ecology of Human development. *American Psychologist*, 32(7). https://doi.org/10.1037/0003-066X.32.7.513

Bronfenbrenner, U. (1979). *The Ecology of Human Development: Experiments by Nature and Design*. Harvard University Press.

Bryson, J. M. (2004). What to Do When Stakeholders Matter. *Public Management Review*, 6(1). https://doi.org/10.1080/14719030410001675722

Burnett, S., Sebastian, C., Cohen Kadosh, K., & Blakemore, S. -J. (2011). The Social Brain in Adolescence: Evidence from Functional Magnetic Resonance Imaging and Behavioural Studies. *Neuroscience & Biobehavioral Reviews*, 35(8). https://doi.org/10.1016/j.neubiorev.2010.10.011

Chapman, R. L., Buckley, L., Sheehan, M., & Shochet, I. M. (2014). Teachers' perceptions of school connectedness and risk-taking in adolescence. *International Journal of Qualitative Studies in Education*, 27(4), 413-431. https://doi.org/10.1080/09518398.2013.771225

Chhuon, V., & Wallace, T. L. (2014). Creating Connectedness Through Being Known. *Youth & Society*, 46(3). https://doi.org/10.1177/0044118X11436188

Cunningham, N. J. (2007). Level of Bonding to School and Perception of the School Environment by Bullies, Victims, and Bully Victims. *The Journal of Early Adolescence*, 27(4). https://doi.org/10.1177/0272431607302940

Davis-Alldritt, L. (2012). School Connectedness/Parent Engagement. *NASN School Nurse*, 27(6). https://doi.org/10.1177/1942602X12462529

Demanet, J., & van Houtte, M. (2012). School Belonging and School Misconduct: The Differing Role of Teacher and Peer Attachment. *Journal of Youth and Adolescence*, 41(4). https://doi.org/10.1007/s10964-011-9674-2

Dotterer, A. M., McHale, S. M., & Crouter, A. C. (2007). Implications of Out-of-School Activities for School Engagement in African American Adolescents. *Journal of Youth and Adolescence*, 36(4). https://doi.org/10.1007/s10964-006-9161-3

Eisenberger, N. I. (2012). Broken Hearts and Broken Bones. *Current Directions in Psychological Science*, 21(1). https://doi.org/10.1177/0963721411429455

Erikson, E. H. (1994). *Identity: Youth and Crisis*. Norton & Co.

Faircloth, B. S., & Hamm, J. V. (2005). Sense of Belonging among High School Students Representing 4 Ethnic Groups. *Journal of Youth and Adolescence*, 34(4). https://doi.org/10.1007/s10964-005-5752-7

Flitcroft, D., & Kelly, C. (2016). An Appreciative Exploration of How Schools Create a Sense of Belonging to Facilitate the Successful Transition to a New School for Pupils Involved in a Managed Move. *Emotional and Behavioural Difficulties*, 21(3). https://doi.org/10.1080/13632752.2016.1165976

Frydenberg, E., Care, E., Chan, E., & Freeman, E. (2009). Interrelationships between Coping, School Connectedness and Wellbeing Erica Frydenberg. *Australian Journal of Education*, 53(3). https://doi.org/10.1177/000494410905300305

García-Moya, I. (2020). *The Importance of Connectedness in Student-Teacher Relationships: Insights from the Teacher Connectedness Project*. Springer International Publishing. https://doi.org/10.1007/978-3-030-43446-5

Garcia-Reid, P. (2007). Examining Social Capital as a Mechanism for Improving School Engagement Among Low Income Hispanic Girls. *Youth & Society*, 39(2). https://doi.org/10.1177/0044118X07303263

Garcia-Reid, P., Reid, R. J., & Peterson, N. A. (2005). School Engagement among Latino Youth in an Urban Middle School Context. *Education and Urban Society*, 37(3). https://doi.org/10.1177/0013124505275534

Goodenow, C. (1993). Classroom belonging among early adolescent students: Relationships to motivation and achievement. *The Journal of Early Adolescence*, 13(1), 21-43. https://doi.org/10.1177/0272431693013001002

Greenwood, L., & Kelly, C. (2019). A Systematic Literature Review to Explore How Staff in Schools Describe How a Sense of Belonging Is Created for Their Pupils. *Emotional & Behavioural Difficulties*, 24(1), 3-19.

Hallinan, M. T. (2008). Teacher Influences on Students' Attachment to School. *Sociology of Education*, 81(3). https://doi.org/10.1177/003804070808100303

Hamm, J. v., Farmer, T. W., Dadisman, K., Gravelle, M., & Murray, A. R. (2011). Teachers' Attunement to Students' Peer Group Affiliations as a Source of Improved Student Experiences of the School

Social-Affective Context Following the Middle School Transition. *Journal of Applied Developmental Psychology*, 32(5). https://doi.org/10.1016/j.appdev.2010.06.003

Hattie, J. (2009). *Visible Learning: A Synthesis of Meta-Analyses Relating to Achievement*. Routledge.

Hawkins, J. D., von Cleve, E., & Catalano, R. F. (1991). Reducing Early Childhood Aggression: Results of a Primary Prevention Program. *Journal of the American Academy of Child & Adolescent Psychiatry*, 30(2). https://doi.org/10.1097/00004583-199103000-00008

Holt, M. K., & Espelage, D. L. (2003). A Cluster Analytic Investigation of Victimization among High School Students. *Journal of Applied School Psychology*, 19(2). https://doi.org/10.1300/J008v19n02_06

Holt-Lunstad, J., Smith, T. B., Baker, M., Harris, T., & Stephenson, D. (2015). Loneliness and Social Isolation as Risk Factors for Mortality. *Perspectives on Psychological Science*, 10(2). https://doi.org/10.1177/1745691614568352

Jennings, G. (2003). An exploration of meaningful participation and caring relationships as contexts for school engagement. *California School Psychologist*, 8, 43–52. https://doi.org/10.1007/BF03340895

Jose, P. E., Ryan, N., & Pryor, J. (2012). Does Social Connectedness Promote a Greater Sense of Well-Being in Adolescence Over Time? *Journal of Research on Adolescence*, 22(2). https://doi.org/10.1111/j.1532-7795.2012.00783.x

Kawamoto, T., Ura, M., & Nittono, H. (2015). Intrapersonal and Interpersonal Processes of Social Exclusion. *Frontiers in Neuroscience*, 9. https://doi.org/10.3389/fnins.2015.00062

Kessler, R. C., Amminger, G. P., Aguilar-Gaxiola, S., Alonso, J., Lee, S., & Ustun, T. B. (2007). Age of Onset of Mental Disorders: A Review of Recent Literature. *Current Opinion in Psychiatry*, 20(4). https://doi.org/10.1097/YCO.0b013e32816ebc8c

Knifsend, C. A., & Graham, S. (2012). Too Much of a Good Thing? How Breadth of Extracurricular Participation Relates to School-Related Affect and Academic Outcomes During Adolescence. *Journal of Youth and Adolescence*, 41(3). https://doi.org/10.1007/s10964-011-9737-4

Legters, N., Balfanz, R., & McPartland, J. (2002). *Solutions for Failing High Schools: Converging Visions and Promising Models*. Department of Education.

Libbey, H. P. (2007). *School Connectedness: Influence Above and Beyond Family Connectedness*. University of Minnesota.

Marraccini, M. E., & Brier, Z. M. F. (2017). School Connectedness and Suicidal Thoughts and Behaviors: A Systematic Meta-Analysis. *School Psychology Quarterly*, 32(1). https://doi.org/10.1037/spq0000192

McClelland, H., Evans, J. J., Nowland, R., Ferguson, E., & O'Connor, R. C. (2020). Loneliness as a Predictor of Suicidal Ideation and Behaviour: A Systematic Review and Meta-Analysis of Prospective Studies. *Journal of Affective Disorders*, 274. https://doi.org/10.1016/j.jad.2020.05.004

McNeely, C., & Falci, C. (2004). School Connectedness and the Transition Into and Out of Health-Risk Behavior Among Adolescents: A Comparison of Social Belonging and Teacher Support. *Journal of School Health*, 74(7). https://doi.org/10.1111/j.1746-1561.2004.tb08285.x

Meece, J. L., & Schaefer, V. A. (2010). School as a Context of Human Development. In J. L. Meece & J. S. Eccles (Eds.), *Handbook of Research on Schools, Schooling and Human Development* (pp. 3–6). Routledge.

Neel, C. G. -O., & Fuligni, A. (2013). A Longitudinal Study of School Belonging and Academic Motivation Across High School. *Child Development*, 84(2). https://doi.org/10.1111/j.1467-8624.2012.01862.x

Neville, H. A., Oyama, K. E., Odunewu, L. O., & Huggins, J. G. (2014). Dimensions of Belonging as an Aspect of Racial-Ethnic-Cultural Identity: An Exploration of Indigenous Australians. *Journal of Counseling Psychology*, 61(3). https://doi.org/10.1037/a0037115

Noble, T., & McGrath, H. (2008). The Positive Educational Practices Framework: A Tool for Facilitating the Work of Educational Psychologists in Promoting Pupil Wellbeing. *Educational and Child Psychology*, 25(2), 119–134.

O'Brennan, L. M., & Furlong, M. J. (2010). Relations Between Students' Perceptions of School Connectedness and Peer Victimization. *Journal of School Violence*, 9(4). https://doi.org/10.1080/15388220.2010.509009

O'Connor, M., Sanson, A., Hawkins, M. T., Letcher, P., Toumbourou, J. W., Smart, D., Vassallo, S., & Olsson, C. A. (2011). Predictors of Positive Development in Emerging Adulthood. *Journal of Youth and Adolescence*, 40(7). https://doi.org/10.1007/s10964-010-9593-7

Organisation for Economic Co-operation and Development. (2017). PISA 2015 Results (Volume III). OECD. https://doi.org/10.1787/9789264273856-en

Osterman, K. F. (2000). Students' Need for Belonging in the School Community. *Review of Educational Research*, 70(3). https://doi.org/10.3102/00346543070003323

Owings, W., & Kaplan, L. (2003). *Best Practices, Best Thinking, and Emerging Issues in School Leadership.* Corwin Press.

Parr, E. J., Shochet, I. M., Cockshaw, W. D., & Kelly, R. L. (2020). General Belonging Is a Key Predictor of Adolescent Depressive Symptoms and Partially Mediates School Belonging. *School Mental Health,* 12(3). https://doi.org/10.1007/s12310-020-09371-0

Patel, V., Flisher, A. J., Hetrick, S., & McGorry, P. (2007). Mental Health of Young People: a Global Public-Health Challenge. *The Lancet,* 369(9569). https://doi.org/10.1016/S0140-6736(07)60368-7

Pfeifer, J. H., & Blakemore, S. -J. (2012). Adolescent Social Cognitive and Affective Neuroscience: Past, Present, and Future. *Social Cognitive and Affective Neuroscience,* 7(1). https://doi.org/10.1093/scan/nsr099

Reschly, A. L., Huebner, E. S., Appleton, J. J., & Antaramian, S. (2008). Engagement as Flourishing: The Contribution of Positive Emotions and Coping to Adolescents' Engagement at School and with Learning. *Psychology in the Schools,* 45(5). https://doi.org/10.1002/pits.20306

Richard, A., Rohrmann, S., Vandeleur, C. L., Schmid, M., Barth, J., & Eichholzer, M. (2017). Loneliness Is Adversely Associated with Physical and Mental Health and Lifestyle Factors: Results from a Swiss National Survey. *PLoS One,* 12(7). https://doi.org/10.1371/journal.pone.0181442

Rico-Uribe, L. A., Caballero, F. F., Martín-María, N., Cabello, M., Ayuso-Mateos, J. L., & Miret, M. (2018). Association of Loneliness with All-Cause Mortality: A Meta-Analysis. *PLoS One,* 13(1). https://doi.org/10.1371/journal.pone.0190033

Rowe, F., & Stewart, D. (2009). Promoting Connectedness Through Whole-School Approaches: A Qualitative Study. *Health Education,* 109(5). https://doi.org/10.1108/09654280910984816

Sakiz, G. (2012). Perceived Instructor Affective Support in Relation to Academic Emotions and Motivation in College. *Educational Psychology,* 32(1). https://doi.org/10.1080/01443410.2011.625611

Samdal, O., Nutbeam, D., Wold, B., & Kannas, L. (1998). Achieving Health and Educational Goals Through Schools—A Study of the Importance of the School Climate and the Students' Satisfaction with School. *Health Education Research,* 13(3). https://doi.org/10.1093/her/13.3.383

Sari, M. (2012). Sense of School Belonging Among Elementary School Students. *Çukurova University Faculty of Education Journal,* 41(1), 1–11.

Schonert-Reichl, K. A., & Lawlor, M. S. (2010). The Effects of a Mindfulness-Based Education Program on Pre- and Early Adolescents' Well-Being and Social and Emotional Competence. *Mindfulness,* 1(3). https://doi.org/10.1007/s12671-010-0011-8

Sebastian, C. L., Tan, G. C. Y., Roiser, J. P., Viding, E., Dumontheil, I., & Blakemore, S. -J. (2011). Developmental Influences on the Neural Bases of Responses to Social Rejection: Implications of Social Neuroscience for Education. *NeuroImage,* 57(3). https://doi.org/10.1016/j.neuroimage.2010.09.063

Shochet, I. M., Smith, C. L., Furlong, M. J., & Homel, R. (2011). A Prospective Study Investigating the Impact of School Belonging Factors on Negative Affect in Adolescents. *Journal of Clinical Child & Adolescent Psychology,* 40(4). https://doi.org/10.1080/15374416.2011.581616

Shochet, I. M., Smyth, T., & Homel, R. (2007). The Impact of Parental Attachment on Adolescent Perception of the School Environment and School Connectedness. *Australian and New Zealand Journal of Family Therapy,* 28(02). https://doi.org/10.1375/anft.28.2.109

Slaten, C. D., Ferguson, J. K., Allen, K.-A., Brodrick, D.-V., & Waters, L. (2016). School Belonging: A Review of the History, Current Trends, and Future Directions. *The Educational and Developmental Psychologist,* 33(1). https://doi.org/10.1017/edp.2016.6

Steiner, R. J., Sheremenko, G., Lesesne, C., Dittus, P. J., Sieving, R. E., & Ethier, K. A. (2019). Adolescent Connectedness and Adult Health Outcomes. *Pediatrics,* 144(1). https://doi.org/10.1542/peds.2018-3766

Stemler, S. E., Bebell, D., & Sonnabend, L. A. (2011). Using School Mission Statements for Reflection and Research. *Educational Administration Quarterly,* 47, 383–420.

Stirling, S., & Emery, H. (2016). *A Whole School Framework for Emotional Well-Being and Mental Health: Supporting Resources for School Leaders.* National Children's Bureau.

Tanti, C., Stukas, A. A., Halloran, M. J., & Foddy, M. (2011). Social Identity Change: Shifts in Social Identity during Adolescence. *Journal of Adolescence,* 34(3). https://doi.org/10.1016/j.adolescence.2010.05.012

Teddlie, C., & Reynolds, D. (2000). *The International Handbook of School Effectiveness Research.* Falmer Press.

Uslu, F., & Gizir, S. (2017). School Belonging of Adolescents: The Role of Teacher–Student Relationships, Peer Relationships and Family Involvement. *Educational Sciences: Theory & Practice.* https://doi.org/10.12738/estp.2017.1.0104

van Ryzin, M. J., Gravely, A. A., & Roseth, C. J. (2009). Autonomy, Belongingness, and Engagement in School as Contributors to Adolescent Psychological Well-Being. *Journal of Youth and Adolescence*, 38(1). https://doi.org/10.1007/s10964-007-9257-4

Walton, G. M., & Brady, S. T. (2017). The Many Questions of Belonging. In A. J. Elliot, C. S. Dweck, & D. S. Yeager (Eds.), *Handbook of Competence and Motivation: Theory and Application* (2nd ed., pp. 272–293). The Guilford Press.

Wang, M. -T., & Eccles, J. S. (2012). Social Support Matters: Longitudinal Effects of Social Support on Three Dimensions of School Engagement from Middle to High School. *Child Development*, 83(3). https://doi.org/10.1111/j.1467-8624.2012.01745.x

Wang, L., Huettel, S., & de Bellis, M. D. (2008). Neural Substrates for Processing Task-Irrelevant Sad Images in Adolescents. *Developmental Science*, 11(1). https://doi.org/10.1111/j.1467-7687.2007.00661.x

Waters, S. K., Cross, D., & Shaw, T. (2010). How Important Are School and Interpersonal Student Characteristics in Determining Later Adolescent School Connectedness, by School Sector? *Australian Journal of Education*, 54(2). https://doi.org/10.1177/000494411005400207

Wentzel, K. R. (1998). Social Relationships and Motivation in Middle School: The Role of Parents, Teachers, and Peers. *Journal of Educational Psychology*, 90(2). https://doi.org/10.1037/0022-0663.90.2.202

Whitlock, J. (2007). The Role of Adults, Public Space, and Power in Adolescent Community Connectedness. *Journal of Community Psychology*, 35(4). https://doi.org/10.1002/jcop.20161

Willms, J. D. (2003). *Student Engagement at School*. OECD. https://doi.org/10.1787/9789264018938-en

World Health Organization. (2014). *Health for the World's Adolescents. A Second Chance in the Second Decade*. Https://Apps.Who.Int/Adolescent/Second-Decade-Files/1612_MNCAH_HWA_Executive_Summary.Pdf.

Wyn, J., Cahill, H., Holdsworth, R., Rowling, L., & Carson, S. (2000). MindMatters, a Whole-School Approach Promoting Mental Health and Wellbeing. *Australian & New Zealand Journal of Psychiatry*, 34(4). https://doi.org/10.1080/j.1440-1614.2000.00748.x

Zimmer-Gembeck, M. J., Chipuer, H. M., Hanisch, M., Creed, P. A., & McGregor, L. (2006). Relationships at school and stage-environment fit as resources for adolescent engagement and achievement. *Journal of Adolescence*, 29(6), 911–933. https://doi.org/10.1016/j.adolescence.2006.04.008

17 Positive psychology and school bullying

Jolanta Burke

Bullying is one of the most insidious school behaviours that threaten young people's self-concept, their engagement with school, life, and overall well-being. This chapter reviews the literature associated with applying positive psychology research to enhance pro-social behaviour and prevent and reduce bullying in schools. Specifically, it focuses on strength-based approaches to bullying and offers practical ways to apply them effectively in schools.

Introduction

School bullying is a growing problem worldwide (Mc Guckin et al., 2013), yet its definition and scope are unclear for the young people, their teachers, parents, not to mention the researchers who specialise in this area (Goldsmith & Howie, 2014). One thing, however, that most stakeholders agree on is the negative impact it has on everyone involved. Targets of bullying report higher levels of depression, anxiety, lower self-esteem, and in extreme cases suicidal ideation (Bucchianeri et al., 2014; Espinoza, 2015; Hansen et al., 2014; Hinduja & Patchin, 2008; Sarkova et al., 2014; Schneider et al., 2013). Nonetheless, they are not the only victims of bullying. Bystanders, who witness bullying are indirectly and repeatedly exposed to the victimisation process, which impacts them in various ways (Twemlow et al., 2004). Children who take on different roles in the bullying process, including being bystanders, are more likely to report depression and suicidal ideation compared with young people not involved in bullying (Rivers & Noret, 2010). Therefore, school bullying is an insidious, ongoing issue that requires urgent action. While positive psychology and school bullying are not usually discussed in tandem, positive psychology offers an opportunity to approach school bullying from a unique perspective and contribute to its eradication in educational institutions.

Theoretical background

Bullying refers to a repetitive, deliberately aggressive, yet unprovoked behaviour demonstrating an imbalance of power, which includes, but is not limited to, verbal and/or physical abuse, exclusion, extortion, or rumour spreading (Olweus, 2003). As such, it is referred to as "traditional

DOI: 10.4324/9781003228158-22

bullying" as opposed to cyber bullying/aggression, which indicates aggressive behaviour via digital media (Corcoran et al., 2015). A meta-analysis of the literature between 1978 and 2013 showed that the prevalence of traditional bullying is reported to be higher than cyber bullying, as it stands at 35%-16%, respectively (Modecki et al., 2014). However, given that young people have ever-increased access to online content, these figures may continue to increase.

Over the last few decades, many initiatives have been introduced in schools to stop and/ or prevent bullying. For example, in the 1990s after a flurry of research about the social impact of bullying (Salmivalli, 1999; Salmivalli et al., 2004), the KiVa programme was implemented in Finland and then tweaked for cultural difference across Europe, the aim of which was to inspire the bystanders to stand up to bullies on behalf of the targets (Garandeau et al., 2014; Yang & Salmivalli, 2015). Other programmes followed suit focusing on the power of social persuasion, e.g. "Zero Violence Brave Club" (Roca-Campos, 2021). A systematic review of over 100 bullying (traditional and cyber) programmes showed a reduction of school bullying by 19-20% and school victimisation by 15-16%, as well as reduction of cyberbullying by 10-15% and cyber victimisation by 14% (Gaffney et al., 2019). While this is an optimistic finding, it also highlights the need for alternative approaches that may be more effective in combatting bullying. We argue that positive psychological approaches may prove beneficial, although more research is required to demonstrate their full potential.

The interest in applying positive psychology to reduce bullying and victimisation in schools is constantly growing (Georgoulas-Sherry, 2021; Richards et al., 2008). There are three main positive psychology approaches suggested by the researchers that may contribute to eradicating school bullying by 2030, which is one of the United Nations Educational, Scientific and Cultural Organisation's (UNESCO) ambitious objectives (UNESCO, 2016). Firstly, given that positive assets, such as resilience, or character strengths are associated with a lower prevalence of bullying and victimisation in schools (Burke & McGuckin, in press; Moore & Woodcock, 2017), researchers suggest that focusing on developing them may enhance pro-social behaviours, thus prevent and reduce bullying in schools. Secondly, programmes that help the targets of bullying cope more effectively with their experiences of bullying may contribute by reducing the effects of bullying on targets (Watson et al., 2017). Thirdly, since implementing well-being programmes for schools, which include evidence-based positive psychology interventions, such as gratitude, result in the reduction of bullying (Richards et al., 2008), and extensive research indicates that who bully often experience mental health issues and report lower levels of well-being than their non-bullying counterparts (Ivarsson et al., 2005; Kumpulainen et al., 1999; Liu et al., 2013; Srabstein & Piazza, 2012), introducing well-being programmes may also help young people develop pro-social skills, thus reducing the incidents of bullying in schools. However, given that bullying incidents are rarely measured as outcomes of positive psychology programmes, there is limited evidence for the effectiveness of positive psychology programmes in reducing bullying. More evidence is required to understand their impact, internal and external factors that contribute to their effectiveness.

Apart from exploring the three emerging fields of research, other positive psychology concepts can also be considered. For example, a meta-analysis study on the impact of parental behaviour on bullying showed that positive parenting protected children from becoming the victims of bullying (Lereya et al., 2013). At the same time, in positive psychology, the latest developments in strength-based parenting demonstrate positive results associated with its impact on such outcomes as improved school belonging, achievement, reduction in stress, and growth (Arslan et al., forthcoming; Waters, 2015; Waters et al., 2019; Zavala & Waters, 2021). Therefore, an opportunity exists to further explore the influence of strength-based parenting on bullying and victimisation. In this chapter, I will present the emerging research associated with the application of strengths in the context of aggression and school bullying.

Strength-based approaches

At least two strength-based programmes have been developed to help young people reduce bullying and victimisation in schools (Gaffney et al., 2019). The first one was the "Strengths in Motion" programme, which helped students identify strengths and apply them to promote pro-social behaviour; in the event of bullying, it encouraged them to use their strengths to cope with it more effectively (Rawana et al., 2011). The second programme aimed to introduce students to cognitive behavioural therapy and used students' strengths to influence the situations they found themselves in their daily school life (Stallard et al., 2013). Both programmes acknowledged the potential of focusing on young people's strengths to develop pro-social behaviour, thus indirectly impacting school bullying.

One of the most remarkable developments in positive psychology was the creation of VIA Character Strengths, which provided young people with the lingo they required to articulate strengths, which is the first, necessary step towards applying them (Niemiec, 2018; Peterson & Seligman, 2004). While there are other strength assessments available (e.g. StrengthScope, Clifton Strengths Assessment, Strengths Profile), VIA character assessment is the only validated and non-commercial tool for strength identification, which is why this chapter will focus solely on it.

Over the years, a few papers have identified a correlation between young people's violent behaviour, aggression, and character strengths. The strengths of prudence, honesty, persistence, and love were highlighted as being associated with pro-social behaviour and fewer externalising problems (Park & Peterson, 2006). Other strengths that may have impacted youth violence were gratitude, forgiveness, sense of meaning, altruism, humility, and prudence (Tweed et al., 2011). Most recently, research with almost 3,000 teenagers demonstrated that prudence, in particular, was the only strength that all children had in common, who were not involved in traditional or cyber bullying or victimisation (Burke & McGuckin, in press). Prudence is a strength responsible for impulse control, acting in a way that is not regretted later (Peterson & Seligman, 2004). Given that bully/victim issues are linked to impulsivity (Walters & Espelage, 2018), this finding offers an opportunity for further research to identify whether helping children develop prudence may reduce bullying and victimisation in schools.

In addition to the bullies and targets of bullying, recent research explored the character strengths of bystanders of bullying. A study with 1,000 young people identified that the strengths of forgiveness and gratitude were associated with bystanders' pro-social behaviours (Garcia-Vazquez et al., 2020). Another study with almost 3,000 participants recognised the strengths of x as being most prevalent in the context of bystanders (Burke & Arslan, forthcoming). Building on these strengths may help empower young people to stand up to school bullies, thus it offers a great opportunity to contribute to UNESCO's (2016) goal of eradicating school bullying by 2030.

Practice

Given the extent of the research on applied positive psychology, many of the interventions can be applied to enhance students' well-being, which may impact well-being. However, further research is required to explore this. In the meantime, below are some of the activities that educators and students can carry out to enhance their pro-social attitudes and behaviours.

"Try this" for educators

Identify your strengths and reflect on your colleagues' strengths. Sometimes, when we overdo our strengths, they become our weaknesses (Niemiec, 2019). Reflect on the strengths you have overused in the past and the impact they had on others. Also, reflect on the strengths that some of your colleagues have overused in the past, which affected you. How can you use your strengths in the future to improve your relationship with others?

"Try this" for students

Introduce the concept of character strengths in your classroom. You may encourage students to complete a strengths assessment (see Suggested Resources). Then, create a strength tree for your class, plotting all student names and their strengths on it. Discuss at length each one of the character strengths paying particular attention to the value that each person adds to the class. This may relate to a different perspective they offer or a quirky behaviour that may be associated with their strengths. Conclude this exercise by highlighting.

Case study

A teacher in a secondary school in Ireland decided to tackle the bullying problem in their school using positive psychology. She divided the class into groups and the group's task was to create a positive profile of each person in their group. Students were encouraged to discuss what is good about their classmates, what they admire about them, and in what way each person contributed to the class. Each profile was then discussed and posted on the notice board. The exercise created high energy in the school and a significant increase in pro-social behaviours in the classroom. During a debrief, students remarked on how embarrassed they felt when hearing about themselves on such positive terms, but they also expressed a lot of gratitude and reported a boost of positive emotions. Most importantly, however, bullying behaviours have decreased significantly after conducting this pro-social activity.

Discussion points

What aspects of positive psychology can be applied to address school bullying and victimisation?
How can you increase pro-social behaviour in your school?

Suggested resources

- Free strength-assessment: www.viacharacter.org
- Niemiec, R. M. (2018). *Character strengths interventions: A field guide for practitioners*. Hogrefe Publishing Corporation.
- Libby, C. (2015). *The end of bullying*? Retrieved from: https://www.livehappy.com/positive-psychology/the-end-of-bullying/

References

Arslan, G., Burke, J., & Majercakova-Albertova, S. (2022). Strength-based parenting and social-emotional wellbeing: Does school belonging matter? Educational and Developmental Psychologist, DOI: 10.1080/20590776.2021.2023494

Bucchianeri, M. M., Eisenberg, M. E., Wall, M. M., Piran, N., & Neumark-Sztainer, D. (2014). Multiple types of harassment: Associations with emotional well-being and unhealthy behaviors in adolescents. *Journal of Adolescent Health, 54*(6), 724–729 6p. doi: 10.1016/j.jadohealth.2013.10. 205

Burke, J. & Arslan, G. (forthcoming). The character strengths of bystanders of bullying and cyberbullying in schools.

Burke, J., & McGuckin, C. (in press). Bullying and character development: An examination of character strengths associated with bullying and cyberbullying in post-primary schools in Ireland. *Journal of Character Education*.

Corcoran, L., Mc Guckin, C., & Prentice, G. (2015). Cyberbullying or cyber aggression? A review of existing definitions of cyber-based peer-to-peer aggression. *Societies, 5*(2), 245–255. doi: 10.3390/soc5020245

Espinoza, G. (2015). Daily cyber victimization among Latino adolescents: Links with emotional, physical and school adjustment. *Journal of Applied Developmental Psychology, 38*, 39–48. doi: 10.1016/j.appdev.2015.04.003

Gaffney, H., Farrington, D. P., Espelage, D. L., & Ttofi, M. M. (2019). Are cyberbullying intervention and prevention programs effective? A systematic and meta-analytical review. *Aggression & Violent Behavior, 45*, 134–153. doi: 10.1016/j.avb.2018.07.002

Garandeau, C., Poskiparta, E., & Salmivalli, C. (2014). Tackling acute cases of school bullying in the KiVa anti-bullying program: A comparison of two approaches. *Journal of Abnormal Child Psychology, 42*(6), 981–991. doi: 10.1007/s10802-014-9861-1

García-Vázquez, F. I., Valdés-Cuervo, A. A., Martínez-Ferrer, B., & Parra-Pérez, L. G. (2020). Forgiveness, gratitude, happiness, and prosocial bystander behavior in bullying. *Frontiers in Psychology, 10*.

Georgoulas-Sherry, V. (2021). Enforcing a positive psychology approach to mitigate bullying: Findings among U.S. children and adolescents from the National Survey of Children's Health. *Journal of Child and Adolescent Psychology, 5*(S1).

Goldsmid, S., & Howie, P. (2014). Bullying by definition: An examination of definitional components of bullying. *Emotional and Behavioral Difficulties, 19*, 210–225. doi: 10.1080/13632752.2013.844414

Hansen, H. H., Hasselgård, C. E., Undheim, A. M., & Indredavik, M. S. (2014). Bullying behaviour among Norwegian adolescents: Psychiatric diagnoses and school well-being in a clinical sample. *Nordic Journal of Psychiatry, 68*(5), 355–361. doi: 10.3109/08039488.2013.845689

Hinduja, S., & Patchin, J. W. (2008). Cyberbullying: An exploratory analysis of factors related to offending and victimization. *Journal of Deviant Behavior, 29*(2), 1–29.

Ivarsson, T., Broberg, A. G., Arvidsson, T., & Gillberg, C. (2005). Bullying in adolescence: Psychiatric problems in victims and bullies as measured by the youth self-report (YSR) and the depression self-rating scale (DSRS). *Nordic Journal of Psychiatry, 59*(5), 365–373. doi: 10.1080/08039480500227816

Kumpulainen, K., Räsänen, E., & Henttonen, I. (1999). Children involved in bullying: Psychological disturbance and the persistence of the involvement. *Child Abuse & Neglect, 23*(12), 1253–1262. doi: 10.1016/S0145-2134(99)00098-8

Lereya, S. T., Samara, M., & Wolke, D. (2013). Parenting behavior and the risk of becoming a victim and a bully/victim: A meta-analysis study. *Child Abuse & Neglect, 37*(12), 1091–1108. doi: https://doi-org.jproxy.nuim.ie/10.1016/j.chiabu.2013.03.001

Liu, X., Lu, D., Zhou, L., & Su, L. (2013). Relationship between bullying, victimization and depression, suicidal ideation. *Chinese Journal of Clinical Psychology, 21*(1), 85–87.

Mc Guckin, C., Cummins, P., & Lewis, C.A. (2013). *School based bullying in Ireland – A cause for concern? A review of research from Northern Ireland and the Republic of Ireland.* Retrieved from http://esource. dbs.ie/copyright

Modecki, K. L., Minchin, J., Harbaugh, A. G., Guerra, N. G., & Runions, K. C. (2014). Bullying prevalence across contexts: A meta-analysis measuring cyber and traditional bullying. *Journal of Adolescent Health, 55*(5), 602–611. https://doi-org.jproxy.nuim.ie/10.1016/j.jadohealth.2014.06.007

Moore, B., & Woodcock, S. (2017). Resilience to bullying: Towards an alternative to the anti-bullying approach. *Educational Psychology in Practice, 33*(1), 65–80. doi: 10.1080/02667363.2016.1233488

Niemiec, R. M. (2018). *Character strengths interventions: A field guide for practitioners.* Boston, MA: Hogrefe Publishing Corporation.

Niemiec, R. M. (2019). Finding the golden mean: The overuse, underuse, and optimal use of character strengths. *Counselling Psychology Quarterly, 32*(3–4), 453–471.

Olweus, D. (2003). A profile of bullying at school. *Educational Leadership, 60*(6), 12–17.

Park, N., & Peterson, C. (2006). Character strengths and happiness among young children: Content analysis of parental descriptions. *Journal of Happiness Studies, 7*(3), 323–341. doi: 10.1007/s10902-005-3648-6

Peterson, C., & Seligman, M. E. P. (2004). *Character strengths and virtues: A handbook and classification.* American Psychological Association; Oxford University Press.

Rawana, J. S., Norwood, S. J., & Whitley, J. (2011). A mixed-method evaluation of a strength-based bullying pre-vention program. *Canadian Journal of School Psychology, 26*(4), 283–300. doi: 10.1177/0829573511423741

Richards, A., Rivers, I., & Akhurst, J. (2008). A positive psychology approach to tackling bullying in sec-ondary schools: A comparative evaluation. *Educational and Child Psychology, 25*(2), 72–81.

Rivers, I., & Noret, N. (2010). Participant roles in bullying behavior and their association with thoughts of ending one's life. *Crisis: The Journal of Crisis Intervention and Suicide Prevention, 31*(3), 143–148. https://doi.org/10.1027/0227-5910/a000020

Roca-Campos, E., Duque, E., Ríos, O., & Ramis-Salas, M. (2021). The zero violence brave club: A successful intervention to prevent and address bullying in schools. *Frontiers in Psychiatry, 12.* doi: https://doi-org. proxy.library.rcsi.ie/10.3389/fpsyt.2021.601424

Salmivalli, C. (1999). Participant role approach to school bullying: Implications for interventions. *Journal of Adolescence, 22*(4), 453–459. doi: https://doi-org.proxy.library.rcsi.ie/10.1006/jado.1999.0239

Salmivalli, C., Kaukiainen, A., Voeten, M., & Sinisammal, M. (2004). Targeting the group as a whole: the Finnish anti-bullying intervention. In P. K. Smith, D. Pepler, & K. Rigby (Eds.), *Bullying in schools: How successful can interventions be?* (pp. 251–273). Cambridge: Cambridge University Press.

Sarkova, M., Bacikova-Sleskova, M., Geckova, A. M., Katreniakova, Z., van den Heuvel, W., & van Dijk, J. P. (2014). Adolescents' psychological well-being and self-esteem in the context of relationships at school. *Educational Research, 56*(4), 367–378. doi: 10.1080/00131881.2014.965556

Schneider, A., von Krogh, G., & Jäger, P. (2013). "What's coming next?" Epistemic curiosity and lurking behavior in online communities. *Computers in Human Behavior, 29*(1), 293–303.

Srabstein, J., & Piazza, T. (2012). Is there a syndrome of bullying? *International Journal of Adolescent Medicine and Health, 24*(1), 91–96.

Stallard, P., Phillips, R., Montgomery, A. A., Spears, M., Anderson, R., Taylor, J., & Sayal, K. (2013). A cluster randomised controlled trial to determine the clinical effectiveness and cost-effectiveness of class-room-based cognitive-behavioural therapy (CBT) in reducing symptoms of depression in high-risk adolescents. *Health Technology Assessment, 17*(47), vii–xvii. doi: 10.3310/hta17470

Tweed, R. G., Bhatt, G., Dooley, S., Spindler, A., Douglas, K. S., & Viljoen, J. L. (2011). Youth violence and positive psychology: Research potential through integration. *Canadian Psychology, 52*(2), 111–121. doi: 10.1037/a0020695

Twemlow, S. W., Fonagy, P., & Sacco, F. C. (2004). The Role of the Bystander in the Social Architecture of Bullying and Violence in Schools and Communities. In J. Devine, J. Gilligan, K. A. Miczek, R. Shaikh, & D. Pfaff (Eds.), *Youth violence: Scientific approaches to prevention.* (Vol. 1036, pp. 215–232). New York Academy of Sciences.

UNESCO. (2016). *UNESCO strategy on: Education for health and well-being: Contributing to the sustaina-ble development of goals.* Retrieved from Paris, France

Waters, L. (2015). The relationship between strength-based parenting with children's stress levels and strength-based coping approaches. *Psychology, 6*(6). DOI: 10.4236/psych.2015.66067.

Walters, G. D., & Espelage, D. L. (2018). Cognitive insensitivity and cognitive impulsivity as mediators of bullying continuity: Extending the psychological inertia construct to bullying behavior. *School Psy-chology Quarterly, 33*(4), 527–536. doi: 10.1037/spq0000240

Waters, L. E., Loton, D., & Jach, H. K. (2019). Does strength-based parenting predict academic achievement? The mediating effects of perseverance and engagement. *Journal of Happiness Studies, 20*(4), 1121-1140.

Watson, H., Rapee, R., & Todorov, N. (2017). Forgiveness reduces anger in a school bullying context. *Journal of Interpersonal Violence, 32*(1642-1657).

Yang, A., & Salmivalli, C. (2015). Effectiveness of the KiVa antibullying programme on bully-victims, bullies and victims. *Educational Research, 57*(1), 80-90.

Zavala, C., & Waters, L. (2021). Coming Out as LGBTQ+: The role strength-based parenting on posttraumatic stress and posttraumatic growth. *Journal of Happiness Studies, 22*(3), 1359-1383.

18 Positive psychology, strengths-based and inclusive practices, and disability

Michael L. Wehmeyer

Positive psychology is the study of optimal human functioning. Disability, throughout most of its history, has been understood within the context of diseases and deficits and, far too often, has not been associated with strengths and abilities. This chapter highlights progress on mindfulness, character strengths, and self-determination as examples of how strengths-based approaches are increasingly impacting disability services and supports.

Introduction

A focus on positive psychology in and strengths-based approaches to disability is a recent phenomenon, although efforts to improve quality of life, promote self-determination, and implement inclusive practices have been part of practice in special education since the late 1980s and early 1990s. When in the early 2000s positive psychology emerged as a discipline, it was at the same time that new ways of thinking about disability were introduced, propelled by the World Health Organization's (WHO) International Classification of Functioning, Disability, and Health (ICF; 2001). The ICF conceptualized disability not as pathology or a disease, but as the outcome of the interaction among health conditions (impairments), personal factors, and environmental factors. Disability, within the ICF, exists only in the gap between what a person can do and what that person wants to do. These so-called person–environment fit models of disability shifted the emphasis in special education away from a focus on remediation and efforts to fix a student and towards strengths-based and inclusive practices (Wehmeyer, 2013). With a worldwide focus on positive education, incorporating the principles and constructs of positive education, strengths-based and inclusive approaches to educating learners with disabilities align even more closely with best practice for all students.

Theoretical background

There have been multiple theoretical and conceptual developments that have propelled a focus on strengths-based and inclusive practices in disability, beginning with the aforementioned emergence of positive psychology and the conceptualization of person–environment

DOI: 10.4324/9781003228158-23

fit models of disability, leading in turn to a focus on positive education, strengths-based approaches, and self-determined learning. Because readers will be familiar with positive psychology from previous chapters in this text, the focus of this section will be on positive education (as a domain of positive psychology) and an examination of how this has been implemented in the field of special education in the form of strengths-based approaches (Wehmeyer, 2019).

Positive education is an outgrowth of the focus on positive psychology. Seligman et al. (2009) defined positive education as "education for both traditional skills and happiness" (p. 293). The table of contents for a handbook on positive education (Kern & Wehmeyer, 2021) identified core capabilities in positive education as focusing on:

- Well-being and flourishing
- Coping skills and resilience
- Character strengths
- Self-determination and self-determined learning
- Positive emotions and playfulness
- Creativity and creative learning
- School belonging
- Positive relationships
- Meaning and purpose
- Positive spirituality
- Mindfulness

Just as positive psychology focuses on optimal human well-being and functioning, the emphasis in positive education is on a student's strengths, interests, abilities, and preferences that lead to well-being and optimal functioning.

Within special education, strengths-based approaches emerged as ways of understanding disability changed. Over most of history, disability was mainly understood as a problem within a person, and interventions and treatments emphasized deficits and disorders (Wehmeyer, 2013). Such conceptualizations situated the person with the disability as the problem to be fixed, cured, or managed. Not surprisingly, people with disabilities were seen as broken, diseased, pathological, aberrant, and so on, as somehow different from other people. Unavoidably, this deficit perspective of disability has led to negative stereotypes about disability and in people with disability experiencing discrimination, segregation, and marginalization (Smith & Wehmeyer, 2012).

The seeds of change were introduced in the late twenty and early twenty-first centuries. First, social models of disability, which emphasized disability as arising "from the discrimination and disadvantage individuals experience in relation to others because of their particular differences and characteristics" (Bach, 2017, p. 40), emerged from a growing disability civil rights movement. Second, as mentioned previously, around the same time, the WHO introduced the ICF, which was a refinement of earlier models of disability that de-emphasized disease and disorder and, instead, conceptualized disability as the outcome of the interaction among health conditions, personal factors, and environmental factors. The ICF is an example of what are referred to as social-ecological or person–environment fit models of disability because they emphasize that disability is not something that resides within a person, but instead resides in the gap between what someone can do and what they want to do.

Interventions within these person–environment fit models take on specific characteristics. First, they begin with a person's abilities, interests, and preferences, that is, their strengths. These *strengths-based approaches* take, as a starting point, assumptions of person–environment fit models of disability that disability is not within a person, but a function of the interaction among personal, health, and environmental factors and, importantly, that with appropriate types, intensities, and levels of support, a person can function successfully in typical contexts. *Supports*, in this context, refer to "resources and strategies that aim to promote the development, education, interests, and personal well-being of a person and that enhance individual functioning" (Luckasson et al., 2002, p. 151). Supports are anything that enhance functioning and promote greater participation and inclusion (Thompson et al., 2017). And it is important to note that strengths-based approaches are intended to improve functioning in typical contexts and supports are defined by the degree to which someone improves participation in the community and life. In fact, the ICF essentially defines disability in terms of the impact of health conditions and personal and environmental factors on a person's activities and participation. *Participation* refers to a person's self-determined involvement in a pattern of life (i.e., roles, life situations, and activities) and occurs in and across contexts and is influenced by multiple personal and environmental factors (Dean et al., 2016).

This, in turn, leads us to one of the positive psychological and positive education constructs that has had considerable focus in the education of learners with disabilities, self-determination, and self-determined learning. In the early 1990s, there was a recognition that if students with disabilities were to be successful in school and post-school life, it would take more than simply teacher-delivered specialized education. Drawing from an emphasis in the disability civil rights movement on self-direction and autonomy, and from research in motivation psychology, research, policy, and practice in special education began to consider ways to involve and engage students themselves in their learning and instruction. This, in turn, led to an emphasis on promoting and enhancing the self-determination of students with disabilities. *Self-determination*, within a special education context, has been defined as a "dispositional characteristic manifested as acting as the causal agent in one's life" (Shogren et al., 2015, p. 258). Within positive psychology, self-determination refers to acting volitionally, where volitional refers to acting based upon conscious choice (Wehmeyer et al., 2017). Essentially, enabling young people to become more self-determined refers to efforts to enable them to make or cause things to happen in their own life. Within education, this focus has turned to efforts to promote self-determined learning in which students take ownership over and direct their own learning. Wehmeyer and Zhao (2020) noted that in self-determined learning:

- Teachers teach students to teach themselves.
- Students learn how to set and achieve goals and make plans.
- Teachers relinquish ownership for learning to the student, not by abdicating all roles in teaching, but by creating learning communities and using teaching methods that emphasize students' curiosity and experiences; that are autonomy-supportive and ensure

that learning is tied to activities that are intrinsically motivating or lead to the attain-ment of goals that are valued and based upon student preferences, interests, and values.

- Teachers provide competence supports by emphasizing mastery experiences, using as-sessment (both teacher-directed and student-directed) to provide supportive feedback, and aligning instruction with students' strengths and abilities.
- Teachers provide relatedness supports by providing choice opportunities, supporting volition, and emphasizing the goal process and not just goal outcomes.
- Students take initiative in learning because learning is meaningful and of personal value to them. They act volitionally because they are provided choices that are meaningful, meaningfully different, and autonomy-supportive (p. 35).

In summary, multiple theoretical and conceptual frameworks have converged to create an emphasis in special education on strengths-based and inclusive practices, which are char-acterized by a focus on, logically, strengths, on supports that enable participation, and on student self-determination and self-determined learning. Practice that has emerged from these innovations emphasizes autonomy-supportive contexts and interventions.

Practice

Practice purpose

The purpose of strengths-based approaches is to enhance learning for all students, to facil-itate inclusive education, and to promote student self-determination and self-determined learning. We do this with both a focus on creating autonomy-supportive classrooms and by teaching students the knowledge and skills that enable them to set and attain goals, solve problems, and advocate for themselves.

"Try this" for educators

The ICF looks at disability as the interaction among health conditions, personal factors, and environmental factors. Person–environment fit models of disability view disability as existing only in the gap between what a person can do and what that person wants to do. One implica-tion from these models for education is that interventions need to focus not only on chang-ing the student in some way but also on creating contexts and implementing instructional strategies that are autonomy-supportive. Research in motivation has identified ways in which teachers can interact with students and create learning communities that enhance autonomy and self-determination (Reeve et al., 2018). Chang et al. (2017) synthesized this research, suggesting that teachers can do the following to promote autonomy and self-determination:

1   Communicate frequently to clarify expectations and acknowledge students' feelings and to ensure that students know what is expected of them and do not have to depend upon the teacher to self-direct learning.
2   Provide multiple choice opportunities by considering the relevance of activities to stu-dents' interests and values and do not rely on controlling events and experiences, such as competitions or evaluations.

3   Encourage and support students to participate actively, rather than being passive observers/absorbers. Such classrooms emphasize student self-direction and active involvement in generating, delivering, and consuming information and content.
4   Provide positive and informational feedback that is constructive but positive, and not negative.
5   Provide guidance that clearly states expectations and the student's role. Structured guidance emphasizes elements of explicit and understandable directions, constructive feedback, and support for students to plan for learning and action.

A deficits-approach to special education has, too often, emphasized teacher control in the classroom, from setting classroom rules to determining what students are supposed to learn and how they are supposed to do it. The research in motivation is clear that when instruction is delivered in a controlling manner, students' motivation and active engagement in learning are undermined, but when the classroom structure is delivered in an autonomy-supportive manner, students' motivation and engagement are enhanced or facilitated (Cheon et al., 2020).

Of course, students need to acquire knowledge and skill that enables them to become more self-determined. As is the case in all areas of teaching and learning, assessment plays an important role in determining what a student knows and needs to learn. In promoting self-determined learning, however, the focus must shift from teacher-directed and controlled assessment to assessment models that actively engage the student in the process. One tool to support teachers to actively engage students with disabilities in assessing their strengths and areas of instructional needs is the Self-Determination Inventory (SDI) assessments (Shogren et al., 2020). The SDI has a student self-report version and a teacher-report version, both of which have been normed with students with and without disabilities. The SDI was developed to operationalize an empirically validated theory of self-determination, Causal Agency theory (Shogren et al., 2015). Both versions provide information about three essential characteristics of self-determined action proposed by Causal Agency theory: volitional action, agentic action, and action-control beliefs. Students and teachers can get information about student strengths and instructional needs in each of these characteristics, as well as on overall self-determination. Normed with adolescents ages 13–22 with and without disabilities, the student-report version is fully online and composed of 51 questions, the majority of which are rated via an online sliding scale that ranges from 0 to 100 with the anchors of Disagree and Agree. Validation of the student report form identified an equivalent factor structure across adolescents with and without disabilities, as well as adequate reliability in both populations (Shogren et al., 2020).

"Try this" for students

Most instructional strategies are teacher-directed. That is, they were designed for use by teachers to teach students. Efforts to develop strengths-based approaches have shifted that emphasis to student-directed and self-determined learning. To that end, Wehmeyer et al. (2000) developed the Self-Determined Learning Model of Instruction (SDLMI). The SDLMI has, in subsequent research, been shown to improve school and post-school outcomes for youth with disabilities as well as to promote student self-determination and self-determined learning (Shogren, Burke et al., 2019; Shogren et al., 2012; Wehmeyer et al., 2012).

A teacher's guide to the SDLMI and instructions on implementation of the model are available (see Suggested resources), so the process will not be discussed in detail in this chapter. Despite the fact that this is a teaching model, and thus intended for use by teachers, it is a teaching model that enables teachers to teach students to, in essence, teach themselves! Teachers teach students to solve a series of problems (What is my Goal?, What is my Plan?, and What have I Learned?) by using a self-regulated problem-solving process to set an educational goal, develop an action plan to reach that goal, identify a self-monitoring process to track their progress towards the goal, and to evaluate that progress, revising their action plan or goal as needed. Students solve these problems by answering a series of four *Student Questions* that vary for each phase to suit the specific problem being solved, but that pose the same four steps in a problem-solving sequence: (1) identify the problem, (2) identify potential solutions to the problem, (3) identify barriers to solving the problem, and (4) identify consequences of each solution. The SDLMI also provides teacher objectives and recommendations for educational supports and strategies that can be used to support the student to answer the questions. Students learn, essentially, how to become self-determined learners.

Another important focus in strengths-based approaches as applied to special education services is to enable students to take greater ownership over their educational planning and decision-making process (Wehmeyer & Zhao, 2020). When students participate in their annual Individualized Education Program (IEP) meeting, there is too often a focus only on what the student has not done well. Instead, the IEP meeting can become a means for students to practice self-determination and self-advocacy skills and to gain a sense of autonomy and competence. Williams-Diehm et al. (2008) found that students who are more self-determined are more likely to participate in their IEP meeting and that participating in the IEP meeting increased student self-determination, so the benefits of such activities are reciprocal. There are a number of resources (see Suggested resources) available for teachers to promote student involvement in educational planning. Of particular importance is to teach students self-advocacy skills as part of promoting student involvement. Students with disabilities need to learn the skills to advocate on their own behalf if they are to be successful both in school and in life. There are ample opportunities for students to practice and learn self-advocacy skills within the context of the educational planning process. Instruction can include a focus on student rights and responsibilities, ways to communicate to get what one wants, citizenship and leadership skills, how to be assertive, and so forth. The IEP meeting provides an ideal situation that students can apply those skills in a, hopefully, safe context.

Finally, there have been efforts to focus on mindfulness and character strengths as positive, strengths-based approaches to supporting students with disabilities (Shogren, Singh et al., 2017; Shogren, Wehmeyer et al., 2017). The VIA Character Strengths framework (see Suggested resources) identified a number of character strengths, from honesty and kindness to perseverance and creativity (see https://www.viacharacter.org/character-strengths for full list and explanations). Strategies in schools to promote student character strengths include having students use their 'signature' (e.g., highest ranked) character strengths each day or by having teachers and others engage in 'strengths-spotting' to identify student character strengths as they are exhibited (Shogren, Singh et al., 2017). Mindfulness practices are those that teach and encourage students to pay attention, through meditation and other practices, on the present moment as a means to support students to handle stress and assume greater agency over their lives. A number of practices, from *meditation on the soles of the feet* to *mindful observation of thoughts* have been shown to be useful when taught to and implemented by students with disabilities (Shogren, Singh et al., 2017).

Case study

The following case study illustrates the implementation of the Self-Determined Learning Model of Instruction, discussed previously.

Background

Jordan is a 17-year-old student who likes participating in Band twice a week after school, playing video games, and helping his dad with projects at their house He receives special education services (under the educational classification of autism spectrum disorders) and lives at home with his parents and younger sister. He has begun working with his transition planning team to create goals to plan for his transition from school to employment or higher education.

Ms. Labelle, Jordan's special education teacher and case manager, recently completed training to implement the SDLMI with students with disabilities, and she will be using it in both small groups and one-on-one with students as part of a class focused on transition planning. She is excited to work with Jordan to set and work towards transition-related goals based on his interests, preferences, and needs.

Preliminary conversation

Ms. Labelle is committed to facilitating interagency collaboration, and so she invited a representative from a local employment services agency (who participates on many of her students' transition planning teams) to support the students in completing a career interests assessment. Jordan plays the keyboard, and he identified music as a passion he would like to turn into a future job or career. He also likes technology and thinks he might like to work with digital devices like laptops, tablets, and smartphones.

Ms. Labelle also introduced several key terms (e.g., self-determination, goal, plan, barrier) using examples related to post-school outcomes like jobs, living arrangements, and community activities. Ms. Labelle supported the students to create a visual chart representing each of these terms that they can easily refer back to while going through the phases of the SDLMI.

Phase 1: Set a goal

STUDENT QUESTION 1: WHAT DO I WANT TO LEARN?

Ms. Labelle supports students in reviewing the results of their career interests' assessment. Jordan is deciding between working on an employment goal related to his interests in music or technology. After talking with a classmate and Ms. Miller, Jordan is able to identify his strengths and needs, communicate his preferences and interests, and prioritize his needs. He decides he's more interested in music and that working with digital devices might be overwhelming, although he could reconsider it in the future.

STUDENT QUESTION 2: WHAT DO I KNOW ABOUT IT NOW?

Ms. Labelle puts guiding questions on the board with visuals, one at a time, to support students in considering what they know about it now. For example, the first question is, "How did you first learn about your goal area?" Jordan shares that he started taking piano lessons when he was 8 years old. From this information, Ms. Labelle helps him think of different jobs related to music – like teaching music, working in a music-related store, or fixing instruments.

STUDENT QUESTION 3: WHAT MUST CHANGE FOR ME TO LEARN WHAT I DON'T KNOW?

Jordan decides he needs to explore each of these options. He's not sure what he would need to do to be prepared to teach music, work at a music store, or fix instruments. Ms. Labelle begins thinking about the supports she might need to provide to enable Jordan to decide if his actions will be focused on capacity building, modifying the environment, or both, and to identify actions he would need to take for each of these job options. She thinks that he may need support choosing strategies to meet his needs.

STUDENT QUESTION 4: WHAT CAN I DO TO MAKE THIS HAPPEN?

After going through a mini-lesson with Ms. Labelle on goal setting, Jordan and his classmates each set a goal. Jordan decides that the best goal for him right now regarding future employment is to explore what actions he would need to take to either be a music teacher, a music store employee, or an instrument technician.

Phase 2: Take action

STUDENT QUESTION 5: WHAT CAN I DO TO LEARN WHAT I DON'T ALREADY KNOW?

Jordan really liked the career interests assessment he did with Ms. Miller, and he's comfortable with her because she's been on his transition planning team for over a year. He decides that he wants to start by meeting with her about each of this job options. In small groups with his classmates, he hears some of them talking about doing job research on the computer, and he decides that will be a good backup plan.

STUDENT QUESTION 6: WHAT COULD KEEP ME FROM TAKING ACTION?

Ms. Labelle reminds the students of the poster they created with examples of barriers. This reminds Jordan that self-management can be a challenge. He really likes playing video games, after all! He also isn't sure how to reach out to Ms. Miller, because someone else always sets up meetings with her. He identifies this as a barrier.

STUDENT QUESTION 7: WHAT CAN I DO TO REMOVE THESE BARRIERS?

Since communication (i.e., reaching out to Ms. Miller) is something Jordan identified as a barrier, Ms. Labelle provides communication instruction on how Jordan can reach out to Ms. Miller. Options include email, phone call, or in person. Jordan realizes that if he chooses talking to Ms. Miller in person, he'll have to wait until the next time he sees her, which might not happen for a while. He also tells Ms. Labelle that he doesn't like talking on the phone. With the support of Ms. Labelle, he concludes that emailing Ms. Miller would be the best way to set up a meeting with her.

STUDENT QUESTION 8: WHEN WILL I TAKE ACTION?

At first, Jordan says that emailing Ms. Miller can wait until his tablet is repaired (the tablet he often uses at home is broken). However, Ms. Labelle supports him with self-scheduling, and he realizes it could be awhile until he has his tablet working again. One of his classmates reminds him of the computer lab that's open to students, so Jordan decides he can start working on his goal during their next transition planning session the following week. When that time arrives, he implements his plan.

Phase 3: Adjust goal or plan

STUDENT QUESTION 9: WHAT ACTIONS HAVE I TAKEN?

Jordan worked with Ms. Labelle to write out the email he would send to Ms. Miller. Then, he went to the computer lab during a later transition planning class and typed and sent the email. Ms. Miller responded, set up a time to come to the school (Ms. Labelle helped Jordan look at his schedule and share times their transition planning class met with Ms. Miller), and they met. Ms. Miller and Jordan looked at job postings for music teachers and music store employees and at music technician programs at the local community college, focusing on skills and qualifications for these jobs or program. From this information and with Ms. Miller's support, Jordan makes a list of actions he would need to take to get a job as music teacher or at a music store or to go to a music technician program.

STUDENT QUESTION 10: WHAT BARRIERS HAVE BEEN REMOVED?

Jordan now has a list of actions for what he would need to do to pursue one of his three music-related job interests. He worked past the barrier of his broken tablet, as well as not wanting to talk on the phone.

STUDENT QUESTION 11: WHAT HAS CHANGED ABOUT WHAT I DON'T KNOW?

Jordan knows he made progress accomplishing his goal of learning the actions he needs to take to pursue a career in music, but he's not sure how to use this information to move forward. Ms. Labelle supports Jordan with decision-making instruction, and he decides that he knows enough about each job and is ready to set a goal to work towards one of them.

STUDENT QUESTION 12: DO I KNOW WHAT I WANT TO KNOW?

Yes! Jordan is excited to say he accomplished his goal, and he's going to work through the SDLMI phases again and will think about what he needs to learn to get a part-time job at a music store, the next goal in his goal sequence.

[Copyright by Shogren, Raley et al. (2019), used with permission.]

Discussion points

1   In what ways do strengths-based and positive approaches change the focus of the education of learners with disabilities?
2   What is self-determination and how is it applicable to the education of learners with disabilities?
3   Why is it important to focus on issues of self-advocacy for students with disabilities?
4   In what ways does self-determined learning differ from how students typically are taught and learn?
5   How might mindfulness and character strengths interventions enhance a focus on positive approaches for students with disabilities?

Suggested resources

- https://selfdetermination.ku.edu/homepage/assessments/ provides online access to the Self-Determination Inventory assessments.
- https://selfdetermination.ku.edu/homepage/intervention/#sdlmi provides access to the Teacher's Guide for the Self-Determined Learning Model of Instruction and to information about the model.
- https://www.ou.edu/education/centers-and-partnerships/zarrow/self-determination-assessment-tools provide access to multiple self-determination assessments.

- https://www.ou.edu/education/centers-and-partnerships/zarrow/choicemaker-curriculum provides access to the ChoiceMaker Self-Determination Curriculum, focusing on choosing and expressing goals and taking action. This includes access to the Self-Directed IEP, which is a student-led IEP program.
- https://www.ou.edu/education/centers-and-partnerships/zarrow/transition-education-materials/whos-future-is-it-anyway provides access to the Whose Future is it Anyway? student self-directed transition planning process.
- https://www.ou.edu/education/centers-and-partnerships/zarrow/transition-education-materials provides access to multiple student involvement and self-determination–related instructional materials.
- https://selfdeterminationtheory.org/application-disability/ provides access to research and resources in motivation theory pertaining to the disability context.
- https://www.imdetermined.org/ provides access to the I'm Determined process to promote self-determined behavior and student involvement.
- https://www.beselfdetermined.com/about/ provides information about and resources for self-determination.
- https://www.palgrave.com/gp/book/9783030645366 provides access to an open-source handbook on positive education.
- https://www.viacharacter.org/reports provides access to the VIA Character Strengths survey and a resource guide to support use of the survey by students with intellectual and developmental disabilities.
- https://www.oxfordhandbooks.com/view/10.1093/oxfordhb/9780195398786.001.0001/oxfordhb-9780195398786 provides information on the Oxford Handbook of Positive Psychology and Disability.
- https://www.springer.com/gp/book/9783319590653 provides information on the Springer Handbook of Positive Psychology in Intellectual and Developmental Disabilities.

References

Bach, M. (2017). Changing perspectives on intellectual and developmental disabilities. In M.L. Wehmeyer, I. Brown, M. Percy, K. A. Shogren, & W. L. A. Fung (Eds.), *A comprehensive guide to intellectual and developmental disabilities* (2nd ed., pp. 35–45). Baltimore, MA: Paul H. Brookes.

Chang, R., Fukuda, E., Durham, J., & Little, T. D. (2017). Enhancing students' motivation with autonomy-supportive classrooms. In M. L. Wehmeyer, K. A. Shogren, T. D. Little, & S. J. Lopez (Eds.), *Development of self-determination throughout the life-course* (pp. 99–110). New York: Springer.

Cheon, S. H., Reeve, J., & Vansteenkiste, M. (2020). When teachers learn how to provide classroom structure in an autonomy-supportive way: Benefits to teachers and their students. *Teaching and Teacher Education, 90*, 103004.

Dean, E. E., Fisher, K. W., Shogren, K. A., & Wehmeyer, M. L. (2016). Participation and intellectual disability: A review of the literature. *Intellectual and Developmental Disabilities, 54*(6), 427–439.

Kern, M. & Wehmeyer, M. L. (2021). *The Palgrave handbook of positive education.* New York: Palgrave Macmillan.

Luckasson, R., Borthwick-Duffy, S., Buntinx, W. H. E., Coulter, D. L., Craig, E. M., Reeve, A., ... Tasse, M. J. (2002). *Mental retardation: Definition, classification, and systems of supports.* Washington, DC: American Association on Mental Retardation.

Reeve, J., Ryan, R. M., & Deci, E. L. (2018). Sociocultural influences on student motivation as viewed through the lens of self-determination theory. In D. M. McInerney & G. A. D. Liem (Eds.) *Big theories revisited 2: Research on sociocultural influences on motivation and learning* (pp. 15–40). Greenwich, CT: Information Age Publishing.

Seligman, M. E. P., Ernst, R. M., Gillham, J., Reivich, K., & Linkins, M. (2009). Positive education: Positive psychology and classroom interventions. *Oxford Review of Education, 35*, 293–311.

Shogren, K. A., Burke, K. M., Antosh, A., Wehmeyer, M. L., LaPlante, T., Shaw, L. A., & Raley, S. (2019). Impact of the self-determined learning model of instruction on self-determination and goal attainment in adolescents with intellectual disability. *Journal of Disability Policy Studies, 30*(1), 22–34.

Shogren, K. A., Little, T. D., Grandfield, E., Raley, S., Wehmeyer, M. L., Lang, K. M., & Shaw, L. A. (2020). The self-determination inventory-student report: confirming the factor structure of a new measure. *Assessment for Effective Intervention, 45*(2), 110–120.

Shogren, K., Palmer, S., Wehmeyer, M. L., Williams-Diehm, K., & Little, T. (2012). Effect of intervention with the self-determined learning model of instruction on access and goal attainment. *Remedial and Special Education, 33*(5), 320–330.

Shogren, K. A., Raley, S. K., Burke, K. M., & Wehmeyer, M. L. (2019). *The self-determined learning model of instruction teacher's guide*. Lawrence, KS: Kansas University Center on Developmental Disabilities.

Shogren, K. A. Singh, N. N., Niemiec, R. M., & Wehmeyer, M. L. (2017). Character strengths and mindfulness. In M. L. Wehmeyer (Ed.), *Oxford handbook of positive psychology and disability*. Oxford, UK: Oxford University Press. DOI:10.1093/oxfordhb/9780199935291.013.77

Shogren, K. A., Wehmeyer, M. L., Palmer, S. B., Forber-Pratt, A. J., Little, T. D., & Lopez, S. J. (2015). Causal agency theory: Reconceptualizing a functional model of self-determination. *Education and Training in Autism and Developmental Disabilities, 50*(3), 251–263.

Shogren, K. A., Wehmeyer, M. L., & Singh, N. (2017). *Handbook of positive psychology in intellectual and developmental disabilities: Translating research into practice*. New York: Springer.

Smith, D. J., & Wehmeyer, M. L. (2012). *Good blood, bad blood: Science, nature, and the myth of the Kallikaks*. Washington, DC: American Association on Intellectual and Developmental Disabilities.

Thompson, J. R. Wehmeyer, M. L., Shogren, K. A., & Seo, H. J. (2017). The supports paradigm and intellectual and developmental disabilities. In K. A. Shogren, M. L. Wehmeyer, & N. N. Singh (Eds.), *Handbook of positive psychology in intellectual and developmental disabilities: Translating research into practice* (pp. 23–35). New York: Springer.

Wehmeyer, M. L. (2013). *Oxford handbook of positive psychology and disability*. Oxford, UK: Oxford University Press.

Wehmeyer, M. L. (2019). *Strength-based approaches to educating all learners with disabilities: Beyond special education*. New York: Teachers College Press.

Wehmeyer, M. L., Palmer, S., Agran, M., Mithaug, D., & Martin, J. (2000). Promoting causal agency: The self-determined learning model of instruction. *Exceptional Children, 66*, 439–453.

Wehmeyer, M. L., Shogren, K. A., Little, T. D., & Lopez, S. J. (2017). *Development of self-determination through the life-course*. New York: Springer.

Wehmeyer, M. L., Shogren, K., Palmer, S., Williams-Diehm, K., Little, T., & Boulton, A. (2012). The impact of the self-determined learning model of instruction on student self-determination. *Exceptional Children, 78*(2), 135–153.

Wehmeyer, M. L., & Zhao, Y. (2020). *Teaching students to become self-determined learners*. Alexandria, VA: ASCD.

Williams-Diehm, K., Wehmeyer, M. L., Palmer, S., Soukup, J. H., & Garner, N. (2008). Self-determination and student involvement in transition planning: A multivariate analysis. *Journal on Developmental Disabilities, 14*, 25–36.

World Health Organization. (2001). *International classification of functioning, disability, and health (ICF)*. Geneva: WHO.

19 Positive solution

Conor Mc Guckin, Mary Quirke, and Patricia McCarthy

This chapter introduces the concepts of Universal Design (UD) and Universal Design for Learning (UDL). With an understanding that "inclusion is everyone's business" (McCarthy et al, 2019), the reader is encouraged to consider how they might develop and implement positive psychology approaches that can be accessed and engaged with by the largest amount of people by interpreting and encompassing UD thinking in all aspects of your work - from inception, through development, to implementation and review.

Theoretical background

What is universal design?

UD is a concept that originated from the field of architecture. It is an approach that seeks to create products and services so that they can be accessed and used by the greatest number of users possible (Mace, 2008). Ron Mace, an architect who had a physical disability, advocated for an approach that moved away from the "add-on" or "reactionary" thinking around inclusion and physical spaces. Together with colleagues, Mace devised seven principles that frame and guide the design process to be inclusive from the outset (Story et al., 1998). However, it is important to recognise that this approach does not seek to negate the need for add-on supports for individuals or groups who might find themselves excluded without them. Therefore, this approach demands a mindful, and perhaps more "positive approach", to inclusion.

The seven principles of UD are:

1 Equitable use - means that the design should be useful and marketable to people with a diverse range of abilities;
2 Flexibility in use - means that the design should be able to accommodate a wide range of individual preferences and abilities;
3 Simple and intuitive - asks whether your design is easy to understand - regardless of the user's knowledge, language skills, or current concentration level;
4 Perceptible information - does the design communicate all of the necessary information effectively to the user, regardless of ambient conditions or the user's sensory abilities?

DOI: 10.4324/9781003228158-24

5 Tolerance for error - means that the design minimises hazards and possible adverse consequences of accidental or unintended actions;

6 Low physical effort - guides us to ensure that the intervention or programme can be used efficiently and comfortably and with a minimum of fatigue for the child or young person;

7 Size and space for approach and use - reminds us that appropriate size and space should be provided for approach, reach, manipulation, and use regardless of the user's body size, posture, or mobility.

When we read the names and initial descriptions of the seven principles, we need to remember that these were designed for architects and designers. However, in a similar manner, we are also architects and designers - but we might need to reinterpret these principles for use in designing and implementing positive psychological interventions in our work.

Even if you have been providing a lot of positive psychology interventions in your work to date, beginning on a UD road does not mean that you need to "reinvent the wheel". Rather, Tobin and Behling's (2018) notion of "plus one" can give you confidence. With a plus one approach, you seek to identify just one area of practice where you could create just one more way of doing something that you currently do, adjusting current approaches to be more in line with the philosophy and practice of UD. From this incremental perspective, this means that UD becomes easy to embed in your ongoing thinking and planning.

Conclusion

So that's it! Or, is it? These UD principles can be easily used as an audit tool for things that we already do, or as a checklist for new approaches or programmes that we wish to develop. Used as a foundational tool for our active inclusion thinking, these seven UD principles really come to life for us in education when we see how they have been developed through UD approaches to the learning environment - e.g., UDL. The next section introduces the various approaches to UD as applied to education and focuses on one particular model (the Center for Applied Special Technology [CAST] model) to demonstrate UDL thinking and practice for both teachers and pupils.

Practice

Universal design for learning: the CAST model

The original architectural and design-based UD thinking has been successfully interpreted for the educational environment. The important development here is that these newer interpretations have been for all learners - not just those with a disability. These new approaches demand that learning environments are designed to be as inclusive as possible - minimising the need for add-on supports - so that a great diversity of learners (including those with a disability) - are included in a more integrative and less stigmatising way (Rose et al., 2006, CAST, 2018).

While there are many models and applications of UD thinking in education (e.g., Universal Design in Education: Bowe, 2000; Universal Design for Instruction: Scott et al., 2003; Universal Instructional Design: Higbee, 2003; Universal Instructional Design: Palmer & Caputo, 2003; Universal Design of Instruction: Burgstahler, 2007), the model of UDL that has a broad appeal is the CAST model of UDL - originally proposed as an iteration of UD by David Rose and Anne Meyer from the Center for Applied Special Technology (CAST) in Wakefield, Massachusetts (Rose & Meyer, 2002).

The CAST model of UDL is attractive as it is easily understood and engages a variety of practitioners in educational settings. The CAST framework is easily understood and adaptable to a variety of curricula and pedagogical practices. It is underpinned by multidisciplinary thinking, drawing upon theories and research from the fields of learning (e.g., Lev Vygotsky) and neuroscience. Importantly, the word "universal" in UD does not serve to mean that there is only one optimal solution for every learner. Rather, it indicates an awareness of the unique nature of each learner and the need to accommodate differences, creating learning experiences that meet the needs of the learner and maximise their ability to progress (Rose & Meyer, 2002). The CAST framework does not set out to present one optimal solution for every learner - rather, it embraces the unique nature of each learner together with the need to engage with difference, creating learning experiences that do not just meet the needs of the learner, but aim to maximise their ability to progress (Rose & Meyer, 2002).

The CAST model is exceptionally practical due to its focus on planning the learning environment to be inclusive of all learners in an increasingly more unifying and less stigmatising way by developing an understanding of all the potential differences (Rose & Meyer, 2006). While UDL asks that inclusive learning environments be designed from the "get-go" (Quirke et al, 2019) - minimising but never negating the need for add-on supports - it does recognise the need for add-on support for some learners. Support or accommodations for learners with a disability are more focused on need: be it the need of the learner or the need of the group. Learners' needs may, in some instances, be better served with a grouped rather than individualised support or reasonable accommodations. This promotes the idea that what works for one learner may work for many learners and improve the learning environment. It is important to remember that UDL emerged from the social and rights-based models of disability - approaches that appreciate how society plans and operates itself may in fact cause barriers, rather than the individual being viewed as a problem that needs to be fixed (i.e., the medical model).

The CAST model of UDL is directed by three interrelated pillars, each focused around a set of principles whereby "flexibility" is the key word in relation to teaching, assessment, and learning environments:

1   Multiple Means of Engagement (the "why" of learning) - enabling learners to engage positively with their learning and to appreciate the value of learning;
2   Multiple Means of Representation (the "what" of learning) - focusing around offering choice in learning;
3   Multiple Means of Action/Expression (the "how" of learning) - considering assessment as part of the process so that learners have a very real choice in how they represent their learning (e.g., multiple options - not just an essay) while meeting curriculum goals and learning outcomes.

The usefulness of the CAST guidelines is that they are being continuously developed - continuously including new understandings about the learning process and the diversity of our learners. This is exciting. It is not often that we encounter theories and models that are truly modern and contemporary. In essence, a positive psychology approach will identify with the CAST model, as it seeks to identify with positive practices and offer hope and meaning, love and inspiration, together with resilience, compassion, and gratitude. If these important positive psychology attributes are combined with the philosophy and practice enshrined in CAST's model of UDL, the result is a learning environment that includes every learner in a positive learning journey - in a more clear and intentional way.

Practice

"Try this" for educators and students

The CAST model: from theory to action

The following examples, based on real experiences, are shared so as to explore some of the ways that both theories can come together in practice. As you read, Kipling's six honest serving-men may help you - their names are Who and What and Why, and When and Where and Which.

- "Who" is being challenged?
    - Who is experiencing the problem?
    - Who can offer a solution?
    - There is in fact multiple who's in every problem - no one is alone.
- "What" is the barrier or issue that is being faced?
    - What is it the teacher or learner is being asked to do?
    - What would you like to see happen?
- Why?
    - Do not aim to be self-reflective - it is more about being self-reflexive.
- "When" can someone start?
    - When is there a need to re-evaluate?
    - Adopt a growth mindset approach.
- "Where" does one start?
    - Where can they find support or other examples of good practice?
- "Which" parts of the UDL framework do you easily identify with?
    - Which parts do you want to explore further?

Case study

Example 1

The following is an example of "Designing Flexibility in Learning Environments". It sets out how a teacher engaged with his pupils as he learned to redesign the learning environment to be as inclusive and engaging as possible.

As an engineering pupil, Mark's experience of his classroom was that it was too busy. Mark had a hearing impairment and felt particularly challenged when there was a lot of background noise. Mark shared his concern with Mr Cotter (his teacher). Mr Cotter met with Mark and his parents. He recognised that Mark had a real interest in the subject and showed real potential for success.

Mr Cotter explored UDL and realised that how his workshop was set up could be changed – giving support to Mark but also increasing flexibility for the other pupils too. For example, in redesigning the workshop, he developed new safety instructions using clear visuals that also incorporated alternative instructions in plain English. Mark was allowed to wear ear plugs when working on theoretical or writing exercises. As a result, Mark felt less fatigued by the environment. This enabled Mark to engage more fully and to both share and engage with his peers in the more practical work. Very soon, the other pupils also requested to wear headphones – they appreciated listening to music when learning! Mr Cotter agreed to a trial period with the pupils. Together, they designed the pace and structure of the class – practical assignments prefaced with clear instruction and written work toward the end. Listening to music meant that all of the pupils engaged more fully in the lessons and were also more relaxed at the end of each lesson. Should he require their attention, Mr Cotter simply turned the lights on and off three times in quick succession – just as Mark's mother did at home!

The learning environment needs to work for both the pupils and the teacher. In today's world, what works for pupils can change and sometimes challenge what we appreciate to be a well organised workshop, laboratory, or classroom. However, redesigning the learning environment with support materials and a little knowledge does help. Would you consider asking a pupil what works at home or when engaging in activities outside of the classroom? In a UDL classroom, teachers are learners too. Does this idea challenge you?

Example 2

The following is an example of "Provision of Accessible Materials" (adopting and appreciating all aspects of the CAST model – doing it in a "plus one" way). It highlights how pupils often know best what works for them, and that tapping into this knowledge can be extremely beneficial for a UDL approach to change.

Ms O'Sullivan was advised that a pupil who was blind would be joining her history class. The pupil would be using assistive technologies and Ms O'Sullivan had no idea what this meant! She had never taught a pupil who was blind or had a visual impairment, and she had a fear of technology. All of this made Ms O'Sullivan very anxious. She was a teacher who prided herself in her organisation skills and had wonderful notes made for her students. She wondered how she could engage with the new pupil – never mind make the notes and learning accessible.

Ms O Sullivan reached out to a trusted colleague from her alma mater. Through this conversation, Ms O'Sullivan learnt about the potential of UDL. While she had heard about UDL previously, she still had the firm belief that her notes, assessment approaches, and teaching methodologies were already "ticking a lot of the boxes". Surely this would be enough?

Ms O'Sullivan quickly recognised that she was going to have to become comfortable with technology that she did not fully understand. She also identified what she did know – her subject, her enthusiasm for teaching, her interest in pupils, and her love of learning.

She organised a meeting with her new student and they discussed what might be needed so as to make learning a pleasurable experience. Some of the things that they considered included: class goals and notes in advance, access to audio learning, permission to use a mobile phone to record in the classroom, and accepting homework by email with extended deadlines. Having a re-read about UDL, Ms O'Sullivan recognised that she needed to redesign her teaching approach – perhaps trying in a "plus one" approach – to move all of her notes online and recording some podcasts. A simple "contract of understanding" around recording in the classroom put her mind at ease as respected boundaries were developed and agreed. In addition, by involving other pupils in the changes, she was able to add to the learning in her classroom.

It was not easy for Ms O'Sullivan to embrace new technologies and approaches. Would this be a challenge for you? How would you work around it? Do you know who you could reach out to when faced with such a challenge?

Conclusion

Designing for the diversity of learners and colleagues (not just teachers) who work in our schools is much more than a simplistic view of special educational needs/disability and requires consideration for a wide range of learners and workers in the contemporary learning organisation. A UD/UDL approach presents opportunities for everyone to fully demonstrate their learning and personal/professional development. A positive psychology approach to this work will enable us to change hearts and minds – both our own and others. As we have noted, there is often a rush to "do" UD/UDL in the absence of thinking about why and how we would want to make changes to our work. In essence, this leads to much heat but little illumination. The net result is that people become frustrated and stop trying to add a "plus one" approach to their work.

We hope that this chapter has given you the confidence to develop your positive psychological approaches in a more equitable manner – recognising that inclusion is everyone's business! A simple rubric to adopt our "Three Laws" – shifting from expert thinking to a more mindful and inclusive thinking:

Law 1: Connect & Try!

Accept that UD/UDL is about "we" – not "me" – with an intentional and cooperative focus on you and your community of learners. Think about both your's and their's attitudes and beliefs. Reflect upon and examine unconscious bias.

Law 2: Listen & Act!

Commit to continually reappraise and re-evaluate your UD/UDL work, recognising that everyone has a "voice" and is an "expert by experience". Commit to listening to all voices.

Law 3: Grow & Share!

Try, try, and try again! Nobody is perfect – accept that you need to grow and learn. Engage with colleagues and a professional learning community to share and learn from others.

Discussion points

- UDL often requires change and as with any new approach, this can be a challenge. Particularly in an environment that is already busy. How do you manage change in your work – particularly if you find you are challenged with time and resources? How would you work around it?
- A less discussed component of the UD and UDL approach is the 'margin for error' – do you, as a professional, allow yourself time to reflect and learn as you seek to include a diversity of learners in your classroom.
- As a professional, do you feel 'included' in the UDL discourse? Who can you engage with and connect with as you add to your thinking and learning?

Suggested resources

- Quirke, M., McCarthy, P., Treanor, D., & Mc Guckin, C. (2019). Tomorrow's disability officer – A cornerstone on the universal design campus. *Journal of Inclusive Practice in Further and Higher Education (JIPFHE)*, 11(1), 29–42. Available at: http://www.tara.tcd.ie/handle/2262/91528
- Story, M. F., Mueller, J. L., & Mace, R. L. (1998). *The universal design file: Designing for people of all ages and abilities*. Raleigh, NC: Center for Universal Design. Retrieved from http://www.ncsu.edu/ncsu/design/cud/pubs_p/pudfiletoc.htm
- CAST. (2018). *Universal design for learning guidelines version 2.2*. Retrieved from http://udlguidelines.cast.org
- Quirke, M., & McCarthy P. (2020). A conceptual framework of universal design for learning (UDL) for the Irish further education and training sector where inclusion is everybody's business. Dublin: SOLAS. https://www.solas.ie/f/70398/x/b1aa8a51b6/a-conceptual-framework-of-universal-design-for-learning-udl-for-the-ir.pdf

References

Bowe, F. G. (2000). *Universal design in education: Teaching non-traditional students*. Westport, CT: Bergin & Garvey.

Burgstahler, S. (2007). Who needs an accessible classroom? *Academe, 93*(3), 37–39. Retrieved from http://www.jstor.org/stable/40253051

CAST. (2018). *Universal design for learning guidelines version 2.2* [graphic organizer]. Wakefield, MA: CAST. Retrieved from http://udlguidelines.cast.org

Higbee, J. L. (2003). *Curriculum transformation and disability: Implementing universal design in higher education*. University of Minnesota: Center for Research on Developmental Education and Urban Literacy.

Mace, R. L. (2008). Ronald L. Mace. Retrieved from: https://projects.ncsu.edu/ncsu/design/cud/about_us/usronmace.htm

McCarthy, P., Quirke, M., & Mc Guckin, C. (2019). *UDL - Can you see what I see …. is it an exclusive model or an inclusive model?* Third Pan-Canadian Conference on Universal Design for Learning: Connecting the Dots - Sharing Promising Practices across Country, 2nd–4th October, 2019, Royal Roads University, Victoria, Canada. Abstracts not published.

Palmer, J., & Caputo, A. (2003). *The universal instructional design implementation guide*. Guelph, ON: University of Guelph.

Quirke, M., McCarthy, P., Treanor, D., & Mc Guckin, C. (2019). Tomorrow's disability officer - A cornerstone on the universal design campus. *Journal of Inclusive Practice in Further and Higher Education (JIP-FHE), 11* (1), 29–42. Available at: http://www.tara.tcd.ie/handle/2262/91528

Rose, D. H., & Meyer, A. (2002). *Teaching every student in the digital age: Universal design for learning*. Association for Supervision and Curriculum Development, 1703 N. Beauregard St., Alexandria, VA 22311-1714 (Product no. 101042).

Rose, D. H., & Meyer, A. (Eds.). (2006). *A practical reader in universal design for learning*. Cambridge, MA: Harvard Education Press.

Rose, D. H., Harbour, W. S., Johnston, C. S., Daley, S. G., & Abarbanell, L. (2006). Universal design for learning in postsecondary education: Reflections on principles and their application. *Journal of Postsecondary Education and Disability, 19*(2), 135–151. Retrieved from: https://www.learntechlib.org/p/77561/

Scott, S. S., McGuire, J. M., & Shaw, S. F. (2003). Universal design for instruction: A new paradigm for adult instruction in postsecondary education. *Remedial and Special Education, 24*(6), 369–379. DOI: https://doi.org/10.1177/07419325030240060801

Story, M. F., Mueller, J. L., & Mace, R. L. (1998). *The universal design file: Designing for people of all ages and abilities. Revised Edition*. Retrieved from: https://files.eric.ed.gov/fulltext/ED460554.pdf

Tobin, T. J., & Behling, K. T. (2018). *Reach everyone, teach everyone: Universal design for learning in higher education*. West Virginia University Press.

Part 6

The road less travelled for well-being strategies

Positive psychology in education thrives; however, it is usually known in schools as an add-on to the current activities. We encourage schools to introduce positive psychology interventions, such as gratitude, acts of kindness, or savouring. Yet, we often do not consider some of the organic ways of helping students and teachers enhance their well-being, which is what this part of the book discusses.

Chapter 20 discusses the why and how of whole-school well-being. Introducing ad hoc interventions to students without properly embedding them in their personal lives may not be as effective as the whole-school approach, which is often the road less travelled for schools. Chapter 21 delves into the pedagogy for well-being, ways in which teachers can enhance their students' and their own well-being by tweaking their pedagogical approaches. Chapter 22 considers the focus on enhancing well-being among teachers. So often, schools, organisations, and governments set up strategies and activities for young people without considering the well-being of teachers. Yet, both teachers' and students' well-being is intertwined (Harding et al., 2019); therefore, a specific focus on ways we can enhance teachers' well-being is necessary. Finally, Chapter 23 introduces a reflection on the meeting of the two worlds: academics and teachers on the road less travelled.

As you read this part, you may reflect on the following:

- How do I look after my health?
- How is health promoted in my school?
- What changes can we all make to the way we introduce the strategy and practice of well-being in our school community.

Reference

Harding, S., Morris, R., Gunnell, D., Ford, T., Hollingworth, W., Tilling, K., ... Kidger, J. (2019). Is teachers' mental health and wellbeing associated with students' mental health and wellbeing? *Journal of Affective Disorders, 253,* 460–466. doi:10.1016/j.jad.2019.03.046

DOI: 10.4324/9781003228158-25

20 The why and how of whole-school well-being

Lucy Hone and Denise Quinlan

The last two decades have witnessed a growing recognition of the importance of taking a system-wide approach to promoting and protecting well-being in educational contexts. This chapter reviews the process of "Navigating Well-being Change", sharing how schools have used it, over time, to create a whole-system approach to well-being that is tailored to their needs and resources, a topic much overlooked so far by the field of positive education.

Introduction

While mental health promotion is now high on schools' agendas (Allen et al., 2018), many are at a loss to know where to begin. Listening to schools has brought two principal challenges to our attention. First, educators can regard well-being promotion too narrowly, erroneously believing that timetabling the explicit teaching of well-being literacy is the primary solution. Second, those who can see the importance of taking a whole-school approach are frequently overwhelmed by the enormity of the task. Some struggle to understand the breadth of what's involved; others, paralysed by an abundance of literature on the topic, tell us they don't know where to start. In response to many requests from schools, we have worked with them to co-create the Navigating Well-being Change process, designed to help schools chart their course, understand the ongoing nature of this work, and assist them each year to review their policies, practices, and procedures and reiterate so they continue to be fit for purpose.

Theoretical background

The why and how of whole-school well-being

While the earliest examples of school well-being programmes focused on the explicit teaching of resilience thinking skills to selected students (Gillham et al., 2007), Geelong Grammar School (GGS) was the first to embark upon a whole-school approach in 2008. With the support of Martin Seligman and a team from the University of Pennsylvania, the staff at GGS committed to professional development around learning and teaching of well-being, took

DOI: 10.4324/9781003228158-26

time away from the traditional core subjects of Mathematics and Science to create space for explicit teaching of 'PosEd', and sought to implicitly promote well-being by embedding well-being practices throughout the school. For more on the school's pioneering journey in Positive Education, see Jacolyn Norrish's book, *Positive education: The Geelong Grammar School Journey* (Norrish & Seligman, 2015). Geelong Grammar School (GGS) has continued to evaluate and develop its whole-school approach, maintaining a focus on staff training in the principles and practices of positive education, and endeavouring to ensure that well-being is explicitly taught and implicitly caught across all areas of the school community since. Other private Australian schools were quick to follow, notably among them, for their research-driven approach and intensive support from practicing academics, were St Peter's Adelaide, Knox Grammar, and Ravenswood School for Girls.

Over the last decade, the value of going beyond just teaching well-being has become widely acknowledged by schools and researchers alike. For example, White and Kern (2018, p. 6) suggest: "The greatest benefit will arise from the combination of caught and taught approaches... Successful positive education programmes blend evidence-based learning and teaching, whole school strategy, and evaluation, and consider pedagogy, philosophical assumptions, and the school's culture". Weare and Nind's (2011) systematic review of mental health promotion in schools also suggests effective programmes balance universal and targeted approaches across the whole school system – including changes to the curriculum, improving school ethos, teacher education, parenting education, community involvement, and coordinated work with outside agencies. Similarly, Gomez-Baya and Gillham (2018, p. 10) agree that: "Multi-year, whole school approaches are likely to have even greater impact than curriculum or classroom-only approaches". Longitudinal studies such as the *Values Education Project* (Lovat et al., 2011) in Australia demonstrate the value: a study including 166 schools and 70,000 students showed programmes using a whole-school approach achieved better results, deeper commitment, and improved sustainability compared to similar programmes not using a whole-school approach.

Whole-school well-being change requires attention to every level of the school's policies, practices, and procedures: from enrolment and induction, through reporting, reviews, curricula design, pedagogy, disciplinary processes, awards systems, timetabling, assessment, coaching and tutoring, psychological safety, and many more. It should also involve all education stakeholders: learners, school staff (not just educators), parents/caregivers, the wider community (including indigenous tribes and elders), governing bodies, external supporting agencies, and policymakers. For a school to genuinely have whole-school well-being, it must be able to say that it values and listens to the needs of every member of its community and gives them opportunities to contribute to the vision and practice of well-being in the school. That also means distributing leadership, responsibility, and agency for well-being.

Enabling well-being across the entire school system is, however, a complex challenge which, like any large-scale culture change, requires long-term prioritisation and considerable investment in time and resources. The research from the fields of Organisational Development, Organisational Change, Positive Organisation Scholarship, and Restorative Practice points clearly to the importance of adopting a process approach for effective, sustainable change. One of the most important truths of this work is that building well-being in your school is as much about the process as the content.

When we consider the scale and scope of change involved, it is not surprising this also requires long-term commitment. Schools that take well-being seriously reorganise the whole system so that well-being is always prioritised, they see the long-term value for all and known their commitment is never completed, but always a work in progress. For whole-school well-being to become an embedded part of school practices and culture – not just a 'bolt on' initiative or the pet project of a principal or single staff – typically requires a decade. Even among early adopting practitioners and researchers who have dedicated the last decade to Positive Education, the general consensus is that schools are mostly still scratching the surface (Scudamore, 2019).

Practice

While it's easy to agree with the science making the case for a whole-school approach to well-being, it's harder to put it into practice. The real world is messy, school budgets are tight, resources are limited, many teachers and students are already operating at capacity, there are always competing priorities, timetables are not often negotiable, assessment pressures can be entrenched, and many stakeholders have set views on how schools 'should' operate and how and what teachers 'should' teach. Against this context, we urge schools to focus their attention on what they can do, where there is appetite, opportunity, and capacity for change, and to set goals for what's realistically achievable.

"Try this" for educators

We find it useful to think of Five Ps here to remind all those involved of the importance of the change process, to put people first by endeavouring to consider different stakeholders' views, and to review the impact on well-being of the school's existing policies, practices, and procedures. We designed the Navigating Well-being Change Wheel (see Figure 6), described below, to cover all five.

The wheel provides a guide to best-practice Process and serves as a reminder of its iterative nature. Many schools we've worked with treat each school year as one cycle around the wheel. The wheel offers reminders and opportunities to make sure the whole-school community is involved in this work, that existing practices are acknowledged and valued, that plans reflect the priorities of all those affected, that there is time for trial and error – all founded on the expectation that initiatives won't always work first time. It also reminds school to monitor progress, to celebrate and share successes, and to schedule time to review learnings each year. Within the confines of this chapter, we review the steps briefly below.

The first year of 'becoming a well-being school' should be about moving around the right-hand side of our wheel. If you're reading this, chances are you've already identified the opportunity and need for change and perhaps also recruited some key people or departments willing to jump on board. Make gathering information – identifying what and who already supports well-being in your school – an essential first step. Ask the different sections of your school community to participate, e.g. staff, students, parents, Board. Use well-being surveys, but also ask people what needs to happen and record what's already good via digital crowd sourcing options like Mentimeter, focus groups, narrative sessions,

Figure 6 Navigating Well-being Change Wheel.

Post-Its on the wall. We use a number of different tools to do this – a Well-being Inquiry based on David Cooperrider's appreciative inquiry method (Whitney & Cooperrider, 2011), a Benchmark Survey we designed to assess existing school practices and a Well-being Audit using Google Sheets (for more details, see Quinlan & Hone, 2020).

The gathering information phase is also a good chance to develop your team. Like all change management, commitment from senior leadership is key. "Unless the principal is deeply involved - and models the learning required in order to enable others to take risks both professionally and also personally in their pedagogy – well-being education will stall in many institutions" explains Mat White, associate professor in the School of Education at the University of Adelaide (Quinlan & Hone, 2020, p. 279). Having senior leadership on board is critical; however, successful, sustained, and embedded change requires the creation of a broad-based representative team. All too often, we have seen enthusiastic educators who are passionate about making a difference create well-being initiatives designed around their own cultural worldviews and beliefs of what is needed. Not only does this fail to take into account the wants, needs, beliefs, resources, and identities of diverse learners, but we've also witnessed change agents working alone frequently burn out, or have their ideas and endeavours siloed by other stakeholders who have been left out of the development process. Remain vigilant to who is interested, who is initially sceptical (and perhaps influential), and who has demonstrated a long-term commitment. Recruitment can include 'shoulder-tapping' individuals whose contribution you believe will be important (perhaps a head of department or senior leader with sufficient influence to make change happen at the organisational level) and external partners can be useful for creating the impetus and initial professional development. The heavy lifting needs to be owned, carried out, assessed, and reiterated internally, however.

Schools move at their own pace through the ten stages of the wheel. Some stages will be brief, others may take longer. If the right-hand side of the wheel is all about gathering information, listening to people, and creating a representative team, the left side is when your school moves into trying out initiatives and focuses on learning and sharing feedback. At some point, it's time for action: get in the Sandpit, implement some initiatives, gather feedback, learn from it, and improve. Whatever you are trialling - different ways to gather student voice, growing student agency around well-being, promoting educator well-being, new strengths-based reporting systems, restorative practices, coaching conversations, introducing learner profiles, new enrolment processes, or introducing inquiry-based learning - design thinking and rapid prototyping are helpful here. The main thing is to learn from what works, what doesn't, and adapt accordingly.

The final three stages of the wheel involve monitoring progress, sharing outcomes, and ensuring there is sufficient time for reflection, review, and a commitment to making the action required. Assess the impact of your initiatives every step of the way. Student well-being assessment is important, but it is also complex and requires some expert assistance, so remember to draw upon the existing evaluation methods that are familiar: classroom observations, learner inquiries, conversations with parents and caregivers, absenteeism, and other national data that is part of existing school practices. Create opportunities for everyone to contribute to the reflection process and input to future adaptations or changes. "If a school is really committed to implementing Positive Education in a sustainable way, it must be prepared to ask hard questions, 'what goes, what do we do less, or possibly what do we even stop doing?' Without courageously addressing these questions, there is a risk that Positive Education is viewed as an add-on, another 'thing to do' rather than a key strategic and philosophical priority", remind Justin Robinson and David Bott from GGS (Quinlan & Hone, 2020, p. 280). Reflecting, reviewing, and reiterating is where the rubber hits the road: where schools have to decide how much they truly want to prioritise well-being. This is the point when you ask yourselves, what changes need to be made to existing policies, practices, and procedures to enable greater well-being in the future?

For many schools, identifying and evaluating existing well-being practices (foundations on which you will build), the people who might champion and lead well-being, the objections and challenges, and the well-being priorities of the different levels of your community might be all you can manage in your first year. Even schools with large budgets and resources are staffed by humans with limited time and energy to make change. It's better to progress slowly, build ownership, and bring people along on this journey together. It's also important not to overload or overwhelm your community - that is not good well-being practice! If you sense that well-being change is causing overload: pause, review, and slow the pace. Not everyone has the budgets that helped some of the famous PosEd schools embark on their journeys! We encourage schools to consider the limitations of their capacity, often limiting school well-being priorities or initiatives to a maximum of three in a year.

"Try this" for students

Four Catholic schools in Christchurch, New Zealand, collaborated on a three-year project exploring the relationship between student agency, well-being, and learning, funded by the Ministry of Education. Seeking to investigate if, given the right opportunities, support, and environment (physical, emotional, spiritual, cultural, social, educational), they could work *with* students to build creative, imaginative, resourceful, and practical dispositions to enhance well-being and learning in their school communities, the teachers involved in the project summarised the key themes they believed should be present in the implementation of any whole-school well-being approach using the RIPPLE acronym described below (M. Martin, personal communication, May 4th 2021).

R – Relationships. Positive learning relationships must be developed by a teacher's shared approach with the learners that acknowledges the identity of the learner and embedding pedagogical practices proven to enhance connection. This study recognised that social, cultural, and environmental power dynamics all impact student well-being.

I – Identity. Teachers need to know, respect, and value learners' identity. This can be done by listening to their voice and creating authentic learning experiences and environments.

P – Participation. Creating an environment that allows for learner's voice to be heard and acted upon; allowing them to be active participants in their learning is vital. This results in increased ownership, agency, and sense of belonging.

P – Pedagogical Know-how. Being adaptive educators that move with the times using pedagogical research and evidence to shift practice is required to be effective in meeting the needs of learners.

L – Leadership. It is crucial that there is collective voice (senior leadership, teacher leadership, and learner leadership) in the decision-making processes that affect the learning environments for all.

E – Environment. A learning environment should reflect the spiritual, emotional, social, cultural, physical, and intellectual needs of its community.

Below we share two case studies from schools who are three years into their well-being journeys. One focuses more broadly on the whole-school journey, the other on one practice they are gradually rolling out across the school.

Case studies

Case study 1

Over a three-year period, ten schools in the Palmerston North East area of New Zealand have worked together as a Community of Learning to focus on well-being. The impetus came originally from the schools' principals, who decided well-being was an area they all valued, and that working together to build capacity and knowledge was likely to have greater impact than working in silos. Carissa Davies, a senior leader at Whakarongo School, took up the Across School Teacher role:

> One of the first steps was to decide how we'd run the professional development (PD) training. We contracted the New Zealand Institute of Wellbeing & Resilience to help guide us through the process and to run our termly PD days because we wanted it to be high quality, research based and also saw the benefit of working with an outside agency to help get staff on board. We focused on the staff first and

planned one PD day in each term designed to build knowledge among our Within School Leads. Each school sent a team, so we had around 30 people in all. We weren't very clear on who should be in those teams initially, which was confusing, but once we cleared that up, there's been great buy-in across our schools since. Having consistent wellbeing leaders delivering the work back in their own schools helps ensure we are always building our knowledge and understanding.

Our first year we focused on promoting staff wellbeing, but we also completed a Benchmark Whole-school Wellbeing Survey provided by the Institute, and individual schools carried out their own Wellbeing Audits using google sheets, to capture the good practices already going on in our schools. In our school we worked as a staff to consider which of the many wellbeing models was the best fit for us, and asked staff to consider 'what does wellbeing mean to you?' While we kept the board of trustees in touch, we decided to focus on upskilling the staff initially, so didn't consult much with students or our community. We celebrated best practice during regular staff meetings dedicated to wellbeing.

Wellbeing has now become embedded in our classroom pedagogy and integrated into our programmes. Each pod runs their own 'hauora' (wellbeing) teaching, tailoring it to the students in different classes and at different year levels – that way we are now drawing in student voice as well as providing greater autonomy for staff.

Now that we have grown staff wellbeing knowledge we are switching focus to our learners, looking to create a long-term plan for wellbeing, identifying our key aims over the next few years and how we might implement these.

The most important lesson for us have been the importance of leadership support and the opportunities that cross-school collaboration provides. It has allowed us to listen to each other, learn from other schools' successes and mistakes, share how we are using some of the free wellbeing resources, as well as supporting each other. It definitely helps that we are geographically close, not too big a group, we can all see the benefit of learning from each other and we all agree on the importance of wellbeing work and can see the value of it.

Case study 2

Claire Howison is the principal of Ararira Springs, a new school built on the edge of Christchurch, New Zealand. Having undergone professional development in wellbeing for two years, Claire was seeking a way to leverage that knowledge to support her staff and ultimately benefit learners. Here she describes the rationale and practice of the school's coaching approach.

In 2018, my first year of being a principal, I had the experience of working with an external appraiser. Having studied coaching the previous year, as part of a leadership paper, I was keen to look for a less traditional approach. I paired with a coach who worked alongside me in my new role, adopting a coaching methodology and framework. As a result, I felt nurtured, supported, but also challenged and accountable. I quickly saw the strengths of the model and implemented a similar structure with our leadership team.

In 2019 our school opened, and we used the coaching framework as part of our appraisal process. Our school mission is, 'it starts with me | māku e whakatika' so the learner taking the lead is central to our practice. Our school values are simply being caring, curious and capable and coaching ticked all these boxes. We designed our professional meeting structure to support coaching with coaching conversations taking priority every third week of the term and no other meetings taking place that week. Each teacher is paired with a coach and we have developed a framework to support the coaching sessions. Each session starts with a check-in and the outcome of this conversation may form the basis of the session, if not, we look to the coachee's goals which have been constructed in the first session. Our teachers love these sessions and they have become an integral part of our professional growth cycle.

Last year we introduced coaching to our senior students. We trained parent volunteers and with teacher volunteers, every year 7 and 8 student was paired with coach. This provided an external person for the student to meet regularly with, check in, identify goals and make steady progress towards these goals. This was hugely successful and will continue again. Students are excited for this to begin again next week.

Wellbeing is central to our practice and coaching sits beautifully alongside this. Coaching provides the opportunity to meet with a trusted person on a regular basis with each session starting on connecting with the coachee ensuring all is well. Coachees feel cared for and coaches develop capability.

Discussion points

- How has your process for well-being promotion shaped up to date? What have you tried? What have you learned?
- When making well-being plans for your school, which stakeholders have you already heard from? Whose voices might you be missing? How can you remedy that?
- Who would be good to have on your well-being team? Who is mandated to challenge existing policies, practices, and procedures?
- How will you communicate that well-being initiatives will involve trial and error – that mistakes are part of learning?
- What organisational opportunities and practices can you put in place to encourage those in the sandpit to share great wins and epic fails with their colleagues?

Suggested resources

- The Educators' Guide to Whole-school Wellbeing: A practical guide to getting started, best-practice process and effective implementation (Taylor & Francis, 2021). https://www.routledge.com/The-Educators-Guide-to-Whole-school-Wellbeing-A-Practical-Guide-to-Getting/Quinlan-Hone/p/book/9780367236052

- Building Whole-school Wellbeing Podcast with Dr Lucy Hone and Dr Denise Quinlan https://nziwr.co.nz/building-whole-school-wellbeing-with-dr-lucy-hone-and-dr-denise-quinlan/
- Wellbeing Learning for Students and Parents Podcast with Dr Ase Fagerlund. https://nziwr.co.nz/wellbeing-learning-for-students-and-parents-with-dr-ase-fagerlund/
- Scudamore, C. (2019). NZIWR podcast, bringing wellbeing to life: Positive education leadership. Available from Apple podcasts, or nziwr.co.nz/podcasts
- Papps, S. (2019). NZIWR podcast, bringing wellbeing to life: The first three years of a wellbeing agenda. Available from Apple podcasts, or nziwr.co.nz/podcasts

References

Allen, K. A., Kern, M. L., Vella-Brodrick, D., & Waters, L. (2018). Understanding the priorities of Australian secondary schools through an analysis of their mission and vision statements. *Educational Administration Quarterly, 54*(2), 249–274. https://doi.org/10.1177/0013161X18758655

Gillham, J. E., Reivich, K. J., Freres, D. R., Chaplin, T. M., Shatté, A. J., Samuels, B., Elkon, A. G. L., Litzinger, S., Lascher, M., Gallop, R., & Seligman, M. E. P. (2007). School-based prevention of depressive symptoms: A randomized controlled study of the effectiveness and specificity of the penn resiliency program. *Journal of Consulting and Clinical Psychology, 75*(1), 9–19. https://doi.org/10.1037/0022-006X.75.1.9

Gomez-Baya, D., & Gillham, J. E. (2018). Positive education: Promoting well-being at school. In J. Velázquez, A. Muñiz, & C. M. Pulido (Eds.), *The Routledge handbook of positive communication: Contributions to an emerging community of research on communication for happiness and social change*. Routledge.

Lovat, T., Clement, N., Dally, K., & Toomey, R. (2011). The impact of values education on school ambience and academic diligence. *International Journal of Educational Research, 50*(3), 166–170. https://doi.org/10.1016/j.ijer.2011.07.008

Norrish, J. M., & Seligman, M. E. (2015). *Positive education: The Geelong grammar school journey*. Oxford Positive Psychology Series.

Quinlan, D. M., & Hone, L. C. (2020). *The educators' guide to whole-school wellbeing: A practical guide to getting started, best-practice process and effective implementation* (1st ed.). Routledge. https://doi.org/10.4324/9780429280696

Scudamore, C. (2019, April 8). *Ten lessons learned from ten years of PosEd*. Presentation at Positive Education NZ Conference. Christchurch, NZ.

Weare, K., & Nind, M. (2011). Mental health promotion and problem prevention in schools: what does the evidence say? *Health Promotion International, 26*(1), 129–169, https://doi.org/10.1093/heapro/dar075

White, M. A., & Kern, M. L., (2018). Positive education: Learning and teaching for wellbeing and academic mastery. *International Journal of Wellbeing, 8*(1), 1–17. https://doi.org/10.5502/ijw.v8i1.588

Whitney, D., & Cooperrider, D. (2011). *Appreciative inquiry: A positive revolution in change*. ReadHowYouWant.com.

21 Pedagogy for well-being

A new model for organic development of well-being in schools

Majella Dempsey and Jolanta Burke

Well-being promotion is of utmost importance in schools worldwide. However, most approaches are associated with providing students with knowledge about well-being and introducing additional interventions to enhance their well-being. This chapter discusses an alternative to these add-on approaches, which are related to designing pedagogies for well-being.

Introduction

The application of positive psychology in education has been thriving over the last decade. Various frameworks have been created (e.g. PERMA-H, FLOURISH, PROSPER) to assist schools in integrating positive psychology research and practice in education (Lai et al., 2018; Noble & McGrath, 2015; Williams, 2011). Many of them derived from adapting well-being models, such as PERMA to the schools' well-being frameworks, teaching the science of well-being, and encouraging the use of positive psychology interventions (see Burke, 2021 for review). Furthermore, specific well-being programmes were created, the objective of which was to teach children happiness, such as Penn Resiliency, SPARKS, or Making Hope Happen (Lopez, 2013; Pluess et al., 2017; Reivich & Gillham, 2010), some encouraged the whole-school approach to introducing well-being (Quinlan & Hone, 2020). While these approaches were useful, they acted as an add-on, often creating additional work for students and teachers alike (Waters, 2021). They also required teachers to have the knowledge and skills to teach positive psychology and/or well-being content. Conversely, little attention was paid to the more organic media for enhancing the school community's well-being, which does not require extra time on the curriculum, nor teachers' additional knowledge relating to well-being, i.e. pedagogies for well-being, which is what this chapter is about.

Theoretical background

Well-being is defined as "a journey of promoting and improving individuals' mental health and conditions so that they can contribute to the school communities' overall well-being, and vice versa" (Burke, 2021, p. 6). The vast majority of well-being interventions in school focus

DOI: 10.4324/9781003228158-27

on psychosocial well-being, yet the most organic way, in which well-being can impact the learning community is via curriculum. Over the last decade, many researchers highlighted the necessity to tweak the current curriculum to help young people engage more actively with positive psychology research. For example, English teachers discuss signature strengths of Shakespeare's King Lear, Religion teachers encourage "meaningful dialogues", while scriptural passages in a school chapel focus on values of courage, forgiveness, or persistence (Quinlan & Hone, 2020; Seligman, 2011). Values education is linked to pro-social behaviour which in turn is linked to enhanced academic achievement (Nielsen, 2010) and is best developed as an integrated curriculum concept rather than as a programme, an event, or an addition to the curriculum (DEEWR, 2008; Waters, 2021). The pedagogical decisions we make as educators can demonstrate that we value young people as autonomous beings with agency and power in their learning.

Pedagogy is understood as the approach to teaching, the instructional methods used, and the method and practice of teaching. It is closely linked to the theory and practice of learning (Leach & Moon, 1999). Pedagogical content knowledge, originally coined by Shulman (1986), is how teachers relate their pedagogical knowledge, what they know about teaching methods and learning to their disciplinary knowledge, and what they know about what they teach in the context of the individuals they teach. Pedagogy is never innocent, it carries its own message (Bruner, 1999). The pedagogical decisions teachers make are crucial because education is a "site where identities are being continually transformed, power is enacted, and learning assumes a political dynamic" (Girouz, 2004, p. 6). By facilitating students' agency to question, to have a voice, to learn to disagree, we can enhance their ability to participate in society. In this chapter, we aim to explore how pedagogy and the choices teachers and students make can be transformational, or indeed the opposite, close down growth and impose a kind of structural violence on learning (Osler, 2006; Winters et al., 2020). At the same time, given that curriculum-making and agency to make pedagogical choices are dependent on structure, culture, and materials (Priestley et al., 2015), these factors need to be considered when designing pedagogies for well-being.

One of the effects of well-crafted pedagogies is their impact on students' well-being resulting in improvement of self-esteem, trust, and respectful behaviour (Noble & McGrath, 2010). These pedagogies include narrative pedagogy of storytelling, which result in meaningful learning (Pulimeno et al., 2020), social pedagogy, which focuses on strength-based informal learning strategies (Petrie, 2020), person-centred pedagogies (Fielding, 2007), and pedagogical well-being (Soini et al., 2010). Despite progress being made in this area, especially in the last few years, we do not have a framework established that would support teachers in implementing pedagogies for well-being. Therefore, we propose a pedagogical well-being framework (Figure 7), which is built on the concept of teacher and student agency in the learning process. The framework consists of four integral parts relating to (1) curriculum choices, (2) pedagogical choices, (3) learning agency, and (4) relationships. Within the social context of schools and universities, student well-being is about feeling part of a community of learners where they have autonomy and the epistemic agency to make decisions about what and how they learn within an environment that supports meaningful relationships with other learners, teachers, and the discipline.

Figure 7 Pedagogical Well-being Framework.

Curriculum choices

Young people respond best when the topic they are learning is relevant and connected to their lives (Damon, 2008; Eisner, 2003). Thus, we can make the curriculum more relevant by using real-world examples in our teaching and sharing clear educational purposes (Tirri, 2011). Confidence and motivation to learn are facilitated when the teacher orchestrates environments where children feel that their learning is relevant and that they play an active part in understanding not just what they are learning, but also why they are learning (Wallace et al., 2005). Deng (2020) describes the role of the teacher as one of the interpreters of the curriculum where they strive to "create 'fruitful meetings' between students and content that gives rise to the cultivation of human powers" (p. 91). It is these fruitful moments that support students' well-being, and it is these human powers that give meaning and purpose to the learning for them. Without this, the student is merely learning facts, they need to see a reason for their learning. Students and teachers should be given space to structure and guide their learning journey in a holistic way (Eisner, 2003). To do this, we need to ask students what do they want to focus on in a particular topic? Find out if there is a particular aspect of a topic that they are particularly interested in and give them choice around how they show what they have learned.

Pedagogical choices – key pedagogies for well-being

Teachers make pedagogical choices when they plan for teaching, these choices are around the material they teach and also how they will organise the teaching. We know from research that well-being within a school is associated with active learning in a collaborative environment that is responsive to an individual's needs (Fielding, 2007; Pulimeno et al., 2020; Pyhältö et al., 2010). Pedagogy must be viewed from a situated perspective, from the perspective of a learning community, where the individual actions and interactions between all participants are seen as part of one process. Leach and Moon (1999) describe this as how

> Participants create, enact and experience – together and separately – purposes, values, and expectations; knowledge and ways of knowing; rules and discourse; roles and relationships; resources, artefacts; and the physical arrangement and boundaries of the setting. All of these together and none of these alone.
>
> (p. 268)

Therefore, while teachers use different pedagogical practices in their classrooms, the application of the process is very context-dependent in each setting, with each teacher, each group of students, different subjects, and different environments.

We propose three powerful ways to organise learning that can support student well-being – (1) building collaboration into the learning process, (2) activating students to self and peer assess their own and other's work through the use of formative assessment, and (3) using pedagogies that support and encourage dialogue and student epistemic agency. To enhance pedagogical well-being, we need to make clear for students why they are learning in this way, explain the purpose of tasks assigned, and facilitate them to use creative ways to respond to the work assigned.

Learning – epistemic agency and well-being

Collaborative learning is often considered effective. When young people learn collaboratively, they develop deeper interpersonal relationships, and this has an impact on behaviour, discourse, and learning (Gillies, 2008; Roseth et al., 2008; Slavin 2010; Topping, 2005) and increases motivation and social skill development (Fung & Howe, 2012; Hänze & Berger, 2007). Lyle (2008) found that collaborative talk leads to cognitive development and promotes communicative competence. If collaborative learning is not planned strategically, teachers will fail to realise the social pedagogical potential of the classroom (Blatchford et al., 2003). It has to be more than just exchanging ideas; teacher-led discourse and peer group interactions in collaborative learning are essential for success (Rojas-Drummond & Mercer, 2003).

The role of discourse in learning has been described in various ways such as dialogic instruction (Renshaw, 2004), dialogical inquiry (Wells, 1999), dialogical pedagogy (Skidmore, 2006), and dialogic teaching (Alexander, 2008). What is common to all of these is a move to students constructing knowledge within the curriculum and a move from teacher-dominated transmission approaches. Improving the quality of classroom dialogue can make a major contribution to enhancing student learning and increasing a sense of belonging, purpose, and epistemic agency (Damon, 2008; Pyhältö et al., 2010; Skidmore, 2006; Stroupe et al., 2018). Dialogue helps to "mediate the cognitive and cultural spaces" between teacher and student, among students, and this has impacts on society and how we view learning (Alexander, 2008, p. 92).

Formative assessment where students are activated as resources for one another through peer assessment and for themselves through self-assessment contributes to how students achieve agency and autonomy in their learning (Black & Wiliam, 2009; William, 2017). This active participation in their learning and ability to make informed decisions on how they learn enhances their sense of coherence and leads to better pedagogical well-being (Pyhältö et al., 2010). Peer assessment and teaching provides students with opportunities to give meaningful feedback to peers and in doing so feel part of other's learning journey.

Relationships - self, others, and discipline

Teachers and students are involved in a complex set of relationships in the classroom. The most obvious one is the student–teacher relationship, however, there are also peer relationships to consider and the learners' relationship with the discipline. We must acknowledge the complex identities, biographies, and histories each of us brings to the pedagogical situation. All learning is relational. Friends and social relationships are very important for young people in their schools (Tirri, 2011). Students want to feel accepted, valued, and to belong to a community, and daily classroom interactions can enhance these feelings or have a negative impact on them (Noble & McGrath, 2010). Attention to building relationships in pedagogical choices is central to student well-being.

Practice

"Try this" for educators

Ahead of teaching, think about your learning intentions for this class, start with the end in mind and scaffold the way for the students where they can take ownership of their learning. To do this, you must get to know your students, their interests, their strengths, and their weaknesses and see the student as a complete, complex, empathetic human being (Buber, 2008). When planning for teaching, think about how you can make the learning more relevant to their interests and collaborative. Can you assign a group task where each individual can contribute to it in a meaningful way? Think about how you might activate students as a resource for each other by incorporating peer teaching and peer feedback into your classes.

"Try this" for students

Set goals for your learning, map out targets on the way to achieving these goals. Think about how you can learn with others, what are the traits you can bring to a group to enhance their learning. Give and ask for feedback on your learning, remember to focus on the task. Give specific feedback on how you might improve peer learning. Think about how you learn best and try to build on these skills while also looking at any gaps you may have. Think about the topics you are interested in and how you might contribute new knowledge to your classes.

Case study

A secondary school was trying to implement changes to enhance students' sense of being personally effective, which is an ability to appraise oneself, evaluate one's performance, receive and respond to feedback, be flexible, and be able to persevere when difficulties arise (Dempsey, 2016). They accomplished it by changing pedagogies. The key pedagogical changes included:

- Peer and self-assessment
- Students devising 80% of their summative assessment, examinations
- Working systematically developing targets
- Reflection on learning

These changes had a phenomenal impact on students' engagement with learning, well-being, and a sense of accomplishment. Students reported increased levels of school belonging, and epistemic agency, whereby they did not seek out answers from the teacher, instead they were able to see themselves as knowledge brokers, all of which had a positive effect on their well-being.

Discussion points

What pedagogies help you boost your positive emotions?
What pedagogies help you connect with others?
What pedagogies help you find meaning?
What pedagogies help you experience a sense of accomplishment?

Suggested resources

Geoff, P. (2018). *How to teach even better: An evidence-based approach.* Oxford: Oxford University Press.
Hargreaves, A., & Shirley, D. (2021). *Well-being in schools: Three forces that will uplift your students in a volatile world.* Tascd, MN: ASCD.
Waters, L. (2021). Positive education pedagogy: Shifting teacher mindsets, practice, and language to make wellbeing visible in classrooms. Access from: https://link.springer.com/chapter/10.1007/978-3-030-64537-3_6

References

Alexander, R. (2008). *Towards dialogic teaching* (4th ed.). Dialogos.

Black, P., & Wiliam, D. (2009). Developing the theory of formative assessment. *Educational Assessment, Evaluation and Accountability, 21*(1), 5-31.

Blatchford, P., Kutnick, P., Baines, E., & Galton, M. (2003). Toward a social pedagogy of classroom group work. *International Journal of Educational Research, 39*, 153-172.

Bruner, J. (1999). Folk pedagogies. In J. Leach & B. Moon (Eds.), *Learners and pedagogy.* Paul Chapman.

Buber, M. (2008). *I and thou.* Howard Books.

Burke, J. (2021). *The ultimate guide to implementing wellbeing programmes for school.* London: Routledge.

Damon, W. (2008). *The path to purpose: How young people find their calling in life.* The Free Press.

Department of Education, Employment and Workplace Relations (DEEWR) (2008). *At the heart of what we do: Values education at the centre of schooling: The final report of the values education good practice schools project - Stage 2.* [Report for The Australian Government Department of Education, Employment and Workplace Relations (DEEWR)]. Melbourne: Curriculum Corporation. Available at: http://www.valueseducation.edu.au/values/default.asp?id=16381

Dempsey, M. (2016). *Exploring the impact of a key skills approach to teaching and learning in secondary education.* Thesis. Dublin: Trinity College Dublin.

Deng, Z. (2020). *Knowledge, content, curriculum and didaktik: Beyond social realism.* Routledge.

Eisner, E. W. (2003). Questionable assumptions about schooling. *Phi Delta Kappan, 84*(9), 648-657.

Fielding, M. (2007). The human cost and intellectual poverty of high performance schooling: Radical philosophy, John Macmurray and the remaking of person-centred education. *Journal of Education Policy, 22*(4), 383-409. doi:10.1080/02680930701390511

Fung, D., & Howe, C. (2012). Liberal studies in Hong Kong: A new perspective on critical thinking through group work. *Thinking Skills and Creativity, 7*, 101-111.

Gillies, R. (2008). The effects of cooperative learning on junior high school students' behaviours, discourse, and learning during a science-based learning activity. *School Psychology International, 29*, 328-347.

Giroux, H. A. (2004). Public pedagogy and the politics of neo-liberalism: Making the political more pedagogical. *Policy Futures in Education, 2*(3-4), 494-503. doi:10.2304/pfie.2004.2.3.5

Hänze, M., & Berger, R. (2007). Cooperative learning, motivational effects, and student characteristics: An experimental study comparing cooperative learning and direct instruction in 12th grade physics classes. *Learning and Instruction, 17*, 29-41.

Lai, M. K., Leung, C., Kwok, S. Y. C., Hui, A. N. N., Lo, H. H. M., Leung, J. T. Y., & Tam, C. H. L. (2018). A multidimensional PERMA-H positive education model, general satisfaction of school life, and character strengths use in Hong Kong senior primary school students: Confirmatory factor analysis and path analysis using the APASO-II. *Frontiers in Psychology, 9.* doi:10.3389/fpsyg.2018.01090

Leach, J., & Moon, B. (1999). *Learners & pedagogy.* Paul Chapman.

Lopez, S. J. (2013). Making hope happen in the classroom. *Phi Delta Kappan, 95*(2), 19-22. doi:10.1177/003172171309500205

Lyle, S. (2008). Learners' collaborative talk. In M. Martin-Jones, A. -M. de Mejia, & N. Hornberger (Eds.), *Encyclopaedia of language and education Vol. 3: Discourse and education* (pp. 279-290). Springer.

Nielsen, T. (2010). Toward pedagogy of giving for wellbeing and social engagement. In T. Lovat, R. Toomey & N. Clement (Eds.), *International research handbook on values education and student wellbeing.* Springer Press.

Noble, T., & McGrath, H. (2010). The third pillar of the student wellbeing pedagogy: Positive educational practices. In T. Noble & H. McGrath (Eds.), *Teacher education and values pedagogy: A student wellbeing approach* (pp. 54-74). David Barlow Publishing.

Noble, T., & McGrath, H. (2015). PROSPER: A new framework for positive education. *Psychology of Wellbeing, 5*(2). doi:10.1186/s13612-015-0030-2

Osler, A. (2006) Excluded girls: Interpersonal, institutional and structural violence in schooling. *Gender and Education, 18*(6), 571-589, doi:10.1080/09540250600980089

Petrie, P. (2020). Taking social pedagogy forward: Its fit with official UK statements on promoting wellbeing. *International Journal of Social Pedagogy, 9*(1), 1-13. doi:10.14324/111.444.ijsp.2020.v9.x.017

Pluess, M., Boniwell, I., Hefferon, K., & Tunariu, A. (2017). Preliminary evaluation of a school-based resilience-promoting intervention in a high-risk population: Application of an exploratory two-cohort treatment/control design. *PLoS One, 12*(5), 1-18. doi:10.1371/journal.pone.0177191

Priestley, M., Biesta, G., & Robinson, S. (2015). *Teacher agency: An ecological approach.* Bloomsbury.

Pulimeno, M., Piscitelli, P., Miani, A., Colazzo, S., Mazza, A., & Colao, A. (2020). Narrative pedagogy to promote health and wellbeing in school setting: An approach proposed by UNESCO chair on health education and sustainable development. *Health Promotion Perspectives, 10*(1), 1–2. doi:10.15171/hpp.2020.01

Pyhältö, K., Soini, T., & Pietarinen, J. (2010). Pupils' pedagogical well-being in comprehensive school–significant positive and negative school experiences of Finnish ninth graders. *European Journal of Psychology in Education, 25*, 207–221. https://doi.org/10.1007/s10212-010-0013-x

Quinlan, D., & Hone, L. (2020). *The educators' guide to whole-school wellbeing: A practical guide to getting started, best-practice process and effective implementation.* Routledge.

Reivich, K., & Gillham, J. (2010). Building resilience in youth: The Penn resiliency program. *Communique, 38*(6), 1–17.

Renshaw, P. D. (2004). Dialogic learning teaching and instruction. In J. van der Linden & P. Renshaw (Eds.), *Dialogic learning.* Dordrecht: Springer. https://doi.org/10.1007/1-4020-1931-9_1

Rojas-Drummond, S, & Mercer, N. (2003). Scaffolding the development of effective collaboration and learning. *International Journal of Educational Research, 39*, 99–111.

Roseth, C. J., Johnson, D. W., & Johnson, R. T. (2008). Promoting early adolescents' achievement and peer relationships: The effects of cooperative, competitive, and individualistic goal structures. *Psychological Bulletin, 134*(2), 223–246.

Seligman, M. E. P. (2011). *Flourish: A new understanding of happiness and well-being – And how to achieve them.* Nicholas Brealey.

Shulman, L.S. (1986). Those who understand: Knowledge growth in teaching. *Educational Researcher, 15* (2), 4–14.

Skidmore, D. (2006). Pedagogy and dialogue. *Cambridge Journal of Education, 36*(4), 503–514.

Slavin, R. E. (2010). Co-operative learning: What makes group-work work? In H. Dumont, D. Instance, & F. Benavides (Eds.), *The nature of learning using research to inspire practice.* Paris: OECD.

Soini, T., Pyhalto, K., & Pietarinen, J. (2010). Pedagogical well-being: Reflecting learning and well-being in teachers' work. *Teachers and Teaching: Theory and Practice, 16*(6), 735–751.

Stroupe, D., Caballero, M. D., & White P. (2018). Fostering students' epistemic agency through the co-configuration of moth research. *Science of Education, 1,* 25. https://doi.org/10.1002/sce.21469

Tirri, K. (2011). Holistic school pedagogy and values: Finnish teachers' and students' perspectives. *International Journal of Educational Research, 50,* 159–165.

Topping, K. J. (2005). Trends in peer learning. *Educational Psychology, 25*(6), 631–645.

Wallace, B., Maker, J., Chandler, S., & Cave, D. (2005). *Thinking skills and problem-solving – an inclusive approach: A practical guide for teachers in primary schools.* New York: David Fulton Publishers.

Waters, L. (2021). Positive education pedagogy: Shifting teacher mindsets, practice, and language to make wellbeing visible in classrooms. In K. M. L. & W. M. L. (Eds.), *The Palgrave handbook of positive education.* Palgrave Mcmillan.

Wells, G. (1999). *Dialogic inquiry towards a sociocultural practice and theory of education.* Cambridge University Press.

William, D. (2017). *Embedded formative assessment* (2nd ed.). (Strategies for Classroom Assessment That Drives Student Engagement and Learning). Bloomington: Solution Tree Press.

Williams, P. (2011). Pathways to positive education at Geelong grammar school integrating positive psychology and appreciative inquiry. *AI Practitioner, 13*(2), 8–13.

Winters, N., Eynon, R., Geniets, A., Robson, J., & Kahn, K. (2020). Can we avoid digital structural violence in future learning systems? *Learning, Media and Technology, 45*(1), 17–30.

22 Well-being of school teachers

Elaine Wilson and Jude Brady

Teaching is an intellectually demanding and emotionally charged role which requires high levels of professional knowledge, understanding, and skills. Teacher well-being is a complex multifaceted construct which has a temporal dimension, as teachers grow over a life course of teaching. This chapter explores options to contribute to the overall well-being of educational professionals.

Introduction

At the time of writing there is a global pandemic impacting drastically on every country of the world and on schools in particular. This crisis has had a huge effect on the well-being of all teachers and students everywhere. However, what is beginning to emerge is that despite adversity, teachers as people have the propensity to learn, to internalize, to use reason, to engage in evaluative thought, and to autonomously care for others, all of which are made possible by a functional self. This chapter will focus on trying to understand a bit more about what teacher's functional self is and the factors which affect teacher well-being.

Theoretical background

What is teacher well-being

Well-being is a much-used term which is difficult to define precisely. A top-level general definition is that well-being is about feeling good and functioning well. Going deeper, positive psychologists have refined the dimensions of well-being into an individual's experience of their life and a comparison of life circumstances with social norms and values. These two dimensions are defined as Subjective Well Being (SWB) and Objective Well Being (OWB) (Diener et al., 1999; Kahneman et al., 1999). SWB is sometimes referred to as personal well-being and this is gauged by asking people directly about how they think and feel about their own well-being. This can include aspects such as life satisfaction, positive emotions, and whether their life is meaningful. OWB is based on assumptions that humans have basic needs and that these can be measured through self-report methods such as asking people whether they have a specific health condition and by collecting objective measures such as mortality rates and life expectancy

DOI: 10.4324/9781003228158-28

In this chapter, we will focus on the SWB of teachers. Although this dimension is also complex with many interchangeable terms used in the literature, such as "happiness", "thriving", and "flourishing". There are many active theories which focus on emotional (he-donic) well-being, some emphasise the good life (eudaimonic) while others blend hedonic and eudaimonic domains. This is still an emerging active area of research. However, in this short chapter, it will not serve our purpose to discuss all of these important ideas. For teacher scholars of well-being, there are links to reading and references to the important theories in the suggested resources section at the end of this chapter.

We will use the Van Petegem et al. (2005) description of well-being which specifically relates to teaching. That is that teacher well-being is a positive emotional state where there is harmony between the school context and teacher. Van Petegem et al. describe this as the interaction between place and people where teachers are "capable of attuning to their own needs and expectations to specific context factors and demands of the school" (p. 35) and must feel they fit with the school in which they work.

Table 4 presents a summary of the key factors, set out a series of questions, which have been reported to have an effect on teacher well-being. This question could be used by teachers and school leaders to review teacher well-being holistically. The questions are nested, with teacher self at the centre, moving out to consider classroom dynamics and the wider whole school context. Well-being is also influenced by teachers' personal life satisfaction circumstances as well as factors which impinge on teachers work which are external to the school, such as how supportive parents are and how the school introduces account-ability measures.

Table 4 presents a summary of the key factors, set out a series of questions, which have been reported to have an effect on teacher well-being.

Teacher self-evaluation

This chapter will draw on the well-established blended hedonic and eudaimonic self-determination theory. Self-determination theory (SDT) has an extensive empirical evidence base in a wide range of contexts (Ryan et al., 2021). The main tenet of SDT is that people need three basic psychological, social, and emotional experiences to function well. These domains are defined as the need to experience autonomy, competence, and relatedness in their day-to-day roles.

When all three of these interrelated domains are in place, then a teacher is more likely to enjoy their work and be committed to developing their practice and in turn are more likely to stay on in the classroom to make a difference to children's learning. This is how we are defining having high levels of teacher well-being. Hobson and Maxwell (2017) showed that for early careers, teachers' **relatedness** was the most important SDT domain. Relatedness or a sense of belonging is vital for new teachers as they embark on their career. Believing that you are part of a team supported by people who care about you is a great motivating factor particularly in times of adversity (Brady & Wilson, 2020; Fox & Wilson, 2009).

Hobson and Maxwell identified **competence** as the next most important factor for early career teachers. As highly qualified graduates, it is really important that new teachers believe they are doing a good job and that their teaching makes a difference to student's

Table 4 Teacher Well-being Contributory Factors

Personal life satisfaction (OWB)

Are my personal circumstances supportive of my career?
Am I free from external stressors?
Do I have financial security?

Beyond school factors

Are the parents of children in my school supportive of my teaching and the school's role in the education of their children?
Are the accountability measures in force helping me to know what I do well and how I can get better at my job?

Within school factors

Teacher self-evaluation

Do I enjoy my work and am I committed to constantly improving my practice so that my students can grow and achieve high standards?

Relatedness

Do I feel I belong in this classroom and school?
Do I feel supported and cared for by school leaders?

Competence

Do I believe I do a good job? Do my students learn my subject well?
Does my line manager think I am doing a good job and provide me with helpful feedback?

Autonomy

Do I perceive I have some control over what I can teach and how I can organise my classroom?
Do I feel like I am trusted to do a good job?

Wider school context

Are the school leaders supportive of my personal development at my stage of my teaching career?
Do I have access to a mentor or critical friend as I progress in my teaching career?
Is the school a collegial and convivial place to work?
Does the school ethos align with my own personal values?
Does the leadership support me to do meaningful work?

Classroom dynamics

Do I have good relationships with my students?
Is there a positive work climate in my lessons?
Do I have good access to the resources I need to teach my subject well?
Do I have a manageable workload?

learning of their subject. However, teachers at all stages of their careers want to do their best for students and that is why it is vital that all teachers are allowed the opportunity to carry on learning about how to teach their subject and their students well. Competence is about having high **self-efficacy**. Klassen et al. (2013) showed that teachers' high self-efficacy partially reduced the effect of stress caused by student poor behaviour and from the debilitating effects of having a heavy workload. Feeling competent seemed to lessen the way in which work stress influenced well-being and in turn the commitment to continue teaching.

The final SDT domain, **autonomy** is the one which is less clear cut. This domain was identified as being the least important by early careers teachers. Deci et al. (2021) define autonomy as feeling trusted to have control over what teachers do in classrooms. Hobson and Maxwell's study found that early careers teachers had higher levels of well-being when they had fewer assessment style lesson observations which were not followed up with constructive or limited feedback. Furthermore, well-being is enhanced by being able to move away from prescriptive lesson planning requirements and to have control of the teaching approaches used. So, in effect, this means that teachers are trusted as professionals to make choices about how to teach classes in the way teachers believe is most appropriate for their students. As teachers gain experience, they also want to have increased influence on the decision-making processes in the school.

Hobson and Maxwell's UK-based study also recorded strong evidence that on the one hand where early careers teachers are judged by external Ofsted inspectors, to be 'performing' effectively, then this had a positive impact on their well-being by increasing self-efficacy and therefore beliefs about competence. On the other hand, Hobson and Maxwell's study, and more recent work by Brady and Wilson (2021), revealed that this was far outweighed by the negative emotional impact of subjecting teachers to intense scrutiny and additional work preparing for 'inspection'. There is very strong evidence that the hard accountability system in operation in England has a serious negative effect on teachers at all stages of their career (Brady & Wilson, 2021).

School relationship and collegial teams

Teachers' self-perspectives cannot be isolated entirely from the classroom context or the wider issues beyond the school, because teacher well-being is also shaped by a wider range of both environmental and contextual factors. Teacher well-being is more likely to be positive where school leaders create a trusting supportive collaborative culture where the day-to-day interactions focus on meaningful work which supports students' learning. Such positive work environments are open and honest (Brady & Wilson, 2020; Owen, 2016). In convivial environments, teachers want to do a good job and ask for help to do their job better. In collegial school cultures, school leaders encourage teachers to ask for help and provide support to help them learn how to improve (Fox & Wilson, 2015; Wilson & Demetriou, 2007). Asking for help ought not to be considered as a sign that teachers are failing but rather that teachers need further training and support. All teachers want to do their best. However, learning to become a teacher is context-specific and so when teachers move to new schools, they will need to learn how to fit into the new context (Wilson, 2013). In supportive school environments, leaders set up support systems which help teachers to bounce back to overcome difficulties.

Such a supportive trajectory promotes teacher growth and so teachers are more likely to flourish (Vella & Pai, 2009). The alternate path leads to unwellness and in extreme circumstances to teacher **burn out** and mental illness (Education Support, 2020). Indeed, there is a growing recognition that to flourish all teachers ought to be learning all the time too. To this end, it is one of the main roles of the school leaders to look after their most valuable assets, that is their teaching team. This can be achieved through creating a teacher support team where new teachers are allocated a mentor or a buddy system for more experienced teachers. The remit of this group is to have a specific concern for the promotion of teacher well-being. In supportive school environments, teachers work together to develop their practice, often in school-based professional learning research communities where expansive cultures are based around collegiality and trust. This means that teachers can constantly update their professional knowledge and skills together and be able to access other external sources of knowledge and support (Fuller & Unwin, 2003; Wilson & Sharimova, 2019).

This learning community approach to professional development may appear to add to teacher's workload. However, National Fountion for EducationalResearch (NFER) researchers have suggested that teacher workload is not just the number of hours teachers work, but rather can also be conceptualised as teachers feeling in control of their work or having autonomy. Indeed, NFER's recent research on teachers' sense of professional autonomy shows that autonomy is a key part of the relationship mitigating the effects of unmanageable workload with job satisfaction, and retention (Worth & Van den Brande, 2020).

Ultimately, it is essential that school leaders ensure that teachers' workloads are manageable, and that they are provided with opportunities to improve their knowledge and skills of time scheduling and how to manage workload, so that teachers and school leaders can achieve a satisfactory work-life balance.

Implications of COVID for teacher well-being

The immediate impact of the global pandemic has been that families have been forced to work from home and to homeschool or care for their children simultaneously. This has unlocked a different discourse around teachers, teaching, and schooling. Teachers and schools have stepped up and worked together to rapidly learn to teach in an online environment. Despite many teachers not having the skills or resources to teach their lessons, we have witnessed a situation of growing together. Cooperrider and Fry (2012) described this as 'consonant flourishing or growing together that happens naturally and reciprocally to us when we actively engage in or witness the acts that help others flourish, or the world as a whole to flourish' (p. 8). In the positive psychology literature, the concept of 'mirror flourishing' offers a post pandemic expansion of how we might interpret what has taken place during the COVID disruption. This idea might help us learn how we could come out of this pandemic situation in a better place in terms of teacher well-being. In essence, 'mirror flourishing' describes what happens when individuals, whether alone or together with others, focus their energy on 'doing good' for others in the broader social context, connecting and leveraging their strengths in the service of improving the world beyond themselves and the walls of their individual organization, they actually in turn activate mechanisms that support their individual well-being and flourishing (Cooperrider & Fry, 2012). The concept of mirror flourishing that is emerging in the organisational sciences transfers elegantly into education and supports the benefits of expanding the Seligman PER-MA-H model developed further by Norrish et al. (2013) to recognise that contributing to the collective well-being of others also expands individual well-being. Teacher researchers will find links to more information about these ideas in the reference section.

Many teachers acknowledged increased gratitude from parents generally. Parent perception surrounding teachers and their lack of confidence in the profession, which is often encouraged by the media, has generally changed and had a positive influence on how teachers are being evaluated. So, now is the time to capitalise on the good will and reset how teachers and leaders conceptualise teacher well-being. Leaders ought to think deeply about the negative impact of hard accountability on teacher well-being and consider the negative effects of inspections. During the online homeschooling phase, these hard accountability measures were suspended. Schools continued to function despite a lack of time and resources because professional teachers stepped up, pulled together for the greater good of the children. Wise school leaders will learn from this and will not allow their schools to revert to the hard accountability systems which has had such a negative effect on teachers' well-being.

Practice

Table 5 provides some reflective questions for new teachers, experienced teachers, and school leaders.

Table 5 Reflective Questions for New and Experienced Teachers

New teacher	Experienced teacher
Have you been inducted fully into the school 'rights and rituals' and know who to consult when difficulties arise?	Do you feel supported by the school leadership when issues arise in your classrooms and beyond?
Do you have a mentor who you trust to support you to improve your teaching?	Do you have the opportunity to support new teachers and to share your experience with newer members of the team?
Does your mentor give you positive feedback and areas for development as well as set up training activities to learn how to do things differently?	Have you been given training in how to support a new teacher to develop?
Do people acknowledge the changes an improvement you make to your teaching?	Are you given recognition for this mentoring role?
Are you included in decision-making processes?	Do you believe you have autonomy in how you teach in your own classroom? Are you trusted to get on with things in your own way in your own classroom?
Do you feel part of the wider school community?	Do you contribute to the wider school community and feel you belong in a collegial team?
Are the things you are asked to do meaningful for students learning and not just to satisfy hard accountability requirements?	Do you have a say in what is classified as meaningful work in the school?

(Continued)

New teacher	Experienced teacher

School leadership

Are genuine efforts made to promote trusting and collegial school environments in which teachers feel psychologically safe?

Do leaders really know their staff and know what they are good at and what they might need support with?

Is there an active coaching and mentoring programme in place for all teachers?

Are teachers provided with generic school focused professional learning to help them develop their time and workload management?

Do teachers have opportunities to undertake learning activity in relation to their individual learning and subject development needs?

Are teachers fully involved in decision-making and provided with opportunities for new challenges?

Is the accountability system in place humane, purposeful and supports the development of teaching and learning?

Are teachers appropriately and fairly rewarded for the work they do and the level of responsibility they hold?

Are all teachers provided with opportunities and support for career progression?

The next section shares results from a recent study which compares working conditions for teachers in highly selective independent schools with teachers in state-funded non-selective schools with students across a full attainment range.

Case study

Teacher well-being in independent and state schools is there a difference?

Contextual background

In England, at the time of writing, there is a big problem with teacher recruitment and retention. Data collected by the UK government's workplace survey shows that the number of full-time, qualified teachers starting work in state schools has fallen since 2015 – from 45,450 to 42,430 in 2017, and since 2011, the overall number of teachers has in general not kept pace with increasing pupil numbers. This means the ratio of qualified teachers to pupils has increased from 17.8 in 2011 to 19.1 in 2019.

Alongside the recruitment of new teachers, the retention of existing teachers is a key component in maintaining teacher numbers. A total of 39,675 FTE qualified teachers left the state-funded sector in the 12 months to November 2019, a 'leavers rate' of 9.2%. However, 21.7% of newly qualified entrants to the sector in 2017 were not recorded as working in the state sector two years later. The five-year out-of-service rate for 2014 entrants was 32.6%, the highest rate during the current series, which dates back to 1997. The ten-year out-of-service rate for 2009 entrants was 38.8%; this is also the highest rate since 1997.

In 2018, Brady carried out a survey of more than 800 teachers from across England to try to identify the school factors which might help improve teachers' job satisfaction (Brady, & Wilson, 2021). The survey report[1] compares working conditions in England's state and independent schools to identify what contributes to teachers' job satisfaction and identify what might improve working conditions for all teachers in order to address the national teacher retention crisis.

The findings

It is probably not surprising to learn that independent school teachers are more satisfied and less stressed than their state counterparts. However, it might be more interesting to learn that, during term time, teachers in both state and independent schools work a similar number of hours each week. Furthermore, when senior leaders are included in the data analysis, there is no significant correlation between job satisfaction and working hours for full-time teachers. However, when senior leaders are excluded from the analysis, there is a significant correlation between job satisfaction and working hours for the state school classroom teachers and middle leaders.

Although independent school teachers have longer holidays and smaller classes, the nature of the work teachers are asked to undertake and more importantly the ways in which teachers are 'monitored' does make a big difference to overall job satisfaction.

Many of the state school teachers who took part in the survey reported feeling that much of their work is meaningless and linked directly to hard accountability inspection of schools. Teachers gave examples of time spent on activity which did not contribute to children's learning, such as: colour coding complex seating plans, triple marking children's work, and providing evidence of verbal feedback written into exercise books. These books were inaccessible to the children most of the time and were designed to be "inspection ready". School leaders conducted book marking inspections, and brief on-the-spot observations, which were termed "climate" or "learning walks". Leaders argued that these checks were to ensure that teachers are ready for Ofsted and are following school policies. However, these extra tasks did not actually contribute to either the teachers' learning or students' education but did create an extra burden for teachers. Such hard accountability approaches diminish teacher autonomy which in turn reduces job satisfaction. Teachers in independent schools were also monitored but this was carried out as a formative process of professional learning rather than as an accountability mechanism.

Brady's takeaway message

Schools looking to improve teachers' job satisfaction might consider evaluating the purpose and audience for existing marking and feedback policies alongside their internal auditing processes. If the extra work burden is not making tangible improve-ments to both teachers' and students' learning, then leaders might want to think carefully about why they would risk damaging trusting and collegial working relation-ships with teachers.

In summary

Ultimately, when teachers' well-being is not considered to be important, teach-ers may not feel that they belong or are valued by a school. Teachers who don't believe they are doing a good job and are also required to carry out meaningless work will not flourish. Over the course of time, these teachers will either stay in their post and become unwell or what is more likely to be the case, they will leave the school. Some teachers may move to a different school but many more will leave the profession. This is a needless tragic waste of talent and government resources.

Discussion points

1   **Good is Good enough. Strive for excellence rather than perfection.**

Perfectionism can be defined as striving for flawlessness and setting up excessively high standards for performance accompanied by a tendency to be overly critical (He-witt & Flett, 1991).

Having high standards is not necessarily problematic in itself and indeed can promote self-efficacy. However, being a perfectionist can impede optimal function-ing or be associated with problems such as anxiety and depression. In schools, it can be linked to significant psychological distress. Perfectionists have a tendency to self-defeating thoughts and behaviours associated with high ideals, not realistic goals. These tendencies are often mistakenly seen as desirable or even necessary for success. Strategies which support excellence over perfectionism include: setting re-alistic and reachable goals and then setting subsequent goals in a sequential manner. Experimenting with 'standards' for success, perhaps 80% or even 60%. Focussing on the *process* of doing an activity not just the end result. Evaluating success in terms of what is accomplished.

Q 1. Do you or a member of your team have perfectionist tendencies? How might you help them to focus on excellence rather than perfection whilst taking on a new school project?

2   **Consider the factors which influence job satisfaction.**

According to Bakker and Demerouti (2007), job-demands-resources (JD-R) model, supportive resources include those factors of the work environment that facilitate and enrich people's working lives (Figure 8). As discussed earlier, the support of school leaders is instrumental in building teacher's resilience, in the face of challenges such

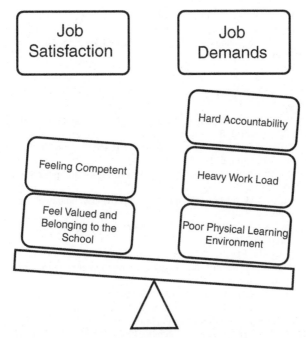

Figure 8 Job Demands – Resources Model for Teacher Well-being.

as problematic student behaviour. An important component of that support and trust building is the consistent practice of fair procedure within the work environment. Another important resource often reported by engaged workers is a sense of having an effective balance between work and non-work lives. Dollard and Bakkers' (2010) work has shown that an organisation's psycho-social safety climate (PSC) linked to teachers' self-determination well-being significantly predicted teachers' levels of both work engagement and burnout.

Q2. What are the main job demands and enrichment factors for your position in your school context?

3   **Looking after your own well-being?**
     How do you fit the following activity into your life?
     –   Physical exercise?
     –   Connecting with family, friends, and colleagues?
     –   Life work balance? Switching off from work?
     –   Reflecting on what is going well in your job and what you need more help to improve?
     –   Congratulating yourself on what is going well?

Suggested resources

Centre of Self Determination Theory. https://selfdeterminationtheory.org/theory/
Seligman's PERMA theory of wellbeing and workshops. https://ppc.sas.upenn.edu/learn-more/perma-theory-well-being-and-perma-workshops

Annual Teacher Wellbeing index. https://www.educationsupport.org.uk/resources/research-reports/teacher-wellbeing-index-2020

OECD Framework for measuring wellbeing and progress. https://www.oecd.org/statistics/measuring-wellbeing-and-progress.htm

References

Bakker, A., & Demerouti, E. (2007). The job demands-resources model: State of the art. *Journal of Managerial Psychology, 22*(3), 309-328.

Brady, J., & Wilson, E. (2020). Teacher wellbeing in England: Teacher responses to school-level initiatives. *Cambridge Journal of Education, 51*(1), 45-63.

Brady, J., & Wilson, E. (2021). Comparing sources of stress for state and private school teachers in England. *Improving Schools*, 1-16.

Cooperrider, D., & Fry, R. (2012). Mirror flourishing and the positive psychology of sustainability. *The Journal of Corporate Citizenship, 46*, 3-12.

Diener, E., Suh, E., Lucas, R., & Smith, H. (1999). Subjective well-being: Three decades of progress. *Psychological Bulletin, 125*, 276-302.

Dollard, M., & Bakker, A. (2010). Psychosocial safety climate as a precursor to conducive work environments, psychological health problems, and employee engagement. *Journal of Occupational and Organisational Psychology, 83*(3), 579-599.

Education Support. (2020). *Teacher wellbeing index 2020.* Accessed 12/10/2021 https://www.educationsupport.org.uk/sites/default/files/teacher_wellbeing_index_2020.pdf

Fox, A., & Wilson, E. (2009). 'Support our networking and help us belong!': Listening to beginning secondary school science teachers. *Teachers and Teaching, 15*(6), 701-718.

Fox, A., & Wilson, E. (2015). Networking and the development of professionals: Beginning teachers building social capital. *Teaching and Teacher Education, 47*, 93-107.

Fuller, A., & Unwin, L. (2003). Fostering workplace learning: Looking through the lens of apprenticeship. *European Educational Research Journal, 2*(1), 41-55.

Hewitt, P. L., & Flett, G. L. (1991). Perfectionism in the self and social contexts: Conceptualization, assessment, and association with psychopathology. *Journal of Personality and Social Psychology, 60*, 456-470.

Hobson & Maxwell. (2017). Supporting and inhibiting the well-being of early career secondary school teachers: Extending self-determination theory. *British Educational Research Journal, 43*(1), 168-191.

Kahneman, D., Diener, E., & Schwarz, N. (Eds.). (1999). *Well-being: The foundations of hedonic psychology.* New York: Russell Sage Foundation.

Klassen, R., Wilson, E., Fiu, A., Hannok, W., Wong, M., & Wongsri, N. (2013) Work stress and occupational commitment of pre-service teachers in four countries: The mediating effect of self-efficacy. *European Journal of Psychology of Education, 28*(4) 1289-1309.

Norrish, J. M., Williams, P., O'Connor, M., & Robinson, J. (2013). An applied framework for positive education. *International Journal of Wellbeing, 3*(2), 147-161.

Owen, S. (2016). Professional learning communities: Building skills, reinvigorating the passion, and nurturing teacher wellbeing and "flourishing" within significantly innovative schooling contexts. *Educational Review, 68*(4), 403-419.

Ryan, R., Deci, E., Vansteenkiste, M., & Soenens, B. (2021). Building a science of motivated persons: Self-determination theory's empirical approach to human experience and the regulation of behavior. *Motivation Science, 7*(2).

Van Petegem, K., Creemers, B., Rossel, Y., & Aelterman, A. (2005). Relationships between teacher characteristics, interpersonal teacher behaviour and teacher wellbeing. *Journal of Classroom Interaction, 40*(2), 34-43.

Vella, S. L. C., & Pai, N. B. (2019). A theoretical review of psychological resilience: Defining resilience and resilience research over the decades. *Archives of Medicine and Health Sciences, 7*(2), 233-239.

Wilson, E. (2013). Higher education academy. Learning to teach; Supporting research-informed teacher education in a changing policy environment. Learning to teach. https://www.heacademy.ac.uk/sites/default/files/resources/LearningToTeach_Part1_Final.pdf

Wilson, E., & Demetriou, H. (2007). New teacher learning; Substantive knowledge and contextual factors. *Curriculum Journal, 18*(3), 213-229.

Wilson, E., & Sharimova, A. (2019). Conceptualizing the implementation of lesson study in Kazakhstan within a social theory framework. *International Journal for Lesson and Learning Studies, 8*(4), 320-333.

Worth, J., & Van den Brande, J. (2020). Teacher autonomy: How does it relate to job satisfaction and retention. Retrieved from NFER 12/10/2021 https://files.eric.ed.gov/fulltext/ED604418.pdf

Note

1 https://bit.ly/3yR7Yk9

23 Expertise

The problem with experience

David Bott

This chapter suggests that empirical, scientific evidence can be highly valuable for well-being-oriented teachers. However, we must acknowledge that, perhaps, the most important, relevant, and constructive evidence that can help evolve our craft might come from the people who best understand teaching: teachers.

Introduction

Having supported educators from over 1,000 schools in the last ten years and having spent 15,000 hours teaching kids in three different countries, and having interviewed and consulted with some of the best teachers and school leaders in the world, the one thing that I've come to understand about teaching more than perhaps any other is this: it's a real thing. School teaching is an incredibly complex, nuanced, unique, challenging craft that requires years and years of toil and refinement to move towards mastery.

Those of you who have chalked up significant classroom experience will understand this. Those of you who are new to teaching or slightly removed from the 'chalk-face' may appreciate this, but the felt truth of this may be slightly illusive – in the same way that I can somewhat appreciate what it must be like to be a chef, painter, or architect, but I have no elemental connection to the reality of those crafts.

And because teaching is a craft, it is about as far from a science as you can get. Broadly speaking, the human sciences are attempting to develop theories that are abstracted, idealised, and value-free.

Abstracted: Scientific theories do not deal in particularities; rather, specific details are often omitted in favour of larger generalisations. Variables are isolated, controlled, or eliminated.

Idealised: Scientific theories do not deal in reality; rather, subtle distortions are commonly adopted that reflect nature as it would be in a perfect state.

Value-free: Scientific theories do not deal with subjective standards; rather, morals and principles are commonly ignored in favour of impartial observation and measurement. A guiding principle of theory is to describe the world as it is, not as it ought to be.

By contrast, the practice and craft of teaching is contextualised, naturalistic, and value-laden.

DOI: 10.4324/9781003228158-29

Contextualised: Practice necessarily embraces and leverages the infinite variables of each unique classroom experience.

Naturalistic: Practice does not deal in idealisation; rather, perfect forms must commonly be abandoned in favour of the rich and messy reality. Variables are embraced and celebrated.

Value-laden: Practice does not deal in value-free description; rather, nearly every school teaching activity is imbued with conceptions of what is good/bad or right/wrong.

Importantly, it takes only a moment to recognise that although theory and practice – science and craft – overlap and profoundly influence one another, the two are necessarily distinct entities that, at times, can become unhelpfully conflated.

And this is why, as highly professional educators, we should embrace the symbiosis of well-being science and practice but we must also do the work of filtering, distilling, translating, and contextualising any potentially helpful scientific findings that might be of benefit to us we personally refine our craft. This 'work' is what "applying" the science means. It's hard. And it can only be done in any sustained and profound way by the people who understand teaching the best – teachers themselves.

To examine this further, let's explore the concept of 'evidence-based practice'.

Within medical research, there are two classes of experiments: in vitro and in vivo. In vitro (Latin for 'in the glass') denotes experiments that are conducted outside of the body, often with cells or tissue cultures in petri dishes or test tubes. In vivo (Latin for 'in the living') denotes experiments that are conducted within living beings.

Nearly, all newly developed pharmaceuticals begin with in vitro experimentation, as this allows researchers to more easily isolate compounds to determine how they function and interact. Interestingly, of the hundreds of newly developed drug compounds each year that prove effective when tested in vitro, an estimated 90% become either inert or harmful when tested in vivo.

For example, Thalidomide was a drug marketed to pregnant women during the late 1950s as a remedy for morning sickness. Unfortunately, when taken during the first trimester of pregnancy, this drug proved to be highly toxic to the developing foetus, leading to an untold number of infant deaths and birth defects around the world.

Following this tragedy, in vitro research was employed to determine that the Thalidomide molecule comes in two unique configurations, each an asymmetrical mirror of the other (much like our left and right hands are asymmetrical mirrors of each other). Importantly, this work revealed that only the left-hand form of thalidomide prevents morning sickness, while only the right-hand form causes birth defects. Here, it appears in vitro research has solved a major problem: if we were to develop a purely left-hand version of Thalidomide, then we could safely harness the benefits of this drug without adverse side effects.

In fact, drug makers have tried this. Unfortunately, modern (and now mandatory) in vivo drug testing has revealed that as soon as the beneficial left-hand Thalidomide molecule enters the human body, it has a 50/50 chance of spontaneously flipping into the toxic right-hand configuration. Although nobody is certain why this sudden shift occurs, it serves as a poignant example of how something that proves effective in a petri dish is not guaranteed to work in the body.

Interestingly, this phenomenon works the other way as well. In the early 1920s, at a time when bacterial infections like pneumonia and streptococcus were often fatal, scientists were working hard to develop effective treatments. The first successfully synthesised antibacterial agent was called Prontosil – a drug credited with saving millions of lives while earning its inventor Gerhard Domagk the Nobel Prize in Medicine.

But here's the twist: Prontosil has no effect in vitro. When Domagk tested this compound against bacteria in a test tube, nothing happened. It was only after he tested Prontosil in vivo (including with his own six-year-old daughter, who had contracted a severe streptococcal infection from an unsterilised needle) that the antibacterial properties came to light. This serves as a wonderful example of how something that proves effective in the human body might produce no results in a petri dish.

What's going on here? Why is there such a marked disconnect between test tubes and bodies; between cell cultures and people; and sometimes, between well-being research and real classrooms?

As you've likely noticed, despite more than a decade of intense effort trying to apply well-being research in the classroom, we have witnessed only limited impact on teacher practice. The sad truth is that, although validated well-being research and scientific findings may inspire or influence how educators choose to approach certain situations, it can never directly drive teacher practice.

The reason for this harkens back to why medical researchers must undertake both in vitro and in vivo experimentation if they ever hope to cure disease: prescriptive translation.

Emergence

Within science, 'prescriptive translation' refers to the process of using data or findings generated in one field to guide actions, thoughts, and behaviours in a different field – for example, using findings from biochemistry to drive social epidemiology interventions. Put simply, prescriptive translation seeks to answer the elusive question so many people ask after reading a piece of scientific research: 'What does this mean for me?'

To understand the process of prescriptive translation, there are two foundational concepts we must first explore.

The first is Levels-of-Organisation. This concept states that when small entities are combined, larger and more complex entities are formed. As a biological example, when many cells are combined, a tissue is formed. When many tissues are combined, an organ is formed. This continues upwards through an organ system, an organism, a population, a community, etc. Put simply, each new level-of-organisation is composed of material from the previous level.

The second concept we need to understand is Emergence. This concept states that as we move up levels-of-organisation, new properties arise that are neither present nor predictable in earlier levels.

For example, picture a yellow circle sitting alongside a red circle. Now, imagine that you knew everything there was to know about the yellow circle: every yellow-molecule, every yellow-atom, every yellow-particle. In this instance, with absolutely perfect knowledge of yellow, would you have any idea that a colour called orange exists? Of course not, because orange is not in yellow.

Now flip it. Imagine you knew everything there was to know about the red circle. Again, with absolutely perfect knowledge of red, would you have any idea that a colour called orange exists? As before, you wouldn't, because orange is not in red.

So, where exactly does orange exist? Orange emerges only when yellow and red are brought together and allowed to interact. Pull the two apart and orange doesn't split itself evenly among yellow and red – it disappears completely and can no longer be meaningfully discussed. This is the crux of emergence.

Let's return to our earlier example. When many cells combine to form a tissue, valuable properties like permeability, malleability, and mineralisation emerge. Importantly, none of these properties exist in any individual cell; they arise only when many cells interact. Similarly, when many tissues combine to form an organ, valuable functions like digestion, circulation, and respiration emerge. Again, none of these functions exist in any individual tissue; they arise only when many tissues interact.

This is why 90% of clinical trials don't survive in vivo testing. When a drug is developed in the lab, it may perform flawlessly on isolated cells or tissues within a petri dish. But, once that same drug is introduced into a larger organ, system, or different organism, there's every chance emergent properties will interfere with that performance triggering unintended and unpredictable consequences (such as left-hand thalidomide spontaneously flipping into a right-hand configuration).

This same effect can be seen when transferring well-being science concepts to different settings. In a recent conversation with a colleague at an international school, I learned that a short, seemingly innocuous, five-minute, guided mindfulness 'body-scan' meditation in an 8th-grade classroom went wrong when it traumatically rekindled experiences of childhood physical abuse for two students.

Despite what the 'evidence' might seem to indicate, mindfulness mediation, character-strength spotting, gratitude journaling, growth mindset, flow triggers, random acts of kindness – they all have effects that are emergent – heavily dependent on context. They can be transformative for many students in some schools – and potentially have a vastly different effect for others.

From the well-being journal to the classroom

Within education, the levels-of-organisation we typically draw upon to shape teaching practice are the brain (neuroscience), the individual (well-being science), and the group (education). Nothing surprising here.

Problems begin to arise when we are confronted with emergence. More specifically, once a brain comes together with other organs to form a person (i.e. we move from neuroscience to psychology), a number of hugely important properties emerge: movement, behaviour, emotions, consciousness, cognition. Many neuroscientists will never discuss these properties because they are not processes of an individual brain; they only arise when multiple organs interact and can only be meaningfully discussed at the psychological level.

To be fair, behaviours, emotions, and cognitions undoubtedly have neural correlates (regions of the brain that play a role in their emergence). However, this does not mean these properties exist in or are driven by those parts of the brain. This is analogous to recognising that removing the spark plugs from an engine will cause a car to stop accelerating – but it does not follow that acceleration exists in the spark plugs themselves. Acceleration emerges only via the interaction of many car parts and cannot be reduced to, predicted by, or explained through any single part.

Continuing on, once many people come together to form a unique social environment like a school or classroom, a number of new properties emerge: communication, relationships, social observation, behavioural mimicry, culture. Again, the reason why psychological researchers have long struggled to coherently explain and predict these phenomena is that they do not exist in any single individual; they only arise when many individuals interact and can only be meaningfully discussed at the educational level.

Emergence is the reason why attempts to move neuroscientific or even well-being science research into the classroom can fall flat. It's not that the data or ideas are wrong – it's that strategies born in a controlled laboratory or isolated school context, or even a meta-analysis of multiple contexts, can never reliably account for the emergent properties that will arise in your unique classroom or school.

Mindset theory is a classic example of a beautifully elegant scientific theory and set of interventions, backed by empirical data, that have failed to produce the real-world impact on academic learning that researchers initially hoped and predicted. To use Carol Dweck's own words, "In the beginning, as I have freely admitted, we did not recognise the complexity of the implementation". In a complex system like a classroom, emergence will always interface with theory and can easily derail it.

So where does this leave us?

In summary, as we open the door of each school or classroom, properties emerge that are not necessarily predictable and explainable by data generated in previous contexts. This means, in order for well-being science concepts to be practically useful within the classroom, teachers must prescriptively translate them to their unique context.

Which leaves us with one final issue: evidence-based practice. Over the last decade, there has been an incredible push to make teaching an 'evidence-based' profession. Although this isn't necessarily a bad thing, it does lead to one very important question:

"Whose evidence do you mean?"

Through this discussion, you've likely come to recognise that evidence is not a singular entity owned and controlled by scientific researchers; but rather, it's a concept that changes and gets redefined across divergent fields. Evidence to a lawyer (precedence) is very different than evidence to an anthropologist (stories and myths). Evidence to a neuroscientist (blood-flow) is very different than evidence to a positive psychologist (questionnaires). Importantly, none of this evidence is wrong, but it's only meaningful within the context and emergent properties of each relevant field, application, or craft.

This means evidence-based practice within well-being education must be defined by teachers and for teachers. Although I can't predict how the profession will ultimately choose to define evidence (qualitative; quantitative; expert judgement; student feedback; etc.), I do know that teachers are the only ones qualified to make this decision.

Once it is recognised that research is largely defined by and confined to the field in which it was developed, it becomes clear that well-being educators must begin to systematically document their attempts at prescriptive translation within the classroom. This does not mean teachers must become scientific researchers; it simply means that teachers must methodically organise and collect information concerning the impact of varied well-being practices, strategies, and interventions within their classroom. This process will generate the evidence needed to push back against unqualified incursions and establish professional control amongst teachers.

One final point to consider concerns consistency. Currently, in the realm of Positive Education, there are thousands of teachers working in hundreds of different classrooms across the globe to bring well-being science to life in their contexts. With such a massive teaching force, how can we ever expect to achieve any semblance of professional coherence? Well, here's where it might make sense to steal a page from the book of science.

Scientific research is chaotic. According to several estimations, there are 10 million practicing scientists publishing over 2 million research articles per year using thousands of different measures, techniques, and interventions. Despite this, scientific research remains highly integrated and coherent. How? Because all scientific researchers document their work in exactly the same format and they make it accessible in exactly the same repositories. It doesn't matter that they're all studying different (and oftentimes conflicting) things, the simple fact that they can all easily access and decode each other's work allows the entire endeavour to attain coherence without any oversight.

If well-being-oriented teachers ever truly hope to build a strong body-of-knowledge, then it's essential that a consistent means of presenting and disseminating work amongst practitioners is established. It does not matter that every well-being teacher chases different passions, explores different techniques, and works in different classrooms – so long as every teacher's work is consistently organised and made available via a central repository, coherence will emerge without the need for top-down mechanisms.

Centralised peak bodies such as the International Positive Education Network (IPEN) and Australia's Positive Education Schools Association (PESA) are working on this challenge but there is still some way to go. It's a difficult but crucial problem to solve if applied well-being science is to have the impact globally that I have seen it have in dozens of individual schools around the world.

Every day, I have the privilege of working with and supporting highly dedicated professional teachers who are striving – largely in isolation – and succeeding – largely in isolation – to translate well-being science into strategies and practices that are impacting their students and communities in powerful ways. The field is reaching a level of maturity where well-being educators can stand on their own feet – shoulder to shoulder with their researcher counterparts.

Through emergence, prescriptive translation, and a consistent framework of documentation and dissemination, well-being teachers can begin to build a reservoir of knowledge unique and relevant to the profession of teaching. Once a profession-specific body-of-knowledge has been established that upcoming and future practitioners can unambiguously refer to, we will begin to see an evolution of the craft driven by the only people qualified to do it: teachers.

Part 7

Conclusion

Andrea Giraldez-Hayes and Jolanta Burke

Because you are reading the conclusion, we assume that you have read all or most of this book. We hope you have enjoyed it as much as we did when reading each chapter and engaging in meaningful conversations with the authors. Endings are moments of reflection. Therefore, we would like to invite you to reflect on the knowledge you have gained reading this book, the skills you may have developed, the discussions you probably engaged in with colleagues or other people and, most importantly, the actions you will take to apply positive psychology in schools as a result of your reading.

At this point, you may have some answers and probably new questions about what is positive psychology, and how it can be applied in schools? Why positive psychology in schools? Can teachers help students to flourish and thrive if they do not start by themselves? Assuming they start by themselves, how do they support students? Is it enough to add some activities to the curriculum or, conversely, it is necessary to develop well-being programmes or embed well-being as the school's hallmark? In this book, we tried to answer these and other questions by offering various theories, methods, models, and perspectives. After providing an overview of positive psychology and its application in schools, chapters in Part II considered one of the basic human needs –connecting with others. Students and teachers spend many hours in schools, and as suggested by Delors (UNESCO, 1996), one of the four pillars of education should be learning to live together. However, the paradox of an increasingly interconnected world is that more people, at all ages, including children and teenagers, experience loneliness (Rotenberg & Hymel, 1999) or difficulties in creating meaningful connections. In this context, as Chris Peterson, one of the "fathers" of positive psychology, used to say, "Other people matter. Period" (IAAP, 2013). Therefore, using different approaches and perspectives, including self-confidence, courage, strengths, or coaching, these chapters aim to promote reflection and offer evidence-based ideas to increase health and well-being by promoting better relationships in schools. It has also been argued that to connect with others truly, we must first connect with ourselves (Klussman et al., 2021). Therefore, Part III aimed to promote the reflection around topics such as meaning, compassion, and meditation. Those two sections, together with Part V, which includes topics such as belonging, bullying, or Universal Design for Learning (UDL) presented from the lenses of positive psychology, focused on perspectives directly related with students', teachers', and other members of the community intra- and interpersonal development, which in turn would have an impact on their well-being.

DOI: 10.4324/9781003228158-31

We also wanted to explore topics that are rarely included in the literature, such as creativity and playfulness as approaches and essential positive psychology interventions in schools. It is also worth noticing that in this book, we have focused primarily on the psychological aspects of well-being. However, let us not forget that our minds sit in our bodies, which affect us significantly and should not be ignored. Worldwide, non-communicable diseases kill 41 million people each year, which is equivalent to 71% of all deaths (WHO, 2021). Four conditions, in particular, are responsible for over 80% of global deaths: (1) cardiovascular diseases, e.g. heart attacks and strokes (17.9 million), (2) cancers (9.3 million), (3) respiratory diseases, e.g. asthma (4.1 million), and (4) diabetes (1.5 million). Given that non-communicable diseases refer to chronic diseases deriving from a combination of genetic, physiological, environmental, and behavioural factors, many of them are preventable.

Lifestyle medicine is a rapidly emerging medical field that focuses on developing daily habits and practices that prevent and treat disease (Egger, Binns, Rossner, & Sagner, 2017). World Health Organization has been promoting this approach for almost a century, yet most of the medical and mental health professionals continued to focus primarily on cures (Seligman & Csikszentmihalyi, 2000). Lifestyle medicine acknowledges that behavioural changes can help us pave the way towards a healthier life. The six pillars of that change are improvement in nutrition, increase in physical activity, enhancement of sleep quality, managing stress effectively, developing relationships and ceasing tobacco use and other unhealthy habits (Collings, 2020). When applied effectively, they can improve the health of generations to come.

While research in lifestyle medicine has been developing rapidly since the 1980s (Rippe, 2019), it focuses mainly on the physical aspects of well-being. This is why, in recent years, it has merged with the field of positive psychology, creating a more comprehensive perspective on health (Burke, Dunne, Meehan, O'Boyle, & van Nieuwerburg, 2022; Lianov, Fredrickson, Barron, Krishnaswami, & Wallace, 2019). Even though this book has not focused on the somatopsychic aspects of well-being as well as psychosomatic effects of positive psychology applied in education, future research needs to explore this link with more care and help us incorporate the well-being of the whole person, not only their minds.

As we work on this book's final details, we are all dreaming of the end of a pandemic that had one of the most challenging effects on students and teachers. We hope the book will contribute to restoring their well-being and designing school projects based on some of the main findings in positive psychology.

References

Burke, J., Dunne, P., Meehan, T., O'Boyle, C., & van Nieuwerburg, C. (2022). *Positive psychology and health: 50+ research-based tool for enhancing wellbeing*. London: Routledge.

Collings, C. (2020). On your mark, get set, go! It's time to elevate all six pillars of lifestyle medicine ... Starting with physical activity! *American Journal of Lifestyle Medicine, 14*(6), 612–614.

Egger, G., Binns, A., Rossner, S., & Sagner, M. (Eds.). (2017). *Lifestyle medicine: Lifestyle, the environment and preventive medicine in health and disease* (3rd ed.). London: Academic Press.

IAAP. (2013). *Obituaries. Christopher Peterson "Other People Matter"*. https://deepblue.lib.umich.edu/bitstream/handle/2027.42/96673/aphw12007.pdf?sequence=1

Klussman, K., Nichols, A. L., Curtin, N., Langer, J., & Orehek, E. (2021). Self-connection and well-being: Development and validation of a self-connection scale. *European Journal of Social Psychology*. https://doi-org.libproxy.ucl.ac.uk/10.1002/ejsp.2812

Lianov, L. S., Fredrickson, B. L., Barron, C., Krishnaswami, J., & Wallace, A. (2019). Positive psychology in lifestyle medicine and health care: Strategies for implementation. *American Journal of Lifestyle Medicine, 13*(5). doi:10.1177/1559827619838992

Rippe, J. M. (2019). *Lifestyle medicine* (3rd ed.). London/New York: Routledge.

Rotenberg, K. J., & Hymel, S. (Eds.). (1999). *Loneliness in childhood and adolescence.* Cambridge University Press.

Seligman, M. E. P., & Csikszentmihalyi, M. (2000). Positive psychology: An introduction. *American Psychologist, 55*(1), 5–14. doi:10.1037/0003-066X.55.1.5

UNESCO. (1996). *Learning the treasure within; Report to UNESCO of the International Commission on Education for the twenty-first century.* UNESCO Dirigal Library. https://unesdoc.unesco.org/ark:/48223/pf0000102734?posInSet=8&queryId=fdce52d4-96d3-4d97-9679-c3467dfb7628

WHO. (2021). *Non-communicable diseases.* Retrieved from https://www.who.int/news-room/fact-sheets/detail/noncommunicable-diseases

Index

Note: **Bold** page numbers refer to tables and *italic* page numbers refer to figures.

accolade courage 46
Action Character Strengths Survey 36
active-constructive response 26
active-destructive response 26
active listening 65
activity-based groups 13
adverse childhood experiences (A.C.E.s) 14–15
Afghanistan National Institute of Music (ANIM) 138
Afghan musical heritage 137–138
Allen, K. A. 161, 162
Ardi, H. 153
arousal theory 142–143
Arslan, G. 75
art: benefits 126; community art 127–128; for educators 129; integration 128–129; participatory art 127–128; PERMA model 126; positive psychology 125; self-esteem 127; for students 129; and well-being, in schools 126–127
Ashton-Hay, S. 153
ASPIRE 14, 16–17
attention-based training (ABT) 105–106, *106*, 109, 111
aware-explore-apply model 53
awareness 25

Baily, John 138
Baines, E. 144
Bakker, A. 228
Bandura, A. 30, 31, 38
Barrett, L. F. 151
Bates, Bob 127
Beghetto, R. 129

behaviour change science 107
behaviourist approach 15–16
Behling, K. T. 193
belonging sense, primary schools 11–12
Blatchford, P. 144
Bott, David 207
Brady, J. 223, 227–228
British Psychological Society 144
Bronfenbrenner, U. 161–162, 167
Brown, S. 143
Brownlee, K. 54
Bruner, J. 143
Brunzell, T. 15
Bryne, R. W. 82
Burke, J. 63, 66, 115

Carmichael, N. 81
Causal Agency theory 184
CBIs *see* compassion-based initiatives (CBIs)
Center for Applied Special Technology (CAST) model: applications 193; guidelines 194–195; inclusive learning environments 194; principles 194; theory 195
Chang, R. 183
character strengths 36, 116
Chemi, T. 128
Children's Self-efficacy Scale 36
Chockalingam, M. 47
civil courage 46
classroom-based strengths programme: application 56; automatic and unconscious strengths 55; inductive approach 55; noticing strengths 56; owning and valuing strengths 55

Clough, P. J. 33

CMT *see* compassionate mind training (CMT)

coaching: active listening 65; defined 64; peer coaching 67; positive psychology 63–64, 66–67; PPIs 64, 66; questions 65; rapport 65; school community 63; in schools 66; self-awareness 64; skills 64–66; trust 65

collaborative learning 215

collective student efficacy (CSE) 31

collective teacher efficacy (CTE) 31–32, 35

communication, with families 11

community art 127–128

Community of Learning 208–209

compassion 95–96; benefits 85; caring behaviours 82; CBIs 81, 84, 86; in classroom setting 92; CMT 85, 89, 91; cognitive competency 82–83; for educators 87–91; empathy skills 84; ethos of 84; gratitude 104; life tasks 83; monopoliser 93–95; motivational system 83; MSCC 86; physical and mental health 81; physiological analyses 85; prosocial behaviour 81, 82; PSHE curriculum 85–86, 91, 96; qualitative analyses 85; regal walking 91–92; self-compassion 89–91; soothing rhythm breathing 87–89; for students 91–95

compassionate mind training (CMT) 85, 89, 91

compassion-based initiatives (CBIs) 71, 81, 84, 86

concentration-based meditation 103–104

conscious awareness 82

contextual wellbeing 16

cooperative learning 13

Cooperrider, D. 206, 224

courage: accolade 46; approach-oriented cognition 47; blended 46; civil 46; cognitive/subjective component 44–45; defined 45; education-related narrative 48; for educators 47–48; moral 46; physical 45–46; process 46, 47; psychological 46; public speech 49; social rejection/exclusion 48; social risk 48; for students 48; vital 46; workplace social 46

COVID-21 4, 40, 86, 98, 136

creativity 123; and arts 125–130; EG 150–154; music 134–141; play 142–147

CSE *see* collective student efficacy (CSE)

Csikszentmihalyi, M. 143

CTE *see* collective teacher efficacy (CTE)

cultural democracy 127

culture, psychological strengths 58–59

curriculum choices, well-being 214–215

Darewych, O. H. 126

Deci, E.L. 223

decision-making processes 223

deficit-based approach 104

Demerouti, E. 228

Deng, Z. 214

deprivation 15

Designing Flexibility in Learning Environments 195–196

Dewey, John 125

Diagnostic and Statistical Manual (DSM) of Mental Disorders 116

disability *see* strength-based approaches

Dutton, J. E. 24

Dweck, C. S. 236; failure day 145; spaghetti marshmallow tower challenge 146

Early Childhood Education Curriculums 144

early school experiences 10–11

education: courage in 44–49; distance 4; needs 91, 12; in primary schools 91–18; strengths 52–60

EG *see* emotional granularity (EG)

Ekman, P. 151

emotional awareness 39

emotional differentiation *see* emotional granularity (EG)

emotional distress 16

emotional granularity (EG): constructivist theories 151; core affect 151; culture-bound psychiatric illnesses 151–152; defined 150; for educators 153; lexicography 152, 153; LRH 151; multicultural societies 153; social and emotional learning 150; for students 153–154

Engert, V. 104, **104**

evidence-based coaching conversations 35–36

evidence-based practice 233, 236

exam-related anxiety 101

experiential learning 154

expertise: abstracted 232; contextualised 233; evidence-based practice 233, 236; idealised 232; IPEN 237; levels-of-organisation 234,

235; mindfulness body-scan meditation 235; naturalistic 233; PESA 237; prescriptive translation 234; school teaching 232; value-free 232; value-laden 233; well-being journal, classroom 235-237

Farson, R. 65
formative assessment 216
Frankl, V. 74-75
Fredrickson, B. L. 67
friendships: benefits 24; hedonic and eudaimonic well-being 24; high-quality connections 24; pleasure and utility 23; primary schools 13-14
Fry, R. 224

Gallup 52, 116
Geelong Grammar School (GGS) 203-204
Gilbert, P. 83
Gillham, J. E. 204
Giraldez-Hayes, A. 126
Goddard, R. D. 31
Gomez-Baya, D. 204
Gray, P. 142, 143, 146-147
Green, Ashley 120
Greenwood, L. 162
Grounded Theory 152
Growth Mindsets 143-146
Guerrero, Rosemin 120

Hallam, S. 135, 137
Hanna, S. A. 77
Harvey, C. 86, 95
Hattie, J. 31, 35
Henrich, J. 152
Himonides, E. 135, 137
Hobson, Andrew J. 221, 223
Holmgren, N. 59
Hone, L. C. 117
Hook, P. 64
Howard, M. C. 45
human connection 21; coaching conversations 63-67; courage, positive education 44-49; education strengths 52-60; positive relationships 23-26; self-confidence 26-40; self-efficacy development 26-40

human rights-based approach 127
Hwang, H. S. 151

importance, positive relationships 25
inclusion 157; positive approach 192; positive psychology 159-167, 173-176
inclusive practices 180, 183; *see also* strength-based approaches
Individualized Education Program (IEP) 185
individual teacher efficacy 32
inquiry-based learning 207
International Positive Education Network (IPEN) 237

job-demands-resources (JD-R) model 228, *229*

Kang, K. A. 76
Karr, J. 85
Kelly, C. 162
KiVa programme 174
Klassen, R. 223
Klussman, K. 71
Kramer, A. 47

Leach, J. 215
Ledertoug, M. 58
Lee, J. 126
lexicography 152, 153
life meaning 74, 75
lifestyle medicine 238
Lim, Y. S. 76
linguistic relativity hypothesis (LRH) 151
Linley, P. A. 52
Lissing, J. 104
logotherapy 76-78
Loinaz, E. S. 153
Lomas, T. 63
loss and family breakdown 14-15
Lottman, T. J. 53
Louis, T. 126
LOVA 130
Lovtsevich, G. N. 153
Lyle, S. 215
Lythcott-Haims, J. 145

Mace, Ron 192
Madden, W. 66

Maratos, F. A. 85, 86
Maslow's hierarchy of needs 24
Matsumoto, D. 151
Mattaraso, F. 127
mattering wheel 24-25
Maxwell, Bronwen 221, 223
McGinn, Mary Ruth 130
meaning-centered interventions 77
meaning, in life 74, 75
meditation-based tools: ABT 105-106, *106*,
    109; anxiety 110; behaviour change science
    107; benefits 102, 103; body scan 106-107;
    Buddhism 102; Christianity 102; for educators
    109; exam-related anxiety 101; long-term
    reward 108; mindfulness 104; modern stress
    102-103; positive psychology 104-105;
    purpose and motivation 108; RCSI winter
    school 110-112; short-term reward 108; for
    students 109-110; thinking process 102-103;
    time and position 108; track improvement
    108; types 103-104, **104**
mental toughness 40; 4C model 32-33, *33*;
    components 32; defined 32; interventions
    33-34; learning activities 32
metacognition 82, 83, 103
Metcalf, E. -M. 153
Meyer, A. 194
micro skills of compassionate communication
    (MSCC) 86
mindfulness 104, 185, 186, 235
mindset theory 236
Minton, S. J. 77
Moon, B. 215
Moore, Niamh 120
Moors, T. 139
moral courage 46
multi-component positive psychology
    interventions (MPPIs) 34
music: Afghan musical heritage 137-138;
    functions 134-135; positive impact,
    well-being 137; RCTs 136; singing, without
    voice box 138-139; socio-economic status 136;
    Sounds of Intent project 139-140; systematic
    approaches 135; technology role 140-141

National Fountion for Educational Research
    (NFER) 224
Navigating Well-being Change Wheel 205-207,
    206

New General Self-efficacy Scale 36
Niemiec, R. M. 59, 104, 118-119
Nind, M. 204
non-cognitive factors 29
Norrish, J. M. 15, 225
Norton, P. J. 45, 47

Objective Well Being (OWB) 220
Ockelford, A. 134
Otake, K. 67

Panksepp, J. 143, 146
participatory art 127-128
passive-constructive response 26
passive-destructive response 26
Passmore, J. 63
peer assessment and teaching 216
peer coaching conversations 67
peer mentoring 36
Penn Resiliency Program (PRP) 128
Personal, Social, Health and Economic
    Education (PSHE) curriculum 85-86, 91, 96
PESA *see* Positive Education Schools
    Association (PESA)
Peterson, C. 52, 116
physical courage 45-46
Piaget, Jean 143
play: arousal theory 142-143; British
    Psychological Society 144; Early Childhood
    Education Curriculums 144; for educators
    and students 145-147; emotional balance 142;
    Growth Mindsets 143-146; mental rules 142;
    Play Club 147; positive education 144; positive
    psychology 143; postmodern theories 143;
    socio-constructivist theory 143
PLCs *see* Professional Learning Communities
    (PLCs)
PMLD *see* profound and multiple learning
    difficulties (PMLD)
pose, understanding, responsibility, and
    enjoyment (PURE) model 74, 77
PosEd schools 207
positive education: play 144; whole-school well-
    being 204, 205, 207
Positive Education Schools Association
    (PESA) 237
positive postcards home 12
positive psychology 237; applications 4, 115-116;
    art 125; bullying 173-176; defined 3; disability

180-189; happyology 5; inclusive practices 180-189; meditation 104-105; origin of 3; play 143; positive education 115; positive solution 192-198; in primary schools 91-18; RCSI winter school 110-111; research-based practice 5; school communities 1; in schools 159-167; strengths-based approaches 180-189; well-being 212; youth life 74

positive psychology intervention (PPI) 64, 66, 117, 201

positive relationships: awareness 25; capitalisation 25; for educators 25-26; friendships 23-24; importance 25; mattering 25; motivation theories 24; reliance 25; romantic relationship 23; school community 23; school-related relations 23; for students 26; TCK 24-25; types 24; work-related relationship 23

positive schools: distance education 4; global education 3

poverty 15

Prilleltensky, I. 25

Prilleltensky, O. 25

primary schools: A.C.E.s 14-15; ASPIRE 14, 16-17; behaviourist approach 15-16; belonging sense 11-12; communication with families 11; early school experiences 10-11; educational needs 91, 12; friendship 13-14; interaction 91-10; personal bests 13; SEL 13-14; skills and abilities 13; whole-child 91-10, 16-17; whole-school wellbeing 91-10, 16-17

process courage 46, 47

Proctor, C. 117

professional development (PD) training 208-209

Professional Learning Communities (PLCs) 40

profound and multiple learning difficulties (PMLD) 140

prosocial behaviour 15, 21, 174-176; compassion 81, 82; well-being 213

Provision of Accessible Materials 196-197

PRP see Penn Resiliency Program (PRP)

PSC see psycho-social safety climate (PSC)

PSHE curriculum see Personal, Social, Health and Economic Education (PSHE) curriculum

psychological courage 46

psychological strengths: awareness of 59; classroom-based strengths programme 55-56; culture 58-59; defined 52; early

years/preschool 53; for educators 60; high school 53-54; intervention 58; learning activities 59; New Zealand population 58; positive impact 54; primary/intermediate school 53-54; programmes and evidence 52-53; shared language 58; for students 60; teacher perspective 56-58; working experiences 54

psycho-social safety climate (PSC) 229

public speech, courage 49

PURE model see pose, understanding, responsibility, and enjoyment (PURE) model

Pury, C. L. S. 48

questions, coaching conversations 65

Rachman, S. J. 44-45

randomised controlled trials (RCTs) 136

rapport, coaching conversations 65

Rashid, T. 54

Rate, C. R. 45

RCSI winter school: course content 110-111; qualitative assessment 111-112; quantitative assessment 111

reliance, positive relationships 25

research 1, 3-6, 91, 11, 25, 29, 47, 54, 71, 74, 103-105, 116, 117, 136, 174, 183, 224

resilience 3, 4, 15, 32, 38, 40, 54, 76, 127, 203

Riedel Bowers, N. 126

Robinson, Justin 207

Robinson, K. 123

Roffey, S. 15

Rogers, C. 65

Rose, D. H. 194

Russell, J. A. 151

Sapir, E. 151

Sapir-Whorf Hypothesis 151

Sarigul, E. 153

school see school belonging; school bullying

school belonging: in adolescence 159-160; defined 160-161; for educators **163-164**; emotional support 166; evidence-base 162, **163-164**; macrosystem's effect 162; outcomes 161; psychological pain 159; rapid confirmatory literature review 162, **164-165**; social support 166; socioecological model 161-162; for students **164-165**; vulnerability 160 school bullying: defined 173–174; depression 173; for educators 176; KiVa programme 174; pro-social behaviours 174–176; strength-based approaches 175; for students 176; suicidal ideation 173; VIA Character Strengths 175; victimisation 174, 175; well-being programmes 174

SEL *see* social emotional learning (SEL)

self-awareness 56

self-concept 13

self-confidence 29; defined 30; *see also* self-efficacy

self-connection: compassion 81–96; defined 71; meditation-based tools 101–112; strengths-based interventions 115–120; youth life 73–78

self-conscious strengths 55

self-determination 182, 183, 184, 229

Self-Determination Inventory (SDI) assessments 184

self-determination theory (SDT) 24, 221; autonomy 223; competence 221, 223; relatedness 221; self-efficacy 223

Self-Determined Learning Model of Instruction (SDLMI) 184–185; action 187–188; goal 187; implementation 186; plan adjustment 188–189; preliminary conversation 186

self-efficacy 29; arousal level 30, 34; beliefs 30; defined 30; for educators 34–35; mastery experiences 30, 31, 34, 35; mental toughness 32–34, *33*; outcomes and benefits 31–32; social persuasion 30, 31, 34; for students 35–36; vicarious experiences 30, 31, 34, 36

Seligman, M. E. P. 3, 52, 116, 181, 203, 225

shared language, psychological strengths 58

Shulman, L. S. 213

signature strengths 119

Singer, T. 104, **104**

singing, without voice box 138–139

social and emotional development 10

Social Cognitive Theory (Bandura) 30

social emotional learning (SEL) 13–14

socio-constructivist theory 143

Sounds of Intent project 139–140

Specific, Measurable, Achievable, Relevant, Timely (SMART) goals 33, 35

Spreitzer, G. M. 24

strengths: decision-making process 185; deficits-approach 184; disability civil rights movement 182; educational planning 185; for educators 183–184; ICF 180–183; interventions 182; person-environment fit models 180–183; positive education 181, 182; purpose of 183; school bullying 175; self-determination 182, 183, 184; social models of disability 181; for students 184–186; supports 182; WHO 180, 181

strength-based parenting 174–175

strengths- and solution-focused approach 14

strengths-based interventions: benefits 117–118; Character Day 118; character strengths 116; for educators 118–119; positive psychology 115; psychological ingredients 116; signature strengths 119; strengths blindness 117; for students 119–120; VIA 116–117

Strengths-Based Resilience programme 54

student assessment 36

students: art 129; compassion 91–95; courage 48; EG 153–154; meditation-based tools 109–110; play 145–147; positive relationships 26; psychological strengths 60; school belonging **164–165**; school bullying 176; self-efficacy 35–36; strengths 184–186; strengths-based interventions 119–120; well-being 217; whole-school well-being 207–208; youth life 76

Subjective Well Being (SWB) 220, 221

Synergistic Change Model 34

Taipei European School (TES) 36; approaches 38; arousal level 39; mastery experiences 38–39; mission 37; outcomes 40; PERMAH model 37; social persuasion 40; vicarious experiences 39; well-being framework 37, *37*; well-being strategy 37, *38*

teacher-delivered specialized education 182

teacher efficacy 31, 35

teacher-led discourse 215

teachers: burn out and mental illness 224; in classroom 57–58; collegial teams 223–224; COVID implications 224–225; critical thinking skills 57; learning strengths 57; noticing changes 56–57; reflective questions 225, **225–226**; school relationship 223–224; self-evaluation 221, 223; well-being 91, 16, 220–221, **222**, 226–228

third culture kids (TCK) 24–25

Tobin, T. J. 193

trauma 15

Trom, P. 66

trust, coaching conversations 65

unconscious strengths 55
universal design (UD) 192–193, 197–198
Universal design for learning (UDL) 193–198

values in action inventory (VIA) 116–119
values in action inventory (VIA) Character
Strengths: honesty and kindness 185; school
bullying 175
Values in Action Inventory of Strengths (VIA-IS)
116–117
Van Petegem, K. 221
victimisation 174, 175
vital courage 46
Vygotsky, Lev 143

Waters, L. 144, 145
Weare, K. 204
Wehmeyer, M. L. 182
Weiss, B. J. 45
well-being: collaborative learning 215;
curriculum 214–215; defined 212; for
educators 216; formative assessment 216;
interventions 212–213; journal, classroom
235–237; learning discourse 216; learning
process 213; pedagogical choices 215;
pedagogical content knowledge 213;
pedagogical framework 213, *214*; peer
relationships 216; positive psychology 212;

pro-social behaviour 213; school bullying 174;
school teachers 220–228; for students 217
Whitmore, J. 64
whole-school well-being: coaching framework
210; Community of Learning 208–209; for
educators 205–207, *206*; evidence-based
learning and teaching 204; explicit teaching
203–204; GGS 203–204; large-scale culture
change 204; positive education 204, 205,
207; RIPPLE 208; for students 207–208
Whorf, B. L. 151
Williams-Diehm, K. 185
Wilson, E. 223
Wong, P. T. P. 75, 77
workplace social courage 46

Yıldırım, M. 75
youth life: academic-based outcomes 73;
characteristics 75; components 74, *74*;
development stages 75; for educators 76–77;
intervention services 73; life meaning 74, 75;
logotherapy 74, 76–78; meaning-centered
interventions 77; positive psychology 74;
PURE model 75, 77; school-based prevention
73; social and career roles 73; for students 76

zero-tolerance authoritarian approach 15
Zhao, Y. 182
Zinbarg, R. 47

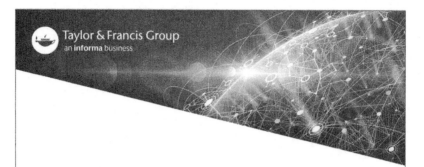